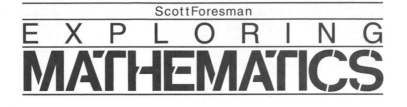

ScottForesman

EXPLORING MATHEMATICS

AUTHORS

L. Carey Bolster
Coordinator of Mathematics
Baltimore County Public Schools
Towson, Maryland

Clem Boyer
Coordinator of Mathematics, K-12
District School Board of Seminole County
Sanford, Florida

Thomas Butts
Associate Professor,
Mathematics Education
University of Texas at Dallas
Richardson, Texas

Mary Cavanagh
Math/Science Coordinator
Solana Beach School District
Solana Beach, California

Marea W. Channel
Mathematics Resource Teacher
Los Angeles Unified School District
Los Angeles, California

Warren D. Crown
Associate Professor of
Mathematics Education, Rutgers,
The State University of New Jersey
New Brunswick, New Jersey

Jan Fair
Mathematics Department
Allan Hancock College
Santa Maria, California

Robert Y. Hamada
District Mathematics Specialist, K-12
Los Angeles Unified School District
Los Angeles, California

Margaret G. (Peggy) Kelly
Associate Professor
California State University, San Marcos
San Marcos, California

Miriam Leiva
Professor of Mathematics
University of North Carolina at Charlotte
Charlotte, North Carolina

Mary Montgomery Lindquist
Callaway Professor of Mathematics Education
Columbus College
Columbus, Georgia

William B. Nibbelink
Professor, Division of Early Childhood and
Elementary Education, University of Iowa
Iowa City, Iowa

Linda Proudfit
University Professor of Mathematics
and Computer Education, Governors State
University, University Park, Illinois

Cathy Rahlfs
Mathematics Coordinator
Humble Independent School District
Humble, Texas

Rosie Ramirez
Assistant Principal
Highland Elementary School
Silver Spring, Maryland

Jeanne F. Ramos
Assistant Principal
Nobel Middle School
Northridge, California

Gail Robinette
Vice-Principal
Fresno Unified School District
Fresno, California

David Robitaille
Head, Department of Mathematics
and Science Education
University of British Columbia
Vancouver, British Columbia,
Canada

James E. Schultz
Project LITMUS
University of Georgia
Athens, Georgia

Richard Shepardson
Professor, Division of Early Childhood
and Elementary Education
University of Iowa
Iowa City, Iowa

Jane Swafford
Professor of Mathematics
Illinois State University, Normal, Illinois

Benny Tucker
Dean, School of Education and Human Studies
Union University
Jackson, Tennessee

John Van de Walle
Professor of Education
Virginia Commonwealth University
Richmond, Virginia

David E. Williams
Former Director of Mathematics Education
School District of Philadelphia
Philadelphia, Pennsylvania

Robert J. Wisner
Professor of Mathematics
New Mexico State University
Las Cruces, New Mexico

Multicultural Reviewers

Cherry McGee Banks
University of Washington
Seattle, Washington

Armando Ayala
Director of Bilingual Education
Placer County, California

Diane Deckert Jost
Field Museum of Natural History, Chicago, Illinois

**Patricia Locke
(Ta Wacin Waste Win)**
Lakota, Chippewa Educator
Wakpala, South Dakota

Vicky Owyang Chan
Multicultural Educator
Fremont, California

Seree Weroha
Kansas State University, Manhattan, Kansas

Efrain Melendez
Dakota School, Los Angeles, California

Linda Skinner
Choctaw Educator, Edmond, Oklahoma

ScottForesman

Editorial Offices: Glenview, Illinois   Regional Offices: Sunnyvale, California • Tucker, Georgia • Glenview, Illinois • Oakland, New Jersey • Dallas, Texas

CONSULTANTS

Reading
Robert A. Pavlik
Professor, Reading/Language Arts Department
Cardinal Stritch College
Milwaukee, Wisconsin

At-Risk Students
Edgar G. Epps
Marshall Field Professor of Urban Education
Department of Education
University of Chicago
Chicago, Illinois

Limited-English-Proficient Students
Walter Secada
Department of Curriculum and Instruction
University of Wisconsin
Madison, Wisconsin

Mainstreaming
Roxie Smith
Associate Provost
Northwestern University
Evanston, Illinois

Gifted Students
Christine Kuehn Ebert
Associate Professor of Education
University of South Carolina
Columbia, South Carolina

CRITIC READERS

Tony Barajas
Grace M. Nicholson School
Montgomery, Illinois

Jean (Bagley) Brennan
Johnson School
Nahant, Massachusetts

Jonathan Brinkerhoff
Shell Beach Elementary School
Pismo Beach, California

Leonor Esquivel Chavera
Zavala Special Emphasis Elementary School
Corpus Christi, Texas

Howard Cohn
Lone Star Elementary School
Jacksonville, Florida

Beverly Ireland
Loomis School
Loomis, California

Mary Jaramillo
Austin Elementary School
Odessa, Texas

Lin Jennings
Longoria Elementary School
Brownsville, Texas

Robert Leyva
Hellbeck Elementary School
Pueblo, Colorado

Rosemary Marich
Youngstown City Schools
Youngstown, Ohio

Feliciano Mendoza
Miles Avenue School
Huntington Park, California

Ann Marie O'Leary
Peter Muschal School
Bordentown, New Jersey

Vincent F. Rozen
Norwood Avenue Elementary School
Cranston, Rhode Island

Jan Sands
Western Oaks Elementary School
Bethany, Oklahoma

Diane C. Yee
Jefferson Year Round School
Oakland, California

Acknowledgments appear after the index.

Contents

Chapter 3 Two-Digit Addition and Subtraction

Chapter 4 Three- and Four-Digit Addition and Subtraction

Chapter 5   Time, Measurement, and Geometry

Chapter 6   Multiplication Concepts

Chapter 7 Multiplication Facts

Chapter 8 Geometry and Measurement

Chapter 9 Division Concepts

Chapter 10 Division Facts

Chapter **13** Multiplication Computation

Chapter **14** Statistics, Graphing, and Probability

Chapter 15 Division Computation

WELCOME TO
E X P L O R I N G
MATHEMATICS

Mathematics is valuable and interesting. The next ten pages describe some of the ways your book will help you explore and discover more of the wonders of mathematics.

Your book will help you build your

Math Power

Build your math power by doing
Problem Solving and Critical Thinking

You will use math to solve problems all your life. When you solve problems in your book, you will do more than find answers. You will learn how to think mathematically.

In Chapter 1, tell the page numbers where you first find these.

1 "Problem-Solving Guide"
- Understand
- Plan and Solve
- Look Back

2 "Tips for Problem Solvers"

3 An exercise called "Critical Thinking"

Build your math power by looking for

Connections

Your book will help you explore connections. You will see connections between math and the real world. Multicultural connections show the part mathematics plays in many cultures and societies.

In Chapter 2, tell the page numbers where you first find these headings.

4 Consumer Connection

5 Science Connection

6 Career Connection

7 Multicultural Connection

*Build your math power
by working on*

Number Sense and Using Data

You want your work with numbers to make sense. You need to be able to understand numbers, estimate, and do mental math. To read and use data, you will gather, organize, display, and study data.

1 Find a chapter that begins with a Number Sense Project about school lunches. Then find where this project is continued. (Hint: Find the Problem-Solving Workshop within the chapter.) On what page is the project continued?

2 On page 92, what kind of estimation is used?

3 On what page is the Data File that you'll use with Exercise 25 on page 96?

Scott, Fore

NUM
SENS

WORKSHOP

Build your math power by using
Calculators and Computers

Calculators and computers can help you solve problems and learn mathematics. It's important to know when calculators can help you and when they are not needed.

4 On page 24, what math topic does a calculator help you learn?

5 On page 229, what math topics does a computer help you learn?

6 Which exercises on page 143 ask you to tell whether or not you would use a calculator?

7 What pages in the Independent Study Handbook explain how to use a calculator?

Use your book to help you
Do Your Best

To do your best,
Expect to Succeed

When you want to learn something, it helps to believe in yourself. Whether you are learning a sport, a musical instrument, or mathematics, a positive attitude can make a big difference.

To do your best,
Build Your Understanding

When you understand what you're doing, you do it better and remember it longer. So it pays to study the "Build Understanding" part of the lessons.

1 On page 18, why is it easy to see what new math words are being taught?

To do your best, learn ways to do
Independent Study

You can learn how to study math even when a teacher is not there to help.

2 On page 4, look to the right of the words "Check Understanding." On what page can you find another example for that lesson?

3 On page 5, look to the right of the word "Practice." On what page can you find more practice for that lesson?

4 There is an Independent Study Handbook in the back of your book. On what page does the "Math Study Skills" section begin?

5 Name the first and last words defined in the glossary on page 563.

Your book will help you through
Active Learning

You'll learn math by doing
Math Activities

Activities help you understand math. Some activities use materials that help you show numbers, measure objects, do experiments, explore shapes, or solve problems.

1 What materials are used in the activity on page 36?

2 Use your "Math Sketcher" or a ruler to draw a picture that shows two equal parts of a rectangle.

Doing math includes
Reading, Writing, Talking, Listening

Reading, writing, talking, and listening in math class will help you think mathematically.

3 In Chapter 1, tell the page number where these first occur.

"Talk About Math"

"Write About Math"

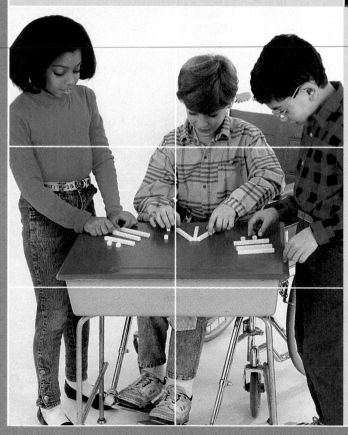

A good way to learn is by
Working in Groups

In real life and in math class, people can often solve problems better by working together.

4 How many students should work together in a group to do the "Building Hundreds" activity on page 36?

5 In the "Explore As a Team" on page 163, what is the "Tip for Working Together"?

To have a math adventure, catch the spirit of
Exploration

Be a Math Explorer and discover new things. Look for patterns. Check out your hunches, and try different ways to solve problems.

6 On what pages in Chapter 2 do you explore patterns in numbers with a number chart?

7 In "Explore Math" on page 47, what are you asked to do in problems 20–21?

A key ingredient to learning math is
Enjoying Math

Your book will help you
Enjoy Math at School

The explorations in your book will help you discover and enjoy mathematics.

1 In Chapter 8, what pages ask you to explore folding and cutting paper?

2 Fold a sheet of paper in half. Cut half of an apple with scissors or by tearing. Unfold the paper. Do you have a whole apple?

To make math a part of your life
Enjoy Math at Home

Outside of school, share math ideas with others and continue to explore math your whole life.

3 In the Math-at-Home Activity on page 131, how many dry beans are used?

4 Play this estimation game with someone at home. Choose items such as light switches. Guess how many are in your house. The player with the closest estimate scores 1 point. Repeat this with 4 other items. The player with the most points wins.

Using Basic Facts

Did You Know: In 1990, about 1 out of 3 children in the world were first-born. In Bolivia, 1 out of 6 children were first-born. In Japan, Poland, and the United States, about 1 out of 2 were first-born.

Number-Sense Project

Estimate
Estimate how many children in your class are the oldest child in their family.

Gather Data
Write down your estimate. Then take a class count to see how many children actually are the oldest in their families.

Analyze and Report
Was your estimate too high or too low? Compare with other students. Compare your actual results with the information given on page 2.

3

Number Sense

Build Understanding

Numbers can be used in many ways.

Numbers are used to *count*.

Numbers are used to *label*.

Numbers are used to *measure*.

Numbers are used to tell *order*.

■ **Talk About Math**   What are some other examples of how numbers are used?

Check Understanding

For another example, see Set A, pages 28–29.

For each picture, tell if the number is used to count, to label, to measure, or to tell order.

1.

2.

3.

Practice

For More Practice, see Set A, pages 30–31.

For each picture, tell if the number is used to count, to label, to measure, or to tell order.

4.

5. Oak Dale Exit 1½ Miles

6. 12 MUFFINS

7. 14

8. 5:00

9. 6th STREET

10. HOME 34 / VISITOR 32

11. FM 92 98 102 / AM 7 10 12

12.

Read each sentence. Tell how each number is used.

13. There are 37 cars in the parking lot.

14. The hockey game was in the 2nd period of play.

Problem Solving

Solve each problem.

Mrs. Lindsay bought theater tickets.

15. How many different numbers are used on the tickets?

16. How is each number used?

SEC	ROW	SEAT
2	B	15

42nd STREET

8 PM   AUG 6 1989

$10 50

Addition and Subtraction

Build Understanding

Activity

More or Less
Materials: Small objects for counting

A.a. Show 4 objects.
Show 3 more.
How many objects are there in all?

b. Write the basic fact.   **4 + 3 = 7**
Addends ———⌐———⌐   ⌐ Sum

c. Make a table to record your work.

	+3
4	7

d. Show a number of objects.
Show 3 more.
Use the table to record your work.

e. Repeat step **d** two more times using a
different number of objects each time.

B.a. Show 10 objects.
Take 4 away.
How many objects are left?

b. Write the basic fact.   **10 − 4 = 6**
↑ ⌐ Difference

c. Make a table to record your work.

	−4
10	6

d. Show a number of objects.
Take 4 away.
Use the table to record your work.

e. Repeat step **d** two more times using a
different number of objects each time.

■ **Write About Math**   Write a word problem using
one of the facts you completed in Example A or B.

For another example, see Set B, pages 28–29.

Check Understanding

Tell the rule for each table in Exercises 1–3. Use the rule to complete the table for Exercises 4–7.

1.

6	14
2	10
8	16
9	17

2.

10	3
8	1
14	7
7	0

3.

1	3
3	5
5	7
7	9

	−4
4. 11	
5. 4	
6. 13	
7. 6	

Practice

For More Practice, see Set B, pages 30–31.

Use the rule given. Find the missing numbers.

	+5
8. 6	
9. 8	
10. 0	
11. 2	

	−2
12. 5	
13. 9	
14. 4	
15. 2	

	+6
16. 6	
17. 8	
18.	13
19.	9

	−7
20. 14	
21.	1
22.	8
23. 7	

Follow the arrows. Find the missing number for each circle.

24. ⑨ → +5 → ○
   ↑   ↓
−1   −7
   ↑   ↓
 ○ ← +3 ← ○

25. ④ → +3 → ○
   ↑   ↓
−2   +8
   ↑   ↓
 ○ ← −9 ← ○

26. ⑩ → −2 → ○
   ↑   ↓
+3   −4
   ↑   ↓
 ○ ← +3 ← ○

Problem Solving

Critical Thinking   Solve each problem.

27. Write three basic facts in which zero is added to a number. Explain what happens when zero is added to a number.

28. Mai picked 6, 9, 5, and 7 apples from 4 different trees. She gave away 3 apples from each tree. How many apples did she keep from each tree?

Operation Sense

Build Understanding

ACTIVITY

The Case of the Sticky Cover-up!
Materials: Objects of the same size

Sticky Fingers stuck stickers on numbers and symbols. Help Mathy Sleuth solve the case.

A. What number is under the 🌵 in 4 + 🌵 = 9?

Think about a number you can add to 4 to get 9.

a. Arrange 4 objects in a row. In another row, add one object at a time until there are 9 objects altogether.

b. Count the objects in the second row.

4 + 5 = 9

B. What symbol is under the ☼ in 5 ☼ 3 = 2?

a. Use 5 objects. Add 3 objects. Do you get 2?

b. Take away 3 objects. Do you get 2?

5 − 3 = 2

c. What numbers added together are the same as or *equal* 7?

2 plus 5 equals 7. 3 + 4 = 7
7 is the same as 6 plus 1.

■ **Talk About Math** How do you know that 6 − 2 = 2 is false? How do you know that 6 − 4 = 2 is true?

Check Understanding

For another example, see Set C, pages 28–29.

Use your objects to tell what number or symbol is under each sticker in Exercises 1–3.

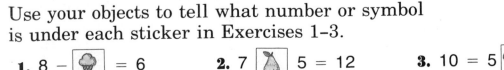

1. 8 − 🍦 = 6   **2.** 7 🍐 5 = 12   **3.** 10 = 5 🌳 5

Practice

For More Practice, see Set C, pages 30–31.

Tell what number or symbol is under each sticker.

4. 1 = 9 − 🕯

5. 0 🌙 4 − 4

6. 🌷 − 2 = 8

7. 6 = 🖌 + 5

8. 11 = 3 👩 8

9. 6 + 🍀 = 6

10. 7 = 7 − ⚓

11. 8 🏠 6 + 2

12. 5 + 🐸 = 5

13. 2 🍎 8 = 10

14. ❤ − 7 = 5

15. 9 🌈 8 + 1

16. 3 🍃 6 − 3

17. 11 ✏ 7 = 4

18. 4 = 4 🐞 0

Problem Solving

Write a number sentence using all of the given
numbers and symbols. **Remember** that the values
on each side of the "=" sign must be the same.

19. 1, 5, 6, −, =

20. 3, 9, 6, −, =

21. 12, 5, 7, +, =

22. 7, 10, 3, +, =

23. 1, 4, 3, −, =

24. 9, 11, 2, +, =

25. 5, 2, 3, −, =

26. 4, 12, 8, +, =

27. 1, 6, 7, −, =

Explore ———— **Math**

28. Suppose 👁 + 🎼 = 8.
What could be under the
stickers?

29. Suppose 🍐 − 🌳 = 5.
What could be under the
stickers?

30. Can there be more than one answer for
Problems 28 and 29? Why or why not?

Using a Problem Solving Guide

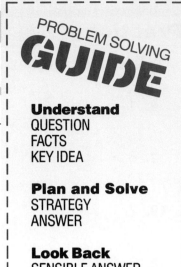

Build Understanding

Solving a problem is like taking a trip. There may be more than one way to get an answer. Sometimes you need to start over. The Problem-Solving Guide is like a map that can help you find your way.

Mr. Barker teaches gym. He is taking stock of his gym equipment. Of 8 mats, 3 are old. How many are new?

Understand
QUESTION
FACTS
KEY IDEA

Plan and Solve
STRATEGY
ANSWER

Look Back
SENSIBLE ANSWER
ALTERNATE APPROACH

Understand
QUESTION _____
What are you asked to find?

FACTS _____
What facts are given?

KEY IDEA _____
How are the facts
and question related?

Plan and Solve _____
STRATEGY
What can you do to solve
the problem?

ANSWER _____
Give the answer in a sentence.

Look Back _____
SENSIBLE ANSWER
Did you check your work?

ALTERNATE APPROACH _____
Is there another way to get
the same answer?

Understand
QUESTION   How many mats are new?

FACTS   8 mats in all. 3 are old.

KEY IDEA   The other mats are new.

Plan and Solve
STRATEGY   Subtract to find how many are new.

$$\begin{array}{r} 8 \\ -\,3 \\ \hline 5 \end{array}$$

ANSWER   There are 5 new gym mats.

Look Back
SENSIBLE ANSWER   Use addition to check your answer. $5 + 3 = 8$

■ **Talk About Math**   Can you think of a different way to solve the problem?

Check Understanding

1. What are the three steps of the Problem-Solving Guide?

Answer each question about the problem at the right.

2. What are you asked to find?

3. What unit label will you use for the answer?

I have 4 aluminum bats and I see 7 wooden ones. How many bats are there in all?

Practice

Answer each question about the problem below.

4. What facts are given?

5. Rewrite the problem in your own words.

6. The answer is 5. Give this answer in a sentence.

7. Complete this sentence. "The answer to Question 6 makes sense because . . ."

There are only 7 basketballs. I need 12 for use in the gym. How many do I need to buy?

Solve each problem. Use the Problem-Solving Guide to help you.

8. There are 8 tennis rackets and 6 badminton rackets. How many children can play either sport at the same time?

9. Mr. Barker had 12 volleyball nets. He lent 3 of them to another school. How many nets did he have left?

10. Mr. Barker had 5 soccer balls that needed to be inflated. He had 9 soccer balls that had enough air. How many soccer balls did he have in all?

Families of Facts

Build Understanding

Number sentences that are related make up a *family of facts.*

A.

One family of facts is:
5 + 4 = 9
4 + 5 = 9
9 − 5 = 4
9 − 4 = 5

B.

One family of facts is:
1 + 1 = 2
2 − 1 = 1

c. Mental Math Families of facts can help you remember basic facts. If you know that 4 + 2 = 6, you can use the family of facts to recall that 2 + 4 = 6, 6 − 2 = 4, and 6 − 4 = 2.

■ **Write About Math** Write 3 families of facts like the one in Example B. What is special about these fact families?

Check Understanding

For another example, see Set D, pages 28–29.

Write the family of facts for each picture.

1.

2.

3. Write the family of facts for 5, 5, 10.

12

Write the family of facts for each picture.

4.

5.

6.

7.

A
L
G
E
B
R
A
Copy and complete each number sentence.

8. 9 + 6 = ▦   **9.** 3 + 7 = ▦   **10.** 8 + 0 = ▦

   15 − 6 = ▦   10 − 7 = ▦   8 − 8 = ▦

    6 + 9 = ▦   10 − 3 = ▦   8 − 0 = ▦

   15 − ▦ = 6   ▦ + 3 = 10   ▦ + 8 = 8

Write the family of facts for the numbers in each exercise.

11. 2, 4, 6   **12.** 3, 5, 8   **13.** 4, 7, 11   **14.** 2, 9, 11

15. 14, 8, 6   **16.** 1, 7, 6   **17.** 9, 3, 6   **18.** 8, 0, 8

19. 5, 0, 5   **20.** 3, 3, 6   **21.** 5, 5, 10   **22.** 12, 7, 19

Copy. Then write each answer. Circle the fact
that does not belong to the family.

23. 12 − 5   **24.** 9 − 4   **25.** 16 − 7   **26.** 15 − 8
       5 + 8   5 + 4   9 − 7   8 + 7
      13 − 5   4 + 5   7 + 9   15 − 9
       8 + 5   9 − 5   16 − 9   7 + 8
      13 − 8   5 + 5   9 + 7   15 − 7

13

Number Sense Suppose that two numbers of a family of facts are 7 and 1.

27. Name a number that could be the third number in that family of facts.

28. What other number could the third number be?

Mixed Practice Find each answer. **Remember** to watch the signs.

29. $\begin{array}{r} 5 \\ +7 \\ \hline \end{array}$	**30.** $\begin{array}{r} 8 \\ -2 \\ \hline \end{array}$	**31.** $\begin{array}{r} 12 \\ -\ 4 \\ \hline \end{array}$	**32.** $\begin{array}{r} 16 \\ -\ 8 \\ \hline \end{array}$	**33.** $\begin{array}{r} 9 \\ +3 \\ \hline \end{array}$	**34.** $\begin{array}{r} 6 \\ +6 \\ \hline \end{array}$
35. $\begin{array}{r} 13 \\ -\ 6 \\ \hline \end{array}$	**36.** $\begin{array}{r} 1 \\ +9 \\ \hline \end{array}$	**37.** $\begin{array}{r} 10 \\ -\ 2 \\ \hline \end{array}$	**38.** $\begin{array}{r} 4 \\ +6 \\ \hline \end{array}$	**39.** $\begin{array}{r} 17 \\ +\ 7 \\ \hline \end{array}$	**40.** $\begin{array}{r} 7 \\ -3 \\ \hline \end{array}$

Problem Solving

Critical Thinking Find the missing numbers.

41. I am the largest number in my family of facts. The other two numbers are 3 and 5. Who am I?

42. There are only two different numbers in my family of facts. The largest number is 8. Who are we?

TIPS FOR PROBLEM SOLVERS

Be confident so you can do your best.

Solve each problem.

43. Use one of the facts you wrote for Exercises 11–22 to write a word problem.

44. Kim has 6 people in her family. There are 2 less people in Meg's family. How many people are in the girls' families altogether?

45. Use Data Look at the way the apples are arranged on the top of page 4. Write a family of facts for the picture.

14

For each picture, tell if the numbers are used
to count, to label, to measure, or to tell order.

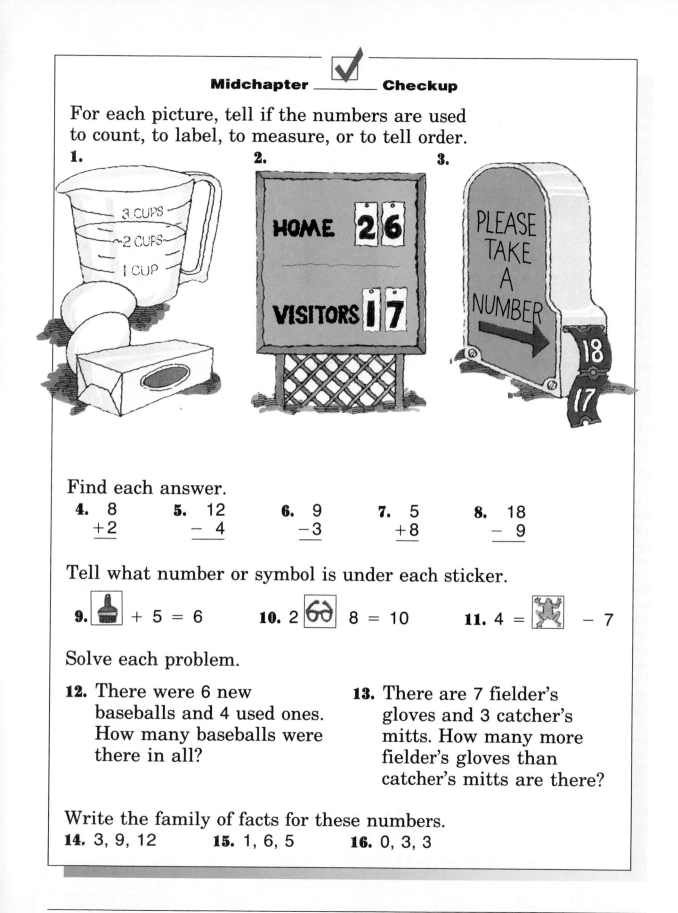

1.

2.

HOME 26

VISITORS 17

3.

PLEASE TAKE A NUMBER

18

17

Find each answer.

4. 8
   +2
_____

5. 12
   − 4
_____

6. 9
   −3
_____

7. 5
   +8
_____

8. 18
   − 9
_____

Tell what number or symbol is under each sticker.

9. ▢ + 5 = 6

10. 2 ▢ 8 = 10

11. 4 = ▢ − 7

Solve each problem.

12. There were 6 new
baseballs and 4 used ones.
How many baseballs were
there in all?

13. There are 7 fielder's
gloves and 3 catcher's
mitts. How many more
fielder's gloves than
catcher's mitts are there?

Write the family of facts for these numbers.
14. 3, 9, 12   **15.** 1, 6, 5   **16.** 0, 3, 3

Problem Solving WORKSHOP

Explore as a Team

1. Use 36 white cards. Write each of the numbers 1–9 on a separate card. There will be 4 sets. Mix well and make a pile face down on the table.

2. Use 17 pink cards. Write each of the numbers 2–18 on separate cards. Each team member gets 4 of these and places them face up on the table.

TIPS FOR WORKING TOGETHER

Help keep your group on task.

3. Then each member draws white cards in turn trying to make an addition basic fact for the numbered pink cards he or she has. Once played, the white cards cannot be moved.

4. When one member has made facts for all 4 numbers, talk about which facts were easiest to make. Which were the hardest?

5. Repeat the process and see if your statements for Exercise 4 are still correct.

Explore with a Computer

Use the *Graphing and Probability Workshop Project* with this activity.

1. Look around your classroom. Count the number of circles, rectangles, and triangles you find. For example, a book looks like a rectangle. Write how many of each shape you find.

2. At the computer, type the number of each shape in the table.

3. Select the **Bar graph** option. What does the graph show?

Number-Sense Project

Look back at pages 2–3. Choose the number sentence from those below that best describes each family pictured on pages 2–3. Explain why.

1. 4 + 1 = 5   **2.** 2 + 2 = 4
3. 2 + 3 = 5   **4.** 1 + 3 = 4

Critical Thinking Activity

Place the numbers 1–9 in the squares to make sums of 15. The sum of each row, column and diagonal must be 15.

15

→15
→15
→15

15 15 15   15

Even and Odd

Build Understanding

That's Odd!

Materials: Small objects for counting

What makes a number even or odd?

An assembly line can produce more than 500 cans per minute.

a. Take 6 objects. Try to separate them into 2 equal piles.

b. Take 9 objects. Try to separate them into 2 equal piles.

c. Repeat a and b using 4, 5, 7, 8, 10, 11, 12, and 13 objects.

d. Which numbers can make two even piles with none left over?

These are called ***even numbers.***

e. Which numbers must have one left over?

These are called ***odd numbers.***

■ **Talk About Math** Can you think of any other ways to tell if a number is even or odd?

Check Understanding

For another example, see Set E, pages 28–29.

For each number, tell whether it is even or odd and why. Use objects if you need them.

1. 8   **2.** 5   **3.** 17   **4.** 54   **5.** 33   **6.** 50

Practice

For More Practice, see Set E, pages 30–31.

Tell if each number is odd or even.

7. 23   **8.** 42   **9.** 98   **10.** 701   **11.** 114   **12.** 85

13. 234   **14.** 467   **15.** 105   **16.** 76   **17.** 67   **18.** 77

Mental Math   Find each sum.

19. 4 + 2   **20.** 6 + 8   **21.** 2 + 6   **22.** 4 + 8   **23.** 8 + 2

24. 1 + 5   **25.** 7 + 9   **26.** 7 + 5   **27.** 3 + 1   **28.** 9 + 1

29. 9 + 4   **30.** 6 + 7   **31.** 3 + 8   **32.** 6 + 9   **33.** 8 + 5

Problem Solving

Calculator   Use a calculator to find each sum.
Tell if the sum is odd or even.

34. 327 + 659   **35.** 108 + 214   **36.** 1,357 + 2,468
   145 + 731   324 + 602   3,414 + 4,319

Number Sense   Use Exercises 34–36. What is the sum of

37. two even numbers?   **38.** two odd numbers?

39. an even and an odd number?

40. Critical Thinking   Will the sum be
odd or even if you add two even
numbers and one odd number? two
odd numbers and one even number?

Skills _____ Review   pages 4–5

Write a sentence using the numbers and words
in each exercise.
1. 6 days   **2.** 1st place   **3.** 21 cents   **4.** 3 o'clock

Use Data from a Picture

Build Understanding

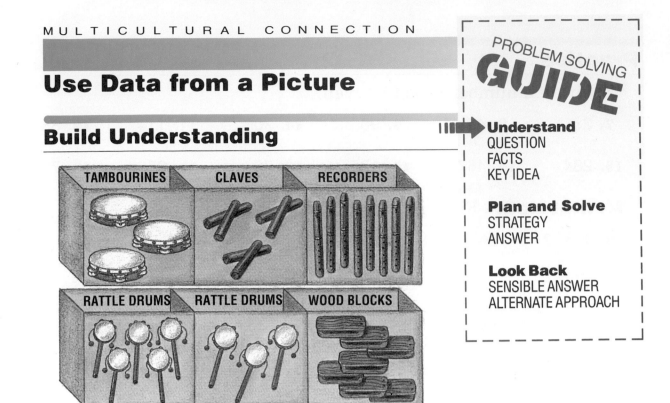

PROBLEM SOLVING GUIDE

▶ **Understand**
QUESTION
FACTS
KEY IDEA

Plan and Solve
STRATEGY
ANSWER

Look Back
SENSIBLE ANSWER
ALTERNATE APPROACH

The music room has many different instruments from around the world. How many rattle drums are there in the boxes?

▶ **Understand**   QUESTION   How many rattle drums are there?

FACTS   One box has 5 rattle drums. One box has 3 rattle drums.

KEY IDEA   You can add to find how many rattle drums there are in all.

Plan and Solve

$5 + 3 = 8$

There are 8 rattle drums in the boxes.

Look Back   You can also find the answer by counting the rattle drums in the two boxes.

Panpipes are made of a series of hollow pipes. Sounds are made by blowing across the pipes.

■ **Talk About Math**   If each student uses two claves, how many students are needed to use all the claves in the box?

Check Understanding

Use the pictures on page 20 to solve the problems.

1. How many recorders are there?

2. How many wood blocks are there?

3. Are there more recorders or wood blocks?

4. Are there more panpipes or tambourines?

Practice

Use the pictures on page 20 and the pictures below to solve the problems.

5. How many thumb pianos are there in all?

6. How many tambourines are there in all?

7. How many more recorders are there than panpipes?

8. Are there more castanets or wood blocks?

9. Which instruments are kept in more than one box?

10. Which instruments are made of wood only?

11. Claves and maracas are used in music from Latin America. How many claves and maracas are there altogether?

What is the total number of instruments that can be played by

12. blowing?   **13.** shaking?   **14.** tapping?

Ordering Events

Build Understanding

Tell how to put the pictures in order.

Which is the first picture? Why?

Which is the second picture? Why?

Which is the third picture? Why?

Which is the last picture? Why?

When the pictures are *in order,* they show a *sequence* of events.

■ **Write About Math** List some things you do each day. Put them in order.

Check Understanding

For another example, see Set F, pages 28–29.

Put each set of pictures in order.

1.

2.

Practice

For More Practice, see Set F, pages 30–31.

Order the following according to the rule.

3. Put in alphabetical order: carrot, apple, potato, celery.

4. Put in numerical order from least to greatest: 8, 1, 5, 3, 6.

5. Put in order by height, shortest first: puppy, goat, gorilla, giraffe.

6. Put in order beginning with Sunday: Friday, Tuesday, Sunday, Thursday.

7. Put in alphabetical order: meal, money, mat, mule.

8. Put in numerical order from greatest to least: 10, 13, 8, 17.

9. Put in order of size, smallest first: baseball, basketball, soccerball.

10. Put in order by age, youngest first: teenager, toddler, senior citizen, infant.

Problem Solving

Write these sentences in the correct order.

11. Jack shoveled the snow.
It snowed a lot.
Jack put on his snow boots.
It was beginning to snow.

12. Marti left for school.
Marti ate breakfast.
Marti woke up.
Marti got out of bed.

Critical Thinking Tell the rule used to order the words.

13. Morning, noon, night

14. Penny, dime, quarter

Find a Pattern

Build Understanding

Have you ever played a game using a calculator?

On his calculator, Pablo entered 4. Then he pushed three other keys which he called his secret key sequence. This is what the display showed.

PROBLEM SOLVING GUIDE

Understand
QUESTION
FACTS
KEY IDEA

Plan and Solve
STRATEGY
ANSWER

Look Back
SENSIBLE ANSWER
ALTERNATE APPROACH

Here you see other numbers Pablo entered along with this secret key sequence. The display for each is shown. Can you tell what Pablo's secret key sequence is?

Enter	Display
4	7
7	10
3	6
0	3

Understand   The secret key sequence does the same thing to each number keyed in.

Plan and Solve   STRATEGY   Look for a pattern. Each display is 3 more than the number keyed in.

4 + 3 = 7
7 + 3 = 10
3 + 3 = 6
0 + 3 = 3

ANSWER   Pablo is using the sequence ⊞ 3 ⊜.

Look Back   Use addition to check the key sequence with each number given. Do your answers match the display numbers?

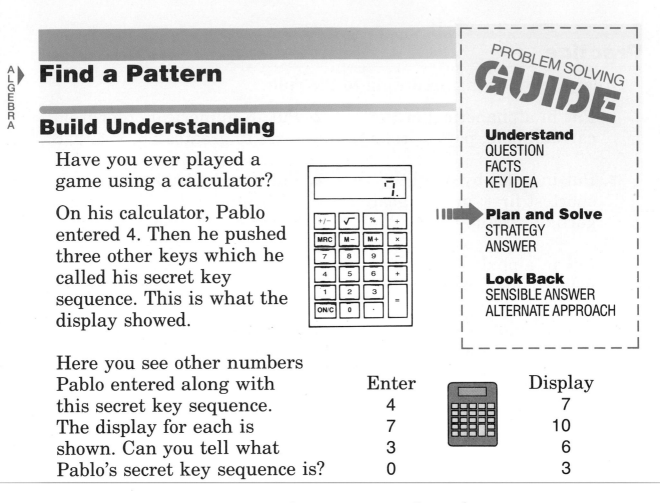

■ **Write About Math** Try Pablo's key sequence with 3 other numbers. Is the display always 3 greater than the number you keyed in?

Check Understanding

Answer each question.

1. Rachel's secret sequence is ⊕ 9 ⊜. What display will she get if she enters 3? 5? 7? 9?

2. Amy's secret key sequence is ⊖ 5 ⊜. What display will she get is she enters 5? 8? 10? 14?

Practice

Tell what key sequence was used.

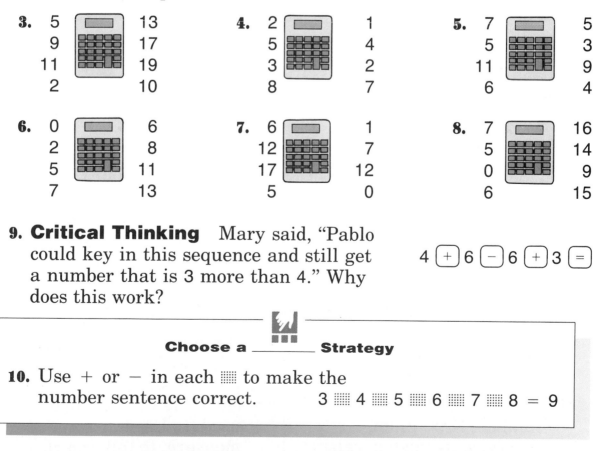

3.
5	13
9	17
11	19
2	10

4.
2	1
5	4
3	2
8	7

5.
7	5
5	3
11	9
6	4

6.
0	6
2	8
5	11
7	13

7.
6	1
12	7
17	12
5	0

8.
7	16
5	14
0	9
6	15

9. Critical Thinking Mary said, "Pablo could key in this sequence and still get a number that is 3 more than 4." Why does this work?

4 ⊕ 6 ⊖ 6 ⊕ 3 ⊜

Choose a ____ Strategy

10. Use + or − in each ▦ to make the number sentence correct. 3 ▦ 4 ▦ 5 ▦ 6 ▦ 7 ▦ 8 = 9

Skills Review

Read each sentence. Tell if the number is used to count, to label, to measure, or to tell order.

1. Joe walks 6 blocks to school.

2. Hannah sits in the 2nd row.

Use the rule given. Find the missing numbers.

		+4
3.	6	▦
4.	1	▦
5.	8	▦
6.	3	▦

		−6
7.	7	▦
8.	9	▦
9.	12	▦
10.	10	▦

Tell what number or symbol is under each strawberry.

11. $4 + 🍓 = 13$

12. $6 🍓 2 = 8$

Write the family of facts for the numbers in each exercise.

13. 3, 3, 0   **14.** 15, 9, 6

Tell if each number is odd or even.

15. 25   **16.** 91   **17.** 40

18. Put in order by size, smallest first: plum, cherry, watermelon, raisin.

Problem-Solving Review

Solve each problem.

19. Begin with 5. Subtract 2. Add 5. Subtract 4. Add 3. What number results?

20. Put in alphabetical order: hamster, dog, fish, cat.

21. Use the picture to answer. If each of 5 people takes one sandwich, how many sandwiches will be left?

22. Dexter bought 3 notebooks and 6 pencils. How many items did he buy?

23. What number will you get if you subtract 5 from 6? from 8? from 10? from 12?

24. **Data File** Use data from pages 104–105. How many more runs did the Mets score than the Pirates?

25. **Make a Data File** Look through a newspaper or magazine. Cut out and label pictures or sentences that show the ways numbers are used (to label, to count, to measure, to tell order).

Read each sentence. Tell if the number is used to count, to label, to measure, or to tell order.

1. There were 15 children at the party.

2. Maria's is the 2nd house.

3. Urich's birthday is May 6.

4. The dog weighs 45 pounds.

Use the rule given. Find the missing numbers.

	+3	
5.	6	
6.	5	
7.	7	
8.	0	

	−9	
9.	12	
10.	9	
11.	18	
12.	15	

	−5	
13.		5
14.	7	
15.	11	
16.		1

	+6	
17.	9	
18.		8
19.		11
20.	7	

Tell what number or symbol is under each bug.

21. $8 + \text{🐞} = 8$

22. $4 \text{🐞} 8 = 12$

23. $3 = \text{🐞} - 6$

24. $9 - 9 \text{🐞} 0$

25. $7 = 11 \text{🐞} 4$

26. $14 = \text{🐞} + 6$

Write the family of facts for the numbers in each exercise.

27. 5, 6, 11

28. 15, 8, 7

29. 5, 0, 5

30. 4, 10, 6

31. 9, 3, 6

32. 12, 7, 5

Tell if each number is odd or even.

33. 33   **34.** 78   **35.** 601   **36.** 95   **37.** 312   **38.** 49   **39.** 30

Order the following according to the rule.

40. Put in numerical order from least to greatest: 6, 2, 5, 9, 1

41. Put in alphabetical order: math, gym, spelling, reading

Reteaching

Set A pages 4–5

Numbers are used in many ways.

To count:
There are 4 boys and 4 girls.

To label:
We live on Third Street.

To measure:
The car is 8 feet long.

To tell the order of things:
The Cubs came in 1st.

Remember that a number, such as a date, can be used in more than one way.

Read each sentence. Tell if the number is used to count, to label, to measure, or to tell order.

1. We stayed in room 837 at the Peabody Hotel.

2. I was born on October 17.

Set B pages 6–7

The rule in this table says: "add 4."

Find the missing numbers.

	+4
6	▨
9	▨
7	▨
4	▨
▨	4

6 + 4 = 10

9 + 4 = 13

7 + 4 = 11

4 + 4 = 8

0 + 4 = 4

Remember that the addends are the numbers used to find the sum.

Use the rule given. Find the missing numbers.

1.

	+7
2	▨
8	▨
▨	13
5	▨

2.

	+6
4	▨
9	▨
7	▨
▨	12

Set C pages 8–9

What number is under the ■ ?

$$7 + \blacksquare = 12$$

Show 7 objects. ▢▢▢▢▢▢▢

Now add 1 object at a time until there are 12 objects. ▢▢▢▢▢

The second row has 5 objects. So
$$7 + 5 = 12.$$

Remember that there are several combinations of numbers that name the same number.

Tell what number is under each sticker.

1. $4 + \blacksquare = 13$

2. $\blacksquare + 9 = 16$

Set D   pages 12–14

Here is the family of facts for 4, 6, and 10.

$6 + 4 = 10$
$4 + 6 = 10$
$10 - 6 = 4$
$10 - 4 = 6$

If you know the basic fact, you can use it to write the other facts.

Remember that you can use families of facts to help you remember basic facts.

Write the family of facts for each picture.

1.

2.

Set E   pages 18–19

Which groups of objects can be separated into 2 equal parts?

4 ☐☐☐☐

5 ☐☐☐☐☐

6 ☐☐☐☐☐☐

7 ☐☐☐☐☐☐☐

Numbers that can make 2 equal parts are even numbers. Numbers that cannot are odd numbers.

Remember that you can make an even number into an odd number by adding one to the even number.

Tell if each number is odd or even.

1. 11   **2.** 20   **3.** 22   **4.** 49

5. 33   **6.** 64   **7.** 109   **8.** 240

Set F   pages 22–23

Write the names of the following states in alphabetical order.

Massachusetts   California
Texas   Florida
California   Massachusetts
Florida   Texas

Now write the names in order according to the number of letters from least to greatest.

Texas   5 letters
Florida   7 letters
California   10 letters
Massachusetts   13 letters

Remember that there are things you do that must be done in a certain order. Other events are put in an order according to a rule.

Order the following according to the rule.

1. Put in alphabetical order: banana, onion, cucumber

2. Put the items in Exercise 1 in order according to the number of letters from least to greatest.

More Practice

Set A pages 4–5

Read each sentence. Tell if the number is used
to count, to label, to measure, or to tell order.

1. He is over 6 feet tall.

2. It is 5 miles to the mall.

3. The parking lot can hold 380 cars.

4. They were moved to room 218.

5. José hit a home run in the eighth inning.

6. Alice has a ticket for the game on September 28.

7. She scored 20 points in the game.

8. She has grown 2 inches this year.

Set B pages 6–7

Use the rule given. Find the missing numbers.

	+4
1.	3
2.	8
3.	7
4.	4
5.	5

	−6
6.	2
7.	9
8.	6
9.	7
10.	8

	+8
11.	5
12.	8
13.	6
14.	10
15.	8

	−8
16.	12
17.	3
18.	2
19.	14
20.	8

Set C pages 8–9

Tell what number or symbol is under each sticker.

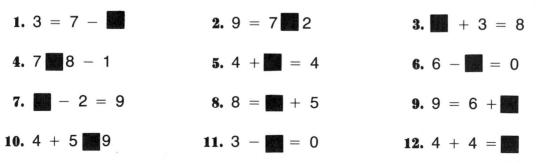

1. 3 = 7 − ■

2. 9 = 7 ■ 2

3. ■ + 3 = 8

4. 7 ■ 8 − 1

5. 4 + ■ = 4

6. 6 − ■ = 0

7. ■ − 2 = 9

8. 8 = ■ + 5

9. 9 = 6 + ■

10. 4 + 5 ■ 9

11. 3 − ■ = 0

12. 4 + 4 = ■

Set D pages 12–14

Write the family of facts for each picture.

1. [dice image]

2. [dice image]

Copy and complete each number sentence.

3. 6 + 7 = ▦
13 − 6 = ▦
7 + 6 = ▦
13 − ▦ = 6

4. 7 + 4 = ▦
11 − 4 = ▦
11 − 7 = ▦
▦ + 7 = 11

5. 8 + 5 = ▦
13 − 8 = ▦
13 − 5 = ▦
▦ + 8 = 13

Copy and write each answer. Circle the fact that does not belong to the family.

6. 13 − 6 =
6 + 5 =
11 − 5 =
11 − 6 =
5 + 6 =

7. 8 − 5 =
5 − 3 =
8 − 3 =
5 + 3 =
3 + 5 =

8. 6 + 8 =
14 − 8 =
14 − 6 =
8 − 6 =
8 + 6 =

9. 12 − 9 =
12 − 3 =
9 − 3 =
3 + 9 =
9 + 3 =

Mixed Practice Find each answer.

10. 6
+7

11. 9
−2

12. 12
−3

13. 4
+9

14. 16
−7

15. 9
+9

Set E pages 18–19

Tell if each number is odd or even.

1. 17   **2.** 36   **3.** 84   **4.** 91   **5.** 68   **6.** 120

Mental Math Find each sum.

7. 2 + 7   **8.** 8 + 7   **9.** 4 + 9   **10.** 7 + 3   **11.** 6 + 5

Set F pages 22–23

Order the following according to the rule.

1. Put in numerical order from least to greatest: 9, 4, 7, 2, 6.

2. Put in alphabetical order: goat, donkey, tiger, elk.

Enrichment

Missing Sums and Addends

Complete this addition table.
To find the missing addend for
Exercise 25, use subtraction.

8 is the sum of 3 plus what?
12 is the sum of 7 plus what?
10 is the sum of 5 plus what?

All three answers should be the
same. If not, check your
subtraction.

	+	3	7	5	9	6	8
1.–6.	6						
7.–12.	8						
13.–18.	7						
19.–24.	9						
25.–28.		8	12	10			
29.–34.	4						

Find the correct sums or addends for
this addition table.

	+			3			
41.–47.							13
48.–53.			12			11	
54.–59.	5	9					
60.–65.		8			9		
66.–70.	8			15		16	
71.–77.					9		
78.–83.						17	15

Chapter 1 Review/Test

1. Tell if the number in the picture is used to count, to label, to measure, or to tell order.

2. Use the rule + 4. Find the missing number.

	+ 4
7	11
4	
2	6

Add or subtract.

3. 9
     +5

4. 10
      − 6

5. 7
     +8

Tell what sign belongs in each box.

6. 8 ▒ 5 + 3   **7.** 16 ▒ 7 = 9

8. Which fact does not belong to the family?

6 + 8 = 14
14 − 6 = 8
8 − 6 = 2
8 + 6 = 14
14 − 8 = 6

Tell if each number is odd or even.

9. 57   **10.** 238   **11.** 99

12. How many more squares are there than triangles?

13. Put in order from the beginning of the day: lunch, supper, afternoon snack, breakfast.

14. Look at the numbers in the top row. Tell what pattern was used to get the numbers in the bottom row.

8	1	7	10	25
12	5	11	14	29

Read this problem. Then answer the questions below.

A school owns 9 microscopes. It will need 9 for the new school year. How many must it buy?

15. What facts are given?

16. The answer is 0. Write this answer in a sentence.

17. ■ **Write About Math** In Exercise 8, tell *why* the fact you chose does not belong to that family.

Place Value

2

Did You Know: Sometimes, all the houses on one side of the street have odd numbers. All the houses on the other side of the street have even numbers.

Number-Sense Project

Estimate

Predict the address of the buildings closest to the home or apartment you live in.

Gather Data

Draw a picture of your house or apartment. Also draw the 2 nearest neighbors on your side of the street. Put your street number under your house. Predict the house numbers for your 2 neighbors. Check to see what they are when you go home.

Analyze and Report

Did you know your house or apartment number? Did you predict the house numbers of your neighbors correctly? Correct the numbers in your drawing. Put the pictures up for others to see.

Understanding Hundreds

Build Understanding

Building Hundreds
Materials: ones, tens, hundreds
Groups: 4 students

Do you think there are really
a hundred fish in this
aquarium? It is hard to tell.

TROPICAL PET LAND
BIG FISH SALE
We have hundreds of fish!

Use ones, tens, and hundreds to help
you see one hundred.

a. How many tens can you cover with 32 ones?

32 ones   3 tens 2 ones

b. How many tens do 56 ones cover?

c. How many hundreds can you cover with 21 tens?

21 tens   2 hundreds 1 ten

d. How many hundreds do
37 tens cover?

■ **Talk About Math**
Explain why 138 ones is
equal to 1 hundred,
3 tens, and 8 ones.

Check Understanding

For another example, see Set A, pages 66–67.

Use tens and ones to make as many tens as you
can. Then use **|** and • to record your work.

1. 30 ones   **2.** 34 ones   **3.** 41 ones   **4.** 18 ones

5. 50 ones   **6.** 12 ones   **7.** 35 ones   **8.** 27 ones

9. Look at Exercises 1 and 2. How are they different?

Use tens and hundreds to make as many
hundreds as you can. Then use ☐ and **|** to
record your work.

10. 30 tens   **11.** 33 tens   **12.** 19 tens   **13.** 35 tens

14. 26 tens   **15.** 50 tens   **16.** 43 tens   **17.** 24 tens

18. Look at Exercises 10 and 11. How are they different?

Practice

For More Practice, see Set A, pages 68–69.

Use tens and ones to make as many
tens as you can. Use **|** and • to record
your work.

19. 20 ones   **20.** 22 ones

21. 33 ones   **22.** 42 ones

23. 37 ones   **24.** 40 ones

25. 24 ones   **26.** 13 ones

27. 44 ones   **28.** 56 ones

29. 10 ones   **30.** 28 ones

Use ones, tens, and hundreds to make as many hundreds as you can. Use □, l, and • to record your work.

31. 40 tens   **32.** 20 tens   **33.** 31 tens   **34.** 13 tens

35. 28 tens   **36.** 21 tens   **37.** 39 tens   **38.** 25 tens

39. 34 tens   **40.** 11 tens   **41.** 15 tens   **42.** 29 tens

43. 23 tens   **44.** 18 tens   **45.** 32 tens   **46.** 16 tens

47. 19 tens 42 ones

48. 27 tens 38 ones

Problem Solving

Mental Math   Solve each problem.

49. The pet store wants no more than 5 fish in each small fish bowl. One small bowl has 13 fish in it. How many fish should be taken out of the bowl?

50. Julio will give Juan 7 tropical fish for his birthday. Juan already has 9 tropical fish. How many tropical fish will Juan have after Julio gives him his birthday present?

Reading ———— Math

Numbers and Symbols   Write each sentence using numbers and symbols.

1. three plus five is eight

2. four plus nine is thirteen

3. fifteen minus nine is six

4. two plus seven is nine

5. five minus four is one

6. nine minus seven is two

7. seven plus eight is fifteen

8. nine minus zero is nine

9. six plus seven is thirteen

10. twelve minus six is six

Hundreds, Tens, and Ones

Build Understanding

The Spring Carnival Committee at Moss School sold tickets for rides. There were rolls of one hundred tickets, strips of ten tickets, and single tickets.

The third graders bought 4 rolls, 3 strips, and 2 singles. How many tickets did they buy?

CARNIVAL TICKETS BOUGHT

Grade	Rolls	Strips	Singles
Third	4	3	2
Fourth	3	8	7
Fifth	0	9	3

What do you like to do at a carnival?

4 hundreds	3 tens		2 ones
Expanded form ⟶ **400**	**+**	**30** + **2**	
Standard form ⟶		**432**	

four hundred thirty-two

The third graders bought 432 tickets.

■ **Talk About Math** Can the value of the digit in the tens place ever be greater than the value of the digit in the hundreds place? Explain.

Check Understanding

For another example, see Set B, pages 66–67.

Use □, I, and • to draw the hundreds, tens, and ones.
Then write the number in standard form for Exercises 1 and 3.

1. 200 + 40 + 5   **2.** 340   **3.** four hundred seven

Practice

For More Practice, see Set B, pages 68–69.

Tell how many hundreds, tens, and ones.
Then write the number in standard form.

4.   **5.**   **6.**

7. two hundred eleven   **8.** one hundred sixty   **9.** seventy-nine

10. three hundred one   **11.** fifty-two   **12.** four hundred ten

Number Sense   Tell whether the 3 is the
hundreds digit, the tens digit, or the ones digit.
Then write the numbers in expanded form.

13. 734   **14.** 386   **15.** 473   **16.** 230   **17.** 703   **18.** 301

19. 238   **20.** 235   **21.** 394   **22.** 123   **23.** 361   **24.** 513

Problem Solving

Solve each problem.

25. The sixth graders bought 4 single
tickets and 7 rolls. How many
tickets did they buy?

26. The seventh graders bought 20 more
tickets than the sixth graders. How
many tickets did they buy?

TIPS FOR PROBLEM SOLVERS

Organize your work
to help you think clearly.

Comparing Numbers

Build Understanding

This chart shows the heaviest fish ever caught.

Which fish was heavier, the Atlantic Tuna or the Halibut?

Find the information in the table. Compare the two numbers.

Fish Records	
Type of Fish	Weight
Atlantic Tuna	375 pounds
Blue Shark	437 pounds
Halibut	350 pounds
Pacific Tuna	435 pounds
Striped Marlin	494 pounds
Sturgeon	468 pounds

Show: Atlantic Tuna 375 pounds

Halibut 350 pounds

Think: 375 ⬚ 350 The hundreds digits are the same.

375 ⬚ 350 The tens digits are not the same.
7 tens is more than 5 tens.
So 375 is more than 350.

Write: 375 > 350 or 350 < 375

The Atlantic Tuna is heavier than the Halibut.

Remember:
> means "greater than."
< means "less than."

■ **Talk About Math** How do you think a sentence using < could be changed to a sentence using >? Explain your answer.

Check Understanding

For another example, see Set C, pages 66–67.

Replace ▦ with < or >. For each exercise, tell
which digits you have to compare.

1. 298 ▦ 476   **2.** 246 ▦ 229   **3.** 421 ▦ 429   **4.** 598 ▦ 601

Practice

For More Practice, see Set C, pages 68–69.

Replace ▦ with < or >.

5. 495 ▦ 476   **6.** 702 ▦ 698   **7.** 89 ▦ 203   **8.** 573 ▦ 578

9. 286 ▦ 276   **10.** 437 ▦ 582   **11.** 27 ▦ 502   **12.** 9 ▦ 85

13. 58 ▦ 580   **14.** 272 ▦ 227   **15.** 36 ▦ 630   **16.** 252 ▦ 225

17. 62 ▦ 107   **18.** 332 ▦ 323   **19.** 56 ▦ 65   **20.** 607 ▦ 670

21. 77 ▦ 571   **22.** 8 ▦ 71   **23.** 645 ▦ 647   **24.** 33 ▦ 324

Mental Math   Find each sum.

25. 9 + 8   **26.** 7 + 5   **27.** 6 + 7

28. 9 + 4   **29.** 3 + 8   **30.** 6 + 9

31. 4 + 6   **32.** 5 + 8   **33.** 4 + 7

Problem Solving

Use the chart on page 42. Tell which fish is heavier.

34. Sturgeon or Atlantic Tuna   **35.** Blue Shark or Pacific Tuna

Critical Thinking   Find each answer.

36. What is the least three-digit number with a 2 in the tens place? Explain your answer.

37. Write a 3-digit number whose tens digit is 4 and whose ones and hundreds digits add up to 2.

Ordering Three-Digit Numbers

Build Understanding

Double-Dutch rope jumping was brought to America by Dutch people who settled in New York.

Lia, Nikaya, Danielle, and Tiffany are members of a Double-Dutch rope jumping team. To find out how fast each girl jumps, judges count the number of times each girl's left foot touches the ground in two minutes. Make a list of the girls in order from most jumps to least jumps.

Number of Jumps in Two Minutes

Person	Lia	Nikaya	Danielle	Tiffany
Jumps	238	106	302	142

3 hundreds	2 hundreds	1 hundred	
302	238	142	Use the hundreds digits to order. If the hundreds digits are the same, compare the tens.
		106	
	142 > 106		4 is greater than 0.
	142 > 106		So 142 is greater than 106.

The jumpers in order are Danielle, Lia, Tiffany, and Nikaya.

■ **Write About Math** Write 128, 120, and 123 from least to greatest. Tell what you do when the hundreds digits and the tens digits in each number are the same.

Check Understanding
For another example, see Set D, pages 66–67.

Write the numbers between

1. 125 and 129.　　　　**2.** 831 and 837.　　　　**3.** 97 and 104.

Practice

For More Practice, see Set D, pages 68–69.

Write the numbers between

4. 821 and 827. **5.** 457 and 462. **6.** 194 and 202.

Write these numbers in order from least to greatest.

7. 298   289   982   **8.** 123   321   276   **9.** 928   789   901

10. 495   549   555   **11.** 783   79   832   **12.** 307   703   730

13. 60   72   136   156   **14.** 543   453   545   455

15. 136   163   135   168   **16.** 93   309   390   319

17. 584   504   575   540   **18.** 630   639   936   976

Problem Solving

Solve each problem.

19. Rope kicking is a game played in China. Players kick a rope that is raised higher until only one player can reach it. Sue's kick reached 119 cm, Lin's 115 cm, and Lee's 120 cm. Who kicked the highest?

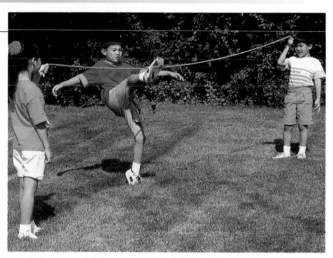

20. In the game in Exercise 19, Lee's last kick was higher than Lin's, but not as high as Sue's. How high could his last kick have been?

21. In another rope kicking game, Sue's last kick was 100 cm. Lin's highest kick was 5 cm higher than Sue's. How high was Lin's kick?

22. Number Sense Tamara's Double Dutch jumping score got smudged. It looked like 1 ▓ 4. Lucy's score was 196. Which girl made more jumps? Explain your answer.

Patterns in Numbers

Build Understanding

Nimble Numbers
Groups: Partners

Number charts can help you
see patterns in numbers.
Imagine crossing out each of
these counting numbers in a
hundreds number chart.
What patterns do you see?

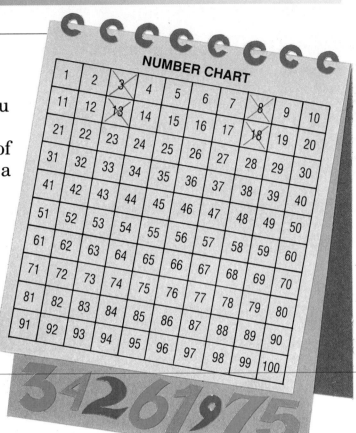

NUMBER CHART

a. Start with 3. Count by
fives.

b. Start with 12. Count by
twos.

c. Start with 27. Count by
tens.

■ **Talk About Math** Tell why you think it
might be useful to count in ways other than
counting just one thing at a time.

Check Understanding

For another example, see Set E, pages 66–67.

Explain how you can use the number
chart to find a number that is

1. 10 less than 37.   **2.** 5 less than 28.   **3.** 2 less than 75.

4. Pick any number in the chart less
than 91. Compare it to the number
just below it. What can you say
about the two numbers?

Practice

For More Practice, see Set E, pages 68–69.

Count by twos.

5. Begin at 14. Count to 24.　　**6.** Begin at 6. Count to 12.

7. Begin at 9. Count to 19.　　**8.** Begin at 26. Count to 38.

Count by fives.

9. Begin at 15. Count to 40.　　**10.** Begin at 25. Count to 55.

11. Begin at 4. Count to 34.　　**12.** Begin at 8. Count to 43.

Count by tens.

13. Begin at 30. Count to 100.　　**14.** Begin at 12. Count to 42.

Describe each pattern. Then find the missing numbers.

15. 6, 11, 16, 21, ▦, ▦　　**16.** 17, 19, 21, ▦, ▦

17. 39, 49, 59, 69, ▦, ▦　　**18.** 83, 87, 93, 97, ▦, ▦

Problem Solving

Explore ——— Math

Count to 20 first by 2s and then by 5s.
What numbers do you say both times you count?

19. Write down the numbers from 1 to 20.

20. Start with 2. Count by 2s. Circle each number.

21. Start with 5. Count by 5s. Put a square around each number.

22. Which numbers have a square *and* and a circle?

Rounding to Tens and Hundreds

Build Understanding

A. In this model train display, the
distance from the water tower to
the train station is 271 centimeters.

A *rounded number* tells
about how many. Round 271 to
the nearest hundred.

Think of the number line as a roller coaster.
The hundreds are at the bottoms of the hills.

Imagine a marble at 271. It would roll forward
to 300. 271 rounded to the **nearest hundred** is
300. The water tower is about 300 centimeters
from the station.

B. Round 271 to the nearest ten.

Think of the number line as a roller coaster again.
Now all of the tens are at the bottoms of the hills.

If you put a marble at 271, it would roll back to 270.
271 rounded to the **nearest ten** is 270.

■ **Talk About Math**   Explain when you might round
283 to the nearest ten and when you might round 283 to
the nearest hundred. Why were the situations different?

Check Understanding

For another example, see Set F, pages 66–67.

Solve.

Round to the nearest ten.

1. Use the hundreds roller coaster to round 121 to the nearest hundred.

2. 48   **3.** 327   **4.** 961

5. 156   **6.** 227   **7.** 514

Practice

For More Practice, see Set F, pages 68–69.

Round each number to the nearest hundred.

8. 299   **9.** 116   **10.** 529   **11.** 904   **12.** 672

13. 416   **14.** 790   **15.** 149   **16.** 151   **17.** 458

18. 587   **19.** 364   **20.** 721   **21.** 885   **22.** 89

Round each number to the nearest ten.

23. 724   **24.** 116   **25.** 281   **26.** 71   **27.** 613

28. 19   **29.** 403   **30.** 368   **31.** 537   **32.** 837

33. 491   **34.** 348   **35.** 122

36. 399   **37.** 2

Midchapter ✓ Checkup

Find each answer.

1. Give the missing number: 40 ones = ▦ tens

2. Tell what the 5 means in 586.

3. Replace ▦ with < or >: 402 ▦ 204

4. Write 123, 321, and 312 in order from least to greatest.

5. Count by twos. Begin at 62. Count to 74.

6. Round 437 to the nearest hundred.

Explore as a Team

1. You may count up to only 10 beans. Estimate the number of beans in each picture.

a.

b.

2. Each person in the group should reach into a bowl of beans and take out a handful.

3. Estimate the number of beans in each handful. Find the actual number to check your estimates.

TIPS FOR
WORKING TOGETHER

Remember, you can disagree without being disagreeable.

Real-Life Decision Making

You are paying for a toy with 40 pennies. You want to make it easy for the clerk to count the pennies to see that they are all there. How will you arrange them on the counter?

Problem Solving WORKSHOP

Number-Sense Project

Look back at pages 34-35.
In the pictures below, some buildings do not have house numbers.
What could they be? Write your prediction.

1.

2.

Visual Thinking Activity

1. How many ducks are in the pond?

2. How many ducks are inside the fence?

3. How many ducks are inside the fence and in the pond?

Use Logical Reasoning

Build Understanding

Ms. Rucker, a photographer, took pictures of the students. One picture was of Dan, May, and Carl. The numbers on their shirts made a three-digit number.

The hundreds digit was the sum of the tens and ones digits. The ones digit was double the tens digit.

PROBLEM SOLVING GUIDE

Understand
QUESTION
FACTS
KEY IDEA

➡ **Plan and Solve**
STRATEGY
ANSWER

Look Back
SENSIBLE ANSWER
ALTERNATE APPROACH

In what order did they appear in the picture?

Understand Who stood first, second, and third in the picture? You can work with the digits 6, 4, and 2 to find the three-digit number that fits the clues.

➡ **Plan and Solve** STRATEGY   Use logical reasoning.

6 is the sum of 4 and 2. It must be the hundreds digit. 2 doubled is 4. It must be the ones digit. The number is 624.

ANSWER   The order is Dan, Carl, and May.

Look Back Check again to see that the number fits all of the clues.

▪ **Talk About Math** Explain why you should check the number to see if the digits fit all the clues.

Check Understanding

Carl, Sue, and Sam posed for a different picture. Their shirts made a three-digit number that was less than 500. The tens digit was the sum of the hundreds and ones digits. In what order did they appear in the picture?

1. What are Carl's, Sue's, and Sam's numbers?

2. Which digit should be the sum of the other two?

3. Which of the student's numbers is the sum of the other two?

4. What two three-digit numbers can you write using 7 as the tens digit?

5. Which of the two numbers you wrote is less than 500?

6. How were the students lined up?

Practice

These groups of students also posed for pictures. How were they lined up?

7. The number made by Carl, Amy, and Sue was more than 400. The ones digit was more than the tens.

8. The number made by Sam, Amy, and Sue was less than 400. The ones digit was 2 less than the tens digit.

Two groups of three students covered their faces and posed for mystery pictures. Name the students in the order in which they appeared in each picture.

9. The number they made was between 500 and 600. The tens digit was 3 more than the ones digit.

10. The number they made was between 200 and 300. The ones digit was 4 less than the tens.

Understanding Thousands

Build Understanding

A. While visiting a pencil factory, the third-grade class observed how pencils are packed.

First, 100 pencils are packed in each box. Then, 10 boxes are packed in each case. How many pencils are there in each case?

a. Each hundred represents a box of pencils. How many hundreds would represent a case?

10 hundreds would represent a case.
There are 1 thousand pencils in each case.

100 PENCILS

| 100 pencils | 100 pencils | | 100 pencils | 100 pencils |
| 100 pencils | 100 pencils | 100 pencils | 100 pencils | 100 pencils |

b. How many thousands can be made from 38 hundreds?

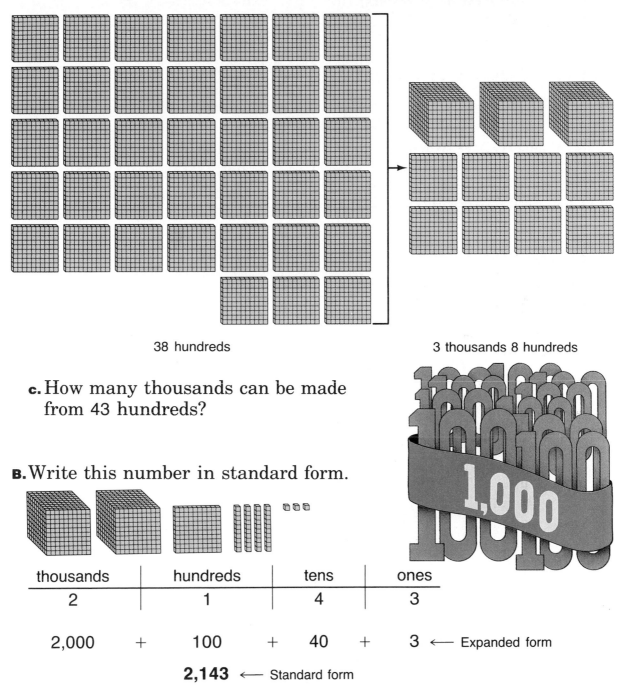

38 hundreds

3 thousands 8 hundreds

c. How many thousands can be made from 43 hundreds?

B. Write this number in standard form.

thousands	hundreds	tens	ones
2	1	4	3

2,000 + 100 + 40 + 3 ⟵ Expanded form

2,143 ⟵ Standard form

two thousand, one hundred forty-three

■ **Talk About Math** Explain what 0 means in 4,902.

55

Check Understanding

For another example, see Set G, pages 66–67.

Write the word that will complete each sentence.

1. 10 tens = 1 ___?___

2. 10 ones = 1 ___?___

3. 10 hundreds = 1 ___?___

4. 20 tens = 2 ___?___

5. Write the standard form.

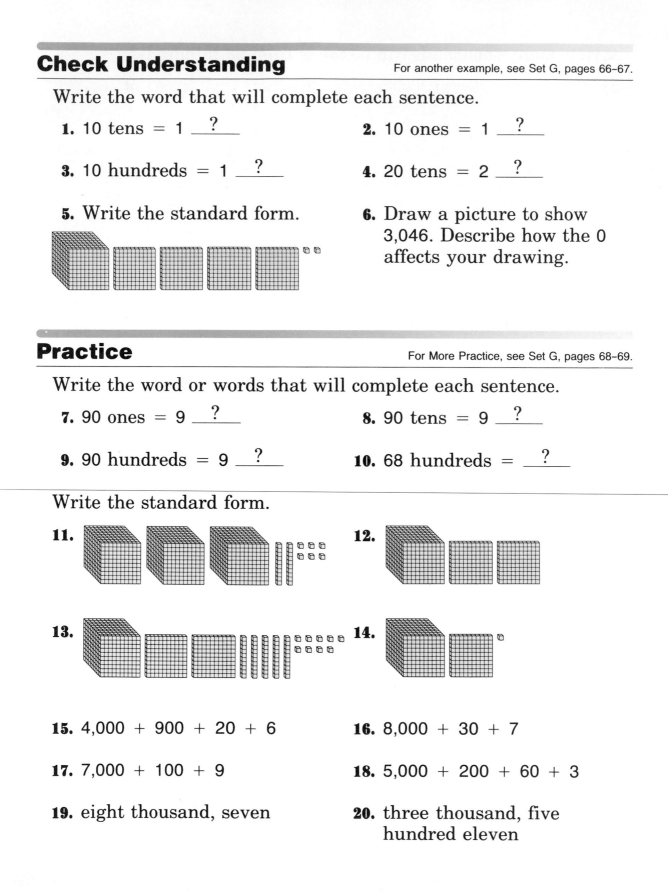

6. Draw a picture to show 3,046. Describe how the 0 affects your drawing.

Practice

For More Practice, see Set G, pages 68–69.

Write the word or words that will complete each sentence.

7. 90 ones = 9 ___?___

8. 90 tens = 9 ___?___

9. 90 hundreds = 9 ___?___

10. 68 hundreds = ___?___

Write the standard form.

11.

12.

13.

14.

15. 4,000 + 900 + 20 + 6

16. 8,000 + 30 + 7

17. 7,000 + 100 + 9

18. 5,000 + 200 + 60 + 3

19. eight thousand, seven

20. three thousand, five hundred eleven

Write the digit that is in the

21. hundreds place of 5,402.

22. thousands place of 9,003.

23. tens place of 6,207.

24. thousands place of 4,996.

25. ones place of 7,348.

26. hundreds place of 3,475.

27. thousands place of 8,160.

28. tens place of 2,531.

29. hundreds place of 1,789.

30. ones place of 5,680.

Calculator Write the answer you think a calculator would give. Then use a calculator to check your answers.

31. 2000 [+] 300 [+] 70 [+] 5 [=]

32. 8000 [+] 200 [+] 10 [+] 3 [=]

33. 4000 [+] 60 [+] 9 [=]

34. 5000 [+] 800 [+] 6 [=]

35. 7000 [+] 70 [=]

36. 3000 [+] 100 [+] 7 [=]

37. 700 [+] 40 [+] 8 [=]

38. 400 [+] 50 [+] 2 [=]

Skills ⎯⎯⎯ **Review**   pages 6–7

Write the number that is one less.

1. 46   **2.** 18   **3.** 51   **4.** 22   **5.** 30   **6.** 80

Mental Math   Add or subtract.

7. 3	**8.** 7	**9.** 5	**10.** 11	**11.** 7	**12.** 9
+1	−1	+4	− 8	−5	+6

Comparing and Ordering Numbers

Build Understanding

A. Mary lives in Los Angeles. Her classmates have pen pals in all of the cities in this chart. Mary decided to find out whose pen pal lives farthest away.

Which city is farther from Los Angeles, Atlanta or Cincinnati?

Distance from Los Angeles	
Atlanta	2,182 miles
Chicago	2,054 miles
Cincinnati	2,179 miles
New Orleans	1,883 miles
Minneapolis	1,889 miles
San Francisco	387 miles

2,179 miles — Cincinnati

2,182 miles — Atlanta

Los Angeles

Cincinnati is 2,179 miles from Los Angeles.

Atlanta is 2,182 miles from Los Angeles.

Think:

2,182 ⬚ 2,179   The thousands digits are the same.

2,182 ⬚ 2,179   The hundreds digits are the same.

2,182 ⬚ 2,179   The tens digits are not the same. 8 tens is greater than 7 tens. So 2,182 is greater than 2,179.

Write: 2,182 > 2,179   or   2,179 < 2,182

Atlanta is farther from Los Angeles than Cincinnati is.

B. Find the distances from Los Angeles for New Orleans, Minneapolis, and San Francisco. List them in order from greatest to least.

1,889   **1,883**   **387**

■ **Talk About Math** Describe how you can order the numbers in Example B from least to greatest.

Check Understanding

For another example, see Set H, pages 66–67.

Replace ▦ with < or >. For each exercise, tell which digits you have to compare.

1. 5,148 ▦ 4,185   **2.** 3,456 ▦ 3,459   **3.** 7,041 ▦ 7,401

Practice

For More Practice, see Set H, pages 68–69.

Replace ▦ with < or >.

4. 6,450 ▦ 6,504   **5.** 9,205 ▦ 9,250   **6.** 5,079 ▦ 5,709

7. 5,398 ▦ 6,000   **8.** 5,298 ▦ 928   **9.** 4,398 ▦ 4,397

10. 6,239 ▦ 6,293   **11.** 3,079 ▦ 3,709   **12.** 7,001 ▦ 6,999

13. 8,111 ▦ 7,999   **14.** 2,984 ▦ 2,894   **15.** 1,610 ▦ 1,620

16. 4,763 ▦ 4,933   **17.** 5,352 ▦ 5,351   **18.** 3,628 ▦ 4,928

Mixed Practice Write these numbers in order from least to greatest.

19. 6,705   6,075   6,507   675   **20.** 498   4,972   49   489

21. 4,279   7,942   4,297   987   **22.** 56   506   6,052   6,502

Write the numbers between

23. 294 and 302   **24.** 547 and 552   **25.** 921 and 929

Problem Solving

Solve each problem.

26. Critical Thinking Use the digits 8, 3, 9, and 5. Write the greatest four-digit number you can.

27. Use Data Look at the chart on page 42. Which is heavier, the Atlantic Tuna or the Pacific Tuna?

Ten-Thousands and Hundred-Thousands

Build Understanding

A. The Helfmans have had their car for five years. Look at the odometer and find how many miles the car has been driven.

ten-thousands	thousands	hundreds	tens	ones
9	8	0	0	0

Think: The digits 9 and 8 show how many thousands.
Read: ninety-eight thousand
Write: 98,000

The car has been driven 98,000 miles.

B. What number is 1,000 more than 99,000?

Think: One more thousand makes 100 thousand.
Read: one hundred thousand
Write: 100,000

C. Write 431,756 in words.
Think about a place-value chart.

hundred-thousands	ten-thousands	thousands	hundreds	tens	ones
4	3	1	7	5	6

four hundred thirty-one thousand, seven hundred fifty-six

■ **Write About Math** Write a sentence telling the meaning of 0 in the numbers 508,161 and 580,161. Write a second sentence telling the difference in those meanings.

Check Understanding

For another example, see Set I, pages 66–67.

Find each answer.

1. 41,000 means ▦ thousands.
2. What number is 1,000 more than 23,000?

3. Write ninety thousand in standard form.

Practice

For More Practice, see Set I, pages 68–69.

Write the numbers in words.

4. 423,156   5. 237,095   6. 409,127   7. 813,006

8. 934,756   9. 728,123   10. 316,342   11. 244,500

Number Sense Tell what the 1 means in each number.

12. 31,000   13. 49,618   14. 12,425   15. 88,291

16. 137,772   17. 220,891   18. 314,842   19. 100,008

Write each number in standard form.

20. twenty-eight hundred

21. thirty-two hundred

22. five hundred sixty thousand

23. eight hundred thirty thousand

24. four hundred forty thousand, seven

25. six hundred twenty thousand, ten

26. fifty thousand, one hundred twelve

27. nine hundred thousand, twenty-eight

28. three hundred forty-two thousand, one hundred five

29. two hundred seventy-three thousand, five hundred sixty-nine

Give Sensible Answers

Build Understanding

Johnny is a third grader at Lincoln School. His hobby is collecting baseball cards.

Johnny had just 75 cents. He bought a pack of cards. How much money did he have left?

50 cents   75 cents   1 dollar

Understand Johnny had just 75 cents to begin with.

Plan and Solve You know that Johnny must end up with less money than he started with.

Look Back SENSIBLE ANSWER Look at the answer choices to see which one makes the best sense. 75 cents is the same amount Johnny started with. 1 dollar is more than Johnny had at the beginning. 50 cents is the only answer choice that is less than 75 cents.

ALTERNATE APPROACH You could model the problem using play money.

PROBLEM SOLVING
GUIDE

Understand
QUESTION
FACTS
KEY IDEA

Plan and Solve
STRATEGY
ANSWER

➤ **Look Back**
SENSIBLE ANSWER
ALTERNATE APPROACH

■ **Talk About Math** The students rode in a school bus to the baseball game. Naomi guessed there were about 400 students on each bus. Explain why this is not a reasonable answer.

Check Understanding

Johnny plays baseball every day. About how many hours does he play baseball each week?

1 hour   10 hours   100 hours

Answer these exercises to help you choose a sensible answer.

1. Guess how many hours Johnny plays baseball each day.

2. If Johnny plays that much each day, how many hours would he play all week?

Practice

Choose the most sensible answer.

3. Johnny has 423 cards in his collection. His friend, Luis, has many more. How many cards does Luis have?

373   425   480

4. In one game, Johnny's team scored 7 runs but lost. How many runs did the other team score?

5   7   9

5. Johnny once saw his favorite player, Eric Davis, hit a home run. How far did the ball go?

4 feet   400 feet   4,000 feet

6. Johnny's mother bought tickets to a baseball game for her family of 4. How much did the tickets cost?

$500 $50 $5

Critical Thinking   Solve each problem.

7. The sum of Johnny's age and the age of his brother James is 12. Who is older, Johnny or James? Explain your answer.

8. The number of feet a ball went was between 300 and 400. The ones digit was 4. The tens digit was 3 less than the ones digit. How far did the ball go?

Skills Review

Use □, I, and • to show how many hundreds, tens, and ones are in

1. 56 ones.   **2.** 35 tens.

Write the number in standard form.

3. one hundred sixteen

4. fifty-seven

5. six thousand thirty-two

6. four hundred ten thousand, seventy-eight

Replace ▦ with < or >.

7. 683 ▦ 652   **8.** 94 ▦ 312

9. 7,120 ▦ 7,242

10. 8,030 ▦ 830

Write these numbers in order from least to greatest.

11. 145   83   276   297

12. 607   624   875   823

13. Begin at 26. Count by twos to 40.

14. Round 478 to the nearest hundred.

15. Round 62 to the nearest ten.

Problem-Solving Review

Solve each problem.

16. Together Karen and Elaine have 13 seashells. Elaine has 1 more than Karen. How many shells does each girl have?

17. Nikki walked to the movie she saw and walked home. How long was she gone?

15 minutes   3 hours
1 hour

18. Look for a pattern. Find the missing numbers.

6	7	10	13	4	8
↓	↓	↓	↓	↓	↓
2	3	6	▦	▦	▦

19. I am an even amount of money. I am greater than 2 dimes but less than a quarter. You can make me with 4 coins. What am I?

20. **Data File** Use data from pages 104–105. List the golf scores from the lowest score to the highest score.

21. **Make a Data File** Look through newspapers or magazines for numbers in the ten-thousands or hundred-thousands. Which are easier to find?

Cumulative Skills Review · Chapters 1 and 2

Read each sentence. Tell if the number is used to count, to label, to measure, or to tell order.

1. There are 2 gallons of milk.

2. Mr. Boyle parked in row 6.

Tell what number or symbol is under each bow.

3. $7 - \text{🎀} = 3$

4. $4 + 6 \; \text{🎀} \; 10$

5. $14 = 8 \; \text{🎀} \; 6$

Write the family of facts for the numbers in each exercise.

6. 7, 3, 10

7. 4, 13, 9

8. 1, 5, 4

9. 7, 0, 7

Put each list in order by size, smallest first.

10. rabbit, pony, mouse, giraffe

11. desk, book, school, eraser

Tell if each number is odd or even.

12. 26

13. 303

14. 71

15. 85

16. 124

17. 90

Write the number in standard form.

18. four hundred twenty

19. ten thousand, forty-six

Replace ▦ with $<$ or $>$.

20. 421 ▦ 457

21. 163 ▦ 63

22. 2,411 ▦ 2,104

Write these numbers in order from least to greatest.

23. 235   124   46   163

24. 2,476   2,434   266   2,716

Find the missing numbers.

25. 55, 60, 65, 70, ▦, ▦

26. 34, 36, 38, 40, ▦, ▦

27. 26, 36, 46, 56, ▦, ▦

28. 41, 43, 45, 47, ▦, ▦

Round each number to the nearest ten.

29. 812

30. 46

31. 342

32. 15

33. 8

34. 403

Reteaching
Set A   pages 36–39

Cover 2 tens with 21 ones.
You will have 1 one left over.

21 ones   2 tens   1 one

Remember that it takes 10 ones to make 1 ten and 10 tens to make 1 hundred.

Make as many tens as you can. Use l and • to record your work.

1. 33 ones   **2.** 52 ones

Set B   pages 40–41

How many hundreds, tens, and ones are in this number? Write this number in standard form.

three hundred   forty-five
3 hundreds   4 tens 5 ones

300   +   40 + 5

345 ← Standard form

Remember that the value of the tens digit cannot be greater than the value of the hundreds digit.

Tell how many hundreds, tens, and ones. Then write the number in standard form.

1. eighty-two **2.** six hundred nine

Set C   pages 42–43

Replace ⁂ with < or >.

436 ⁂ 429

The hundreds digits are the same. The tens digits are not the same. Since 3 tens is more than 2 tens,

436 > 429 or 429 < 436.

Remember that the symbol > or < points to the smaller number. Replace ⁂ with < or >.

1. 375 ⁂ 362   **2.** 88 ⁂ 141

3. 418 ⁂ 425   **4.** 695 ⁂ 702

Set D   pages 44–45

Write these numbers in order from least to greatest.

683   429   432   517

Use the hundreds   683   517   429
digits to order.   432
Compare the tens: 429 ⁂ 432.
Since 2 < 3, 429 < 432.
Order: 429   432   517   683

Remember to compare the tens if the hundreds digits are the same. Write these numbers in order from least to greatest.

1. 481   396   224   368

2. 80   45   181   165

Set E pages 46–47

Describe this pattern. Then find the missing numbers.

3, 7, 11, 15, ▦, ▦, ▦

Begin with 3. Then count by 4s. The missing numbers are 19, 23, and 27.

Remember that finding a pattern can make counting easier.

Describe the pattern. Then find the missing numbers.

1. 4, 7, 10, 13, ▦, ▦

Set F pages 48–49

Round 436 to the nearest ten.

435
430 436 440

If you put a marble at 436, it would roll forward to 440.

Remember that the tens are at the bottom of the hills when you round to the nearest ten.

Round each to the nearest ten.

1. 34   **2.** 119   **3.** 342

Set G pages 54–57

Write 3,000 + 100 + 20 + 2 in standard form.

3,122 ⟵——— Standard form

Remember that it takes 10 hundreds to make 1 thousand. Write the standard form.

1. 5,000 + 300 + 40 **2.** 9,000 + 4

Set H pages 58–59

Compare 4,286 and 4,276.

The thousands digits and the hundreds digits are the same.

Since 8 > 7, 4,286 > 4,276

Remember that > means greater than and < means less than.

Replace ▦ with < or >.

1. 8,362 ▦ 8,371   **2.** 6,459 ▦ 6,549

Set I pages 60–61

Write 618,432 in words.

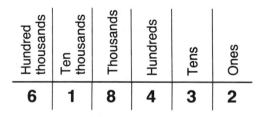

Hundred thousands	Ten thousands	Thousands	Hundreds	Tens	Ones
6	1	8	4	3	2

six hundred eighteen thousand, four hundred thirty-two

Remember to think about a place-value chart when you read a number. Write the number in standard form.

1. four hundred sixty thousand, two hundred twenty-seven

More Practice

Set A   pages 36-39

Use tens and ones to make as many tens
as you can. Then use l and • to record
your work.

1. 43 ones   **2.** 50 ones   **3.** 16 ones   **4.** 36 ones

Use hundreds, tens, and ones to make as
many hundreds as you can. Use □, l, and • to
record your work.

5. 30 tens   **6.** 10 tens   **7.** 24 tens   **8.** 44 tens

Set B   pages 40-41

Tell how many hundreds, tens, and ones.
Then write the number in standard form.

1. six hundred two   **2.** nine hundred fifty   **3.** ninety-eight

Number Sense   In the following exercises,
tell whether the 4 is the hundreds digit, the
tens digit, or the ones digit.

4. 864   **5.** 249   **6.** 461   **7.** 947   **8.** 804

Set C   pages 42-43

Replace ▦ with < or >.

1. 542 ▦ 536   **2.** 409 ▦ 381   **3.** 368 ▦ 386   **4.** 78 ▦ 219

5. 127 ▦ 172   **6.** 62 ▦ 620   **7.** 501 ▦ 510   **8.** 82 ▦ 28

Set D   pages 44-45

Write the numbers between

1. 432 and 438.   **2.** 346 and 351.   **3.** 296 and 304.

Write the numbers in order from least to greatest.

4. 640   82   721   726   **5.** 60   81   123   103

6. 402   390   405   309   **7.** 841   826   796   791

Set E pages 46–47

1. Begin at 9. Count by twos. Count to 21.

2. Begin at 6. Count by fives. Count to 31.

Describe each pattern. Then find the missing numbers.

3. 11, 15, 19, 23, ▦, ▦   **4.** 23, 28, 33, 38, ▦, ▦

Set F pages 48–49

Round each number to the nearest hundred.

1. 377   **2.** 212   **3.** 664   **4.** 706   **5.** 539

For Exercises 6–10, round Exercises 1–5 to the nearest ten.

Set G pages 54–57

Write the standard form.

1. 6,000 + 400 + 30 + 5   **2.** 7,000 + 90 + 6

3. 2,000 + 300 + 9   **4.** six thousand, eighty-nine

Write the digit that is in the

5. hundreds place of 8,304.   **6.** tens place of 7,408.

Set H pages 58–59

Replace ▦ with < or >.

1. 3,841 ▦ 3,481   **2.** 2,084 ▦ 2,048   **3.** 9,642 ▦ 9,643

Set I pages 60–61

Number Sense   Tell what the 3 means in each number.

1. 42,739   **2.** 38,149   **3.** 53,904   **4.** 87,423

Write each number in standard form.

5. nineteen thousand, five hundred sixteen

6. one hundred thirty-two thousand, eight hundred six

Enrichment

Millions and Billions

About two hundred forty-four million, six hundred thousand people live in the United States.

How would you write that number in standard form?

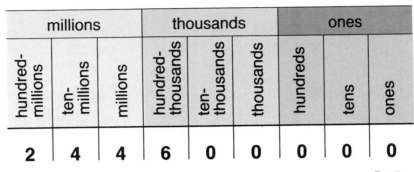

millions			thousands			ones		
hundred-millions	ten-millions	millions	hundred-thousands	ten-thousands	thousands	hundreds	tens	ones
2	4	4	6	0	0	0	0	0

Write: **244,600,000** ⟵ Standard form
Use commas to separate each set of 3 digits.

Start at the right.
The first set of 3 digits tells how many ones.
The second set of 3 digits tells how many thousands.

The third set of 3 digits tells how many *millions.*

Write each number in standard form.

1. Four hundred sixty-one million, seven hundred forty thousand, six hundred

2. Seven hundred eighty-one million, five hundred fifty-two thousand, seventeen

3. Eight hundred seven million, four hundred thousand, eight hundred ninety-four

4. Nine hundred seventy million, three hundred thousand, forty-six

The next set of 3 digits greater than millions is *billions.*
Write each number in standard form.

5. One hundred four billion, four hundred fifty-one thousand

6. Three billion, twenty million, one hundred thirty thousand

Chapter 2 Review/Test

Use □, |, and • to show how many hundreds, tens, and ones are in

1. 62 ones.   **2.** 78 tens.

3. Write the standard form for nine thousand, eight hundred forty-one

In 357,801, which number is in

4. the hundreds place?

5. the hundred-thousands place?

6. the ten-thousands place?

Replace each ⊞ with < or >.

7. 427 ⊞ 348

8. 2,976 ⊞ 3,951

9. Write the numbers in order from least to greatest.

581   642   539

10. Write the numbers as you count by twos from 66 to 74.

11. Round 76 to the nearest ten.

12. Round 542 to the nearest hundred.

13. Write a three-digit number using the digits 3, 6, and 9. The hundreds digit is the sum of the tens and ones digits. The ones digit is greater than the tens digit.

14. Anna's team scored 5 goals and won. Choose the most sensible answer for the number of goals the other team scored.

3 goals   5 goals   7 goals

Read this problem. Then answer the question below.

Gil weighs 72 pounds. His sister Tammy weighs 58 pounds. Which of them weighs more?

15. Choose the question that has the same meaning as the question in the problem.

a. How much more does Gil weigh than Tammy?

b. Does Gil weigh more than 60 pounds?

c. Who weighs more, Gil or Tammy?

16. ■ **Write About Math** Explain what the 0 means in 591,048.

Two-Digit Addition and Subtraction

3

Did You Know: During your lifetime you eat about 60,000 pounds of food. This is the equivalent in weight of six elephants.

Number-Sense Project

Estimate

The sandwiches shown are tuna, hamburger, pita, peanut butter with jelly, and turkey sub. Estimate how many of each sandwich your classmates would choose for lunch.

Gather Data

Write down your estimates. Then take a count of your classmates to see how many would choose each sandwich.

Analyze and Report

Were your estimates accurate? What information might have helped you make more accurate estimates?

Choose an Operation

Build Understanding

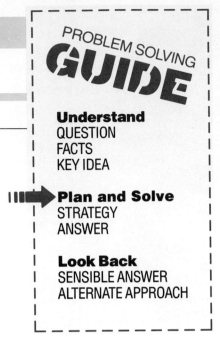

At an international doll fair, Mr. Stein displayed dolls from 16 countries and Mrs. Ozu displayed dolls from 9 countries. Mr. Stein displayed dolls from how many more countries than Mrs. Ozu?

Understand   To find out how many more countries Mr. Stein displayed dolls from than Mrs. Ozu did, you need to compare.

IIII→ **Plan and Solve**   STRATEGY   Choose an operation. Subtract to find out how much greater 16 is than 9.

$$16 - 9 = 7$$

ANSWER   Mr. Stein displayed dolls from 7 more countries than Mrs. Ozu did.

Look Back   You can check the answer by adding.

$$9 + 7 = 16$$

■ **Talk About Math**   How can drawing a picture help you solve an addition or subtraction problem?

Japan

Africa

Guatemala

North American
Hopi Indian

Check Understanding

Solve the problem by answering Exercises 1–2.

On Monday, Susan made 8 cornhusk dolls. On Tuesday, she made 2 more than she made on Monday. How many cornhusk dolls did Susan make on Tuesday?

1. Did Susan make more or less dolls on Tuesday? Should you add or subtract?

2. How many cornhusk dolls did Susan make on Tuesday?

Cornhusk dolls were made in England, where they were used as good luck charms.

Practice

Solve each problem.

3. Kuri has 8 Russian stacking dolls and 6 Pueblo kachina dolls. How many dolls does she have in all?

4. If Kate collects 3 more straw dolls, she will have 10. How many straw dolls does Kate have?

5. In Japan, children display their dolls on March 3. Chisako displayed 12 dolls this year. Last year she displayed 9 dolls. How many more dolls did she display this year?

6. Jane has dolls from 8 countries. Nan has dolls from 3 more countries than Jane. From how many countries does Nan have dolls?

Choose a _____ Strategy

Which Is in Front?

7. Laura placed dolls from four countries on a table. The dolls from Guatemala were behind all the other dolls. The dolls from Russia were behind the dolls from Portugal and in front of the dolls from Thailand. Which dolls were displayed in front?

Renaming for Addition and Subtraction

Build Understanding

Fill the Baskets
Materials: Place-value materials (tens and ones)
Groups: 3–5 students

A. Judy fills baskets at her family's apple orchard. She puts 10 apples in each basket.

Show her work with place-value materials, using a ten for each basket and a one for each apple.

a. Suppose Judy has 27 apples. Think about putting them in baskets. Show the different ways Judy can group these apples. Then write your results.

THINK	0 baskets 27 apples	1 basket 17 apples	2 baskets 7 apples
SHOW			
WRITE	0 tens 27 ones	1 ten 17 ones	2 tens 7 ones

b. Suppose Judy has 2 baskets of apples. Think about taking the apples out of the baskets. Show what happens when you empty each basket. Then write the results.

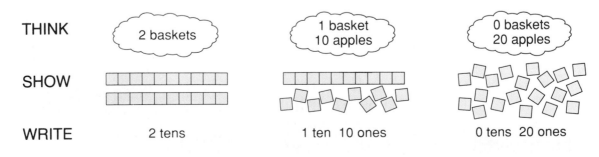

THINK	2 baskets	1 basket 10 apples	0 baskets 20 apples
SHOW			
WRITE	2 tens	1 ten 10 ones	0 tens 20 ones

B. At one point on Monday, Judy had filled 7 baskets and had 13 more apples. How many full baskets did she have when she was all finished? Use place-value materials to show her work.

Tens	Ones
7	13

Tens	Ones
8	3

C. On Tuesday, Judy filled 6 baskets and had 7 apples left. Then her dog, Applesauce, knocked over one of the baskets. How many full baskets and single apples did she have then?

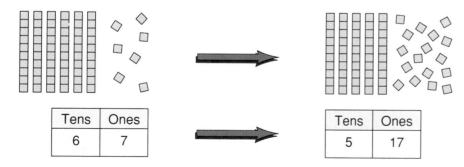

Tens	Ones
6	7

Tens	Ones
5	17

■ **Talk About Math** Look again at the numbers in Examples B and C. What happened to the number of tens in each example? What happened to the number of ones?

Check Understanding

For another example, see Set A, pages 98–99.

Number Sense Use tens and ones or draw a picture to show how you got your answer.

1. How many tens can you make from 14 ones? How many ones are left over?

2. How many ones do you have when you take apart a ten?

Practice

For More Practice, see Set A, pages 100–101.

Copy and complete each sentence. Use tens and ones if you need them.

2 tens 16 ones is the same as

3. ▦ tens 6 ones.　　4. 1 ten ▦ ones.　　5. ▦ tens 36 ones.

Use tens and ones. Make all the new tens you can. How many tens and ones do you have now?

6. Tens	Ones
6	12

7. Tens	Ones
4	16

8. Tens	Ones
5	10

9. 3 tens 14 ones　　10. 7 tens 23 ones　　11. 2 tens 20 ones

Use tens and ones. Trade 1 ten for 10 ones. How many tens and ones do you have now?

12. Tens	Ones
7	3

13. Tens	Ones
6	2

14. Tens	Ones
2	9

15. 5 tens 4 ones　　16. 9 tens 0 ones　　17. 1 ten 5 ones

Mixed Practice Add or subtract.

18. 9 + 8　　19. 15 − 7　　20. 12 − 5　　21. 6 + 7　　22. 8 + 7

23. 7 + 3　　24. 6 + 6　　25. 10 − 6　　26. 16 − 9　　27. 18 − 9

28. 9 + 9　　29. 17 − 8　　30. 5 + 6　　31. 6 + 9　　32. 14 − 8

Problem Solving

TENS	ONES
5	7

Judy and Brian went to gather apples. Judy started with 5 full baskets and 7 single apples. How many baskets and apples did she have after the event in each problem occurred? Draw a picture for each problem.

33. Brian gave her 6 more apples.

Tens	Ones
5	?

34. She filled another basket.

Tens	Ones
?	?

35. Brian gave her 6 more apples.

Tens	Ones
?	?

36. A customer bought 2 baskets.

Tens	Ones
?	?

Critical Thinking Solve each problem.

37. Kim had 6 full baskets and 2 single apples. Jon had 2 more full baskets and 3 more single apples than Kim. How many baskets and single apples did Jon have?

38. Ann gathered 7 full baskets and 8 single apples. Charles gathered 18 less apples than Ann. How many full baskets did Charles gather?

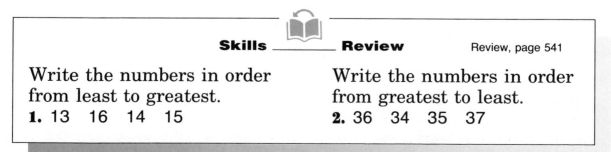

Skills _____ Review   Review, page 541

Write the numbers in order from least to greatest.
1. 13   16   14   15

Write the numbers in order from greatest to least.
2. 36   34   35   37

Two-Digit Addition

Build Understanding

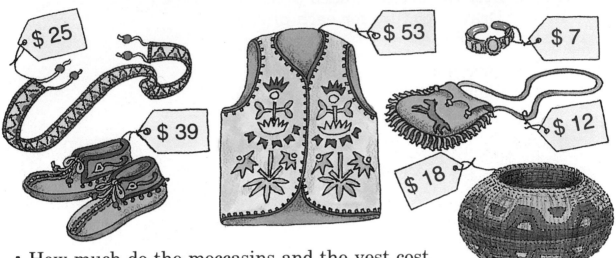

A. How much do the moccasins and the vest cost together? To find the cost of two items, you need to add. Find 39 + 53.

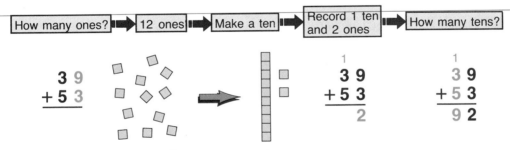

| How many ones? | ➡ | 12 ones | ➡ | Make a ten | ➡ | Record 1 ten and 2 ones | ➡ | How many tens? |

```
              1              1
  3 9       3 9          3 9
+ 5 3      + 5 3        + 5 3
              2            9 2
```

The moccasins and vest cost $92.

B. Find 12 + 25.

| How many ones? | ➡ | 7 ones | | Record 7 ones. | ➡ | How many tens? |

```
  1 2      Cannot      1 2          1 2
+ 2 5      make      + 2 5        + 2 5
           a ten.        7          3 7
```

■ **Talk About Math**   Look at Examples A and B. How can you tell whether you will need to make a ten?

Check Understanding

For another example, see Set B, pages 98–99.

1. Use the information on page 80. Would you need to make a ten to find the cost of the pouch and the bracelet? the basket and the belt?

Find the sums. **Remember** to draw a picture if it will help you.

2. 62 + 27   **3.** 74 + 8   **4.** 56 + 46   **5.** 7 + 81   **6.** 84 + 16

Practice

For More Practice, see Set B, pages 100–101.

Find the sums.

7. 63
+ 29

8. 48
+ 51

9. 53
+ 28

10. 70
+ 16

11. 26
+ 18

12. 42
+ 39

13. 85
+ 12

14. 45
+ 45

15. 27
+ 38

16. 87
+ 5

17. 4 + 17   **18.** 54 + 3   **19.** 32 + 65   **20.** 34 + 47   **21.** 17 + 39

22. 10 + 3   **23.** 28 + 9   **24.** 46 + 15   **25.** 71 + 24   **26.** 50 + 30

Mental Math   Find each answer. Watch the signs.

27. 5 + 5   **28.** 18 − 9   **29.** 13 − 4   **30.** 7 + 6   **31.** 7 + 8

32. 17 − 8   **33.** 11 − 7   **34.** 8 + 9   **35.** 6 + 3   **36.** 16 − 9

Problem Solving

Solve each problem.

37. How much would the basket and the bracelet cost together?

38. Scott's mom spent $57 in the store. What two things did she buy?

TIPS FOR PROBLEM SOLVERS

Compare problems to help you relate new problems to ones you've solved before.

Addition: Mental Math

Build Understanding

Mrs. Delgrado's class has a mental math contest every week. The students use different addition strategies.

A. Mary and Bobby use place value to find 35 + 23.

Mary breaks apart both numbers.

Bobby breaks apart only the second number.

$$30 + 20 = 50$$
$$5 + 3 = 8$$
$$50 + 8 = 58$$

$$35 + 20 + 3 =$$
$$55 + 3 = 58$$

B. Alice is great with problems like 39 + 25.

39 is 1 less than 40.
$$40 + 25 = 65$$
1 less than 65 is 64.

■ **Talk About Math** Which method do you like best? Why? Can you think of another way to add mentally?

Check Understanding

For another example, see Set C, pages 98–99.

Find each sum mentally. Tell which method you used.

1. 27 + 19   **2.** 67 + 32   **3.** 28 + 49   **4.** 36 + 42   **5.** 49 + 12

Practice

For More Practice, see Set C, pages 100–101.

Find each sum mentally. Tell which method you used.

6. 52 + 30   **7.** 37 + 20   **8.** 43 + 40   **9.** 65 + 19   **10.** 26 + 13

11. 25 + 43   **12.** 63 + 28   **13.** 57 + 29   **14.** 22 + 56   **15.** 65 + 43

16. 67 + 19   **17.** 39 + 58   **18.** 27 + 12   **19.** 19 + 74   **20.** 39 + 24

21. 13 + 45   **22.** 27 + 32   **23.** 14 + 39   **24.** 16 + 51   **25.** 38 + 12

Mixed Practice   Use paper and pencil or mental math to solve.

26. 17 − 9   **27.** 85 + 9   **28.** 8 + 8   **29.** 27 + 27   **30.** 66 + 18

31. 7 + 6   **32.** 24 + 63   **33.** 18 − 9   **34.** 42 + 16   **35.** 14 − 8

Explore _____ Math

A
L
G
E
B
R
A

Find each missing number. **Remember** to use mental math strategies to help you.

36. 37 + ▦ = 67   How many more tens are needed?

37. ▦ + 17 = 19   How many more ones are needed?

38. ▦ + 35 = 39   **39.** 34 + ▦ = 94   **40.** 72 + ▦ = 92

41. ▦ + 42 = 49   **42.** 48 + ▦ = 88   **43.** ▦ + 29 = 79

Three or More Addends

Build Understanding

This treasure map was shown in a book about Redbeard the Pirate's secret island.

How many steps is it from the dock to the anchor using the stone path?

Since there are 3 sections to the stone path, add the amounts together. Find 15 + 25 + 32.

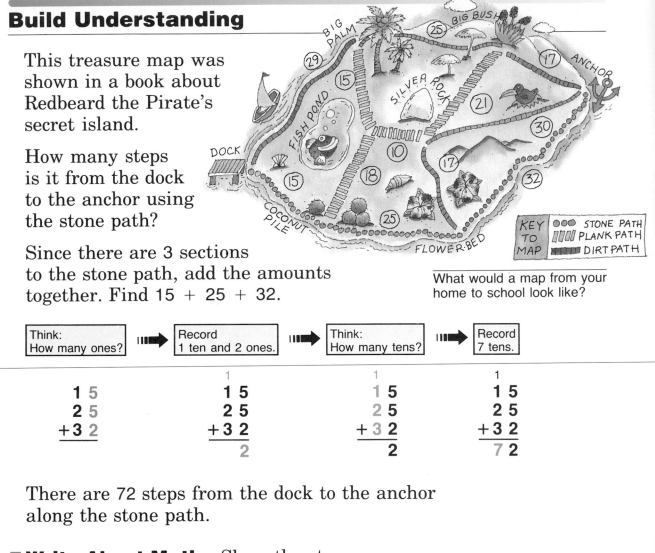

What would a map from your home to school look like?

Think: How many ones?		Record 1 ten and 2 ones.		Think: How many tens?		Record 7 tens.

$$
\begin{array}{r}
1\ 5 \\
2\ 5 \\
+3\ 2 \\
\end{array}
\qquad
\begin{array}{r}
{\scriptstyle 1} \\
1\ 5 \\
2\ 5 \\
+3\ 2 \\
\hline
2 \\
\end{array}
\qquad
\begin{array}{r}
{\scriptstyle 1} \\
1\ 5 \\
2\ 5 \\
+3\ 2 \\
\hline
2 \\
\end{array}
\qquad
\begin{array}{r}
{\scriptstyle 1} \\
1\ 5 \\
2\ 5 \\
+3\ 2 \\
\hline
7\ 2 \\
\end{array}
$$

There are 72 steps from the dock to the anchor along the stone path.

■ **Write About Math** Show the steps you would use to find 25 + 7 + 39. Explain why it is important to line up the digits correctly. Then add.

Check Understanding

For another example, see Set D, pages 98–99.

Find each answer.

1. 56 + 18 + 17   **2.** 49 + 24 + 8   **3.** 29 + 6 + 22 + 25

Practice

For More Practice, see Set D, pages 100–101.

Find these sums.

4. 47 + 23 + 14   **5.** 52 + 28 + 12   **6.** 9 + 35 + 28

7. 65 + 8 + 21   **8.** 37 + 46 + 13   **9.** 26 + 6 + 32

10. 44 + 35 + 4   **11.** 39 + 7 + 43   **12.** 6 + 34 + 23 + 8

13. 27 + 55 + 9   **14.** 8 + 42 + 16   **15.** 14 + 3 + 19 + 5 + 20

Mixed Practice   Find each sum mentally.

16. 45 + 33   **17.** 50 + 28   **18.** 17 + 65   **19.** 20 + 14

20. 62 + 18   **21.** 47 + 37   **22.** 34 + 34   **23.** 59 + 11

Write these numbers in order from least to greatest.

24. 629   686   601   672   **25.** 202   301   311   212

26. 564   465   456   546   **27.** 134   142   143   124

Midchapter ✓ Checkup

Solve each problem.

1. Jaime had 9 marbles. Bob had 6. How many more marbles did Jaime have than Bob?

2. Mark had 4 model cars at home and 5 at school. How many did he have in all?

Find the missing number.

3. 6 tens 8 ones = 5 tens ▦ ones

Find each sum mentally.

4. 29 + 34   **5.** 42 + 50

Add. **Remember** to line up the digits correctly.

6. 16 + 8   **7.** 35 + 35   **8.** 17 + 39 + 4   **9.** 6 + 23 + 34

Problem-Solving Workshop

Real-Life Decision Making

Here is a treasure map. The map shows a ■, a drawing, and the name of a landmark where treasures are buried. You may pick up one treasure from each landmark you visit.

1. What is the fewest number of steps to the crossbar from Start? (Each θ is one step.)

2. If you took the fewest steps from Start to the flower, how many treasures could you pick up?

3. You may take up to 100 steps to collect treasures. Decide which landmarks you will visit.

tetherball

slide

tree

bush

well

rock

statue

flower

Start

crossbar

86

Number-Sense Project

Look back at pages 72-73.
The counts for sandwiches ordered by two grades are shown in this chart.

Sandwich Count		
Sandwich	Grade 3	Grade 4
Hamburger	13	14
Tuna	8	7
Pita	11	10
Peanut Butter with Jelly	6	9
Turkey sub	5	7

1. How many tuna sandwiches were ordered by both grades?

2. Suppose there are 60 students in each grade. Use that information and this chart to show how many students brought their own lunches that day.

3. What was the most popular sandwich? The least popular sandwich?

Explore with a Computer

Use the *Spreadsheet Workshop Project* for this activity. Find out how many boys and girls are in classes in your school. Enter the information into a spreadsheet form. The spreadsheet form will show the sum of the data you type. Think about the totals the spreadsheet form shows. Are the totals reasonable?

Number of Boys and Girls			
Class	Boys	Girls	Total

Two-Digit Subtraction

Build Understanding

A. What is the sale price of the hat?

The sale price is $17 less than the original price so you need to subtract. Find 32 − 17.

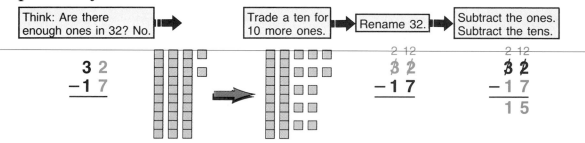

| Think: Are there enough ones in 32? No. | ➡ | Trade a ten for 10 more ones. | ➡ | Rename 32. | ➡ | Subtract the ones. Subtract the tens. |

$$\begin{array}{r} 3\ 2 \\ -1\ 7 \\ \hline \end{array}$$

2 12
$$\begin{array}{r} \cancel{3}\ \cancel{2} \\ -1\ 7 \\ \hline \end{array}$$

2 12
$$\begin{array}{r} \cancel{3}\ \cancel{2} \\ -1\ 7 \\ \hline 1\ 5 \end{array}$$

The sale price of the hat is $15.

B. Find 57 − 12. You can use addition to check your answer.

| Are there enough ones in 57? Yes. | ➡ | Subtract the ones. | ➡ | Subtract the tens. |

Check by adding.

$$\begin{array}{r} 5\ 7 \\ -1\ 2 \\ \hline \end{array}$$
$$\begin{array}{r} 5\ 7 \\ -1\ 2 \\ \hline 5 \end{array}$$
$$\begin{array}{r} 5\ 7 \\ -1\ 2 \\ \hline 4\ 5 \end{array}$$

These two numbers should be the same.

$$\begin{array}{r} 1\ 2 \\ +4\ 5 \\ \hline 5\ 7 \end{array}$$

■ **Talk About Math** Explain how you can use addition to check subtraction. Then tell how you might use subtraction to check addition.

Check Understanding

For another example, see Set E, pages 98–99.

1. Use the information on page 88. Would you need to rename to find the sale price of the dress? the pants?

Find each difference. **Remember** to draw a picture to help you.

2. 75 − 36 **3.** 34 − 21 **4.** 78 − 36 **5.** 82 − 59 **6.** 37 − 25

Practice

For More Practice, see Set E, pages 100–101.

Find each difference.

7.	92 − 29	**8.**	99 − 48	**9.**	81 − 28	**10.**	86 − 70	**11.**	40 − 39

12.	81 − 39	**13.**	57 − 12	**14.**	70 − 45	**15.**	75 − 28	**16.**	92 − 5

Mixed Practice Find the sum or difference.

17.	24 + 16	**18.**	85 − 71	**19.**	40 + 19	**20.**	63 − 44	**21.**	13 − 7

22. 32 + 49 **23.** 48 − 9 **24.** 26 + 35 **25.** 31 − 24 **26.** 60 − 40

27. 87 − 29 **28.** 34 + 48 **29.** 57 + 13 **30.** 54 + 17 **31.** 20 − 13

Problem Solving

Use the information on page 88. What is the sale price of the

32. wooden shoes? **33.** dress? **34.** dress and hat?

35. Use Data Use the data on page 80 to find how much more the basket costs than the bracelet.

36. 🖩 Calculator What 3-digit number and 2-digit number have a sum of 161 and a difference of 109?

Subtraction: Mental Math

Build Understanding

The students in Mrs. Delgrado's class also use different mental math strategies to subtract.

A. To solve 57 − 23, both Mary and Bobby use place value. They break apart the second number.

B. Alice is great with problems like 56 − 19.

57 − 20 = 37

37 − 3 = 34

19 is 1 less than 20.
56 − 20 = 36
1 more than 36 is 37.

■ **Talk About Math**   Which method do you like best? Why? Can you think of another way to subtract mentally?

Check Understanding

For another example, see Set F, pages 98–99.

1. Number Sense   Explain how Alice's method works. For what kinds of exercises would it work best?

Find each difference mentally. Tell which method you used.

2. 57 − 30   **3.** 96 − 40   **4.** 57 − 18   **5.** 35 − 19   **6.** 25 − 19

Practice

For More Practice, see Set F, pages 100–101.

Find each difference mentally. Write which method you used.

7. 63 − 20   **8.** 56 − 30   **9.** 83 − 40   **10.** 38 − 23   **11.** 84 − 23

12. 54 − 31   **13.** 57 − 29   **14.** 42 − 26   **15.** 53 − 38   **16.** 82 − 14

17. 48 − 11   **18.** 74 − 19   **19.** 28 − 9   **20.** 42 − 27   **21.** 34 − 15

22. 65 − 15   **23.** 86 − 69   **24.** 34 − 18   **25.** 73 − 15   **26.** 58 − 50

Mixed Practice   Use paper and pencil or mental math to solve.

27. 48 − 33   **28.** 62 − 51   **29.** 25 − 12   **30.** 97 − 52   **31.** 41 − 29

32. 28 + 37   **33.** 65 − 45   **34.** 52 + 37   **35.** 79 + 13   **36.** 39 − 18

37. 65 − 11   **38.** 24 + 9   **39.** 73 + 21   **40.** 52 + 23   **41.** 63 − 54

Problem Solving

Tell whether you would use mental math or paper and pencil to solve each problem. Then find the answer.

42. Jan has 28 yellow counters, 92 blue counters, and 55 red counters. How many counters does she have in all?

43. Ricky has 28 counters. Ellen has twice that many. How many counters do they have in all?

44. Mark had 48 counters. He used 19 of them. How many did he have left?

A L G E B R A ▶ **Critical Thinking**   Replace each ▦ with the digit 2, 3, 6, or 8 to make the given sum or difference. Do not use any digit more than once in any exercise.

45.
```
  ▦ ▦
− ▦ ▦
─────
  4 5
```

46.
```
  ▦ ▦
+ ▦ ▦
─────
  9 1
```

47.
```
  ▦ ▦
+ ▦ ▦
─────
  6 4
```

48.
```
  ▦ ▦
− ▦ ▦
─────
    8
```

Estimation

Build Understanding

A. Jiro is a reporter for the local newspaper. He often estimates the attendance at PTA® meetings for his articles.

He used front-end estimation to report attendance for the first two meetings.

First Meeting   Second Meeting

3 1   **4 6**   Use only the first digit
 ↓   ↓   of each number. Make
3 0   +   **4 0**   =   **70**   the other digit zero.

Jiro reported that more than 70 people attended those meetings.

B. The editor at the newspaper used a different estimation method.

First Meeting   Second Meeting

3 1   **4 6**   Increase the first digit of
 ↓   ↓   each number by 1. Make
4 0   +   **5 0**   =   **90**   the other digit zero.

She wrote that fewer than 90 people attended the meetings.

The PTA® (Parent Teacher Association®) was started in 1897 to help school children.

C. Use front-end estimation to subtract.

5 1   **3 9**   Use only the first digit
 ↓   ↓   of each number. Make
5 0   −   **3 0**   =   **20**   the other digit zero.

■ Talk About Math

Using Examples A and B, tell why the actual attendance must fall between 70 and 90.

Check Understanding

For another example, see Set G, pages 98–99.

Answer each question.

1. Do you think a front-end estimate for an addition exercise will always be less than the actual sum?

2. Why can a front-end estimate for a subtraction exercise be more or less than the actual answer?

Estimate each answer.

3. 85 − 27   **4.** 16 + 38   **5.** 67 + 85   **6.** 39 − 22   **7.** 12 + 49

Practice

For More Practice, see Set G, pages 100–101.

Estimate each answer.

8. 98 − 42   **9.** 76 − 15   **10.** 35 + 39   **11.** 58 + 19   **12.** 27 − 11

13. 72 − 46   **14.** 44 + 52   **15.** 84 − 19   **16.** 27 + 32   **17.** 38 + 29

Use front-end estimation to find each answer. Tell whether the estimate is more or less than the actual answer.

18. 56 + 14   **19.** 89 − 26   **20.** 78 − 31   **21.** 23 + 75   **22.** 84 − 57

23. 76 − 62   **24.** 57 − 39   **25.** 23 + 19   **26.** 41 + 56   **27.** 76 − 34

Tell whether the sum will be greater than or less than 100.

28. 36 + 55   **29.** 44 + 44   **30.** 16 + 98   **31.** 24 + 39   **32.** 78 + 25

Reading ———— Math

Vocabulary The actual attendance in Examples A and B falls between 70 and 90. This is called the *range.*

60   70   80   90   100

For Exercises 10, 11, 14, 16, and 17 above, find the range.

Deciding When an Estimate Is Enough

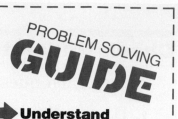

PROBLEM SOLVING
GUIDE

IIII➡ **Understand**
QUESTION
FACTS
KEY IDEA

Plan and Solve
STRATEGY
ANSWER

Look Back
SENSIBLE ANSWER
ALTERNATE APPROACH

Build Understanding

Suppose you have 50¢. You need paper and crayons. Will you have enough money?

IIII➡ **Understand**   QUESTION   Do you have enough money to buy paper and crayons?

FACTS   Paper costs 38¢. Crayons cost 21¢. You have 50¢.

KEY IDEA   To see if you have enough money, you don't have to find the exact amount. You can estimate the cost of the paper and crayons. Then compare to see if your estimate is greater than or less than 50¢.

Plan and Solve   Estimate the cost by rounding.

$$\begin{array}{r} 3\,8 \\ +2\,1 \\ \hline \end{array} \quad \begin{array}{l} \text{rounds to} \rightarrow \\ \text{rounds to} \rightarrow \end{array} \quad \begin{array}{r} 4\,0 \\ +2\,0 \\ \hline 6\,0 \end{array}$$

The estimated cost is about 60¢. You do not have enough money to buy both paper and crayons.

Look Back   You can also use front-end estimation.

$$\begin{array}{ccc} 38 & + & 21 \\ \downarrow & & \downarrow \\ 30 & + & 20 = 50 \end{array}$$

The actual cost will be more than 50¢.

School Supplies

Pencil	7¢
Scissors	33¢
Ruler	14¢
Crayons	21¢
Eraser	12¢
Paper	38¢
Pen	18¢
Glue	18¢

■ Talk About Math Do you think front-end estimation will always be helpful in estimating whether or not you have enough money? Why or why not?

Check Understanding

Suppose you have 30¢.

1. Do you have enough money to buy glue and a pen? How did you decide?

2. You need to buy a pen. Do you have enough money to buy more items? What ones?

Practice

Suppose you have 25¢. Do you have enough money to buy the following items? Tell how you know.

3. Pen and eraser

4. Ruler and glue

5. Pencil and eraser

6. Glue and eraser

Choose as many items as possible that you can buy for

7. 37¢.　　8. 48¢.　　9. 98¢.　　10. 75¢　　11. 89¢.　　12. $1.

Choose a _____ Strategy

Betty's Blocks
13. Betty stacked all her blocks in the shape of a staircase. The highest step was 8 blocks high. How many blocks did she use?

Skills Review

Rename. Make all the new tens you can.

1. 4 tens 13 ones

2. 3 tens 26 ones

Rename. Trade 1 ten for 10 ones.

3. 9 tens 3 ones

4. 7 tens 1 one

Find the sums.

5. 21
   + 37

6. 73
   + 19

7. 62
   + 28

8. 56 + 19 + 5

9. 14 + 9 + 62 + 10

Find each difference.

10. 42
    − 21

11. 91
    − 67

12. 88
    − 39

Find each sum or difference mentally.

13. 69 + 18   **14.** 46 + 27

15. 68 − 50   **16.** 73 − 29

Estimate each answer.

17. 78 − 56   **18.** 37 + 15

19. 61 − 38   **20.** 49 + 53

Problem-Solving Review

Solve each problem.

21. Write the next 3 numbers in the pattern.

1,268   1,278   1,288

22. Mrs. Archer used coupons worth 25¢ and 20¢. How much did she save?

23. A clown doll costs $16 and a cowboy doll costs $12. A Pilgrim doll costs $1 more than the difference between the prices of the other two dolls. What is the cost of the Pilgrim doll?

24. Every ticket with a 7 in the tens place and a 5 in the ones place is a winning ticket. Which of these tickets are winners?

| 1,857 | 2,875 | 8,075 | 3,587 |

25. Data File Use data from pages 104–105. What is the difference between the high temperature in Seattle and the high temperature in Atlanta?

26. Make a Data File Cut out all the coupons from a supermarket flier. Estimate how much you would save if you used all the coupons.

Cumulative Skills Review • Chapters 1-3

Write the family of facts for the numbers in each exercise.

1. 7, 3, 10   **2.** 4, 9, 13   **3.** 0, 6, 6   **4.** 4, 4, 8

Tell if each number is odd or even.

5. 12   **6.** 59   **7.** 85   **8.** 94

Replace each ▦ with $<$ or $>$.

9. 84 ▦ 244   **10.** 780 ▦ 681   **11.** 143 ▦ 413

12. 935 ▦ 1,042   **13.** 5,980 ▦ 5,009   **14.** 9,342 ▦ 8,243

Write the numbers as you count by fives.

15. Begin at 10. Count to 50.   **16.** Begin at 35. Count to 60.

Write the number in standard form.

17. three hundred seventy   **18.** eight thousand, five hundred

19. two hundred thousand, ten   **20.** ten thousand, twenty-two

Round each number to the nearest hundred.

21. 376   **22.** 606   **23.** 129   **24.** 750   **25.** 243

Find each sum.

26.	**27.**	**28.**	**29.**	**30.**	**31.**
56	74	28	37	50	34
+31	+16	+64	+48	+26	+27

Find each difference.

32.	**33.**	**34.**	**35.**	**36.**	**37.**
86	77	62	44	70	53
−42	−38	−58	−25	−32	− 6

Estimate each answer.

38. 47 − 29   **39.** 35 + 26   **40.** 27 + 19   **41.** 71 − 13

Reteaching

Set A   pages 76–79

You have 2 tens and 5 ones. You can trade 1 ten for 10 ones.

So 2 tens 5 ones = 1 ten 15 ones.

Remember that you can trade ones for tens if you have 10 or more ones. Trade 1 ten for 10 ones. How many tens and how many ones do you have now?

1.	Tens	Ones
	5	2

2.	Tens	Ones
	3	4

Set B   pages 80–81

Find 34 + 17.
Add the ones: 7 + 4 = 11. Trade the 11 ones for 1 ten and 1 one. Then add the tens.

$$\begin{array}{r} 34 \\ + 17 \end{array} \Longrightarrow \begin{array}{r} 1 \longleftarrow \text{1 ten} \\ 34 \\ + 17 \\ \hline 51 \longleftarrow \text{1 one} \end{array}$$

Remember that adding the ones will tell you whether you need to make a ten.

Find the sums.

1.	46	**2.**	34	**3.**	58
	+ 25		+ 45		+ 25

Set C   pages 82–83

Find 38 + 34. Use place value. Break apart both numbers.

$$\begin{array}{r} 38 \\ +34 \end{array} \Longrightarrow \begin{array}{r} 30 \\ +30 \\ \hline 60 \end{array} \begin{array}{r} 8 \\ +4 \\ \hline 12 \end{array} \Longrightarrow \begin{array}{r} 60 \\ +12 \\ \hline 72 \end{array}$$

Remember to use the method you like when you add mentally.

Find each sum mentally.

1. 47 + 40   **2.** 35 + 57

Set D   pages 84–85

Find 12 + 25 + 36.
Add the ones: 2 + 5 + 6 = 13

Record 13 ones as
1 ten 3 ones

$$\begin{array}{r} 1 \\ 12 \\ 25 \\ + 36 \\ \hline 3 \end{array}$$

Now add
the tens.

$$\begin{array}{r} 1 \\ 12 \\ 25 \\ + 36 \\ \hline 73 \end{array}$$

Remember to line up the digits correctly.

Find these sums.

1. 26 + 7 + 30   **2.** 32 + 37 + 14

3. 43 + 18 + 24   **4.** 29 + 8 + 42

Set E pages 88–89

Find 43 − 15.
You cannot subtract the ones.

Trade 1 ten for 10 ones.

43 ——————→3 tens   13 ones

```
        3 13
 43      43
-15     -15
        28
```

Remember to use addition to check your answer.

Find each difference.

1. 83 − 44	**2.** 76 − 35	**3.** 52 − 20
4. 50 − 28	**5.** 37 − 16	**6.** 30 − 19

Set F pages 90–91

Find 56 − 28 mentally.
Think: It is easy to subtract 30.

```
 56    ⇒    56
-28        -30
           26
```

Since 30 is 2 more than 28, the actual difference will be 2 more than 26. 2 more than 26 is 28.
So 56 − 28 = 28.

Remember that if you subtract more at the beginning, you have to add more to find the actual difference.

Find each difference mentally.

1. 47 − 30	**2.** 83 − 50	**3.** 29 − 18
4. 56 − 33	**5.** 36 − 28	**6.** 34 − 18

Set G pages 92–93

Estimate the sum by using front-end estimation.

```
 36    ⇒    30
+47        +40
           70
```

Now estimate the sum by increasing the first digit of each number by 1.

```
 36    ⇒    40
+47        +50
           90
```

The actual sum is between 70 and 90.

Remember that an estimated sum will always be less than the actual sum when you use front-end estimation.

Estimate each answer.

1. 46 + 32	**2.** 68 + 25	**3.** 29 + 27
4. 89 + 12	**5.** 31 + 48	**6.** 76 + 25

More Practice

Set A   pages 76–79

Use your place-value materials. Make all the new tens
you can. How many tens and ones do you have now?

1.	Tens	Ones
	3	11

2.	Tens	Ones
	7	14

3.	Tens	Ones
	6	18

4. 4 tens 13 ones   **5.** 5 tens 24 ones   **6.** 6 tens 30 ones

Use your place-value materials. Trade 1 ten
for 10 ones. How many tens and ones do you have now?

7.	Tens	Ones
	4	6

8.	Tens	Ones
	8	4

9.	Tens	Ones
	9	7

10. 6 tens 3 ones   **11.** 5 tens 8 ones   **12.** 3 tens 5 ones

Mixed Practice   Add or subtract.

13. $6 + 9$ **14.** $17 - 9$ **15.** $11 - 6$ **16.** $4 + 7$ **17.** $7 + 7$

18. $8 + 6$ **19.** $16 - 7$ **20.** $17 - 8$ **21.** $15 - 6$ **22.** $8 - 8$

Set B   pages 80–81

Find the sums.

1.	**2.**	**3.**	**4.**	**5.**
36	71	64	27	60
+26	+17	+29	+19	+13

6. $5 + 19$ **7.** $67 + 2$ **8.** $43 + 36$ **9.** $56 + 19$ **10.** $46 + 45$

Set C   pages 82–83

Find each sum mentally. Write which method you used.

1.	**2.**	**3.**	**4.**	**5.**
38	49	34	52	64
+20	+40	+27	+36	+29

6.	**7.**	**8.**	**9.**	**10.**
48	38	81	78	46
+17	+21	+16	+15	+26

Set D pages 84–85

Find these sums.

1. 28 + 6 + 20   **2.** 44 + 26 + 13   **3.** 27 + 32 + 7

4. 56 + 9 + 32   **5.** 24 + 39 + 14   **6.** 36 + 8 + 23

7. 6 + 39 + 52   **8.** 33 + 55 + 10   **9.** 47 + 24 + 12

Set E pages 88–89

Find each difference.

1. 74 − 47	**2.** 66 − 52	**3.** 32 − 19	**4.** 50 − 22	**5.** 73 − 30
6. 41 − 28	**7.** 75 − 15	**8.** 56 − 29	**9.** 60 − 35	**10.** 46 − 9

11. 76 − 41   **12.** 80 − 34   **13.** 84 − 8   **14.** 33 − 4   **15.** 72 − 38

Set F pages 90–91

Find each difference mentally. Write which
method you used.

1. 38 − 20	**2.** 86 − 40	**3.** 46 − 21	**4.** 87 − 34	**5.** 92 − 50
6. 63 − 22	**7.** 48 − 19	**8.** 34 − 28	**9.** 84 − 17	**10.** 56 − 39

Set G pages 92–93

Estimate each answer.

1. 68 − 24	**2.** 84 − 32	**3.** 46 + 36	**4.** 39 + 26	**5.** 39 − 14
6. 53 − 37	**7.** 68 − 49	**8.** 33 + 63	**9.** 34 + 45	**10.** 46 + 36

Tell whether the sum will be greater than or less than 100.

11. 48 + 39   **12.** 96 + 21   **13.** 66 + 32   **14.** 34 + 42   **15.** 52 + 39

Enrichment

Missing Digits

Lupita's wet puppy shook himself and got water drops on her math homework. Help her find each digit covered by the water drops. Look for number clues.

$$\begin{array}{r} 3\ 5 \\ -\ 1\ \square \\ \hline 1\ 9 \end{array}$$

CLUE: Look at the ones column.
5 ones − ⬤ ones = 9 ones
5 ones − ⬤ = 9 doesn't seem possible.

THINK: Maybe the top number was renamed and the ⬤ was subtracted from 15 ones.

15 ones − ⬤ ones = 9 ones
15 − ⬤ = 9

TRY: Try 6. It works!

$$\begin{array}{r} 3\ 5 \\ -\ 1\ 6 \\ \hline 1\ 9 \end{array}$$

Complete each exercise. **Remember** to look for number clues.

1.
$$\begin{array}{r} 5\square \\ -\ 2\ 3 \\ \hline 3\ 5 \end{array}$$

2.
$$\begin{array}{r} 3\ 9 \\ +\ 2\square \\ \hline 6\ 2 \end{array}$$

3.
$$\begin{array}{r} 7\ 4 \\ -\ \square 7 \\ \hline 2\ 7 \end{array}$$

4.
$$\begin{array}{r} 5\square \\ +\ 3\ 8 \\ \hline 9\ 3 \end{array}$$

5.
$$\begin{array}{r} 2\ 7 \\ -\ \square 8 \\ \hline 9 \end{array}$$

6.
$$\begin{array}{r} 3\square \\ +\ \square 4 \\ \hline 8\ 2 \end{array}$$

7.
$$\begin{array}{r} 2\square \\ -\ 1\ 6 \\ \hline 7 \end{array}$$

8.
$$\begin{array}{r} 7\ 6 \\ +\ \square 1 \\ \hline 9\square \end{array}$$

9.
$$\begin{array}{r} 3\ 9 \\ +\ 2\square \\ \hline 6\ 2 \end{array}$$

10.
$$\begin{array}{r} \square 6 \\ -\ 2\square \\ \hline 4\ 9 \end{array}$$

11.
$$\begin{array}{r} 7\square \\ -\ 3\ 4 \\ \hline \square 0 \end{array}$$

12.
$$\begin{array}{r} \square 2 \\ -\ 2\ 7 \\ \hline 6\square \end{array}$$

102

Chapter 3 Review/Test

Rename. Make all the new tens you can.

1.	Tens	Ones
	2	18

2.	Tens	Ones
	7	10

Rename. Trade 1 ten for 10 ones.

3.	Tens	Ones
	3	8

4.	Tens	Ones
	5	2

Add.

5. 65
   + 17

6. 26
   + 24

7. 19
   + 19

8. Add 28 + 41 mentally. Write which method you used.

Add.

9. 45 + 13 + 12

10. 32 + 20 + 19 + 6

Subtract.

11. 83
    − 59

12. 61
    − 24

13. 27
    − 9

Find each difference mentally. Write which method you used.

14. 74 − 19   15. 55 − 37

Estimate each sum or difference.

16. 68 + 27   17. 51 − 32

18. Mr. Cruz baked 24 muffins. He baked 11 more rolls than muffins. How many rolls did Mr. Cruz bake?

19. You have 75¢. Can you buy a 45¢ pad and a 49¢ pen?

Read this problem. Then answer the question below.

Ella had 37 crayons. She gave 16 of them to Cal. How many crayons did she have left?

20. Choose the sentence that correctly answers the problem.

   a. Ella has 21 more crayons than Cal.

   b. Ella has 21 crayons left.

   c. Together, Ella and Cal have 37 crayons.

21. ■ **Write About Math**
Explain the method you used to estimate in Exercise 17.

1. Baseball Scores

American League
Indians 1, White Sox 0
Red Sox 5, Brewers 1
Tigers 5, Yankees 3
Orioles 7, Blue Jays 5
Angels 4, Rangers 3
Athletics 4, Royals 3
Mariners 3, Twins 1

National League
Cubs 5, Cardinals 1
Phillies 5, Expos 3
Mets 7, Pirates 3
Astros 3, Reds 0
Padres 3, Giants 0
Dodgers 3, Braves 1

1. Chart
Baseball scores
for October 1, 1989.

2. Chart
The best score in a game of
golf is the lowest score.

3. Weather Map
The high temperature
and low temperature is
recorded for each city.
The first number is the
high temperature. The
second number is the low
temperature.

4. Bar Graph
The graph shows the
number of hours the
computers are used
each day.

The British Open 1989
Past Champs

Year	Winner	Score
1980	Tom Watson	271
1981	Bill Rogers	276
1982	Tom Watson	284
1983	Tom Watson	275
1984	Seve Ballesteros	276
1985	Sandy Lyle	282
1986	Greg Norman	280
1987	Nick Faldo	270
1988	Seve Ballesteros	273

2. Golf Champs

104

3. Weather Map

Seattle
76/54

70°

80°

90°

90°

90°

Rapid City
90/65

Minneapolis
85/64

80°

San Francisco
73/52

Chicago

New York
87/7

90°

100°

90°

Denver
87/59

80°

80°

Los Angeles
79/66

90°

110°

100°

90°

Atlanta
88/71

Dallas
90/68

Miami
90/77

50°

100°

60°

Conditions

○ Fair

◑ Partly Cloudy

● Cloudy

▨ Rain

▦ Snow

Static front

Warm front

Cold front

Ⓗ High pressure

Ⓛ Low pressure

4. Bar Graph

School District # 25
Daily Computer Use

School	Hours
Spring School	4
Goodwell Middle School	6
Park School	2
Oak School	4
Frost School	3

Hours: 2 4 6 8

Cumulative Review/Test, Chapters 1–3

Give the letter for the correct answer.

1. Tell what number or sign belongs in the box.

8 = 8 − ▦
A 1   **B** 0   **C** 8   **D** 16

2. Add.

  7
+3

A 4
B 11
C 9
D 10

3. Add.

  9
+8

A 17
B 16
C 15
D 1

4. Subtract.

 15
− 6

A 11
B 8
C 9
D 7

5. Which fact does not belong to the family?

A 9 + 5 = 14   **B** 14 − 5 = 9
C 9 − 5 = 4   **D** 14 − 9 = 5

6. Which numbers are written in order from least to greatest?

A 11	12	10	14	13
B 10	11	12	13	14
C 12	11	10	14	13
D 14	13	12	11	10

7. Which is the hundreds digit in 627?

A 6   **B** 7   **C** 2

8. Which number sentence is true?

A 562 < 332   **C** 562 > 432
B 562 = 432   **D** 532 < 432

9. Which numbers are written in order from least to greatest?

A 563	702	519	681
B 681	563	702	519
C 702	681	563	519
D 519	563	681	702

10. What is the next number when counting by fives?

50   55   60   65   ▦

A 70   **B** 67   **C** 66   **D** 75

11. Arrange these numbers to match the directions.

6   4   2

The ones digit is the sum of the hundreds and tens digits. The hundreds digit is twice as big as the tens digit.

A 246   **C** 642
B 426   **D** 624

12. Which is the thousands digit in 6,789?

A 7   **B** 8   **C** 9   **D** 6

13. What is the standard form?

A 136   **C** 1,365
B 365   **D** 3,165

14. Which is the ten-thousands digit in 387,029?

A 8   **B** 7   **C** 2   **D** 9

15. Choose the most sensible answer.

Macky is 9 years old. His sister is just entering first grade. What is her age?

A 9 years   **C** 12 years
B 6 years   **D** 3 years

16. Solve the problem.

Monday Carl practiced violin for 47 minutes. Tuesday he practiced for 52 minutes. How much longer did he practice on Tuesday than on Monday?

A 77 minutes   **C** 15 minutes
B 5 minutes   **D** 25 minutes

17. Add.

$$\begin{array}{r} 58 \\ +34 \\ \hline \end{array}$$

A 83
B 82
C 94
D 92

18. Add.

$$\begin{array}{r} 17 \\ 26 \\ +44 \\ \hline \end{array}$$

A 86
B 87
C 77
D 98

19. Subtract.

$$\begin{array}{r} 82 \\ -14 \\ \hline \end{array}$$

A 72
B 78
C 68
D 62

Read the problem below. Then answer the question.

Ned has a flock of chickens. He has 21 Rhode Island Reds and 8 Plymouth Rocks. How many more Rhode Island Reds than Plymouth Rocks are there?

20. Which number sentence would you choose to solve the problem?

A $21 - 8 = $ ▦
B $21 + 8 = $ ▦
C $29 - 8 = $ ▦
D $29 - 21 = $ ▦

Three- and Four-Digit Addition and Subtraction

4

Did You Know: Domino toppling was popular in the 1980s. Some people have set up dominoes 12 hours a day for a whole month just to topple them down.

Number-Sense Project

Estimate
Estimate the number of dominoes in this picture.

Gather Data
Count the number of each color. Add these numbers together to find how many in all.

Analyze and Report
Compare your count with your estimate.

Using Money to Rename

Build Understanding

Money Power
Materials: Play money
Groups: 3–5 students

A. Johnny emptied his bank. He wanted to trade his pennies for dimes and his dimes for dollars. He knew that

10 pennies make 1 dime.

10 dimes make 1 dollar.

Suppose Johnny had 2 dollars, 9 dimes, and 15 pennies.

a. Use your play money to show Johnny's money. Then trade 10 pennies for 1 dime.

b. Trade 10 dimes for 1 dollar.

c. Show the final amount: 3 dollars, 0 dimes, and 5 pennies.

Johnny had 3 dollars, 0 dimes, and 5 pennies.

B. Suppose Maxine has 2 dollars, 0 dimes, and 7 pennies. She needs dimes to play the machine at the video arcade.

a. Use your play money to show Maxine's money.

b. Trade 1 dollar for 10 dimes.

c. Show the final amount: 1 dollar, 10 dimes, and 7 pennies.

Maxine will have 1 dollar, 10 dimes, and 7 pennies.

c. Johnny and Maxine wrote the amount of money each had after the trades in the place-value boxes at the right.

$	d	p
3	0	5

Johnny

$	d	p
1	10	7

Maxine

■ **Talk About Math** In Example A, explain what will happen if you start trading with the dimes first.

Check Understanding

For another example, see Set A, pages 142–143.

Use your play money to show each problem. Then record the answer.

1. How many pennies can you get for 1 dime? for 2 dimes?

2. How many dimes can you get for 30 pennies? for 57 pennies?

Practice

For More Practice, see Set A, pages 144–145.

Use your play money. Trade pennies for dimes and dimes for dollars. Record how many dollars, dimes, and pennies you have when you finish.

3.

$	d	p
4	3	12

4.

$	d	p
2	14	5

5.

$	d	p
0	13	4

6.

$	d	p
3	3	17

7.

$	d	p
1	15	11

8.

$	d	p
2	13	10

9.

$	d	p
4	9	12

10.

$	d	p
1	9	10

11.

$	d	p
0	8	23

12.

$	d	p
8	7	20

13.

$	d	p
3	12	9

14.

$	d	p
1	4	11

15.

$	d	p
0	15	5

16.

$	d	p
3	10	2

17.

$	d	p
4	3	24

18.

$	d	p
2	4	19

19.

$	d	p
5	1	10

20.

$	d	p
3	16	7

Use play money for each exercise. Make the trade. Now record how many dollars, dimes, and pennies you have.

21. Trade 1 dime for 10 pennies.

$	d	p
3	5	7

22. Trade 1 dime for 10 pennies.

$	d	p
2	8	1

23. Trade 1 dollar for 10 dimes.

$	d	p
4	3	5

24. Trade 1 dime for 10 pennies.

$	d	p
1	4	0

25. Trade 1 dollar for 10 dimes.

$	d	p
5	0	1

26. Trade 1 dollar for 10 dimes.

$	d	p
1	2	6

Problem Solving

Critical Thinking   Find the mystery numbers.

27. I am a 3-digit number less than 300. My tens digit is less than my hundreds digit and my ones digit is less than my tens digit. Who am I?

28. I am a number between 600 and 700. My ones digit is 4. My tens digit is the difference between my ones and hundreds digits. Who am I?

Choose a _____ Strategy

Fun with Phones

29. Barry's phone number is 176-8204. Find the sum of the digits.

30. Rosa's phone number has some digits that are different from Barry's but the sum is the same. What could the number be?

PROBLEM SOLVING STRATEGIES

Choose an Operation
Find a Pattern
Use Logical Reasoning

Exploring Three-Digit Addition

Build Understanding

Birthday Money
Materials: Play money
Groups: 3–5 students

A. Jim and Joanne put their money together
to buy a birthday present for their mother.
How much did they have altogether?

	$	d	p
Jim's money ⟶	2	8	7
Joanne's money →	1	7	5

a. Use your play money to show each
amount. Put the money together.

b. Trade 10 pennies for 1 dime.

c. Trade 10 dimes for 1 dollar.

d. Show the final amount: 4 dollars, 6 dimes, and 2 pennies.

Jim and Joanne had $4.62 in all.

B. What is the total amount in the place-value box?

$	d	p
2	2	7
+ 1	0	2

a. Use your play money to show both amounts.

b. Put them together.

c. Trade if you can.   Not enough pennies or dimes to trade.

d. Show the final amount with play money:
3 dollars, 2 dimes, and 9 pennies.

There is $3.29 in all.

■ **Talk About Math** Why is it important to start with pennies when trading?

Check Understanding

For another example, see Set B, pages 142–143.

Look at the place-value box. Use your play money to help you answer the questions.

1. Look at these two amounts of money. How many pennies are there altogether?

2. How many dimes can be made? How many dimes are there altogether?

3. How many dollars can be made?

$	d	p
2	4	6
+ 1	5	5

Practice

For More Practice, see Set B, pages 144–145.

Use play money to show each amount of money
in the place-value chart. Trade 10 pennies for
1 dime if you can. Then try to trade 10 dimes
for 1 dollar. Write how much in all.

4.

$	d	p
4	2	7
+ 1	5	6

5.

$	d	p
2	8	1
+ 2	6	4

6.

$	d	p
3	7	9
+ 3	1	0

7.

$	d	p
2	4	5
+ 1	8	6

8.

$	d	p
3	2	6
+ 2	5	3

9.

$	d	p
0	4	5
+ 1	5	7

10.

$	d	p
3	6	2
+ 1	7	0

11.

$	d	p
3	4	2
+ 4	4	9

12.

$	d	p
2	9	5
+ 3	0	5

Number Sense Make up a money addition
problem like the ones in this lesson that makes you

13. trade 10 pennies for a dime.

14. trade 10 dimes for 1 dollar.

15. have no trades.

16. trade both 10 pennies for a
dime *and* 10 dimes for a
dollar.

Problem Solving

Jim and Jamelle played this game.

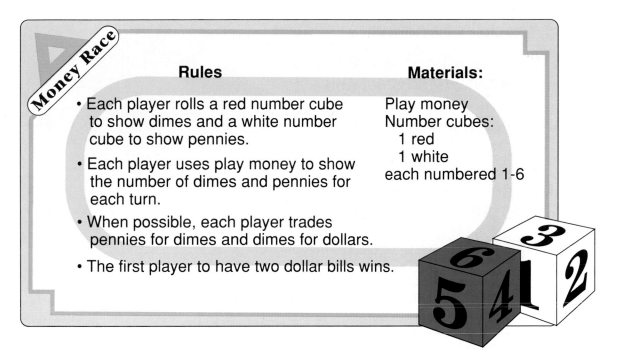

Money Race

Rules

- Each player rolls a red number cube to show dimes and a white number cube to show pennies.

- Each player uses play money to show the number of dimes and pennies for each turn.

- When possible, each player trades pennies for dimes and dimes for dollars.

- The first player to have two dollar bills wins.

Materials:

Play money
Number cubes:
  1 red
  1 white
each numbered 1-6

17. Here are Jim's and Jamelle's rolls. Who won the game?

Jim's rolls	
4	2
1	3
2	6
6	1
4	5
1	2

Jamelle's rolls	
3	6
2	3
6	4
1	2
3	6
4	9

18. Play a game of Money Race with a friend. Play until someone has at least 2 dollar bills.

19. **Critical Thinking** Suppose you roll a 6 and a 2. Would you rather that the red cube show the 6 or the 2? Explain your answer.

TIPS FOR PROBLEM SOLVERS

Think about your own thinking. Pause to ask, "How is this going to help me solve the problem?"

Adding Three-Digit Numbers

Build Understanding

A. Mrs. Wong is a librarian. She just received 472 fiction books and 183 nonfiction books. How many new books did she receive?

Find 472 + 183.

Estimation   472 is about 500. 183 is about 200.
500 + 200 = 700
The answer should be about 700.

There are more than 14,000 public libraries in the United States.

Add the ones.	Add the tens. Rename.	Record.	Add the hundreds.
4 7 2 +1 8 3 ——— 5	4 7 2 +1 8 3 ——— 5 15 tens = 1 hundred and 5 tens	¹ 4 7 2 +1 8 3 ——— 5 5	¹ 4 7 2 +1 8 3 ——— 6 5 5

Mrs. Wong received 655 new books.

B. Find 123 + 271.

Add the ones.	Add the tens.	Add the hundreds.
1 2 3 +2 7 1 ——— 4	1 2 3 +2 7 1 ——— 9 4	1 2 3 +2 7 1 ——— 3 9 4

■ **Talk About Math**   Look at Examples A and B. What extra step did you have to do in Example A? Why was it necessary?

Check Understanding

For another example, see Set C, pages 142–143.

Answer each question to find the missing digits.

1. What number should replace the ▦? the ▦?

2. What does the number for ▦ mean?

3. Find 635 + 147.

```
      ▦
  6 3 5
+ 1 4 7
———————
      ▦
```

Practice

For More Practice, see Set C, pages 144–145.

Find each sum. **Remember** to estimate before you find the exact answer.

4. 539 +247	**5.** 285 +453	**6.** 72 +137	**7.** 403 +382	**8.** 367 +150
9. 690 +153	**10.** 821 +176	**11.** 339 +202	**12.** 264 +570	**13.** 651 +285
14. 369 +528	**15.** 430 +165	**16.** 805 +193	**17.** 56 +751	**18.** 737 +125
19. 247 +481	**20.** 84 +591	**21.** 738 +253	**22.** 387 +418	**23.** 188 +491

24. 127 + 453   **25.** 543 + 345   **26.** 681 + 127   **27.** 328 + 259

28. 325 + 219 + 173   **29.** 189 + 127 + 85   **30.** 109 + 190 + 901

Mixed Practice   Round to the nearest hundred.

31. 541   **32.** 363   **33.** 787   **34.** 852

35. 105   **36.** 945   **37.** 699   **38.** 451

Skills ____ **Review**   Review, page 545

What time is it?

1.   2.   3.   4.

Three- and Four-Digit Addition

Build Understanding

Girl Scout Troop 115 spent the fall collecting aluminum cans to be recycled. They placed containers at two places: one in front of the school and one in the supermarket parking lot.

How many cans altogether did they collect in September?

Find 1,459 + 1,043.

Estimation 1,459 is about 1,500. 1,043 is about 1,000.
1,500 + 1,000 = 2,500
The answer should be about 2,500.

TROOP 115 CAN COLLECTION		
	School	Supermarket
Sept.	1,459	1,043
Oct.	982	586
Nov.	487	325

Add the ones.
Record 12 ones as 1 ten and 2 ones.

$$\begin{array}{r} 1 \\ 1,45\ 9 \\ +\ 1,04\ 3 \\ \hline 2 \end{array}$$

Add the tens.
Record 10 tens as 1 hundred and 0 tens.

$$\begin{array}{r} 1\ 1 \\ 1,45\ 9 \\ +\ 1,04\ 3 \\ \hline 0\ 2 \end{array}$$

Add the hundreds.
Record 5 hundreds.

$$\begin{array}{r} 1\ 1 \\ 1,45\ 9 \\ +\ 1,04\ 3 \\ \hline 5\ 0\ 2 \end{array}$$

Add the thousands.
Record 2 thousands.

$$\begin{array}{r} 1\ 1 \\ 1,45\ 9 \\ +\ 1,04\ 3 \\ \hline 2,5\ 0\ 2 \end{array}$$

There were 2,502 cans collected in September. That is very close to your estimate of 2,500.

■ **Talk About Math** Does the estimate tell you that your answer is correct? Explain.

Check Understanding

For another example, see Set D, pages 142–143.

Estimation Find each answer.

1. Estimate how many cans were collected in October. Then find the exact number. How close was your estimate?

2. Estimate how many cans were collected in November. Then find the exact number. How close was your estimate?

Practice

For More Practice, see Set D, pages 144–145.

Find each sum. **Remember** to estimate first.

3. 4,840 + 1,023	**4.** 6,029 + 1,416	**5.** 5,520 + 715	**6.** 387 + 763	**7.** 398 + 249
8. 6,058 + 819	**9.** 5,727 + 1,609	**10.** 8,731 + 273	**11.** 9,540 + 482	**12.** 8,694 + 457
13. 8,704 + 918	**14.** 5,360 + 315	**15.** 5,462 + 923	**16.** 2,640 + 3,173	**17.** 1,847 + 6,259

18. 3,985 + 632

19. 5,680 + 8,245

20. 4,039 + 962

21. 4,983 + 390

22. 3,519 + 23

23. 387 + 2,980 + 4,257

Explore ——— Math

ALGEBRA

▶ Use the table at the right.

24. Start with 99. Add 11.

25. Record the number sentence in a table.

26. Add 11 to each sum until you reach 198.

27. Describe the pattern you discover in the sums.

Number Sentences		
99 + 11	=	110
110 + 11	=	▨
▨ + 11	=	▨

Choose a Computation Method

Build Understanding

Dan's Cub Scout troop had a pinewood car derby. Each car was judged on speed and style. The chart shows the scores for some of the best cars.

TROOP 157 DERBY

Car	Speed	Style
Firebird	627	812
Gazelle	712	790
Rampage	600	700
Eagle	64	78

A. What was Firebird's total score?

Find 627 + 812.

Calculator This can be a hard problem. You might choose to do it with a calculator:

627 ⊞ 812 ⊜ 1,439

B. Find 600 + 700.

Mental Math This is an easy problem to do with mental math.

Think: 600 + 700 = 1,300

C. Find 64 + 78.

Paper and Pencil This is not a very hard problem, but you might not be able to do it mentally. Use paper and pencil.

$$\begin{array}{r} \overset{1}{}64 \\ +\ 78 \\ \hline 142 \end{array}$$

■ **Talk About Math** How might you be able to find the answer to Example C using a mental math strategy?

Check Understanding

Use paper and pencil, mental math, or a calculator to find each answer. Tell what method you used.

1. 50 + 40	2. 359 + 102	3. 8 + 6	4. 86 + 42	5. 903 + 878

For More Practice, see Set E, pages 144–145.

Practice

Use paper and pencil, mental math, or a calculator to find each answer. Tell what method you used.

6. 603 + 1,457	7. 4 + 2	8. 36 + 20	9. 47 + 12	10. 2,743 + 9,189

11. 86 + 80	12. 563 + 210	13. 67 + 29	14. 4,787 + 1,896	15. 746 + 120

16. 8,354 + 2,498

17. 600 + 320

18. 217 + 328

19. 43 + 51

20. 7,214 + 1,438

21. 673 + 381

22. 6 + 7

23. 37 + 29

24. 5,409 + 2,111

Problem Solving

Use the chart on page 122 to solve each problem.

25. How much greater was Eagle's style score than its speed score?

26. Which car had the greatest total score?

A▶Critical Thinking Find the missing numbers. Within each exercise, the same shape represents the same missing digit.

27. 40▦ + 2▦9 △64	28. 45▦ + 1▦7 △12	29. 45▦ + 1△2 ▦30	30. 7▦3 + 19▦ △59

Use Data from a Picture

Build Understanding

This map shows some of the trails that the pioneers used in the 1800s.

Part of the path from Boston to Independence was called the Mohawk Trail. How many miles was it from Boston to Independence?

PROBLEM SOLVING GUIDE

Understand
QUESTION
FACTS
KEY IDEA

Plan and Solve
STRATEGY
ANSWER

Look Back
SENSIBLE ANSWER
ALTERNATE APPROACH

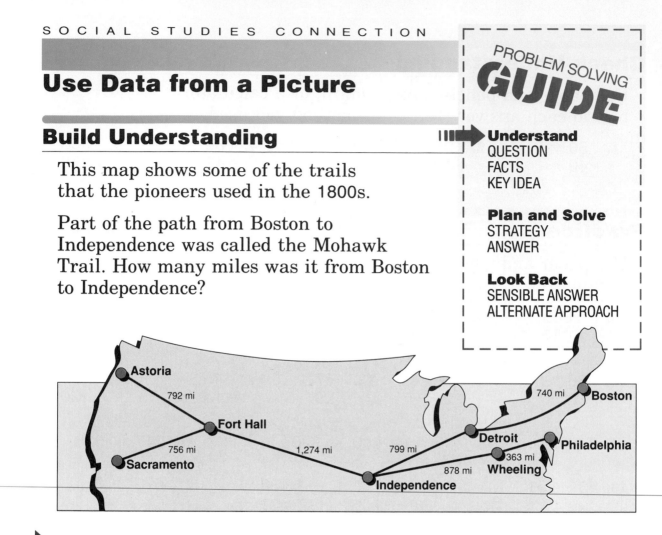

Understand   QUESTION   How far was Independence from Boston?

FACTS   The map shows the information you need. Where do you need to start? Find Boston. Where do you need to go? Find Independence. Can you go directly, or do you need to go through another city? How far is it from Boston to Detroit? How far is it from Detroit to Independence?

KEY IDEA   You are joining the two distances.

Plan and Solve   You should add.

$$\begin{array}{r} 7\,4\,0 \\ +7\,9\,9 \\ \hline 1{,}5\,3\,9 \end{array}$$

It was 1,539 miles from Boston to Independence.

Look Back   Did you use the correct map information?

■ **Write About Math** Is the trip from Boston to Independence longer or shorter than the trip from Philadelphia to Independence? Explain.

Check Understanding

Use the map on page 124 to answer each question.

1. What city must you go through to get from Independence to Astoria?

2. What two smaller trips make the total trip from Independence to Astoria?

3. How long was the Oregon Trail between Independence and Astoria?

Practice

Use the map on page 124 to solve each problem.

4. What city must you go through to get from Independence to Sacramento?

5. What two smaller trips make the total trip from Independence to Sacramento?

6. How many miles is it from Boston to Sacramento?

7. How many miles is it from Philadelphia to Sacramento?

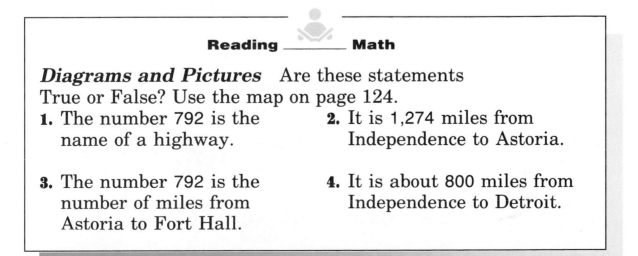

Reading ———— Math

Diagrams and Pictures Are these statements True or False? Use the map on page 124.

1. The number 792 is the name of a highway.

2. It is 1,274 miles from Independence to Astoria.

3. The number 792 is the number of miles from Astoria to Fort Hall.

4. It is about 800 miles from Independence to Detroit.

Exploring Three-Digit Subtraction

Build Understanding

Spending Spree
Materials: Play money
Groups: 3–5 students

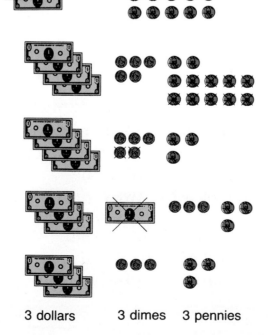

How many kinds of house plants can you name?

A. Toni and Chris had $4.62 to spend. They bought a plant that cost $1.29. How much did they have left?

a. Use your play money to show the amount they started with.

	$	d	p
Their money →	4	6	2
Cost of plant →	1	2	9

b. Try to take away 9 pennies. There are not enough pennies. Trade 1 dime for 10 pennies.

c. Now take away 9 pennies.

d. Take away 2 dimes.

e. Take away 1 dollar.

f. Show the amount left.

Toni and Chris had $3.33 left.   3 dollars   3 dimes   3 pennies

126

B. Suppose you have 3 dollars, 3 dimes, and 3 pennies. Take away 1 dollar, 1 dime, and 2 pennies. How much money is left?

$	d	p
3	3	3
− 1	1	2

a. Show 3 dollars, 3 dimes, and 3 pennies. Take away 2 pennies.

b. Take away 1 dime. Then take away 1 dollar.

c. Show the amount left.

There is $2.21 left.

■ **Talk About Math** Why is it important to take away pennies first? What could happen if you start with the dimes?

Check Understanding

For another example, see Set F, pages 142–143.

Suppose you have 6 dollars, 4 dimes, and 2 pennies. Take away 5 dollars, 9 dimes, and 1 penny.

$	d	p
6	4	2
− 5	9	1

1. Look at these two amounts of money. What would be your first step?

2. Do you need to do any trading to solve this problem?

3. If so, what would you have to trade?

4. What would you get in exchange?

Practice

For More Practice, see Set F, pages 144–145.

Use your play money to show how much you have.
Take away the amount you spend. You may have
to trade a dime for 10 pennies. You may have to
trade a dollar for 10 dimes. Write how much you have left.

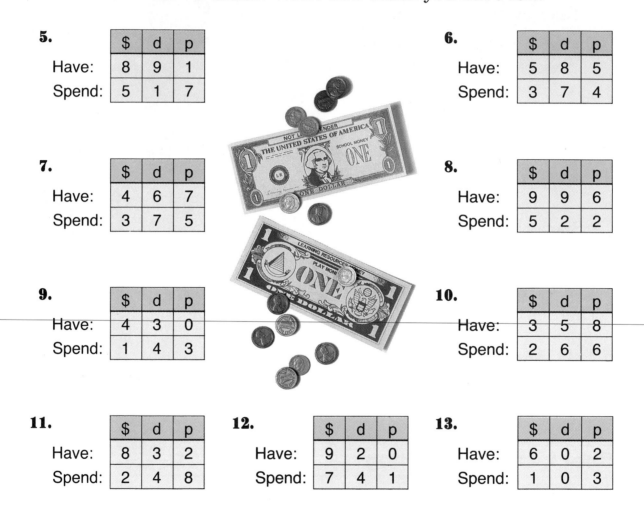

5.

	$	d	p
Have:	8	9	1
Spend:	5	1	7

6.

	$	d	p
Have:	5	8	5
Spend:	3	7	4

7.

	$	d	p
Have:	4	6	7
Spend:	3	7	5

8.

	$	d	p
Have:	9	9	6
Spend:	5	2	2

9.

	$	d	p
Have:	4	3	0
Spend:	1	4	3

10.

	$	d	p
Have:	3	5	8
Spend:	2	6	6

11.

	$	d	p
Have:	8	3	2
Spend:	2	4	8

12.

	$	d	p
Have:	9	2	0
Spend:	7	4	1

13.

	$	d	p
Have:	6	0	2
Spend:	1	0	3

Number Sense Make up a money subtraction
problem like the ones in this lesson that makes you

14. trade a dime for 10 pennies.   **15.** trade a dollar for 10 dimes.

16. trade both a dollar for
10 dimes *and* a dime for
10 pennies.

17. make no trades.

Tell how many dollars, dimes, and pennies
you have if you trade

1. pennies for dimes.

$	d	p
3	6	13

2. 1 dime for 10 pennies.

$	d	p
6	7	8

3. Tell how much you have in all.

$	d	p
1	8	2
3	7	1

4. Tell how much you have left.

$	d	p
4	7	2
1	4	3

Add.

5. 451
    +275

6. 482
    +359

7. 208
    +320

8. 3,086
    +5,027

9. 7,134
    +1,098

Add. Use mental math, paper and pencil, or a calculator
to find each answer. Tell what method you used.

10. 562
     +164

11. 248
     +127

12. 28
      +32

13. 4,274
     +3,899

14. 6,259
     +1,362

15. What is the shortest distance between Woodruff and Slinger?

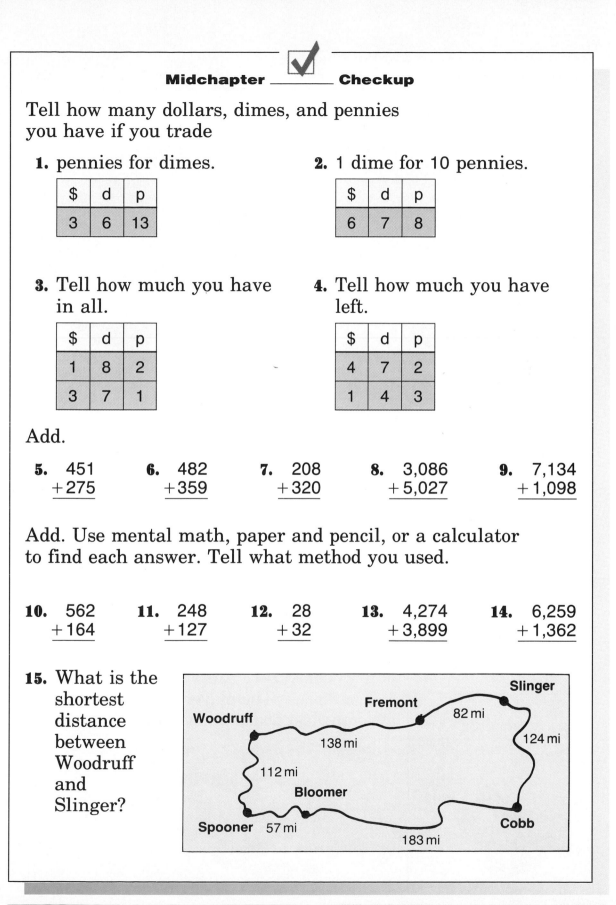

Slinger

Fremont

Woodruff

82 mi

138 mi

124 mi

112 mi

Bloomer

Spooner   57 mi

Cobb

183 mi

Critical Thinking Activity

CLUES

- There are 3 chips in the red box.
- There are 9 chips altogether in the yellow and blue boxes.
- There are 8 chips altogether in the yellow and red boxes.

1. How many chips are in the blue box?

2. How many chips are there altogether?

Hint: Counters may help you.

Math-at-Home Activity

Play this game with someone at home. Put out 21 black-eyed peas or dry beans. Take turns removing 1, 2, or 3 peas. The player who takes away the last pea is the winner.

Number-Sense Project

Look back at pages 108-109.

1. Look at the dots on the green dominoes.

　a. Estimate how many dots there are.

　b. Count the dots.

　c. Was your estimate close to the actual number of dots? Explain how you found your estimate.

2. Look at the red dominoes.

　a. Tell how you could estimate the number of dots. Then give the estimate.

　b. Compare your estimate and method with a classmate. Which one has the better method for estimating?

Explore as a Team

1. Follow the pattern to make bigger and bigger squares.

2. How many yellow squares will be in the next biggest square after d? How many red?

3. Talk and write about number patterns you see.

TIPS FOR
WORKING TOGETHER
Work as a group. If you understand, help another group member. Don't work ahead of the others.

a.

b.

d.

c.

Subtracting Three-Digit Numbers

Build Understanding

Ramón's class is getting ready for a school party. The boys need to make 481 hats. They have already made 124 hats. How many more hats do they have to make?

Find 481 − 124.

Estimation   481 is about 500. 124 is about 100. 500 − 100 = 400 The answer should be about 400.

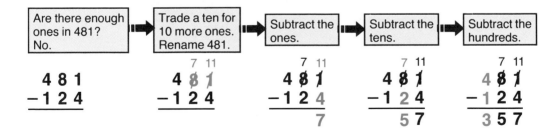

Are there enough ones in 481? No.	Trade a ten for 10 more ones. Rename 481.	Subtract the ones.	Subtract the tens.	Subtract the hundreds.

4 8 1
 − 1 2 4
	7 11
	 4 8̸ 1̸
	 − 1 2 4
		7 11
		 4 8̸ 1̸
		 − 1 2 4
		 ———
		          7
			7 11
			 4 8̸ 1̸
			 − 1 2 4
			 ———
			      5 7
				7 11
				 4 8̸ 1̸
				 − 1 2 4
				 ———
				   3 5 7

The boys have 357 more hats to make. That is close to your estimate of 400.

Check by adding.
$$\begin{array}{r} 4\ 8\ 1 \\ -\ 1\ 2\ 4 \\ \hline 3\ 5\ 7 \end{array}$$
← These two should be the same. →
$$\begin{array}{r} 3\ 5\ 7 \\ +\ 1\ 2\ 4 \\ \hline 4\ 8\ 1 \end{array}$$

■ **Write About Math**   Write a subtraction problem in which you do not have to rename.

Check Understanding

For another example, see Set G, pages 142–143.

Tell if you need to rename the top number in each exercise.
Explain your answer. Then find each difference.

1. 463
-147

2. 406
-134

3. 243
-32

4. 158
-39

5. 762
-481

Practice

For More Practice, see Set G, pages 144–145.

Find each difference. **Remember** to estimate first.

6. 521
-370

7. 654
-108

8. 194
-157

9. 197
-16

10. 585
-469

11. 863
-735

12. 120
-40

13. 654
-542

14. 984
-951

15. 876
-219

16. 724
-115

17. 673
-569

18. 586
-247

19. 850
-334

20. 652
-428

21. 572 − 326

22. 645 − 537

23. 243 − 71

24. 716 − 384

25. 473 − 170

26. 419 − 336

27. 323 − 82

28. 4,930 − 1,052

Mixed Practice   Use paper and pencil or mental
math to find each answer. Tell what method you used.

29. 157
-90

30. 246
$+549$

31. 984
-951

32. 128
$+50$

33. 176
-68

Problem Solving

Solve each problem.

34. 🖩 **Calculator**   What two 3-digit numbers
have a sum of 1,325 and a difference of 367?

35. **Use Data**   Use the chart on page 122.
How many more speed points did
Firebird get than Eagle?

Zeros in Subtraction

Build Understanding

The students in Edgar School were part of a Reading Marathon. The graph shows how many books the students in each grade read.

How many more books did the fifth graders read than the fourth graders?

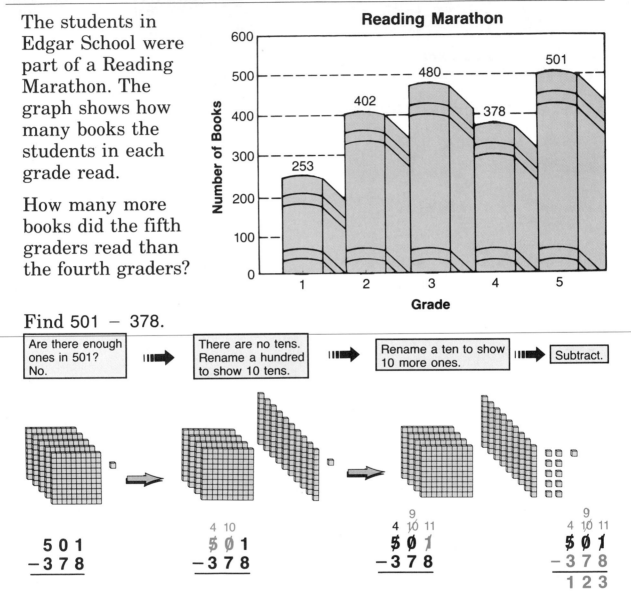

Reading Marathon

Find 501 − 378.

| Are there enough ones in 501? No. | **॥॥⇒** | There are no tens. Rename a hundred to show 10 tens. | **॥॥⇒** | Rename a ten to show 10 more ones. | **॥॥⇒** | Subtract. |

```
                    4 10           9              9
                                 4 10 11        4 10 11
   5 0 1          5 0 1          5 0 1          5 0 1
 - 3 7 8        - 3 7 8        - 3 7 8        - 3 7 8
                                               1 2 3
```

The fifth graders read 123 more books.

■ **Write About Math** Do you always have to rename when there are zeros in a subtraction problem? Write several problems to explain your answer.

Check Understanding

For another example, see Set H, pages 142–143.

In which exercises would you need 10 more ones?
10 more tens? both? Then find the differences.

1. 403 −251	**2.** 673 −205	**3.** 730 −156	**4.** 800 −475	**5.** 436 −138

Practice

For More Practice, see Set H, pages 144–145.

Find each difference.

6. 306 − 57	**7.** 580 −137	**8.** 801 −160	**9.** 507 −372	**10.** 860 −503
11. 402 − 36	**12.** 650 −309	**13.** 700 −160	**14.** 900 −708	**15.** 300 −193
16. 100 − 57	**17.** 201 −118	**18.** 902 −209	**19.** 400 −195	**20.** 504 −337
21. 303 −195	**22.** 703 −512	**23.** 800 −423	**24.** 240 −128	**25.** 509 −327
26. 120 − 59	**27.** 440 −193	**28.** 600 −288	**29.** 908 −719	**30.** 570 −482

Mixed Practice Use paper and pencil or mental math
to find each answer. Then tell which method you used.

31. 673 + 59	**32.** 795 −300	**33.** 472 +758	**34.** 827 −458	**35.** 980 +124

36. 504 − 87   **37.** 638 + 28   **38.** 624 − 24

Three- and Four-Digit Subtraction

Build Understanding

A. Mary McLeod Bethune was a teacher, speaker, and leader. She was born in 1875. In 1904, she started a school for young African American girls that eventually became a college. How old was she in 1904?

Find 1,904 − 1,875.

Are there enough ones in 1,904? No.	→	There are no tens. Rename a hundred to show 10 tens.	→	Rename a ten to show 10 more ones.	→	Subtract.

$$
\begin{array}{r}
1{,}9\,0\,4 \\
-\,1{,}8\,7\,5 \\
\end{array}
\qquad
\begin{array}{r}
{}^{8\;10} \\
1\,9\,0\,4 \\
-\,1{,}8\,7\,5 \\
\end{array}
\qquad
\begin{array}{r}
{}^{\;\;9} \\
{}^{8\;10\;14} \\
1{,}9\,0\,4 \\
-\,1{,}8\,7\,5 \\
\end{array}
\qquad
\begin{array}{r}
{}^{\;\;9} \\
{}^{8\;10\;14} \\
1{,}9\,0\,4 \\
-\,1{,}8\,7\,5 \\
\hline
2\,9 \\
\end{array}
$$

Mary McLeod Bethune was 29 years old when she started her school in 1904.

B. Find 8,006 − 4,927.

Are there enough ones in 8,006? No.	→	There are no tens. There are no hundreds. Rename a thousand to show 10 hundreds.	→	Rename a hundred to show 10 tens.	→	Rename a ten to show 10 more ones.	→	Subtract.

$$
\begin{array}{r}
8{,}0\,0\,6 \\
-\,4{,}9\,2\,7 \\
\end{array}
\quad
\begin{array}{r}
{}^{7\;10} \\
8{,}0\,0\,6 \\
-\,4{,}9\,2\,7 \\
\end{array}
\quad
\begin{array}{r}
{}^{\;\;9} \\
{}^{7\;10\;10} \\
8{,}0\,0\,6 \\
-\,4{,}9\,2\,7 \\
\end{array}
\quad
\begin{array}{r}
{}^{\;9\;9} \\
{}^{7\;10\;10\;16} \\
8{,}0\,0\,6 \\
-\,4{,}9\,2\,7 \\
\end{array}
\quad
\begin{array}{r}
{}^{\;9\;9} \\
{}^{7\;10\;10\;16} \\
8{,}0\,0\,6 \\
-\,4{,}9\,2\,7 \\
\hline
3{,}0\,7\,9 \\
\end{array}
$$

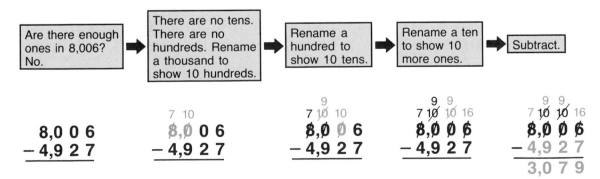

■ **Talk About Math** Tell why addition can be used to check subtraction.

Check Understanding

For another example, see Set I, pages 142–143.

In which of these exercises would you need to rename in the thousands place? Tell why. Then subtract.

1. 5,187
− 3,156

2. 4,672
− 1,826

3. 5,000
− 2,654

4. 6,002
− 3,005

Practice

For More Practice, see Set I, pages 144–145.

Subtract.

5. 434
− 326

6. 7,002
− 3,064

7. 481
− 293

8. 9,004
− 7,539

9. 6,757
− 4,902

10. 8,001
− 1,197

11. 3,926
− 2,842

12. 6,003
− 751

13. 504
− 420

14. 1,005
− 811

15. 9,007 − 4,345

16. 3,502 − 1,201

17. 5,342 − 2,091

Problem Solving

Solve each problem.

18. Dr. Maria Montessori, an Italian physician and educator, was born in 1870. She opened her first preschool when she was 37. What year was this?

19. Lucy Laney was born on April 11, 1854. On January 6, 1886, she opened a school for African American children. How old was she when the school opened in 1886?

20. Critical Thinking Suppose you must rename a hundred to subtract 2,945 − 1,7▦5. What numbers could the missing digit be?

Skills _____ Review   pages 84–85

Find each sum.
1. 72 + 54 + 23
2. 84 + 51 + 92
3. 20 + 34 + 8 + 13

Use Data from a Table

Build Understanding

PROBLEM SOLVING GUIDE

To solve problems, you may need to get information from a table.

Some of the students in Mrs. Shaw's third-grade class made a table to show things about themselves.

Which 9-year-old likes cats best?

▷ Understand
QUESTION
FACTS
KEY IDEA

Plan and Solve
STRATEGY
ANSWER

Look Back
SENSIBLE ANSWER
ALTERNATE APPROACH

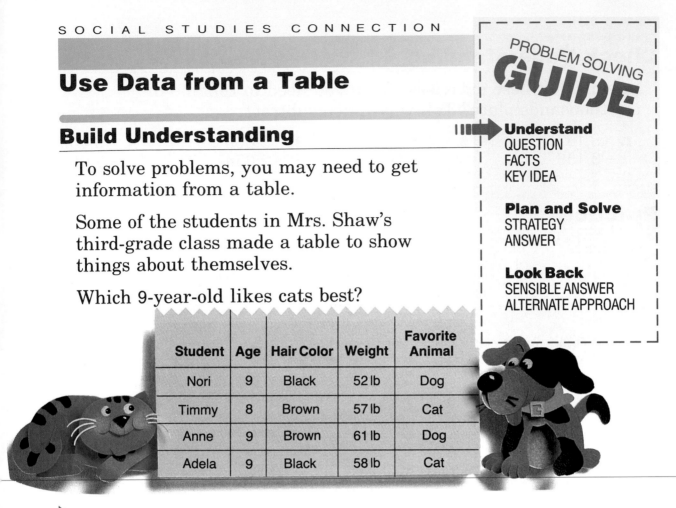

Student	Age	Hair Color	Weight	Favorite Animal
Nori	9	Black	52 lb	Dog
Timmy	8	Brown	57 lb	Cat
Anne	9	Brown	61 lb	Dog
Adela	9	Black	58 lb	Cat

▷ Understand   QUESTION   Which 9-year-old likes cats best?

FACTS   There are many facts in the table. You do not need to use all of them.

KEY IDEA   Pick the facts you need. The first row tells you what information you will find in the chart: each student's name, age, hair color, weight, and favorite animal. You will find the information you want to know in the columns under age and favorite animal.

Plan and Solve   Nori, Anne, and Adela are 9 years old. Adela is the only 9-year-old who likes cats.

Look Back   Have you answered the question? Is there anything else you need to find out?

■ **Talk About Math** Could you have started in another column other than the one for Age? Explain how this would change the way you solved this problem.

Check Understanding

Solve the problem by answering Questions 1–4.

Which 9-year-old has brown hair?

1. What two things have to be true about the student you find?

2. Which two columns do you have to look at?

3. Could Nori be the student? Why or why not?

4. Explain why each of the rest of the students either could or could not be the student.

Practice

Use the table on page 138 to solve each problem.

5. Which student is the youngest?

6. Which student weighs the most?

7. Which student weighing less than 60 pounds has brown hair?

8. Which student with black hair likes cats?

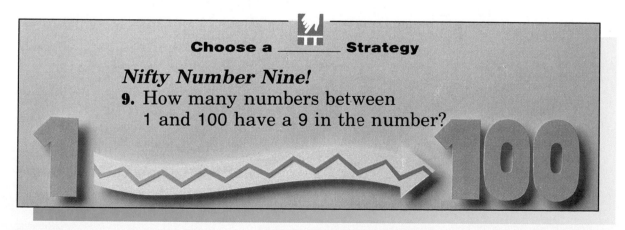

Choose a _____ Strategy

Nifty Number Nine!
9. How many numbers between 1 and 100 have a 9 in the number?

Skills Review

1. Trade 1 dollar for 10 dimes. Write the new amount.
3 dollars, 2 dimes, 6 pennies

Tell how many dollars, dimes, and pennies there are after you add or subtract.

2.

$	d	p
6	3	2
+ 1	7	9

3.

$	d	p
8	3	4
− 3	6	1

Find each sum.

4. 521
      +287

5. 464
      +307

6. 269
      +328

7. 1,204
      +3,818

8. 3,725
      + 681

9. 624
      +299

10. 5,881 + 690

Use paper and pencil, mental math, or a calculator to find each answer. Tell what method you used.

11. 792
       +320

12. 2,547
       + 5,719

13. 56
       +30

Find each difference.

14. 423
       −152

15. 381
       − 257

16. 302
       −196

17. 8,007
       − 3,419

18. 5,020
       − 1,945

Problem-Solving Review

Solve each problem.

19. Westtown has 5,395 people, Eastville has 2,816 people, and Center City has 5,835 people. Which city is the largest?

20. Dana has 7 coins worth 39¢. What coins are they?

21. Mrs. Nova has 3 coupons. She can save 50¢ on cereal if she buys milk too. She can save 30¢ on 2 cans of tuna. She can get a third can of cat food free if she buys 2 cans. What is the least number of items Mrs. Nova will get at the store if she uses all of her coupons?

22. Find the number between 300 and 400. The sum of the hundreds and ones digits is double the tens digit. Their difference is 0.

23. Data File Use data from pages 248–249. Is Anaheim or Los Angeles closer to San Diego? How much closer?

24. Make a Data File Find sale ads for 5 pieces of furniture. Tell the item, the sale price, and the regular price.

Cumulative Skills Review · Chapters 1-4

Read each sentence. Tell if the number is used to count, to label, to measure, or to tell order.

1. Michael invited 6 friends.

2. That is the 2nd book I read.

3. The road is 2 miles long.

4. My library card number is 202.

Order the following according to the rule.

5. Put in numerical order from least to greatest: 4, 2, 6, 1, 3

6. Put in alphabetical order: toad, frog, worm, lizard

Write these numbers in order from least to greatest.

7. 302   320   312   321

8. 4,063   463   630   4,630

Write the numbers as you count by twos.

9. Begin at 12. Count to 24.

10. Begin at 48. Count to 60.

Round each number to the nearest ten.

11. 15

12. 567

13. 312

14. 8

Estimate each answer.

15. 56 − 32

16. 72 − 46

17. 88 + 9

18. 64 + 18

Find each sum or difference.

19. 64
      + 22

20. 48
      + 36

21. 631
      + 239

22. 405
      + 298

23. 535
      + 386

24. 2,567
      +   193

25. 3,546
      + 2,507

26. 6,912
      + 4,828

27. 45
      − 31

28. 78
      − 29

29. 62
      − 46

30. 418
      − 229

31. 806
      − 519

32. 610
      − 579

33. 7,011
      − 5,234

34. 4,400
      − 2,517

Reteaching
Set A   pages 110–113

You have 2 dollars and 1 dime. You need more dimes for the bus. Trade 1 dollar for 10 dimes.

You have 1 dollar and 11 dimes.

Remember that you can trade dimes for dollars if you have 10 or more dimes.

Record how many dollars, dimes, and pennies you have after the trade.

1. Trade 1 dollar for 10 dimes.

$	d	p
4	3	6

Set B   pages 114–117

Find how much money is shown in this chart.

	$	d	p
	3	6	7
+	4	4	8

Add: 7$ 10d 15p

Trade 10 pennies for 1 dime.
7 dollars   11 dimes   5 pennies
Trade 10 dimes for 1 dollar.
   8 dollars   1 dime   5 pennies

Remember to trade pennies for dimes first, if you can. Then trade dimes for dollars if you can. Find how much money is shown in each chart.

1.

	$	d	p
	2	3	6
+	4	5	9

2.

	$	d	p
	3	3	4
+	1	8	7

Set C   pages 118–119

Find 374 + 195.

$$
\begin{array}{r} 374 \\ + 195 \\ \hline 9 \end{array}
\qquad
\begin{array}{r} {}^{1}\ \\ 374 \\ + 195 \\ \hline 569 \end{array}
$$
Record 16 tens as
1 hundred 6 tens

Remember to estimate before you find the exact answer. Find each sum.

1.   364
       + 255

2.   439
       + 380

Set D   pages 120–121

Find 2,084 + 2,547.

$$
\begin{array}{r} {}^{1}\ \\ 2{,}084 \\ + 2{,}547 \\ \hline 1 \end{array}
\qquad
\begin{array}{r} {}^{1\ 1} \\ 2{,}084 \\ + 2{,}547 \\ \hline 31 \end{array}
\qquad
\begin{array}{r} {}^{1\ 1} \\ 2{,}084 \\ + 2{,}547 \\ \hline 4{,}631 \end{array}
$$

Remember to estimate first. Find each sum.

1.   4,165
       + 1,267

2.   5,246
       + 2,375

Set E   pages 122–123

Use a calculator to add large numbers with renaming.

Use mental math to add when there is no renaming.

Use paper and pencil for other addition problems.

Remember to estimate first.

Use paper and pencil or a calculator. Tell what method you used.

1. 2,006
     + 3,997

2. 87
     + 36

3. 30 + 147

Set F   pages 126–128

How much money is left? To subtract pennies, trade 1 dime.

Have:	$	d	p
	7	8	3
Spend:	4	2	6

$	d	p
7	7	13
4	2	6

3 dollars, 5 dimes, 7 pennies: 3$ 5d 7p

Remember to subtract pennies first.
Write how much is left.

1.
$	d	p
6	7	3
3	2	6

2.
$	d	p
3	4	6
1	1	8

Set G   pages 132–133

Find 691 − 563.

                    8 11
Trade a ten for   69̸1
10 more ones.   − 563
                    128

Remember to check by adding. Estimate, then subtract.

1. 637
     − 219

2. 284
     − 146

3. 348 − 140

Set H   pages 134–135

Find 403 − 286.
Rename a hundred to show tens.

3 10   9
403 Rename a ten to   3 10 13
−286 show 10 more ones.   403
                              − 286
                                117

Remember that you may not have to rename when there are zeros. Find each difference.

1. 506
     − 127

2. 202
     − 82

3. 401
     − 103

Set I   pages 136–137

Find 6,007 − 4,135.

              5 10   9
Rename a   6,007   Rename a   5 10 10
thousand. − 4,135   hundred.   6,007
                                  − 4,135
                                    1,872

Remember to check by adding. Subtract.

1. 4,006
     − 1,241

2. 5,006
     − 2,457

More Practice

Set A pages 110–113

Use your play money. Trade pennies for dimes
and dimes for dollars. Record how many dollars,
dimes, and pennies you have when you finish.

1.

$	d	p
3	5	14

2.

$	d	p
4	12	5

3.

$	d	p
2	13	12

Make these sets of money with your play money.
Record how many dollars, dimes, and pennies
you have when you finish trading.

4. Trade 1 dime for
10 pennies.

$	d	p
2	6	8

5. Trade 1 dime for
10 pennies.

$	d	p
4	5	3

6. Trade 1 dollar for
10 dimes.

$	d	p
3	7	2

Set B pages 114–117

Use play money to show each amount of money in the place-value
chart. Trade whenever you can. Write how much in all.

1.

$	d	p
1	4	6
+ 4	3	5

2.

$	d	p
3	3	8
+ 2	7	3

3.

$	d	p
2	5	0
+ 3	8	8

Set C pages 118–119

Find each sum. **Remember** to estimate first.

1. 325
      + 117

2. 174
      + 283

3. 605
      + 384

4. 734 + 375

5. 484 + 519

Set D pages 120–121

Find each sum.

1. 3,641
      + 4,308

2. 5,367
      + 2,027

3. 675
      + 455

4. 5,760 + 465

5. 3,427 + 44

Set E pages 122-123

Use paper and pencil, mental math, or a calculator
to find each answer. Tell what method you used.

1. $1,007$
$+\ \ 898$

2. 785
$+336$

3. 85
$+14$

4. 682
$+317$

5. 74
$+98$

6. $5,284 + 3,469$

7. $300 + 150$

8. $400 + 563$

Set F pages 126-128

Use your play money to show how much you
have. Take away the amount you spend.
Write how much you have left.

1.

	$	d	p
Have:	6	7	2
Spend:	2	4	6

2.

	$	d	p
Have:	2	4	9
Spend:	1	5	3

3.

	$	d	p
Have:	4	3	0
Spend:	2	6	2

Set G pages 132-133

Find each difference. **Remember** to estimate first.

1. 483
-191

2. 274
-238

3. 536
-409

4. 785
-341

5. 340
-160

Set H pages 134-135

Find each difference.

1. 370
-236

2. 408
$-\ \ 49$

3. 500
-240

4. 630
-106

5. 904
-362

6. $400 - 230$

7. $240 - 206$

8. $300 - 109$

9. $608 - 421$

Set I pages 136-137

Subtract.

1. $6,005$
$-2,076$

2. 543
-265

3. 467
-198

4. $8,435$
$-5,713$

5. $3,004$
$-1,265$

6. $5,806 - 3,402$

7. $7,004 - 4,253$

8. $9,463 - 4,082$

Enrichment

Estimation Strategies

Adam has begun collecting stamps from all over the world.

Estimate how many stamps he has in all.

United States: 336

Japan: 256

Mexico: 147

One easy way is to use only the ***front-end*** digits:

$$\begin{array}{r} 3\,3\,6 \\ 1\,4\,7 \\ +\,2\,5\,6 \\ \hline \end{array}$$

3 + 1 + 2 = 6
6 hundreds

Adam has more than 600 stamps in his collection.

A more accurate way is to use the front-end digits and *adjust* the estimate by using the tens digits.

$$\begin{array}{r} 3\,3\,6 \\ 1\,4\,7 \\ +\,2\,5\,6 \\ \hline \end{array}$$

3 + 1 + 2 = 6
6 hundreds

3 + 4 + 5 = 12
12 tens

The tens make at least one more hundred. So a more accurate estimate would be 700 stamps.

Use front-end estimation to estimate each sum.
Adjust the estimate if you can.

1. 517 + 285 + 161

2. 410 + 324 + 19

3. 383 + 242 + 400

4. 253 + 13 + 745

5. 273 + 382 + 29

6. 219 + 86 + 548

7. 112 + 508 + 354

8. 526 + 411 + 689

9. 282 + 860 + 58

10. 36 + 9 + 273

11. 94 + 118 + 6

12. 7 + 50 + 231

Chapter 4 Review/Test

1. Rename 1 dollar as 10 dimes. Write the new amount.

2 dollars, 2 dimes, 7 pennies

Tell how many dollars, dimes, and pennies

2. there are in all.   **3.** are left.

$	d	p
5	4	7
+ 3	6	9

$	d	p
7	2	4
− 5	5	1

Add.

4. 931
     + 54

5. 276
     +481

6. 6,893 + 510

Subtract.

7. 482
     −315

8. 905
     −273

9. 7,261
     −3,521

10. 4,200
      − 374

Use paper and pencil, mental math, or a calculator to find each answer. Tell which method you used.

11. 75
      +20

12. 5
       +3

13. 143
       +869

City-Wide Children's Art Fair
The Most Entries Ever!

Grade	Number of Paintings	Number of Clay Models
2	122	218
3	59	236
4	249	114

Use the data in the picture.

14. Which prize was won by a painting of an animal?

Read this problem. Then answer the questions below.

How many more third graders made clay models than paintings?

15. What facts from the table would you use to solve this problem?

16. Solve the problem above.

17. ■ **Write About Math**
When do you need to rename in order to subtract?

Time, Measurement, and Geometry

5

Did You Know:

Electric clocks came into use in many homes in the 1920s. Digital clocks became popular in the late 1970s. Some of the earliest clocks were sundials and water clocks. They were made many thousands of years ago.

Number-Sense Project

Estimate
Estimate how many clocks you have in your home. Predict: Do your classmates have more digital clocks or more standard clocks in their homes?

Gather Data
Record the number, type, and location of all the clocks in your home.

Analyze and Report
Be ready to add your results to a class chart. Check to see whether you and your classmates have more digital or more standard clocks in your homes.

149

Telling Time: Nearest 5 Minutes and Minute

Build Understanding

About 3,000 years ago, shadow clocks were used in Egypt. Today, clocks and watches are made around the world. The English are known for their chime clocks, the Germans for their cuckoo clocks, and the Swiss for their wristwatches.

Shadow clocks were also called *sundials.* By looking at the way shadows changed, people could tell how much time had passed.

A. Wynona is supposed to wake up at 7:00. She woke up late today. The second clock shows the time she woke up. What time does the second clock show?

The time is 7:00 o'clock.

The time is 7:10 or 10 minutes after 7 o'clock.

Each mark represents 1 minute. Each section represents 5 minutes. There are 60 minutes in 1 hour.

B. The digital and standard clocks to the right show the time Wynona ate breakfast. What time do the clocks show?

The time is 7:27 or 27 minutes after 7 o'clock.

■ **Write About Math** Write the time you woke up this morning in two ways.

Check Understanding

For another example, see Set A, pages 178–179.

Write the letter of the clock that shows the time.

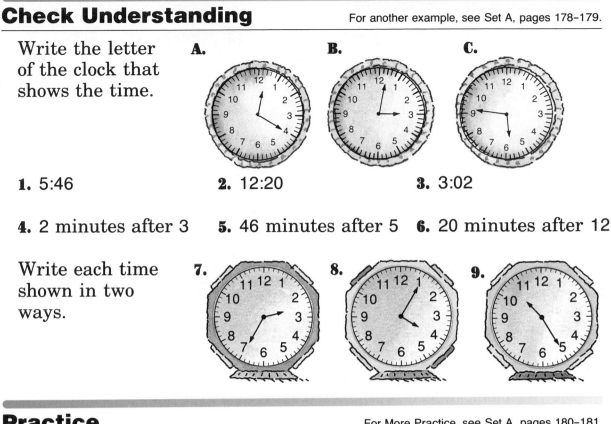

A.   **B.**   **C.**

1. 5:46   **2.** 12:20   **3.** 3:02

4. 2 minutes after 3   **5.** 46 minutes after 5   **6.** 20 minutes after 12

Write each time shown in two ways.

7.   **8.**   **9.**

Practice

For More Practice, see Set A, pages 180–181.

Write the letter of the digital clock that matches the time shown on the standard clock.
Remember that the short hand is the hour hand and the long hand is the minute hand.

10.   **11.**   **12.**   **13.**

A. 6:26   **B.** 8:50   **C.** 12:53   **D.** 4:45

Write each time in two ways.

14. **15.** **16.** **17.**

Mental Math Use a clock showing the current time.

18. What time does the clock show?

19. What time will it be in an hour?

20. What time will it be 10 minutes from now?

21. What time will it be 30 minutes from now?

22. How many minutes is 1 hour and 15 minutes?

23. How many hours is 120 minutes?

Use the clock in Exercise 15 to answer each question.

24. What time did the clock show an hour ago?

25. What time will the clock show in 50 minutes?

Problem Solving

Number Sense Solve each problem.

26. In ancient Rome speakers were allowed to speak for an hour, the time it took the sand to go from one bulb to the other. How many minutes do you think have passed since the hourglass at the right was turned over?

27. Long ago candles were used to tell time in China. If the candle at the right took two hours to burn completely, how many sections would burn in 1 hour and 30 minutes?

Solve each problem.

28. **Estimation** Benjamin Banneker, a mathematician, astronomer, and farmer, built a wooden clock in 1753. His clock kept almost perfect time until the early 1800s. The clock ran properly for about how many years?

29. The Meng family began eating dinner at twenty minutes after six. Draw a clock face showing this time.

30. Roberto read a newspaper in 55 minutes. Flora read it in 1 hour and 10 minutes. How much longer did it take Flora to read the paper?

TIPS FOR PROBLEM SOLVERS

Visualize the problem in your mind to help you understand it better.

31. Pat began to write a letter at 10:30. She finished it 30 minutes later. What time did she finish the letter?

32. Kei and Lee went out to play at 3:15. Their mother told them to come home in 2 hours. What time should they come back?

Reading ——— Math

Vocabulary The hands of a clock always move in the same direction. They move *clockwise.*

1. Which faucet moves clockwise?

2. What do you think the word *counterclockwise* means?

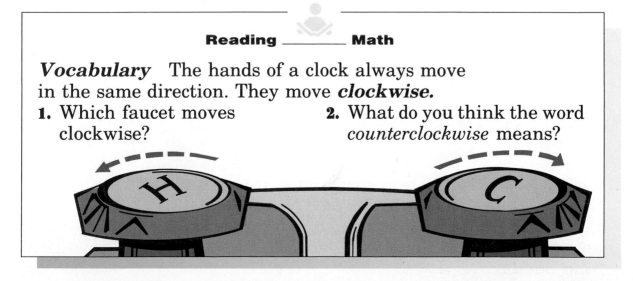

Reading Calendars: Days, Weeks, Months

Build Understanding

Every September the town of New Harmony holds an International Festival. This calendar shows the events of the festival.

August						
S	M	T	W	T	F	S
						1
2	3	4	5	6	7	8
9	10	11	12	13	14	15
16	17	18	19	20	21	22
23	24	25	26	27	28	29
30	31					

October						
S	M	T	W	T	F	S
				1	2	3
4	5	6	7	8	9	10
11	12	13	14	15	16	17
18	19	20	21	22	23	24
25	26	27	28	29	30	31

September

Sunday	Monday	Tuesday	Wednesday	Thursday	Friday	Saturday
		1 Chinese food	2	3	4 Mexican food	5
6	7	8	9	10	11 Italian art	12 Hispanic writing
13	14 Spanish music	15	16 German puppets	17 Russian circus	18	19 African wood carving
20	21 Caribbean steel drum band	22	23 French opera	24	25	26
27	28 Canadian hockey	29 European soccer	30 English rugby			

A. The 7 days of the week are Sunday, Monday, Tuesday, Wednesday, Thursday, Friday, and Saturday.

B. A week begins on Sunday. It ends on Saturday.

■ **Talk About Math** How many days are there from one Sunday to the next? From one Saturday to the next? Use your answers to explain the phrase "a week from Sunday."

154

Check Understanding

For another example, see Set B, pages 178–179.

Use the calendar on page 154 to answer the questions.

1. On what day of the week does the Russian circus perform?

2. What happens on the second Saturday of the month?

Practice

For More Practice, see Set B, pages 180–181.

Use the calendar on page 154 to answer the questions.

3. What happens one week after September 16? What day is that?

4. What happens on the second Friday? What date is that?

5. In what week are the most events held? On what dates does that week begin and end?

6. On August 29, Cal bought a ticket for the festival. What day of the week was that?

7. What is the date 2 weeks after September 29? What is the date 3 weeks before September 2?

Problem Solving

Critical Thinking   Use the calendar on page 154.

8. What date is one week after September 1?

9. Is the date one week after the 1st the same in any month?

10. On what day of the week does October 1 fall?

11. What date is 1 week later than October 1? 2 weeks later? 3 weeks later? 4 weeks later?

12. October 31 is the last date in October. On what day of the week does October end? Use your answer to Exercise 10 to find out.

Customary Lengths: Inches, Feet

Build Understanding

A. Inching Along
Materials: Math Sketcher, 12-inch ruler
Groups: Partners

a. Spread your fingers as shown in the picture. How far do you think one little finger is from the other little finger? Estimate.

b. Have your partner measure the distance. How close was your estimate?

c. Repeat the activity. Measure your partner's hands.

The distance from one little finger to the other is about 12 inches. 12 **inches** (in.) is the same as 1 **foot** (ft).

B.

This ribbon is about 3 inches long to the nearest inch.

C.

This eraser is about $1\frac{1}{2}$ inches long to the nearest half inch.

■ **Write About Math**   Explain what it means
to measure to the nearest inch; the nearest half inch.

Check Understanding

For another example, see Set C, pages 178–179.

1. Measure the length of your shoe to the
nearest inch and to the nearest half inch.

Practice

For More Practice, see Set C, pages 180–181.

Measure the lengths of these objects to the nearest
half inch using your Math Sketcher.

2. your textbook   **3.** your chair seat   **4.** your pencil

Find the distance between the dot by each animal and
the dot by its home. Measure to the nearest half inch.

5. bee   **6.** bird   **7.** fish   **8.** dog

Estimation   Estimate each length. Then
measure each length to the nearest inch.
Use feet and inches when you can.

9. your open math book   **10.** piece of construction paper

11. a bulletin board   **12.** your classroom door

Customary Lengths: Yards, Miles

Build Understanding

The **yard** (yd) and **mile** (mi) are customary units of length. They are used to measure long lengths.

A. Mrs. Awan's stride measures about 1 yard.

1 yard = 3 feet
1 yard = 36 inches

B. Mrs. Awan takes about 1,760 strides to run 1 mile.

1 mile = 1,760 yards
1 mile = 5,280 feet

■ **Talk About Math** Explain what would happen if you tried to use inches to measure a city block.

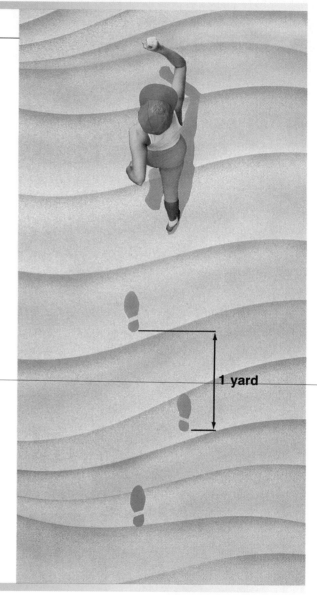

1 yard

Check Understanding

For another example, see Set D, pages 178–179.

Tell whether you would use yards or miles to measure the following.

1. Length of a football field

2. Length of a bus trip

3. Distance from California to China

4. Distance from one street corner to the next

Practice

For More Practice, see Set D, pages 180–181.

Write inches, feet, yards, or miles to tell
which you would use to measure the following.

5. Width of a piece of paper

6. Distance between two towns

7. Depth of a swimming pool

8. Length of a soccer field

9. Length of a classroom

10. Length of a leaf

Copy and complete each sentence.

```
0  1  2  3  4  5  6  7  8  9  10 11 12 13 14 15 16 17 18 19 20 21 22 23 24 25 26 27 28 29 30 31 32 33 34 35 36
```

11. There are ▦ inches in
1 yard.

12. There are ▦ inches in
1 foot.

13. One mile is the same as
▦ feet.

14. Two feet is the same as
▦ inches.

15. There are ▦ yards in
6 feet.

16. Use Data What is the
length in inches of the note
pad on page 94?

Problem Solving

Critical Thinking   Solve each problem.

17. The little finger is also called a
pinky. Suppose you told a friend
that a desk was 17 pinkies long.
Would your friend know exactly
how long that is? Why or why not?

18. Suppose you had a strip of paper that
was 8 inches long. How could you mark
inches on the strip without using a ruler?

Metric Lengths: Centimeters, Decimeters

Build Understanding

A. Measuring Up
Materials: Math Sketcher

Does plant food help plants grow taller? Al chose two plants with stems 4 centimeters long. He fed Plant A. He did not feed Plant B. The picture at the right shows how the plants looked a week later.

a. Measure the stem of each plant from the edge of the cup up to the leaves. Use the centimeter ruler on your Math Sketcher.

b. Subtract the starting length of each plant. How much did each plant grow?

B. Scientists use metric measurements. *Centimeters* (cm) and *decimeters* (dm) are metric units of length.

10 centimeters = 1 decimeter

← one centimeter →
← one decimeter →

Centimeters
1 2 3 4 5 6 7 8 9 10 11 12 13 14 15

■ **Talk About Math** Why should you line up the left edge of the object you are measuring with the zero point on the ruler?

Check Understanding

For another example, see Set E, pages 178–179.

Measure each line segment to the nearest centimeter.

1. ─────────────────────── **2.** ───────────────

3. ──────────────────────────────────────

Practice

For More Practice, see Set E, pages 180–181.

Estimation Without using a ruler, draw a line segment that you think has the length given. Then measure the line segment with a ruler.

4. 1 centimeter   **5.** 8 centimeters   **6.** 6 centimeters

7. 12 centimeters   **8.** 2 decimeters   **9.** 2 centimeters

Measure the lengths of these objects to the nearest centimeter.

10. your shoe   **11.** your textbook   **12.** your chair seat

Problem Solving

13. A stem 8 centimeters long grew 4 centimeters. How long is it now?

14. How could you measure the length of a desk with beans?

Midchapter ✔ **Checkup**

Answer each question.

1. It is 1:30. What time will it be 15 minutes from now?

2. What is the date a week after May 9?

Copy and complete each sentence.

3. One foot is the same as ▦ inches.

4. There are ▦ feet in 1 yard.

5. One decimeter is the same as ▦ centimeters.

Real-Life Decision Making

You can go to the movies if you work in the yard at least 60 minutes. The chart shows what needs to be done and how many minutes each job should take.

1. How many minutes should it take to weed the garden and sweep the driveway?

2. Decide which jobs you will do.

Task	Minutes it should take
weed garden	25
rake leaves	20
sweep driveway	15
water lawn	15
pick vegetables	20

Number-Sense Project

Look back at pages 148-149.
The water clock was invented about 3,000 years ago. It was a glass jar filled with water. Over time the water trickled out of the jar. The water left in the jar showed how much time had passed since the jar was filled.

1. If a water clock contained 6 quarts of water at 8 o'clock in the morning and 2 quarts of water at 12 noon,

    a. how much water had trickled out of the jar?

    b. how much time had passed?

2. For the water clock in Exercise 1, how much water stood for one hour?

Explore as a Team

1. Cut a piece of string that is the length of your height.

2. Guess how many times your shoe will fit along the length of the string. Check your guess.

TIPS FOR **WORKING TOGETHER**

Tell someone when he or she does or says something that helps you.

Math-at-Home Activity

1. Keep a tally of traffic at or near your home. Make a tally mark for each car, bus, or truck that drives by in 10 minutes.

2. Write some things about your tally.

163

Metric Lengths: Meters, Kilometers

Build Understanding

Meters (m) and *kilometers* (km) are metric units of length. They are used to measure long lengths.

A. The length of $3\frac{1}{2}$ pieces of construction paper is about 1 meter.

1 meter = 100 centimeters
1 meter = 10 decimeters

B. The length of 3,500 pieces of construction paper is about 1 kilometer.

1 kilometer = 1,000 meters

■ **Talk About Math** Suppose you were to measure something in meters and then in centimeters. For which measurement would you use *more* units? For which would you use *fewer* units? Explain.

35,000 trees could be saved each year if people recycled used newspapers and boxes.

Check Understanding

For another example, see Set F, pages 178–179.

Tell whether you would use meters or kilometers to measure the following:

1. Length of a city block

2. Length of a picnic bench

3. Distance between cities

4. Length of your school

Practice

For More Practice, see Set F, pages 180–181.

Tell whether you would use centimeters, meters, or kilometers to measure the following:

5. Length of a diving board

6. Length of a baseball bat

7. Distance across Canada

8. Height of a skyscraper

9. Width of a tennis racket

10. Distance along a highway

Copy and complete each sentence.

11. One meter is the same as ▦ centimeters.

12. There are ▦ meters in 1 kilometer.

Number Sense   Copy and complete the sentence.

13. One kilometer is the same as 1,000 meters, so 2 kilometers is the same as ▦ meters.

Mixed Practice   Copy and complete each sentence.

14. There are ▦ feet in 1 yard.

15. In 1 foot there are ▦ inches.

16. One mile is the same as ▦ feet.

17. One meter is the same as ▦ centimeters.

18. In 1 kilometer, there are ▦ meters.

Make a Table

Build Understanding

The class read a story called "Robbery at the Amusement Park." The robber was Sue or Theo or Willa or Fred. Each was at the park on a different day, Wednesday, Thursday, Friday, or Saturday.

The robbery happened on Friday. Was Willa the robber?

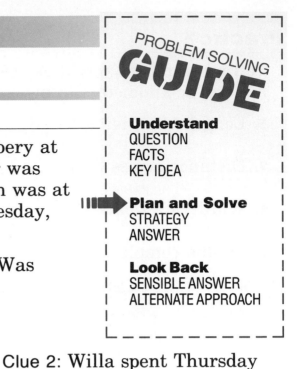

Understand
QUESTION
FACTS
KEY IDEA

➤ **Plan and Solve**
STRATEGY
ANSWER

Look Back
SENSIBLE ANSWER
ALTERNATE APPROACH

Clue 1: No one's name begins with the same letter as the day he or she was at the park.

Clue 2: Willa spent Thursday and Friday at the beach.

Clue 3: Theo was at the park three days before Willa.

Clue 4: Fred was at the park one day after Theo.

Understand Willa is the robber if she was at the park on Friday.

Plan and Solve STRATEGY Make a table. Use the clues. Mark an X when you know a person was not at the park on that day. Use O to show that a person was at the park.

Red x's: Clue 1
Blue x's: Clue 2

Day	Sue	Theo	Willa	Fred
Wednesday			X	
Thursday		X	X	
Friday			X	X
Saturday	X			

ANSWER Willa was at the park only on Saturday. She could not be the robber.

Look Back Are there any clues which have not been used?

■ **Talk About Math**   Suppose you know a person was *not* at the park on Friday. How can this help you decide who the robber was?

Check Understanding

Copy the table on page 166. Fill in more of the table as you answer the questions.

1. Use Clue 3. Put an O in the table to show when Theo was at the park.

2. Put an X in your table for each day when Theo was not at the park.

3. Use Clue 4. When was Fred at the park?

4. For each day, put an O or an X under Fred's name.

Practice

Complete your table to find out who the robber was.

5. How many Xs do you now have in the row for Friday? What do those Xs tell you?

6. Put X or O in every space in your table. Who was the robber?

Use the three clues below to answer the question.

7. Brad, Hannah, Celia, and Don each read a book about a different animal. The animals were a horse, a beaver, a deer, and a cat. Which animal did each child read about?

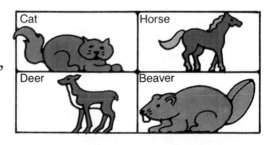

Clue 1: No child's name has the same number of letters as the name of the animal in his or her book.

Clue 2: No child's name begins with the same letter as the name of the animal in his or her book.

Clue 3: Celia's book was not about a deer.

Critical Thinking   Write the missing numbers in each pattern.

8. 2, 4, 6, ▦, 10, ▦

9. 3, 6, ▦, 12, ▦, 18

Perimeter

Build Understanding

Jason is a carpenter. He is putting wood trim around a window. To do this, he needs to know the distance around the window.

Perimeter is the distance around a figure. What is the perimeter of this window?

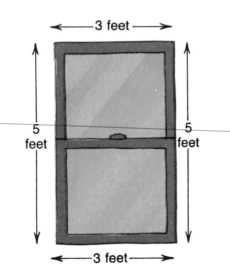

To find the perimeter, add the lengths of the sides.

3 + 5 + 3 + 5 = 16

The perimeter of the window is 16 feet.

■ **Talk About Math** Explain why 16 inches or 16 yards is not a reasonable answer.

Check Understanding

For another example, see Set G, pages 178–179.

Find the perimeter of each window.

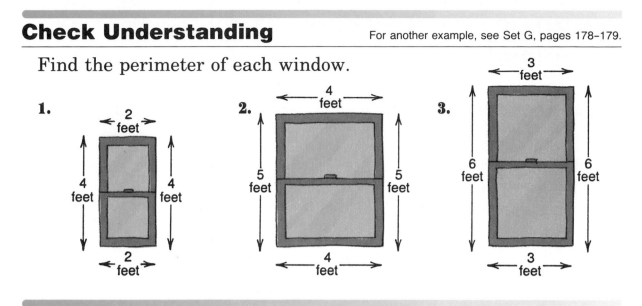

1.

2.

3.

Practice

For More Practice, see Set G, pages 180–181.

Use a ruler to measure the sides of each figure.
Use the units named. Then find the perimeter.

4.

The perimeter is
▦ centimeters

5.

The perimeter is
▦ inches.

6.

The perimeter is
▦ centimeters.

Use paper and pencil or mental math to
find the perimeter of each figure. Tell
which method you used.

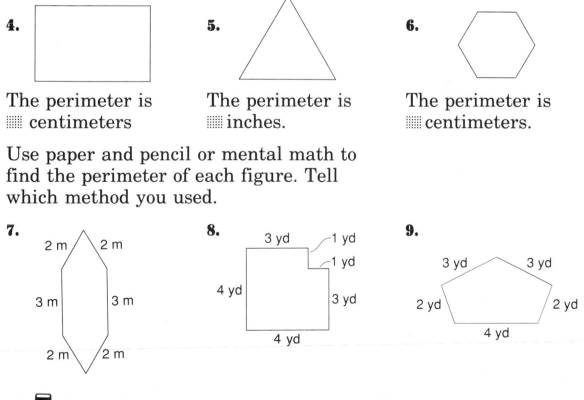

7.
2 m 2 m
3 m 3 m
2 m 2 m

8.
3 yd 1 yd
1 yd
4 yd 3 yd
4 yd

9.
3 yd 3 yd
2 yd 2 yd
4 yd

10. 🖩 **Calculator** The sides of a playground
are 262 feet, 311 feet, 195 feet, and 278 feet
long. Find the perimeter.

Counting Squares to Find Area

Build Understanding

A. Covering the Cover
Materials: math books, play
pennies, paper clips, inch grid
paper, paper rectangles of
various sizes, scissors
Groups: 3 to 5 students

a. Cover one math book with
play pennies. Do not overlap
the pennies. Record how
many pennies you used.

b. Repeat *a* using paper clips.

c. Repeat *a* using squares cut
from inch grid paper.

You can write the answer to *c* as
80 *square inches.*
This tells you the *area* of the cover.

1 in.

1 in.

1 square inch

1 cm

1 cm

1 square centimeter

B. A *square centimeter* is smaller
than a square inch. If you covered
your math book with squares of this
size, would you need more than
80 squares or fewer than 80?

The area of your math book is about
500 square centimeters.

■ **Talk About Math** The answers
for parts *a, b,* and *c* of the Activity
are different. Explain why.

Check Understanding

Work in groups. Cover each object with
1-inch squares. Tell the area.

1. the front cover of your
spelling book

2. the paper rectangle your
teacher gives to your group

Practice

Find the area of each figure in square centimeters.

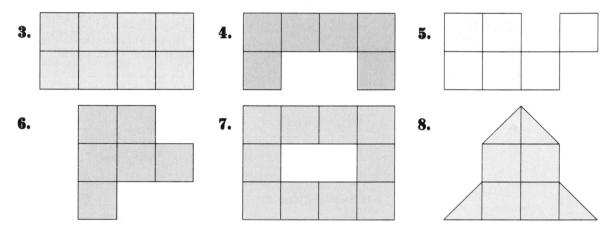

3.

4.

5.

6.

7.

8.

Problem Solving

Explore ——— Math

How could you find the area of your hand?
Try tracing your hand on centimeter grid paper.

9. How many whole boxes are inside your
tracing?

10. How many partial boxes are inside it? About
how many whole boxes do the partial boxes make?

11. What is the area of your hand in
square centimeters?

Deciding When an Estimate Is Enough

PROBLEM SOLVING
GUIDE

Understand
QUESTION
FACTS
KEY IDEA

Plan and Solve
STRATEGY
ANSWER

Look Back
SENSIBLE ANSWER
ALTERNATE APPROACH

Build Understanding

Angela wants 6 streamers for her party. Each streamer will be 12 feet long. Crepe paper comes in rolls of 50 feet or 100 feet. What should Angela buy?

Understand   QUESTION   Will one 50-foot roll be enough?

FACTS   Each streamer will be 12 feet. Rolls of crepe paper are 50 feet or 100 feet.

KEY IDEA   Angela does not need to know the exact number of feet. She needs to know only if one roll of 50 feet is enough.

Plan and Solve   Angela can estimate.

12 feet is a little more than 10 feet.
10 + 10 + 10 + 10 + 10 + 10 = 60 feet

One roll of 50 feet is not enough. Angela must buy one roll of 100 feet.

Look Back   Look at the tens digits. There are 6 tens.

Angela needs at least 60 feet of crepe paper.

$$
\begin{array}{r}
12 \\
12 \\
12 \\
12 \\
12 \\
+\,12 \\
\hline
6
\end{array}
$$

■ **Talk About Math**   Why doesn't Angela need to know the exact number of feet the streamers will be?

Check Understanding

Tell whether you need to find an exact answer or an estimate.

1. You need 5 bows, each 18 inches. Spools of ribbon are 75 inches and 125 inches.

2. Framing is cut to order. You need wood to frame a picture that is 8 inches on each side.

Practice

Tell whether you need to find an exact answer or an estimate. Then tell what Angela should buy for her party.

3. Angela needs string for 4 balloons. Each string is 32 inches. String comes in rolls of 100 or 200 inches.

4. Angela needs fabric for 12 costumes. Each costume uses 3 yards of fabric. Fabric is cut to order.

5. Angela needs ribbon for 5 favors. Each ribbon is 18 inches. Ribbon comes in spools of 100 or 150 inches.

6. Angela needs 6 bows. Each bow is 14 inches. Ribbon comes in spools of 75 or 125 inches.

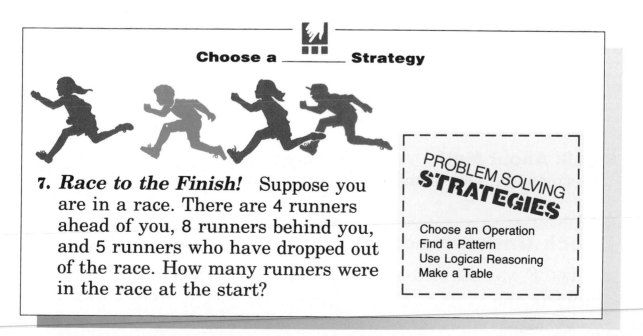

Choose a ▨ Strategy

7. ***Race to the Finish!*** Suppose you are in a race. There are 4 runners ahead of you, 8 runners behind you, and 5 runners who have dropped out of the race. How many runners were in the race at the start?

PROBLEM SOLVING STRATEGIES

Choose an Operation
Find a Pattern
Use Logical Reasoning
Make a Table

Temperature

Build Understanding

When the temperature outdoors is 30°C, do you need a coat?

The thermometers give the temperature in degrees *Celsius* (°C) and *Fahrenheit* (°F). A thermometer measures temperature.

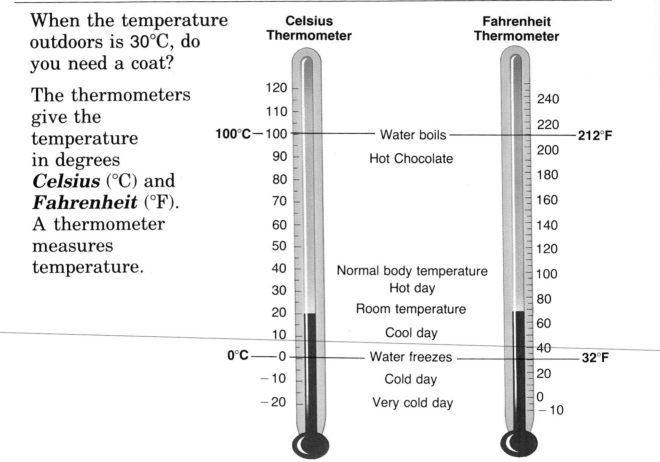

Celsius Thermometer

Fahrenheit Thermometer

100°C — 100 — Water boils — 212°F
Hot Chocolate
Normal body temperature
Hot day
Room temperature
Cool day
0°C — 0 — Water freezes — 32°F
Cold day
Very cold day

You do not need a coat when the temperature is 30°C.

■ **Talk About Math** Are the units on both thermometers the same size? Explain your answer.

Check Understanding

For another example, see Set H, pages 178–179.

1. Is 0°F warmer or colder than 0°C?

2. If −1°F means one degree below zero, what does 5°F mean?

Practice

For More Practice, see Set H, pages 180–181.

Write the temperature in °C or °F.

3. —0°C —10°C

4. —50°C —40°C

5. —100°C —90°C

6. —60°F —50°F

7. —10°F —0°F

8. —100°F —90°F

Estimation Choose the more sensible measure.

9. temperature of a classroom

32°F   69°F

10. a person with a fever

99°C   40°C

11. temperature of hot soup

78°F   179°F

12. blizzard weather

−15°C   15°C

Problem Solving

Ty graphed the temperature at 9:00 every morning.

13. What was the highest temperature?

14. What was the lowest?

15. What was the difference between Monday's and Friday's temperatures?

Temperatures

°C

Days

Skills ———— **Review**   pages 118–119, 132–133

Add or subtract.

1. 665 − 231   **2.** 409 + 356   **3.** 873 + 22   **4.** 803 − 157

Skills Review

1. Give the time on the clock.

April

S	M	T	W	T	F	S
			1	2	3	4
5	6	7	8	9	10	11
12	13	14	15	16	17	18
19	20	21	22	23	24	25
26	27	28	29	30		

2. What is the date of the second Friday, in April?

Choose the more sensible unit of measure.

3. Distance across a gym

  mile   foot

4. Length of a comb

  centimeter   meter

5. Choose the more sensible temperature for iced tea.

  5°C   50°C

Measure your pencil

6. to the nearest half inch.

7. to the nearest centimeter.

8. Find the area in square centimeters.

9. Find the perimeter.

5 ft   5 ft
2 ft   2 ft
9 ft

Problem-Solving Review

Solve each problem.

10. Ed drove 325 miles one day and 378 miles the next. How far did he drive in all?

11. Sheena weighs 70 pounds. Her mother weighs 118 pounds, and her father weighs 162 pounds. Can all three ride together in a boat that can hold 330 pounds?

12. If you need 1 ticket for every 2 adults and 1 ticket for every 3 children, how many tickets do you need for 2 adults and 5 children?

13. Linda is older than Anna. Cathy was born before Anna. Anna is older than Louise. Cathy was born before Linda. Who is the oldest?

14. Will $2 be enough to buy two 49¢ pads and a 98¢ pen?

15. **Data File** Use data from pages 248–249. How much longer is the Amazon River than the Yangtze River?

16. **Make a Data File** Use a newspaper. Record your high and low temperatures for a week. Make a table.

Cumulative Skills Review · Chapters 1-5

Tell if each number is odd or even.

1. 68   **2.** 45   **3.** 107   **4.** 299   **5.** 31   **6.** 124

Write the standard form of each number.

7. thirty-six   **8.** nine hundred seventeen

9. 8,000 + 100 + 2   **10.** 1,000 + 700 + 60 + 8

11. two hundred ten thousand   **12.** sixty thousand, fifty-two

Find each sum or difference mentally.

13. 62 + 20   **14.** 39 + 34   **15.** 87 − 29   **16.** 94 − 45

Find each sum or difference.

17. 1,406 + 226	**18.** 2,448 + 1,239	**19.** 723 + 189	**20.** 4,305 + 3,248
21. 345 − 191	**22.** 671 − 290	**23.** 4,062 − 1,271	**24.** 9,008 − 5,259

25. 23 + 14 + 9   **26.** 47 + 22 + 18   **27.** 7 + 55 + 39 + 4

28. 6,091 + 823   **29.** 792 − 83   **30.** 5,021 − 990

Choose the more sensible measure.

31. height of a window
     meters   kilometers

32. width of your bedroom
     inches   feet

33. length of a river
     yards   miles

34. temperature for snow skiing
     − 10°C   40°C

Measure the line segment to the nearest _____

35. centimeter.   **36.** decimeter.   **37.** inch.   **38.** half inch.

Reteaching

Set A   pages 150–153

Write the time in two ways.

12:35; 35 minutes after 12 o'clock.

Remember that the short hand points to the hour.

1. Write the time in two ways.

Set B   pages 154–155

What day is October 4?

O C T O B E R

Sunday	Monday	Tuesday	Wednesday	Thursday	Friday	Saturday
	1	2	3	4	5	6
7	8	Columbus Day	10	11	12	13
14	15	16	17	18	19	20
21	22	23	United Nations Day	25	26	27
28	29	30	Halloween			

Thursday

Remember that a week begins on Sunday and ends on Saturday. Use the calendar at the left to answer the questions.

1. What day is October 22?

2. What is the date of the third Friday?

Set C   pages 156–157

How long is the pencil to the nearest half inch?

$2\frac{1}{2}$ inches

Remember to line up the end of the ruler with the edge of what you are measuring.

1. Measure the length of your desk to the nearest half inch.

Set D   pages 158–159

The foot and the yard are used to measure lengths that are not as small as a pencil and not as long as the distance between cities.

Remember that 1 mile equals 1,760 yards and also equals 5,280 feet.

1. Would you use inches, feet, yards, or miles to find the length of a car?

Set E   pages 160–161

The width of a large paper clip is 1 centimeter. The length is about 5 centimeters.

1   2   3   4   5

Remember to line up the end of the ruler with the edge of what you are measuring.

Measure each line segment to the nearest centimeter.

1.

2. _____

Set F   pages 164–165

The width of a door is about 1 meter. The width of 1,000 doors is about 1 kilometer.

1 kilometer = 1,000 meters

Remember that it takes more units to measure something in centimeters than in meters.

1. Tell whether you would use centimeters, meters, or kilometers to measure the length of a city block.

Set G   pages 168–169

Find the perimeter of this desk.

←——4 feet——→

2 ft   2 ft

←——4 feet——→

```
  4
  2
  4
+ 2
────
 12 feet
```

Remember that perimeter means the distance around a figure.

1. Find the perimeter of this mirror.

←— 5 ft —→

3 ft   3 ft

←— 5 ft —→

Set H   pages 174–175

What temperature is shown?

Each mark is 1 degree. Start at 30°C and count to 36°C.

— 40°C

— 30°C

Remember that each unit is bigger on the Celsius scale than on the Fahrenheit scale.

1. Write the temperature shown at the right.

— 50°F

— 40°F

More Practice

Set A pages 150–153

Write each time in two ways.

1.   2.

Mental Math

3. The time is 10:20. What time will it be 30 minutes from now?

4. How many minutes is 1 hour and 35 minutes?

Set B pages 154–155

Use the calendar on page 154 to answer these questions.

1. What happens one week after September 21? What day is that?

2. What happens on the third Wednesday? What date is that?

3. Labor Day is the first Monday in September. What date is that?

4. Al's birthday is one week after the French opera. Name the date.

Set C pages 156–157

Measure to the nearest half inch.

1.

2.

Set D pages 158–159

Write inches, feet, yards, or miles to tell which you would use to measure the following.

1. Length of a hairbrush

2. Height of a refrigerator

3. Distance from earth to the moon

4. Length of a football field

Set E   pages 160–161

Estimation   Without using a ruler, draw a line segment that you think has the length given. Then measure the line segment with a ruler.

1. 4 centimeters   **2.** 7 centimeters   **3.** 9 centimeters

Set F   pages 164–165

Tell whether you would use centimeters, meters, or kilometers to measure the following.

1. Length of a toothbrush   **2.** Length of a river

3. Height of tree   **4.** Width of a street

Number Sense   Copy and complete the sentence.

5. One meter is the same as 100 centimeters, so 3 meters is the same as ▦ centimeters.

Set G   pages 168–169

Use paper and pencil or mental math to find the perimeter of each figure.

Tell which method you used.

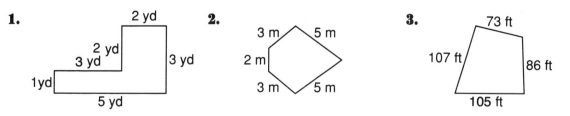

1. 2 yd / 2 yd / 3 yd / 1 yd / 5 yd / 3 yd

2. 3 m / 5 m / 2 m / 3 m / 5 m

3. 73 ft / 107 ft / 86 ft / 105 ft

Set H   pages 174–175

Write the temperature in °C or °F.

1. 20° C / 10° C   **2.** 80° F / 70° F

Estimation   Choose the more sensible measure.

3. Making ice cubes
   50°F   32°F

4. A cup of hot cocoa
   80°C   50°C

Enrichment

Area and Perimeter

Are these two rectangles the same size?

4 cm

3 cm

6 cm

2 cm

1. Find the area of each rectangle.

2. Find the perimeter of each rectangle.

3. Is the area of both rectangles the same?

4. Is the perimeter of both rectangles the same?

Use grid paper to make rectangles for each exercise. Then find the area and perimeter of each. Record your findings in a table.

5. 8 across and 2 down

6. 4 across and 4 down

7. 10 across and 2 down

8. 12 across and 1 down

9. 5 across and 4 down

10. 3 across and 2 down

11. Which rectangles have the same area?

12. Which rectangles have the same perimeter?

13. Do any rectangles have the same area and perimeter?

Exercise	Area	Perimeter
5.		
6.		
7.		
8.		
9.		
10.		

Chapter 5 Review/Test

What time is shown on each clock?

1.

2.

	AUGUST					
S	M	T	W	T	F	S
		1	2	3	4	5
6	7	8	9	10	11	12
13	14	15	16	17	18	19
20	21	22	23	24	25	26
27	28	29	30	31		

3. What is the date of the third Monday in August?

4. Measure the line segment to the nearest inch and centimeter.

Choose the more sensible unit of measure.

5. Length of a truck

   mile   foot

6. Length of a pencil

   centimeter   kilometer

7. Find the perimeter.

8. Find the area of the figure in square centimeters.

9. Choose the most sensible temperature for snow skiing.

   20°F   68°F   90°F

10. John needs string to tie up 6 boxes. For each box he needs 24 inches of string. Should he buy a 100-inch roll of string or a 200-inch roll?

Read this problem. Then make a table to answer the questions below.

Ted, Nan, and Joe are wearing hats. One hat is green, one orange, and one blue. Neither of the boys has a blue hat. Joe wishes he had a green hat. What color is each child's hat?

11. Who has the blue hat?

12. Who has the orange hat?

13. Who has the green hat?

14. ■ **Write About Math** Explain how you would find the perimeter of your classroom.

183

Multiplication Concepts

6

184

Number-Sense Project

Estimate
Estimate how many 2-packs of light bulbs you would need if you replaced every bulb in your house.

Gather Data
Record the number of bulbs you have in your home. How many packages of light bulbs do you need?

Analyze and Report
Make charts with your classmates to compare the number of bulbs you would need with the number of packages you would need.

185

Joining Groups of Equal Size

Build Understanding

What do you like to do at picnics?

Judy bought some of the supplies for the Waller Company picnic. She got 3 six-packs of juice. How many cans of juice did she get?

Add the number in each pack to find the number in all.

6 + 6 + 6 = 18

■ **Talk About Math** Tell how you can find how many cans there would be if Judy bought 30 six-packs of juice.

Each American drinks about $5\frac{1}{2}$ gallons of juice in one year.

Check Understanding

For another example, see Set A, pages 212-213.

Choose all the number names that tell how many there are of each. Use the picture on this page to help you.

1. How many forks?

2. How many plates?

3. How many napkins?

4. How many straws?

A. 2 groups of 100

B. 5 + 5 + 5 + 5

C. 4 groups of 5

D. 10 + 10

E. 100 + 100

F. 4 groups of 20

G. 200

H. 2 groups of 10

I. 20 + 20 + 20 + 20

Practice

For More Practice, see Set A, pages 214–215.

Tell how many.

5. 8 + 8 + 8 + 8   **6.** 9 + 9 + 9   **7.** 6 + 6 + 6 + 6 + 6

8. 5 + 5 + 5   **9.** 7 + 7 + 7 + 7   **10.** 2 + 2 + 2 + 2 + 2

11. 10 + 10 + 10   **12.** 100 + 100   **13.** 10 + 10 + 10 + 10

Mixed Practice Tell which is greater.

14. 5 + 5 or 2 + 9   **15.** 8 − 4 or 3 + 3   **16.** 22 + 22 or 25 + 25

17. 20 + 10 or 34   **18.** 80 or 35 + 35   **19.** 50 − 20 or 20 + 20

Mental Math Tell an easy way to find the answer.

20. 10 + 10 + 10 + 10 + 10 + 10   **21.** 100 + 100 + 100 + 100

Problem Solving

Write an addition sentence for Exercises 22–25.
Use the picture to help you tell how many in all.

22. 4 packages of plates   **23.** 2 packages of napkins

24. 2 packages of forks   **25.** 8 packages of cups

26. Critical Thinking Judy bought 15 packages of spoons and knives. She bought 3 more packages of spoons than knives. How many packages of spoons did she buy?

187

Meaning of Multiplication: Repeated Addition

Build Understanding

A. All the Same
Materials: Small objects
Groups: 3–5 students

How many toy cars are in the picture?

a. Each of you show 3 objects.

b. Tell how many are in 2 groups of 3.
Write an addition sentence.

You can write a multiplication sentence to show 2 groups of 3.

2 × 3 = 6

2   times   3   equals   6

c. Repeat *step b* with 3, 4, and 5 groups of 3. Write an addition and a multiplication sentence for each set.

Use objects to find the number of cars. Write an addition and a multiplication sentence.

B. You can show multiplication in many ways.

$3 \times 8 = 24$
3 times 8 equals 24

3 groups of 8
is the same as 24

3 eights equal 24

three times eight
equals twenty-four

c. 📟 **Calculator** You can use repeated addition to find 4×65.

Press:		You see:	
65	+		*65*
65	+		*130*
65	+		*195*
65	=		*260*

■ **Write About Math** List some things that come in groups. Write multiplication sentences to describe them.

Check Understanding

For another example, see Set B, pages 212–213.

Use the ideas in Example B to help you write 4 sentences to describe each exercise.

1.

2.

3. 4 groups each with 3 toy trucks

4. 6 bags each with 2 toy dinosaurs

Practice

For More Practice, see Set B, pages 214–215.

Write an addition and a multiplication sentence for each exercise. **Remember** to use objects to help you.

5.

6.

7.

8.

9. 5 shelves each with 5 toy dogs

10. 4 bags each with 3 balls

11. 3 boxes each with 9 stuffed animals

12. 2 bags each with 100 marbles

13. 4 boxes each with 200 building blocks

14. 5 checker games each with 24 checkers

Estimation Use what you know about estimating sums to estimate in multiplication. Estimate each answer.

15. 86 + 86 + 86

16. 3 × 32

17. 104 + 104

18. 2 × 197

19. 22 + 22 + 22 + 22

20. 4 × 18

Problem Solving

Solve each problem. Use objects to help you.

21. Jerry saw 3 toy train displays. Each train had 12 cars. How many cars were there in all?

22. Susan bought 4 boxes of tracks for her train set. Each box had 20 pieces of track. How many pieces of track did she buy?

TIPS FOR PROBLEM SOLVERS

Be flexible. If you get stuck, try another idea.

Write a story problem for each exercise.

23. $4 \times 3 = 12$ **24.** $10 \times 6 = 60$ **25.** $100 \times 4 = 400$

Use Data Look at the picture on page 186. Write a multiplication sentence to tell how many

26. forks.   **27.** plates.   **28.** napkins.   **29.** straws.

Visual Thinking Tom folded cards in two and punched holes in them. Then he unfolded the cards. How many holes are there in each card?

30.   **31.**

Exploring Multiplication Using Arrays

Build Understanding

Hurray for Arrays!
Materials: Small objects
Groups: Partners

Bert has some wood carvings. He put them in a display case that has 6 rows with 5 places in each row. How many carvings does he have?

a. Use small objects to show what Bert did.
An **array** shows **rows** and **columns**.

$5 \times 6 = 30$

↑ ↑
└── Number in each group
└── Number of groups

$$5 \leftarrow \text{Number in each group}$$
$$\times\ 6 \leftarrow \text{Number of groups}$$
$$\overline{3\ 0}$$

Bert has 30 carvings.

b. Make an array to show 4 rows of 8 carvings. Write a multiplication sentence to tell how many carvings there are in all.

What hobbies do your classmates like?

■ **Write About Math** List at least 5 things you see displayed as arrays.

Check Understanding

For another example, see Set C, pages 212–213.

Number Sense   True or False. Each exercise matches the array.

1. $3 \times 6 = 18$ **2.** $3 + 3 = 6$

3. $2 \times 9 = 18$ **4.** $6 + 6 + 6 = 18$

5. three fives   **6.** $6 \times 3 = 18$

7. three sixes equal eighteen

Practice

For More Practice, see Set C, pages 214–215.

Write a multiplication sentence for each exercise.
Remember that making arrays may help you.

8. 2 rows of 4   **9.** $3 + 3 + 3$ **10.** 4 sixes   **11.** 5 rows of 7

12. $9 + 9 + 9$ **13.** 4 fours   **14.** 3 rows of 5   **15.** $8 + 8$

16. 5 fives   **17.** 2 rows of 6   **18.** $2 + 2 + 2 + 2$ **19.** 5 twos

20. 4 rows of 8   **21.** 7 threes   **22.** $5 + 5 + 5 + 5$ **23.** $7 + 7 + 7$

24. 6 fours   **25.** 3 rows of 4   **26.** 9 twos   **27.** $8 + 8 + 8$

Problem Solving

Solve each problem.

28. How many wood blocks are in 4 packages if there are 12 blocks in one package?

29. Bert sold 38 carvings. If he started with 214 carvings, how many did he have left?

Explore _____ Math

30. Make as many arrays of 16 objects as you can. Write a multiplication sentence for each array.

31. Repeat Exercise 30 with 36 objects.

Multiplication with Fives

Build Understanding

Number sticks were used for many years throughout the world to count, keep records, and mark the passage of time. The Zuni Indians of North America are an example of one group who wrote numbers by carving notches in sticks or bones.

How many notches do you see?

You can look at them in two different ways.

If you look at the sticks, there are 5 sticks with 4 notches on each stick.

If you look at the rows, there are 4 rows of notches with 5 notches in each row.

You can multiply when all the groups are the same size.

5 × 4 = 20   **4 × 5 = 20**
Think of 5 groups of 4.   Think of 4 groups of 5.

There are 20 notches in all.

■ **Write About Math**   What are some things we count by fives?

Check Understanding

For another example, see Set D, pages 212–213.

For each fact, draw an array and write the answer.

1. 2	**2.** 3	**3.** 4	**4.** 5	**5.** 6	**6.** 7	**7.** 8	**8.** 9
×5	×5	×5	×5	×5	×5	×5	×5

Practice

For More Practice, see Set D, pages 214–215.

Find each answer.

9. 4 $\times 5$	**10.** 3 $\times 5$	**11.** 5 $\times 2$	**12.** 8 $\times 5$	**13.** 6 $\times 5$	**14.** 7 $\times 5$
15. 5 $\times 4$	**16.** 5 $\times 5$	**17.** 2 $\times 5$	**18.** 5 $\times 9$	**19.** 5 $\times 6$	**20.** 5 $\times 7$

21. 5×5 **22.** 5×3 **23.** 5×9 **24.** 8×5 **25.** 4×5

Mixed Practice   Use paper and pencil or mental math to find each answer. Tell which method you used.

26. $46 + 29$ **27.** $191 - 82$ **28.** 5×6 **29.** $489 - 291$

30. $9,836 - 400$ **31.** 9×5 **32.** $3,076 + 925$ **33.** 7×5

Problem Solving

Solve each problem.

34. Long ago, Swiss shepherds notched sticks to count sheep. Suppose they made 5 notches on each stick. How many sticks would they need if they had 30 sheep?

35. How many multiplication sentences can you write for the array at the right?

Explore ———— Math

36. What pattern do you see in Exercises 1–8?

Use the pattern to tell the ones digits in these answers.

37. 5×12 **38.** 5×17 **39.** 5×34 **40.** 5×103

Twos: Doubling

Build Understanding

Have you ever been to a baseball doubleheader? A doubleheader is two games played one right after the other, on the same day.

In one doubleheader, the Cubs played 9 innings in each game. How many innings did they play in all?

There are 2 equal groups of 9. You can multiply.

2 × 9 = 18

The Cubs played 18 innings.

Mets	0	0	1	0	0	2	0	0	1
Cubs	0	0	0	1	1	0	0	0	0

Mets	0	0	0	3	0	0	1	0	0
Cubs	0	0	0	1	1	1	0	0	2

■ **Talk About Math**   Name things that come in doubles or pairs.

Check Understanding

For another example, see Set E, pages 212–213.

1. Could the number 8 come out of the Doubling Machine?

2. Could the number 11 come out of the Doubling Machine?

3. What number comes out of the Doubling Machine when 5 goes in?

For each fact, draw an array and write the answer.

DOUBLING MACHINE

IN	OUT
2	4
3	6
5	
20	40
50	100

4. 2 ×2	**5.** 3 ×2	**6.** 4 ×2	**7.** 5 ×2	**8.** 6 ×2	**9.** 7 ×2	**10.** 8 ×2	**11.** 9 ×2

Practice

For More Practice, see Set E, pages 214–215.

Find each answer.

12. 5
×2

13. 3
×2

14. 2
×8

15. 9
×2

16. 2
×4

17. 2
×7

18. 2
×2

19. 2
×3

20. 2
×9

21. 8
×2

22. 2
×6

23. 4
×2

24. 2 × 6   **25.** 5 × 2   **26.** 8 × 2   **27.** 2 × 7   **28.** 2 × 2

29. 2 × 3   **30.** 4 × 2   **31.** 2 × 9   **32.** 6 × 2   **33.** 2 × 8

A
L
G
E
B
R
A

▶ Find the missing number.

34. 2 × ▦ = 14   **35.** 2 × ▦ = 10   **36.** ▦ × 2 = 8

37. ▦ × 2 = 12   **38.** 2 × ▦ = 6   **39.** ▦ × 8 = 16

40. Number Sense If 20 comes out of the Doubling Machine, what number went in?

41. Which of the numbers from 1 to 20 could come out of the Doubling Machine?

42. What happens when you put 0 in the Doubling Machine?

43. Look at Exercises 4–11. What patterns do you see?

Midchapter ✓ Checkup

For each exercise, draw an array and write an addition and a multiplication sentence.

1. 2 groups of 6   **2.** 3 groups of 9   **3.** 4 groups of 10

Find each answer.

4. 5
×8

5. 6
×5

6. 3
×2

7. 9
×5

8. 2
×7

Explore as a Team

1. Use grid paper to cut out rectangles. *Rule*: Each rectangle must have at least two rows.

2. Can you make rectangles with these numbers of squares?

8 15 11 20 12
7 10 16 30   9

3. Write number sentences for the rectangles you were able to make.

Number-Sense Project

Look back at pages 184-185. Light bulbs come in 2-packs and 4-packs. Suppose you bought 3 of each size package. Then you used 1 light bulb from each package.

1. How many bulbs are left in each package now?

2. How could you use addition to find out how many bulbs are left?

3. How can you use addition and multiplication to find out how many bulbs are left?

Real-Life Decision Making

Your family has many huge baskets full of nuts. You need to put the nuts in bags. Your mother wants about 40 nuts in each bag.

1. You can usually pick up 5 nuts in one handful. How can you use your handfuls to fill each bag with about 40 nuts?

2. What other ways are there to fill the bags with about 40 nuts without counting each nut?

Explore With a Computer

Use the *Number Sense Workshop Project* for this activity.

1. Suppose you are planning a seating arrangement. You have 4 rows and 8 chairs in each row. Make an array to show the chairs in the pattern.

2. In what other pattern can you arrange the same number of chairs to have equal numbers of chairs in each row? Try your plan on the computer.

Draw a Picture

Build Understanding

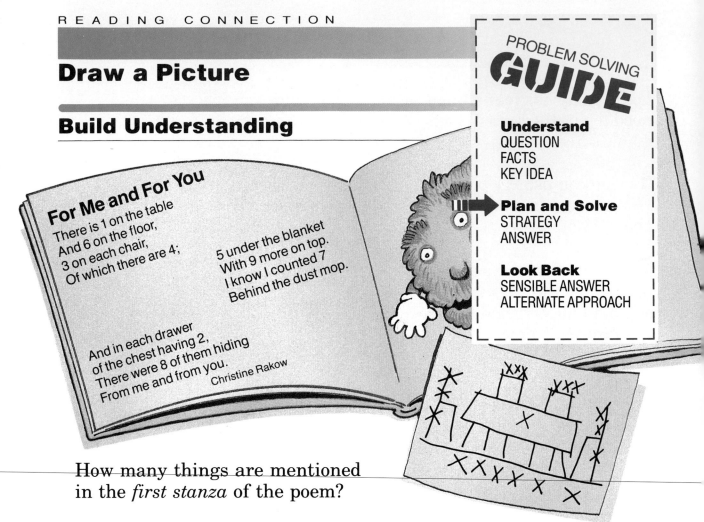

For Me and For You

There is 1 on the table
And 6 on the floor,
3 on each chair,
Of which there are 4;

5 under the blanket
With 9 more on top.
I know I counted 7
Behind the dust mop.

And in each drawer
of the chest having 2,
There were 8 of them hiding
From me and from you.

Christine Rakow

PROBLEM SOLVING
GUIDE

Understand
QUESTION
FACTS
KEY IDEA

Plan and Solve
STRATEGY
ANSWER

Look Back
SENSIBLE ANSWER
ALTERNATE APPROACH

How many things are mentioned
in the *first stanza* of the poem?

Understand   Things are on the table, the floor, and on 4 chairs.

Plan and Solve   STRATEGY   Draw a picture of a table, the floor, and 4 chairs. Draw the number of things on each.

Count how many things in all.

ANSWER   There are 19 things in the first stanza.

Look Back   You could use multiplication to find the number of things on the chairs. Then add that answer to the number of things on the floor and table.

■ **Talk About Math**   What do you think
the things are? How many things
would there be if there were 5 chairs?

Check Understanding

To solve the problem, answer Questions 1–3. Draw a picture to help you.

How many things are in the chest of drawers?

1. How many drawers are in the chest?

2. How many things are in each drawer?

3. How many things are in the chest of drawers?

4. How many things would there be if there were 5 drawers in the chest?

Practice

Solve each problem. Draw a picture to help you.

5. How many things are mentioned in the second stanza?

6. How many things are mentioned in the entire poem?

7. If they shared them evenly, how many things would each person get?

8. If the things are pennies, how many nickels would they be worth?

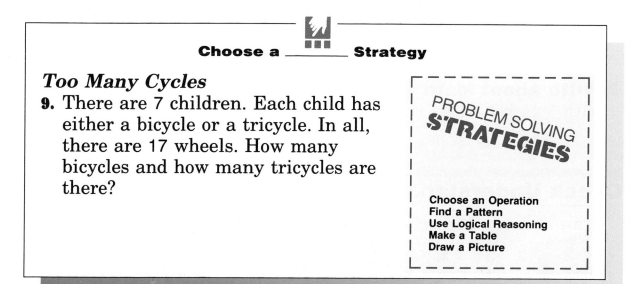

Choose a _____ Strategy

Too Many Cycles

9. There are 7 children. Each child has either a bicycle or a tricycle. In all, there are 17 wheels. How many bicycles and how many tricycles are there?

PROBLEM SOLVING
STRATEGIES

Choose an Operation
Find a Pattern
Use Logical Reasoning
Make a Table
Draw a Picture

Threes: Adding to a Known Fact

Build Understanding

If 8 carrot sticks are put in each lunch, how many are needed for 3 lunches?

You know that 2×8 will tell you how many carrot sticks are needed for 2 lunches. For 3 lunches, add another set of 8 sticks.

2×8

3×8

$3 \times 8 = 24$

You need 24 carrot sticks for 3 lunches.

A balanced diet includes 4 servings of fruits and vegetables each day.

■ **Write About Math** Explain how 8 lunches with 3 carrot sticks is related to the example.

Check Understanding

For another example, see Set F, pages 212–213.

Draw an array for each fact. Find each answer.

1. 2	**2.** 3	**3.** 4	**4.** 5	**5.** 6	**6.** 7	**7.** 8	**8.** 9
$\times 3$	$\times 3$	$\times 3$	$\times 3$	$\times 3$	$\times 3$	$\times 3$	$\times 3$

Practice

For More Practice, see Set F, pages 214–215.

Find each answer.

9.   6
  ×3

10. 8
  ×3

11. 3
  ×2

12. 9
  ×3

13. 3
  ×5

14. 3
  ×3

15. 3×5

16. 3×7

17. 6×3

18. 8×3

19. 3×9

20. 3×2

21. 3×4

22. 7×3

23. 3×3

24. 9×3

Mixed Practice   Find each answer.

25. 2×8

26. 5×5

27. 7×2

28. 9×5

29. 5×2

30. 6×5

31. 2×6

32. 4×2

33. 5×4

34. 3×5

Problem Solving

Number Sense   Solve each problem.

35. Is 2×14 more or less than 3×14?

36. How much more is 3×100 than 2×100?

How much more is

37. 3×9 than 2×9?

38. 3×9 than 3×8?

39. 4×3 than 4×2?

Reading ———— Math

Vocabulary

1. What do *trio, triplet, tricycle, triangle,* and *triple* mean?

2. What do these words have in common?

3. What is the meaning of *tricolor?*

Fours: Doubling a Known Fact

Build Understanding

How many shapes are there in all?

You can double a twos fact to help you multiply by 4.

There are 2 groups of 6 squares. $2 \times 6 = 12$

There are 2 groups of 6 circles. $2 \times 6 = 12$

So 4 groups of 6 shapes is the same as 2×6 plus 2×6.

$$4 \times 6 = 24$$

Factors ———↑   ↑   �l_——Product

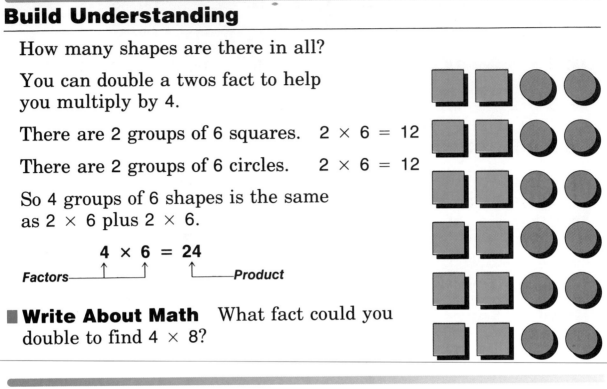

■ **Write About Math** What fact could you double to find 4×8?

Check Understanding

For another example, see Set G, pages 212–213.

For each fact, draw an array and write the answer.

1. 2	**2.** 3	**3.** 4	**4.** 5	**5.** 6	**6.** 7	**7.** 8	**8.** 9
$\times 4$	$\times 4$	$\times 4$	$\times 4$	$\times 4$	$\times 4$	$\times 4$	$\times 4$

What fact could you double to find the products?

204

Practice

For More Practice, see Set G, pages 214–215.

Find each product.

11. 6
    ×4

12. 4
    ×3

13. 4
    ×8

14. 5
    ×4

15. 2
    ×4

16. 4
    ×4

17. 5 × 4

18. 7 × 4

19. 4 × 3

20. 8 × 4

21. 2 × 4

22. 9 × 4

23. 4 × 7

24. 6 × 4

25. 4 × 9

26. 4 × 4

Find the missing factor.

27. 4 × ▦ = 8

28. 4 × ▦ = 16

29. ▦ × 4 = 28

30. 4 × ▦ = 20

31. 4 × ▦ = 24

32. 4 × ▦ = 36

Mental Math   Find each answer.

33. 18 − 9

34. 10 + 10

35. 4 × 7

36. 7 − 2

37. 3 × 5

38. 4 + 6

39. 8 − 5

40. 2 × 8

41. 7 + 8

42. 3 × 9

Problem Solving

Solve each problem.

43. A room has 7 tables. At each table there are 4 chairs. How many chairs are there in all?

44. There are 9 calculators. If 4 are being used, how many are not being used?

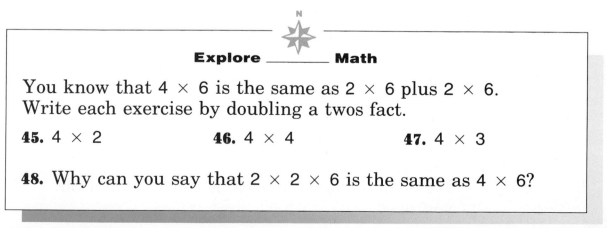

Explore ———— Math

You know that 4 × 6 is the same as 2 × 6 plus 2 × 6. Write each exercise by doubling a twos fact.

45. 4 × 2

46. 4 × 4

47. 4 × 3

48. Why can you say that 2 × 2 × 6 is the same as 4 × 6?

Too Much Information

Build Understanding

How many nature trails are in
the River City Park System?

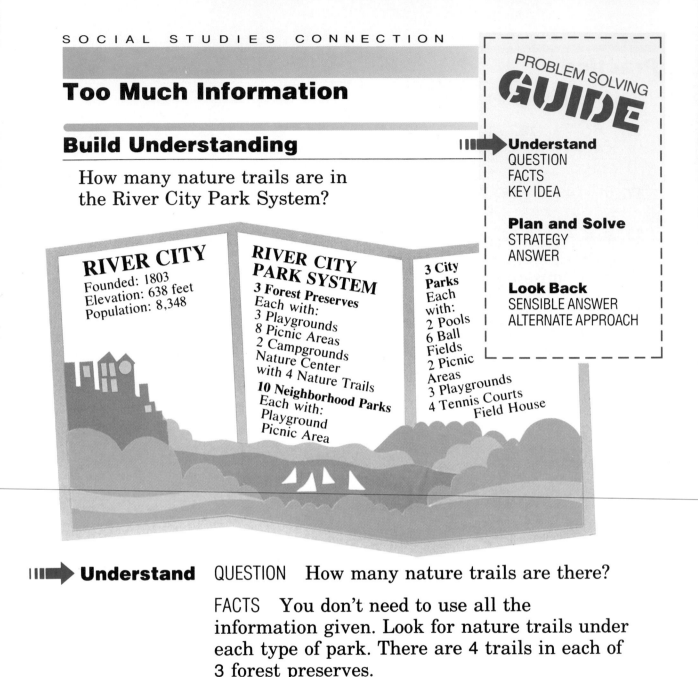

RIVER CITY
Founded: 1803
Elevation: 638 feet
Population: 8,348

**RIVER CITY
PARK SYSTEM**
3 Forest Preserves
Each with:
3 Playgrounds
8 Picnic Areas
2 Campgrounds
Nature Center
with 4 Nature Trails
10 Neighborhood Parks
Each with:
Playground
Picnic Area

**3 City
Parks**
Each
with:
2 Pools
6 Ball
Fields
2 Picnic
Areas
3 Playgrounds
4 Tennis Courts
Field House

PROBLEM SOLVING
GUIDE

Understand
QUESTION
FACTS
KEY IDEA

Plan and Solve
STRATEGY
ANSWER

Look Back
SENSIBLE ANSWER
ALTERNATE APPROACH

Understand   QUESTION   How many nature trails are there?

FACTS   You don't need to use all the
information given. Look for nature trails under
each type of park. There are 4 trails in each of
3 forest preserves.

KEY IDEA   Since the same number of trails are
in each preserve, you can multiply.

**Plan
and Solve** $3 \times 4 = 12$

River City has 12 nature trails.

Look Back   Make sure you have used all the information
you need.

■ **Write About Math**   Draw a picture to show all the different areas one city park has.

Check Understanding

Solve the problem by answering Questions 1–4.

How many playgrounds are in the park system?

1. How many playgrounds are in each forest preserve? How many are in all the forest preserves?

2. How many playgrounds are in each neighborhood park? How many are in all the neighborhood parks?

3. How many playgrounds are in each city park? How many are in all the city parks?

4. How many playgrounds are in the entire River City park system?

Practice

Use the chart on page 206 to solve each problem.

5. How many different types of parks are in the park system?

6. How many ball fields are in the park system?

7. River City had 317 settlers when it was founded. How many more people live in River City now?

8. Are there more nature centers or more field houses in the park system? How many more?

Choose a ⎯⎯⎯⎯ Strategy

No Strings Attached!
9. To cut a string into 8 pieces, how many cuts would you need to make?

207

Zero and One in Multiplication

Build Understanding

A. At the pet shop, Charlie put out 5 empty fish bowls. How many fish are there in all?

5 groups of 0

$0 + 0 + 0 + 0 + 0 = 0$

$5 \times 0 = 0$ There are 0 fish.

B. Charlie put 1 fish in each bowl. How many fish are there in all?

5 groups of 1

$1 + 1 + 1 + 1 + 1 = 5$

$5 \times 1 = 5$ There are 5 fish.

■ **Write About Math** Charlie put another fish in each bowl. Write an addition and multiplication sentence for the picture.

Check Understanding

For another example, see Set H, pages 212–213.

1. **Number Sense** Copy the multiplication sentence ▽ × 0 = ▦. Replace the ▽ with a number between 0 and 15. Find the product.

2. Try Exercise 1 three more times with different numbers.

3. What can you say about multiplying any number by 0?

4. Repeat Exercises 1 and 2 with ▽ × 1 = ▦.

5. What can you say about multiplying any number by 1?

Practice

For More Practice, see Set H, pages 214–215.

Find each product.

6. $\begin{array}{r} 0 \\ \times 5 \\ \hline \end{array}$	**7.** $\begin{array}{r} 0 \\ \times 1 \\ \hline \end{array}$	**8.** $\begin{array}{r} 1 \\ \times 7 \\ \hline \end{array}$	**9.** $\begin{array}{r} 5 \\ \times 0 \\ \hline \end{array}$	**10.** $\begin{array}{r} 1 \\ \times 3 \\ \hline \end{array}$	**11.** $\begin{array}{r} 2 \\ \times 0 \\ \hline \end{array}$
12. $\begin{array}{r} 6 \\ \times 0 \\ \hline \end{array}$	**13.** $\begin{array}{r} 0 \\ \times 0 \\ \hline \end{array}$	**14.** $\begin{array}{r} 1 \\ \times 8 \\ \hline \end{array}$	**15.** $\begin{array}{r} 6 \\ \times 1 \\ \hline \end{array}$	**16.** $\begin{array}{r} 8 \\ \times 0 \\ \hline \end{array}$	**17.** $\begin{array}{r} 1 \\ \times 5 \\ \hline \end{array}$

18. 0×7 **19.** 9×1 **20.** 9×0 **21.** 1×7 **22.** 1×1

23. 2×1 **24.** 0×0 **25.** 1×0 **26.** 0×82 **27.** 36×0

28. 0×61 **29.** 1×32 **30.** 51×1 **31.** 79×1 **32.** 1×45

Mixed Practice   Find each product.

33. $\begin{array}{r} 5 \\ \times 0 \\ \hline \end{array}$	**34.** $\begin{array}{r} 8 \\ \times 2 \\ \hline \end{array}$	**35.** $\begin{array}{r} 7 \\ \times 3 \\ \hline \end{array}$	**36.** $\begin{array}{r} 5 \\ \times 4 \\ \hline \end{array}$	**37.** $\begin{array}{r} 6 \\ \times 2 \\ \hline \end{array}$

38. 4×9 **39.** 5×5 **40.** 6×4 **41.** 2×0 **42.** 4×1

Problem Solving

Write multiplication sentences to help you solve the problems.

43. Lin had 3 bowls with 5 fish in each bowl. He sold 1 bowl of fish. How many fish are left?

44. Lin sold another bowl of fish. How many fish are left?

45. Lin sold the last bowl of fish. How many fish are left?

46. Brian has 2 fish in each of 4 fish bowls. Kevin has 2 fish bowls with 4 fish in each bowl. How many fish do Brian and Kevin have in all?

47. **Use Data**   Tell the number of playgrounds in the neighborhood parks in River City. Use the data found on page 206.

Skills Review

Tell how many.

1. 5 + 5 + 5 + 5 + 5 + 5

2. 2 + 2 + 2 + 2 + 2

Write an addition and a multiplication sentence for each exercise.

3. 3 boxes each with 4 hats

4. 2 bags each with 8 toys

Make an array and write a multiplication sentence for each.

5. 3 nines   **6.** 8 rows of 3

Find each answer.

7. 3 $\times 5$	**8.** 5 $\times 4$	**9.** 6 $\times 2$
10. 8 $\times 3$	**11.** 3 $\times 7$	**12.** 6 $\times 4$
13. 4 $\times 3$	**14.** 0 $\times 7$	**15.** 9 $\times 1$

16. 6×5 **17.** 2×4

18. 9×2 **19.** 3×9

20. 4×8 **21.** 4×4

22. 8×0 **23.** 1×5

Problem-Solving Review

Solve each problem.

24. As the gift shop opened, 7 shoppers arrived. Then 2 more shoppers came in, 5 went out, 4 came in, 3 went out, 6 came in, and 5 went out. How many shoppers are in the shop?

25. What number is more than 2 fives and less than 4 threes?

26. On a video game, Steve scored 105,000 points and Nella scored 96,000 points. In the next game, Nella scored 10,000 points more than her previous game. Is that enough to pass Steve's score?

27. Draw a shape with an area of 3 square units and a perimeter of 8 units.

28. Data File Use data from pages 248–249. What time should Lu catch the bus at the Highland stop to arrive in Chicago at 7:51 A.M.?

29. Make a Data File Record the prices of 5 different brands of the same size box of cold cereal. Order the prices from least to greatest.

Write the family of facts for the numbers in each exercise.

1. 7, 8, 15

2. 4, 12, 8

3. 0, 2, 2

Replace each ▦ with < or >.

4. 782 ▦ 728

5. 65 ▦ 106

6. 125 ▦ 251

Estimate each answer.

7. 58 + 23

8. 84 − 39

9. 67 − 18

10. 45 + 46

Find each sum or difference.

11. 347
   + 171

12. 406
   + 299

13. 9,012
   − 5,961

14. 6,340
   − 3,458

Answer each question.

15. What time is shown on the clock?

16. What date is the fourth Sunday?

October

S	M	T	W	T	F	S
			1	2	3	4
5	6	7	8	9	10	11
12	13	14	15	16	17	18
19	20	21	22	23	24	25
26	27	28	29	30	31	

17. Find the perimeter.

7 cm
6 cm
2 cm
10 cm

18. Find the area in square centimeters.

Complete each sentence.

19. There are ▦ inches in 1 foot.

20. There are ▦ meters in 1 kilometer.

Measure the line segment to the nearest

21. inch.

22. half inch.

23. centimeter.

24. decimeter.

Find each answer.

25. 5
   × 6

26. 7
   × 1

27. 8
   × 2

28. 5
   × 3

29. 4
   × 8

30. 6
   × 4

Set A   pages 186–187

Each table at the picnic has room for 8 people. How many people can sit at 5 tables?

Add the number of people at each table to find the number in all.

$8 + 8 + 8 + 8 + 8 = 40$

Remember that counting by twos is the same as adding twos, counting by threes is the same as adding threes, and so on.
Tell how many.

1. $3 + 3 + 3 + 3 + 3$ **2.** $4 + 4 + 4$

Set B   pages 188–191

There are 3 cartons of eggs. Each carton has 12 eggs. Write an addition and a multiplication sentence to show this.

$12 + 12 + 12 = 36$ $3 \times 12 = 36$

Remember that multiplication is repeated addition.

Write an addition and a multiplication sentence for each.

1. 6 cases each with 8 cans

2. 7 boxes each with 4 bulbs

3. 4 shelves each with 10 books

Set C   pages 192–193

The band was arranged in 4 rows with 7 people in each row. How many people are in the band?

```
x x x x x x x
x x x x x x x
x x x x x x x
x x x x x x x
```
$4 \times 7 = 28$

Remember that rows go across and columns go down.
Make an array and write a multiplication sentence for each.

1. 5 rows of 6   **2.** 4 rows of 9

3. $4 + 4 + 4 + 4$ **4.** 8 fours

Set D   pages 194–195

Write two multiplication sentences for this array.

```
x x x x x x
x x x x x x
x x x x x x
x x x x x x
x x x x x x
```
$5 \times 6 = 30$ $6 \times 5 = 30$

Remember that you can multiply when all the groups are the same size. Find each answer.

1. $\begin{array}{r} 5 \\ \times 8 \\ \hline \end{array}$ **2.** $\begin{array}{r} 5 \\ \times 3 \\ \hline \end{array}$ **3.** $\begin{array}{r} 9 \\ \times 5 \\ \hline \end{array}$

4. 5×4 **5.** 5×2 **6.** 7×5

Independent Study RETEACHING

Set E   pages 196–197

Children's tickets cost $8. Adult tickets cost *double* that amount. How much do adults pay?

$$2 \times 8 = 16$$

An adult ticket costs $16.

Remember that doubling a number means multiplying by 2. Find each answer.

1. 2
     × 5

2. 6
     × 2

3. 7
     × 2

4. 2
     × 9

Set F   pages 202–203

If you eat 3 meals a day, how many meals do you eat in 7 days?

xxx xxx xxx xxx xxx xxx xxx

There are 7 groups of 3.

$$7 \times 3 = 21$$

You eat 21 meals in 7 days.

Remember that multiplying a number by 3 means adding the same number 3 times.
Find each answer.

1. 3
     × 4

2. 7
     × 3

3. 3
     × 2

4. 3
     × 8

Set G   pages 204–205

How many shapes are there in all?

△ △ △ △ △   △ △ △ △ △
△ △ △ △ △   △ △ △ △ △

4 groups of 5 shapes is the same as 2 × 5 plus 2 × 5.
$$4 \times 5 = 20.$$

Remember that the numbers you multiply are called factors. The answer is called the product.

Find each product.

1. 4
     × 6

2. 4
     × 7

3. 9
     × 4

4. 8
     × 4

Set H   pages 208–209

Children can go to the concert free. Adult tickets cost $1. How much does it cost for 4 children?

$$0 + 0 + 0 + 0 = 0 \qquad 4 \times 0 = 0$$

The cost is 0.

How much does it cost for 4 adults?

$$1 + 1 + 1 + 1 = 4 \qquad 4 \times 1 = 4$$

It costs $4 for 4 adults.

Remember that if a factor is 0, the product is 0. If a factor is 1, the product is the other factor.
Find each product.

1. 1
     × 0

2. 7
     × 1

3. 0
     × 2

4. 3 × 1   **5.** 0 × 6   **6.** 1 × 5

More Practice

Set A   pages 186–187

Tell how many.

1. 4 + 4 + 4 + 4   2. 5 + 5 + 5 + 5 + 5   3. 7 + 7 + 7 + 7 + 7

4. 10 + 10   5. 9 + 9 + 9 + 9   6. 100 + 100 + 100

Mixed Practice   Tell which is greater.

7. 9 − 3 or 4 + 4   8. 7 + 4 or 6 + 6   9. 60 or 25 + 25

Set B   pages 188–191

Write an addition and a multiplication sentence for each exercise.

1.   2.

3. 6 bags each with 4 balls   4. 5 shelves each with 5 toy cars

5. 4 boxes each with 8 baseball bats   6. 3 bags each with 200 marbles

Estimation   Use what you know about estimating sums to estimate in multiplication. Estimate each answer.

7. 47 + 47 + 47   8. 4 × 19   9. 96 + 96 + 96

10. 95 × 3   11. 209 + 209   12. 5 × 11

Set C   pages 192–193

Make an array and write a multiplication sentence for each.

1. 4 rows of 9   2. 5 + 5 + 5   3. 4 sevens   4. 5 rows of 6

5. 8 + 8 + 8   6. 4 rows of 2   7. 6 fours   8. 7 + 7

214

Set D pages 194–195

Find each answer.

1. 7
    ×5

2. 5
    ×9

3. 8
    ×5

4. 3 × 5

5. 6 × 5

Mixed Practice Use paper and pencil or mental math to find each answer. Tell which method you used.

6. 7,386 − 300

7. 5 × 5

8. 2,083 + 918

9. 8 × 5

Set E pages 196–197

Find each answer.

1. 2
    ×9

2. 8
    ×2

3. 4
    ×2

4. 7 × 2

5. 2 × 5

Set F pages 202–203

Find each answer.

1. 1
    ×3

2. 3
    ×2

3. 3
    ×3

4. 4 × 3

5. 5 × 3

6. Number Sense What pattern do you see in the answers to Exercises 1–5?

Set G pages 204–205

Find each product.

1. 4
    ×5

2. 7
    ×4

3. 8
    ×4

4. 4 × 2

5. 4 × 6

Mental Math Find each answer mentally.

6. 16 − 8

7. 9 + 9

8. 3 × 7

9. 8 − 2

10. 5 × 2

11. 3 + 7

12. 9 − 4

13. 2 × 9

14. 6 + 5

15. 8 × 3

Set H pages 208–209

Find each product.

1. 3
    ×0

2. 4
    ×1

3. 4
    ×0

4. 2 × 1

5. 8 × 0

Enrichment

Primes and Composites

Only one rectangle can be made with a *prime* number of blocks.

2 is a prime number.   5 is a prime number.

More than one rectangle can be made with a *composite* number of blocks.

4 is a composite number.   12 is a composite number.

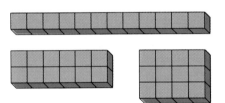

Make as many rectangles as you can for each number. Then copy and complete the chart.

Number	Can you make more than 1 rectangle?	How many rectangles?	Prime or Composite?
1	1 is a special number.		Neither
2	**1.**	**2.**	**3.**
3	**4.**	**5.**	**6.**
9	**7.**	**8.**	**9.**
10	**10.**	**11.**	**12.**
11	**13.**	**14.**	**15.**
15	**16.**	**17.**	**18.**
17	**19.**	**20.**	**21.**
18	**22.**	**23.**	**24.**

Chapter 6 Review/Test

1. Write an addition sentence for this picture.

Write an addition and a multiplication sentence for each picture.

2. ⚬ ⚬ ⚬ ⚬ ⚬ ⚬

3. ◯ ◯ ◯ ◯
◯ ◯ ◯ ◯
◯ ◯ ◯ ◯
◯ ◯ ◯ ◯

Write each product.

4. 3
×5

5. 5
×2

6. 2
×6

7. 7
×2

8. 4
×3

9. 3
×7

10. 5
×4

11. 4
×7

12. 8
×1

13. 1
×9

14. 5
×0

15. 0
×2

16. Which picture can help you find the product for 3 times 4?

a. ★ ★ ★ ★
★ ★ ★ ★

b. ★ ★ ★
★ ★ ★

c. ★ ★ ★
★ ★ ★
★ ★ ★

d. ★ ★ ★ ★
★ ★ ★ ★
★ ★ ★ ★

17. Ramon's aquarium has 2 starfish and 6 guppies. Each starfish has 5 arms. How many arms are there in all?

Read this problem. Then answer the question below.

An ice-cream truck has 4 wheels. If 3 trucks and 4 dogs pass by Jan's house, how many wheels are there in all?

18. Which information is *not* needed to solve the problem?
   a. 4 wheels
   b. 3 trucks
   c. 4 dogs

19. ■ **Write About Math** For the picture you chose in Exercise 16, write a sentence telling how many groups there are and the number in each group.

Multiplication Facts

7

Number-Sense Project

Estimate
Predict how many students in your class have a parent or grandparent who was born as part of a set of twins, quadruplets, or quintuplets.

Gather Data
Find out whether any of your parents or grandparents were part of a set of twins, quadruplets, or quintuplets. Ask an older person in your family, such as a parent or grandparent.

Analyze and Report
Write a summary of the information you collected. Share your findings with other classmates.

Using Order to Multiply with 6 Through 9

Build Understanding

A.

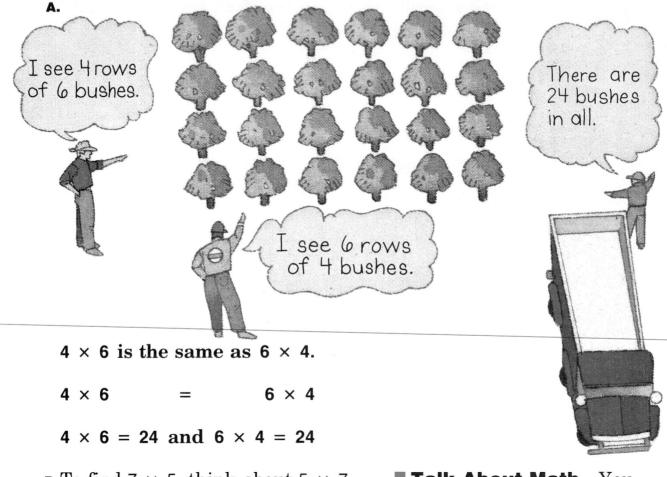

I see 4 rows of 6 bushes.

I see 6 rows of 4 bushes.

There are 24 bushes in all.

4 × 6 is the same as 6 × 4.

4 × 6   =   6 × 4

4 × 6 = 24 and 6 × 4 = 24

B. To find 7 × 5, think about 5 × 7. Count by fives, seven times.

5,   10,   15,   20,   25,   30,   35
  1   2   3   4   5   6   7

5 × 7 = 35 and 7 × 5 = 35

■ **Talk About Math** You can reverse the order of numbers when you multiply. Can you reverse the order when you add? subtract? Explain.

Check Understanding

For another example, see Set A, pages 242–243.

Write two ways to find each product.

1. 8 × 2   **2.** 9 × 3   **3.** 7 × 4   **4.** 6 × 5   **5.** 5 × 8

Practice

For More Practice, see Set A, pages 244–245.

Find each product. **Remember** that you can change
the order of the numbers to help you.

6. 8
    ×4

7. 9
    ×3

8. 6
    ×5

9. 2
    ×8

10. 5
     ×7

11. 9
     ×2

12. 3 × 6   **13.** 4 × 7   **14.** 7 × 3   **15.** 8 × 5   **16.** 5 × 9

17. 7 × 2   **18.** 9 × 4   **19.** 4 × 6   **20.** 3 × 8   **21.** 6 × 2

Mental Math Find each answer.

22. 15 − 6   **23.** 5 × 8   **24.** 9 + 7   **25.** 4 × 5   **26.** 16 − 9

27. 7 + 7   **28.** 3 × 9   **29.** 14 − 6   **30.** 4 × 4   **31.** 7 + 8

32. 13 − 7   **33.** 9 + 7   **34.** 6 × 4   **35.** 15 − 8   **36.** 8 + 6

37. 9 × 4   **38.** 7 + 8   **39.** 17 − 8   **40.** 14 − 7   **41.** 3 × 8

42. 8 + 9   **43.** 16 − 9   **44.** 6 × 3   **45.** 12 − 9   **46.** 5 + 6

47. Number Sense Use repeated addition to find 12 × 3.
Is it easier to add twelve 3s or three 12s?

Problem Solving

Solve each problem.

48. The workers planted 3 rows
of 6 daisies. How many
daisies did they plant?

49. They planted 9 oak and
4 maple trees. How many
trees did they
plant?

50. There is a square foot of land for every
bedding plant. How many square feet
is the area for 5 rows of 8 plants?

Multiplication with 6 Through 9 on the Number Line

Build Understanding

Custom-Designed Fences	
Fence Type	**Section Lengths**
light iron	8 feet
redwood slat	7 feet
stockade	9 feet
heavy iron	6 feet
split rail	10 feet
picket	5 feet

How long is a fence with 5 sections of light iron?

5 × 8 = 40

— number of feet
— number of sections

A fence with 5 sections of light iron is 40 feet long.

■ **Talk About Math** A section of stockade fence is 6 feet high and 9 feet long. Which of the two measures should you use to find how much fencing you need to go around your yard?

Check Understanding

For another example, see Set B, pages 242–243.

1. What is the length of 3 sections of redwood slat fencing?

2. Some **multiples** of 6 are 6, 12, 18, 24, and 30. Give 3 more multiples of 6.

Practice

For More Practice, see Set B, pages 244–245.

Find each product. **Remember** to use a number line if you need it.

3. 4
    ×8

4. 7
    ×3

5. 2
    ×6

6. 8
    ×3

7. 3
    ×9

8. 6
    ×5

9. 5
    ×8

10. 9
    ×2

11. 6
    ×3

12. 9
    ×4

13. 7
    ×5

14. 8
    ×2

15. 4 × 7   16. 6 × 4   17. 9 × 5   18. 7 × 2   19. 3 × 9

Problem Solving

Use the chart on page 222 to solve each problem.

20. How long is a fence with 9 sections of picket boards?

21. How long is a fence with 4 sections of redwood slats?

22. One section of each type of fence is displayed along a wall. How long is the display?

23. The perimeter of a yard is 72 feet. Leaving a 6-foot opening, how much fencing will be needed?

24. How many section lengths of split rail fencing do you need to go around a yard with a perimeter of 80 feet?

25. **Critical Thinking** Would you need more sections of light iron or heavy iron fencing for a fence of 60 feet? Explain.

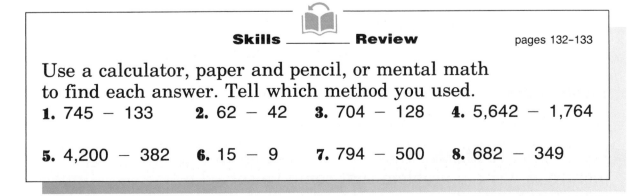

Skills ——— Review   pages 132–133

Use a calculator, paper and pencil, or mental math to find each answer. Tell which method you used.

1. 745 − 133   2. 62 − 42   3. 704 − 128   4. 5,642 − 1,764

5. 4,200 − 382   6. 15 − 9   7. 794 − 500   8. 682 − 349

Choose an Operation

Build Understanding

The Frisbee Club sold Frisbees for $1.00. The amounts collected by the members on Tuesday are shown on the Frisbees below. How much did the boys in the club collect?

PROBLEM SOLVING
GUIDE

Understand
QUESTION
FACTS
KEY IDEA

Plan and Solve
STRATEGY
ANSWER

Look Back
SENSIBLE ANSWER
ALTERNATE APPROACH

BEN $8 DINA $8 KIMI $9 HANK $8 JOSE $8 MARIA $10

Understand There are 3 boys. Each collected $8.

Plan and Solve STRATEGY Choose an operation. Since each boy collected the same amount of money, you can use multiplication to find the answer.

3 × 8 = 24

ANSWER The boys collected $24 dollars.

Look Back Since multiplication is repeated addition, you could use addition to find the answer. 8 + 8 + 8 = 24

■ **Write About Math** Use the information in the picture to write a problem that could be solved by using subtraction.

Check Understanding

Use the picture on page 224. Tell whether you *add*, *subtract*, or *multiply*. Then find each answer.

1. How much did Kimi and Dina collect?

2. How much more did Maria collect than José?

3. Estimation Tell how you could estimate the total amount collected on Tuesday.

Practice

	Ben	Dina	Kimi	Hank	Jose	Maria	Total
Monday	$0	$3	$9	$2	$10	$1	▦
Tuesday	$8	$8	$9	$8	$8	$10	$51
Wednesday	$3	$5	$9	$0	$15	$6	$38
Total	$11	$16	▦	$10	$33	$17	▦

Use the chart to solve each problem. Tell whether you *add, subtract,* or *multiply*. Then find each answer.

4. How much did Kimi collect in all?

5. How much was collected on Monday?

6. How much more did José collect on Wednesday than on Tuesday?

7. How much more was collected on Tuesday than on Monday?

Choose a ——— Strategy

What's the Difference?

8. Find two digits with a sum of 9, a product of 8, and a difference of 7.

Square Products

Build Understanding

Shapely Numbers
Materials: Cubes
Groups: 4 students

Beth and Lia were using cubes to make different designs. Some designs formed squares. They noticed a pattern.

There are some numbers that are called *square products.* Can you tell why?

a. Look at the arrays in the picture. Write a multiplication fact for each.

b. Make arrays to show 6 × 6, 7 × 7, 8 × 8, and 9 × 9. What are the products?

c. What shape is formed by each of the arrays?

d. Make arrays to show 6 × 5, 7 × 4, and 3 × 8. What are the products?

e. What shape is formed by these new arrays?

■ **Write About Math** Using 36 objects, make as many different arrays as you can. Write the multiplication fact for each. Tell which factors make squares and which make rectangles.

Check Understanding

For another example, see Set C, pages 242–243.

1. List the square products for the factors 1 through 9.

2. **Number Sense** You know that 4 × 8 = 32. How can you use this to help you find 8 × 8?

Practice

For More Practice, see Set C, pages 244–245.

Find each product.

3. 4
  ×4

4. 8
  ×8

5. 3
  ×3

6. 7
  ×7

7. 6
  ×6

8. 9
  ×9

9. 5
  ×5

10. 2
  ×2

11. 0
  ×0

12. 1
  ×1

13. 8
  ×8

14. 4
  ×4

15. 2 × 2

16. 0 × 0

17. 5 × 5

18. 1 × 1

19. 10 × 10

20. 8 × 8

21. 3 × 3

22. 9 × 9

23. 6 × 6

24. 7 × 7

Mixed Practice   Find each answer.

25. 9 × 5

26. 3 × 8

27. 5 × 5

28. 2 × 6

29. 7 × 4

30. 8 × 4

31. 7 × 3

32. 9 × 9

33. 5 × 6

34. 3 × 3

Problem Solving

Critical Thinking   Solve each problem.

35. Make arrays to help you find the next two numbers in this pattern.

2   4   8   16   32   ▦   ▦

36. Write a multiplication fact in which the product is two times the product in the fact 3 × 9 = 27. Explain your thinking.

Midchapter ✓ **Checkup**

Find each product.
1. 4 × 8
2. 9 × 9
3. 9 × 5
4. 6 × 6
5. 3 × 8

Tell whether you *add, subtract,* or *multiply.*
6. There are 25, 13, and 37 cards in boxes. How many cards are there in all?

7. Kiri tiled a floor. She used 8 tiles in each of 8 rows. How many tiles did she use?

Visual-Thinking Activity

Which photo did Natalia take?

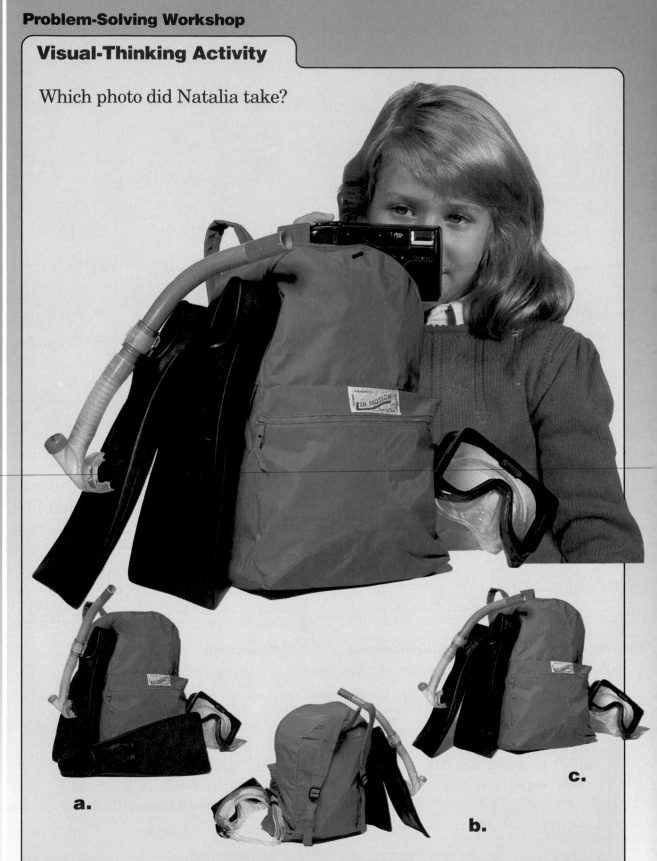

a.

b.

c.

Explore as a Team

1. Use grid paper to draw a secret rectangle. Make each side between 2 and 9 squares long.

2. Cover a part of your rectangle with another piece of paper, hiding parts of two sides of your rectangle.

3. Take turns showing the uncovered part of your rectangles to the rest of your team. Then they can try to figure out how many squares are in the whole rectangle.

TIPS FOR
WORKING TOGETHER
When you are unsure, ask someone in your group for help or say you don't understand.

Explore with a Computer

For this activity use the *Geometry Workshop Project.*

1. Use the **Measure** menu to find the perimeter and area of the rectangle.

2. Use the **Stretch** option to make a different rectangle. Estimate the change in the perimeter and area. Then use the **Measure** menu to check your estimates.

3. Try to stretch the rectangle to make the number of units for the perimeter and the area the same.

Number-Sense Project

Mr. Wong gives each child in his class 8 sheets of colored paper. Does he need more for the Ruiz twins or for the McMahon triplets?

Using Tens to Multiply with 9

Build Understanding

Origami is the Japanese art of folding paper into decorative objects. Suki is making each of her 9 friends a bouquet of 7 origami flowers. How many flowers will Suki make?

Since she plans to give each friend the same number of flowers, she could multiply.

Suki knows that 10 × 7 is 70.
So 9 × 7 is 7 less than 70.

Washi is a thin, Japanese paper that is especially good for the art of origami.

70 − 7 = 63

10 × 7

9 × 7
9 × 7 = 63

Suki will give away 63 flowers.

■ **Talk About Math**   Tell how you can use tens to find 9 × 9.

Check Understanding

For another example, see Set D pages 242–243.

Mental Math   Find each product.

1. How much less than 10 × 8 is 9 × 8?   Find 9 × 8.

2. Complete: 6 × 10 = 60, so 6 × 9 = 60 − ▦.   Find 6 × 9.

Practice

For More Practice, see Set D pages 244–245.

Find each product.

3. $\begin{array}{r} 9 \\ \times 2 \\ \hline \end{array}$ **4.** $\begin{array}{r} 7 \\ \times 9 \\ \hline \end{array}$ **5.** $\begin{array}{r} 9 \\ \times 6 \\ \hline \end{array}$ **6.** $\begin{array}{r} 9 \\ \times 9 \\ \hline \end{array}$ **7.** $\begin{array}{r} 5 \\ \times 9 \\ \hline \end{array}$ **8.** $\begin{array}{r} 9 \\ \times 8 \\ \hline \end{array}$

9. 3×9 **10.** 9×1 **11.** 7×9 **12.** 0×9 **13.** 9×9

14. 5×9 **15.** 9×8 **16.** 6×9 **17.** 9×2 **18.** 9×4

Mental Math   Find each answer.

19. $17 - 9$ **20.** 5×5 **21.** $9 + 6$ **22.** $4 + 8$ **23.** $11 - 3$

24. 4×7 **25.** 7×2 **26.** $12 - 6$ **27.** 3×9 **28.** $8 + 5$

Problem Solving

Draw a picture to help you solve each problem.

29. Suki gave each of her 3 friends 2 pink origami flowers and 4 yellow origami flowers. How many flowers did she give to her friends in all?

30. In Poland, like Japan, paper is folded then cut to make beautiful designs. Sebastian made 10 designs. He made 10 cuts for each design. How many cuts did he make in all?

TIPS FOR PROBLEM SOLVERS

Visualize the problem in your mind to help you understand it better.

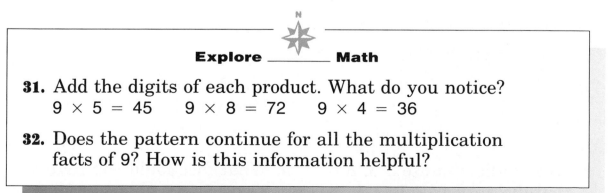

Explore ——— Math

31. Add the digits of each product. What do you notice?
$9 \times 5 = 45$ $9 \times 8 = 72$ $9 \times 4 = 36$

32. Does the pattern continue for all the multiplication facts of 9? How is this information helpful?

The Last Three Facts:
6 × 7, 6 × 8, 7 × 8

Build Understanding

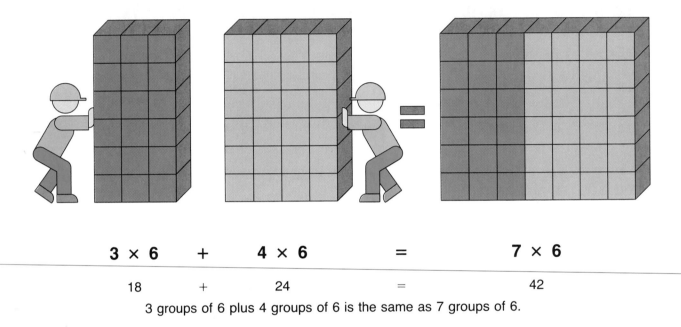

3 × 6	+	4 × 6	=	7 × 6
18	+	24	=	42

3 groups of 6 plus 4 groups of 6 is the same as 7 groups of 6.

$$7 \times 6 = 42$$

■ **Write About Math**   Draw arrays to show two smaller facts that you could use to find 7 × 8.

Check Understanding

For another example, see Set E, pages 242–243.

Number Sense   Answer each question.

1. Which is greater, 4 × 6 or 5 × 6? How much greater? Explain your thinking.

2. Which is less, 7 × 5 or 8 × 5? How much less? Explain your thinking.

3. Explain how to use 3 × 8 to find the answer to 6 × 8.

4. What fact could you find using 5 × 9 plus 4 × 9?

Practice

For More Practice, see Set E, pages 244–245.

ALGEBRA Copy and complete each table.

	× 6			× 7			× 8			× 9
5.	1		**15.**	6		**25.**	2		**35.**	5	
6.	6		**16.**	1		**26.**	9		**36.**	2	
7.	3		**17.**	0		**27.**	4		**37.**	8	
8.	8		**18.**	5		**28.**	7		**38.**	1	
9.	9		**19.**	8		**29.**	0		**39.**	6	
10.	2		**20.**	2		**30.**	3		**40.**	9	
11.	7		**21.**	4		**31.**	1		**41.**	0	
12.	4		**22.**	7		**32.**	6		**42.**	4	
13.	0		**23.**	3		**33.**	8		**43.**	7	
14.	5		**24.**	9		**34.**	5		**44.**	3	

Complete each number sentence.

45. $6 \times \blacksquare = 42$ **46.** $\blacksquare \times 9 = 63$ **47.** $\blacksquare \times 8 = 48$

Mixed Practice Use a calculator, paper and pencil, or mental math to find each answer. Tell which method you used.

48.
$$\begin{array}{r} 521 \\ -\ 70 \\ \hline \end{array}$$

49.
$$\begin{array}{r} 48 \\ -31 \\ \hline \end{array}$$

50.
$$\begin{array}{r} 7 \\ \times 9 \\ \hline \end{array}$$

51.
$$\begin{array}{r} 231 \\ +4{,}160 \\ \hline \end{array}$$

52.
$$\begin{array}{r} 9 \\ \times 3 \\ \hline \end{array}$$

53.
$$\begin{array}{r} 6{,}007 \\ -\ 985 \\ \hline \end{array}$$

54.
$$\begin{array}{r} 4 \\ \times 4 \\ \hline \end{array}$$

55.
$$\begin{array}{r} 936 \\ -846 \\ \hline \end{array}$$

56.
$$\begin{array}{r} 458 \\ +\ 31 \\ \hline \end{array}$$

57.
$$\begin{array}{r} 8 \\ \times 6 \\ \hline \end{array}$$

58. 8×8 **59.** $975 - 620$ **60.** $16 - 7$ **61.** 6×7

62. 1×629 **63.** $27 - 17$ **64.** $86 + 5$ **65.** 0×248

66. $5 + 38$ **67.** 8×3 **68.** 36×1 **69.** $256 + 90$

70. 1 × 9
2 × 9
3 × 9
4 × 9
5 × 9
6 × 9
7 × 9
8 × 9
9 × 9

71. 1 × 99
2 × 99
3 × 99
4 × 99
5 × 99
6 × 99
7 × 99
8 × 99
9 × 99

72. 1 × 999
2 × 999
3 × 999
4 × 999
5 × 999
6 × 999
7 × 999
8 × 999
9 × 999

Use the pattern to write the products.

73. 4 × 9,999

74. 3 × 99,999

75. 5 × 999,999

Problem Solving

Solve each problem.

76. While at camp, Arthur is reading a 360-page book. He has read 88 pages of the book. How many pages does he have left to read?

77. In a craft session, Carla made a button doll. She used 3 cards of buttons. Each card had 8 buttons. How many buttons did Carla use?

78. The chart shows the number of Calories in the breakfast foods served at camp. Jane had milk, cereal, and juice. How many Calories were in Jane's breakfast?

Food	Calories
milk	90
juice	85
toast	95
cereal	195
egg	125

79. Timmy, Mike, Yoshi, and Will are going to summer camp for 2 weeks. Each boy will bring 5 shirts to camp. How many shirts will the 4 friends bring to camp in all?

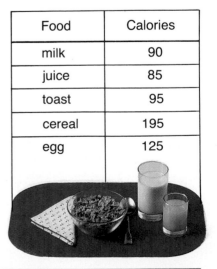

Use Data   Use the chart on page 222 to solve this problem.

80. Carey bought 9 sections of redwood slat fencing and a 9-foot gate to put around his yard. What is the perimeter of the yard?

Choose a _____ Strategy

Bead Necklaces   These necklaces are shaped like triangles. Answer the questions below to find how many beads will be on each side of the sixth necklace and how many beads there will be in the sixth necklace.

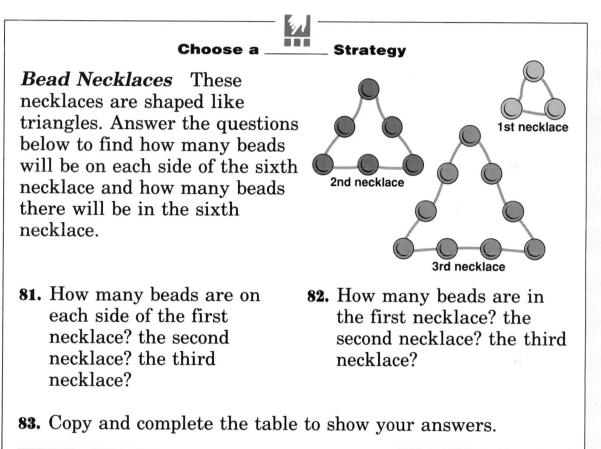

1st necklace

2nd necklace

3rd necklace

81. How many beads are on each side of the first necklace? the second necklace? the third necklace?

82. How many beads are in the first necklace? the second necklace? the third necklace?

83. Copy and complete the table to show your answers.

Necklace	1st	2nd	3rd
Number of beads on each side	2		
Total number of beads	3		

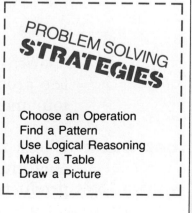

PROBLEM SOLVING
STRATEGIES

Choose an Operation
Find a Pattern
Use Logical Reasoning
Make a Table
Draw a Picture

84. How many beads are on each side of the sixth necklace? How many beads are in the sixth necklace?

Find a Pattern

Build Understanding

Lester found a pattern in the products for multiplication facts for 4. What pattern might he have found?

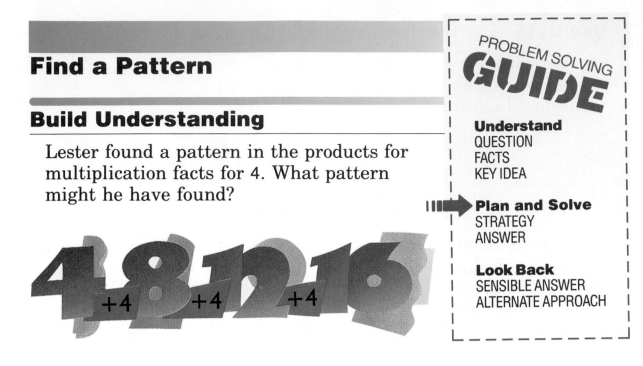

PROBLEM SOLVING
GUIDE

Understand
QUESTION
FACTS
KEY IDEA

||➡ **Plan and Solve**
STRATEGY
ANSWER

Look Back
SENSIBLE ANSWER
ALTERNATE APPROACH

Understand To help find the pattern, you could write the multiplication facts for 4.

1	2	3	4	5	6	7	8	9
×4	×4	×4	×4	×4	×4	×4	×4	×4
4	8	12	16	20	24	28	32	36

||➡ **Plan and Solve** STRATEGY You need to use at least three of the products before you can see if there is a pattern. Look at the products.

To get the second product, add 4.

To get the third product, add 4.

ANSWER The pattern is to add 4. Each number in the products for the multiplication facts for 4 is four more than the number before it.

Look Back Check to see if the pattern continues. Add 4 to each number. Do your answers match the products for the facts of 4?

■ **Talk About Math** In what other ways could you find patterns?

Check Understanding

Look at the ones digit for the products of the following pairs of facts for 4. What do you notice?

1. 1×4 and 6×4 **2.** 2×4 and 7×4 **3.** 3×4 and 8×4

4. Look at the ones digit for the product of 5×4. What should the ones digit for the product of 10×4 be?

5. What is the pattern made by the ones digits in the facts of 4?

Practice

Do Problems 6–8 to find patterns in the multiplication facts for 3, 6, and 8. (Do not use 0 as a factor.)

6. Write the multiplication facts for 3, 6, and 8 in order.

7. For each set of facts, add the digits in each product until you get a one-digit sum.

8. For each set of facts, find the pattern in the sums.

9. Find the pattern made by the sum of the digits in each product of the facts for 9.

10. Critical Thinking If Friday was March 2, what would be the dates of the next 3 Fridays?

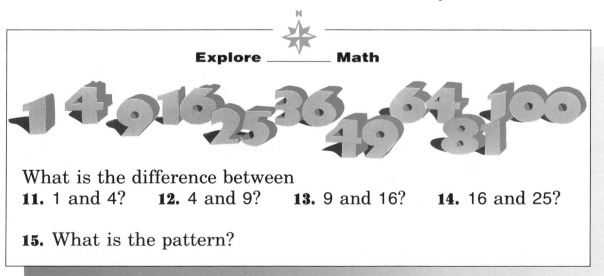

Explore ———— Math

What is the difference between
11. 1 and 4?   **12.** 4 and 9?   **13.** 9 and 16?   **14.** 16 and 25?

15. What is the pattern?

Using Multiplication

Build Understanding

Block Tower
Materials: Cubes
Groups: 4 students

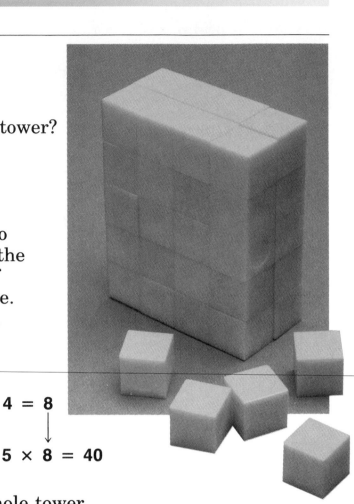

How many cubes are in this tower?

Make the tower. Each layer has 2 rows with 4 cubes in each row. Make 5 layers.

You can use multiplication to find how many cubes are in the tower because the number of cubes in each row is the same. Also, the number of cubes in each layer is the same.

Find $2 \times 4 \times 5$.

First, find the number of cubes in one layer.

$$2 \times 4 = 8$$

Then multiply this answer by the number of layers.

$$5 \times 8 = 40$$

There are 40 cubes in the whole tower.

■ **Talk About Math** Numbers can be multiplied in any order. What would be the best order in which to multiply $2 \times 9 \times 5$? What is the product?

Check Understanding

For another example, see Set F, pages 242–243.

Use cubes or multiplication to find how many in all.

1. Each layer has 2 rows with 3 blocks in each row. Make 7 layers.

2. Each layer has 5 rows with 2 blocks in each row. Make 3 layers.

238

Tell how many layers, how many rows in each layer, and how many in each row. Then find the product.

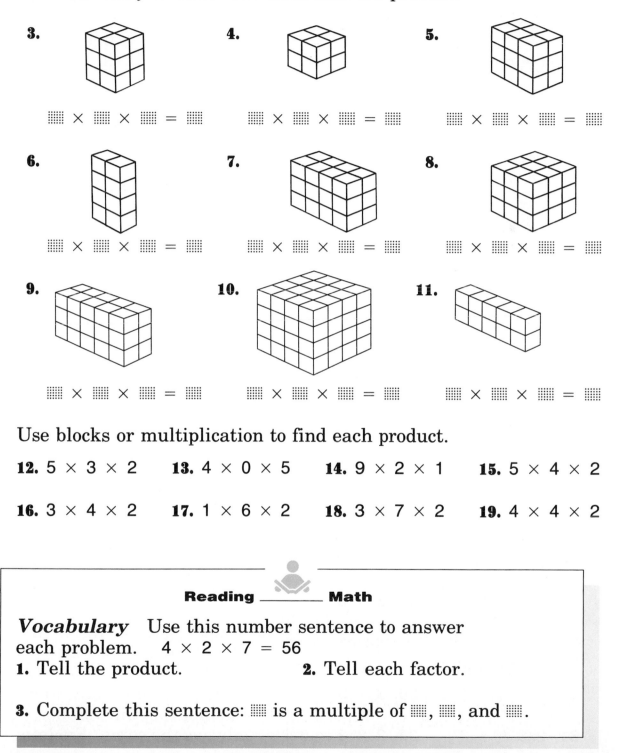

3.

▦ × ▦ × ▦ = ▦

4.

▦ × ▦ × ▦ = ▦

5.

▦ × ▦ × ▦ = ▦

6.

▦ × ▦ × ▦ = ▦

7.

▦ × ▦ × ▦ = ▦

8.

▦ × ▦ × ▦ = ▦

9.

▦ × ▦ × ▦ = ▦

10.

▦ × ▦ × ▦ = ▦

11.

▦ × ▦ × ▦ = ▦

Use blocks or multiplication to find each product.

12. $5 \times 3 \times 2$ **13.** $4 \times 0 \times 5$ **14.** $9 \times 2 \times 1$ **15.** $5 \times 4 \times 2$

16. $3 \times 4 \times 2$ **17.** $1 \times 6 \times 2$ **18.** $3 \times 7 \times 2$ **19.** $4 \times 4 \times 2$

Reading ———— Math

Vocabulary Use this number sentence to answer each problem. $4 \times 2 \times 7 = 56$

1. Tell the product.   **2.** Tell each factor.

3. Complete this sentence: ▦ is a multiple of ▦, ▦, and ▦.

Write two ways to find each product.

1. 5 × 3   **2.** 8 × 2

Find each product.

3. 6
×3

4. 5
×9

5. 8
×5

6. 4
×8

7. 6
×2

8. 4
×6

9. 6
×6

10. 0
×0

11. 9
×3

12. 7
×6

13. 6
×8

14. 7
×8

15. 9 × 9   **16.** 5 × 5

17. 5 × 6   **18.** 9 × 2

19. 7 × 5   **20.** 8 × 3

21. 0 × 9   **22.** 7 × 9

23. 4 × 4   **24.** 4 × 9

25. 3 × 7   **26.** 7 × 7

27. 9 × 8   **28.** 8 × 6

Use blocks or multiplication to find each product.

29. 6 × 4 × 1   **30.** 3 × 0 × 4

31. 2 × 5 × 3   **32.** 2 × 3 × 6

Solve each problem.

33. A number is greater than 350 and less than 400. Its tens digit is 4 times its ones digit. What is the number?

34. Would you use inches or feet to measure a shade for your bedroom window?

35. Each of the Tao quadruplets has 8 hats. How many hats do they have in all?

36. Would it take more postcards or math books to cover your classroom floor? Why?

37. Write the next 3 numbers in the pattern. Describe it using multiplication and using addition.
6, 12, 18, 24, . . .

38. **Data File** Use data from pages 248–249. Jane is making a double-size recipe of baked rice pudding. How much of each ingredient should she use?

39. **Make a Data File** Count the Mondays between July 15 and December 15 on this year's and another year's calendar. Is the number always the same? Explain.

Chapter 7 REVIEW

Tell if each number is even or odd.

1. 54　　　**2.** 67　　　**3.** 82　　　**4.** 25　　　**5.** 99　　　**6.** 48

Write the number in standard form.

7. three hundred two　　　　　　　**8.** fifty-seven

9. four thousand, thirteen　　　　**10.** two hundred six thousand, five

Find each sum or difference.

11. 37 + 19	**12.** 65 + 24	**13.** 75 + 18	**14.** 53 + 38
15. 58 − 29	**16.** 92 − 36	**17.** 31 − 14	**18.** 83 − 45
19. 1,567 + 1,919	**20.** 2,686 + 4,402	**21.** 524 − 333	**22.** 463 − 291

Complete each sentence.

23. There are ▦ inches in 1 foot.　**24.** There are ▦ feet in 1 yard.

25. There are ▦ centimeters in 1 meter.　**26.** There are ▦ meters in 1 kilometer.

Find each answer.

27. 3 × 5	**28.** 5 × 8	**29.** 3 × 6	**30.** 9 × 3	**31.** 4 × 3	**32.** 7 × 4
33. 0 × 5	**34.** 4 × 1	**35.** 1 × 8	**36.** 6 × 5	**37.** 4 × 9	**38.** 9 × 8
39. 7 × 6	**40.** 8 × 7	**41.** 5 × 9	**42.** 4 × 8	**43.** 9 × 9	**44.** 6 × 6

Reteaching

Set A pages 220–221

To find 8 × 4, think about 4 × 8.
Count by fours, eight times.

4, 8, 12, 16, 20, 24, 28, 32
1 2 3 4 5 6 7 8

4 × 8 = 32 and 8 × 4 = 32

Remember that you can reverse the order of the numbers when you multiply.

1. 5
×8

2. 9
×3

3. 7
×6

Set B pages 222–223

One section of fence is 7 feet long. How long is a fence with 4 sections? Use a number line.

4 × 7 = 28
— number of feet
— number of sections

Remember to use the number line if you need help to find a product. Find each product.

1. 5
×7

2. 9
×3

3. 6
×4

4. 3
×8

5. 5
×6

6. 9
×5

Set C pages 226–227

You can make a square array to show 4 × 4. So 4 × 4 is a square product.

Fact: 4 × 4 = 16

Remember that any number multiplied by itself is a square product.

1. 5
×5

2. 8
×8

3. 9
×9

Set D pages 230–231

This array shows how to use tens to find 9 × 6.

10 × 6 = 60

9 × 6 = 54

Remember that 9 × 9 is 9 less than 10 × 9 and that 9 × 8 is 8 less than 10 × 8. Find each product.

1. 9
×3

2. 9
×5

3. 9
×7

4. 4 × 9

5. 9 × 6

6. 9 × 0

Set E pages 232–235

Draw arrays to show two number facts that you can use to find 6 × 8.

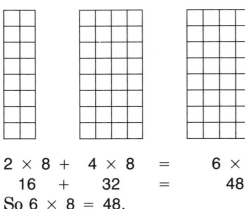

2 × 8 + 4 × 8 = 6 × 8
  16   +   32   =   48
So 6 × 8 = 48.

Remember that you can also use the doubling method to find 6 × 8. You would use (3 × 8) + (3 × 8). Copy and complete each table.

	×	7			×	8
1.	4	▦	**6.**	5	▦
2.	8	▦	**7.**	7	▦
3.	6	▦	**8.**	3	▦
4.	0	▦	**9.**	9	▦
5.	3	▦	**10.**	4	▦

Set F pages 238–239

These blocks show that
    4 × 2 × 3 = 24.

Number of blocks in one layer:

    4 × 2 = 8

Multiply this answer by the number of layers.

    3 × 8 = 24

Remember that you can change the order of the numbers to make the multiplication easier.

Tell how many layers, how many rows in each layer, and how many in each row. Then find the product.

1.

2.

▦ × ▦ × ▦ = ▦   ▦ × ▦ × ▦ = ▦

3.

4.

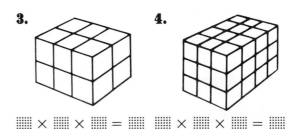

▦ × ▦ × ▦ = ▦   ▦ × ▦ × ▦ = ▦

243

More Practice

Set A   pages 220–221

Find each product. Use the order property to help you.

1. 7	**2.** 3	**3.** 6	**4.** 9	**5.** 8	**6.** 8
×5	×8	×7	×5	×9	×6

7. 2 × 9   **8.** 5 × 6   **9.** 7 × 4   **10.** 6 × 3   **11.** 9 × 4

Mental Math   Find each answer.

12. 14 − 8   **13.** 7 + 5   **14.** 8 × 3   **15.** 15 − 9   **16.** 9 + 9

17. 4 + 8   **18.** 5 × 5   **19.** 7 × 2   **20.** 9 × 3   **21.** 17 − 8

Set B   pages 222–223

1. 4	**2.** 8	**3.** 4	**4.** 7	**5.** 6	**6.** 9
×6	×5	×9	×2	×5	×5

7. 6 × 3   **8.** 7 × 4   **9.** 8 × 3   **10.** 3 × 9   **11.** 5 × 7

Set C   pages 226–227

Find each product.

1. 6	**2.** 3	**3.** 1	**4.** 5	**5.** 2	**6.** 9
×6	×3	×1	×5	×2	×9

7. 8 × 8   **8.** 4 × 4   **9.** 7 × 7   **10.** 9 × 9   **11.** 6 × 6

Set D   pages 230–231

Find each product.

1. 9	**2.** 3	**3.** 9	**4.** 9	**5.** 8	**6.** 6
×4	×9	×1	×2	×9	×9

7. 9 × 7   **8.** 0 × 9   **9.** 9 × 3   **10.** 9 × 9   **11.** 9 × 5

Mental Math   Find each answer.

12. 13 + 8   **13.** 14 − 8   **14.** 8 × 8   **15.** 15 − 9   **16.** 3 × 7

17. 4 × 6   **18.** 5 × 3   **19.** 6 + 9   **20.** 8 × 5   **21.** 12 − 5

Set E   pages 232–235

Copy and complete each table.

	×	6
1.	5	▦
2.	2	▦
3.	7	▦
4.	9	▦
5.	8	▦

	×	7
6.	9	▦
7.	0	▦
8.	5	▦
9.	8	▦
10.	7	▦

	×	8
11.	2	▦
12.	6	▦
13.	3	▦
14.	8	▦
15.	9	▦

	×	9
16.	3	▦
17.	8	▦
18.	1	▦
19.	7	▦
20.	6	▦

Mixed Practice Use a calculator, paper and pencil, or mental math to find each answer. Tell which method you used.

21. $\begin{array}{r} 346 \\ -\ 81 \\ \hline \end{array}$
22. $\begin{array}{r} 483 \\ +5{,}316 \\ \hline \end{array}$
23. $\begin{array}{r} 68 \\ -34 \\ \hline \end{array}$
24. $\begin{array}{r} 7 \\ \times 6 \\ \hline \end{array}$
25. $\begin{array}{r} 37 \\ +23 \\ \hline \end{array}$

26. $610 - 395$
27. 9×9
28. $17 - 9$
29. $76 + 6$

Set F   pages 238–239

Tell how many layers, how many rows in each layer, and how many in each row.

1.
▦ × ▦ × ▦ = ▦

2.
▦ × ▦ × ▦ = ▦

3.
▦ × ▦ × ▦ = ▦

4.
▦ × ▦ × ▦ = ▦

5.
▦ × ▦ × ▦ = ▦

6.
▦ × ▦ × ▦ = ▦

Use blocks or multiplication to find each product.

7. $6 \times 2 \times 2$
8. $8 \times 3 \times 1$
9. $9 \times 3 \times 0$
10. $2 \times 9 \times 5$

Enrichment

Multiplying with Greater Numbers

You can use multiplication facts and what you know about place value to multiply greater numbers.

Here is how Pete found 7×14.

He thought of 14 as $10 + 4$.

Then he multiplied 7×10 and 7×4.

He added the products to find 7×14.

$$7 \times 10 = 70$$
$$7 \times 4 = \underline{28}$$

Add

$$98$$

$$7 \times 14 = 98$$

Find each product.

1. 8×12 **2.** 6×18 **3.** 5×16 **4.** 4×19 **5.** 7×13

6. 9×14 **7.** 3×17 **8.** 8×15 **9.** 7×16 **10.** 6×12

Copy and complete the multiplication table.

	×	0	1	2	3	4	5	6	7	8	9	10	11	12
11.	0													
12.	1													
13.	2													
14.	3													
15.	4													
16.	5													
17.	6													
18.	7													
19.	8													
20.	9													
21.	10													
22.	11													
23.	12													

Chapter 7 Review/Test

1. A section of fence is 6 feet long.

1 section of fence

Feet 1 2 3 4 5 6

Which product shows the length of 4 sections of the fence?

a. 4 × 7   **b.** 6 × 4   **c.** 4 × 8

Find each product.

2. 6
   × 3

3. 6
   × 6

4. 8
   × 6

5. 7
   × 5

6. 9
   × 7

7. 8
   × 8

8. 6
   × 7

9. 7
   × 8

10. 9
    × 9

11. 6
    × 9

12. 8
    × 9

13. 9
    × 2

14. Write the multiplication facts for 8 in order, starting with 0 × 8. What pattern is made by the ones digits?

15. How many layers? How many rows? How many in each row? How many in all?

▦ × ▦ × ▦ = ▦

Tell whether you would add, subtract, or multiply to solve each problem.

16. A laundromat has 3 rows of dryers. There are 5 dryers in each row. How many dryers are there in all?

17. Carlos has 3 model airplanes, 2 model spaceships, 4 model helicopters, and 1 model space station. How many models does he have in all?

18. All of the neighborhood children are having a bicycle parade. If there are 8 rows and 5 children in each row, how many are riding in all?

19. Solve Problem 18.

20. ■ **Write About Math**
Write the next two numbers in this pattern. Explain how you found the missing numbers.
4 9 16 25 ▦ ▦

Data File

1. Mileage Guide
Read across the row and down the column to find the distance in miles between two cities.

2. Chart
The chart shows the seven longest rivers in the world.

3. Bus Schedule
This bus takes passengers to the train station.

4. Recipe Card
This is a recipe for rice pudding.

5. Recipe Card
This is a recipe for making bread modeling dough.

1. NILE (Africa)
   4,000 miles (6,437 km)

2. MISSOURI-MISSISSIPPI (United States)
   3,968 miles (6,420 km)

3. AMAZON RIVER (South America)
   3,900 miles (6,276 km)

4. OB RIVER (Russia)
   3,200 miles (5,149 km)

5. YANGTZE KIANG (China)
   3,100 miles (4,988 km)

6. AMUR RIVER (Eastern Asia)
   2,900 miles (4,667 km)

7. CONGO RIVER (Africa)
   2,900 miles (4,667 km)

2. River Chart

	Los Angeles	Santa Barbara	Palm Springs	San Diego	Anaheim	San Francisco	Las Vegas
Los Angeles	0						
Santa Barbara	97	0					
Palm Springs	105	206	0				
San Diego	121	225	149	0			
Anaheim	29	105	88	90	0		
San Francisco	387	334	573	497	403	0	
Las Vegas	269	387	273	330	295	676	0

1. Mileage Guide

248

ROUTE 602

WEEK DAY MORNING

1 ABBEYWOOD	2 GLEN/LAKE	3 HIGHLAND	4 SALEM	5 SCHAUMBERG	6 WISE	7 ROSELLE STATION	Trains to Chicago TRAIN LEAVES ROSELLE	TRAIN ARRIVES CHICAGO
5:32 A.M.	5:37 A.M.	5:48 A.M.	5:49 A.M.	5:54 A.M.	6:01 A.M.	6:12 A.M.	6:17 A.M.	7:02 A.M.
6:20 A.M.	6:25 A.M.	6:33 A.M.	6:37 A.M.	6:42 A.M.	6:49 A.M.	7:00 A.M.	7:10 A.M.	7:51 A.M.
6:50 A.M.	6:55 A.M.	7:03 A.M.	7:07 A.M.	7:12 A.M.	7:19 A.M.	7:30 A.M.	7:38 A.M.	8:18 A.M.

3. Bus Schedule

5. Recipe Card

4. Recipe Card

BAKED RICE PUDDING

4 eggs   1 cup sugar   1 quart milk
1 teaspoon cinnamon   2 cups cooked rice

2 tablespoons butter

1. Preheat oven to 250 degrees F. butter 9 x 13 inch baking dish.
2. Break eggs into bowl and beat lightly with beater or fork.
3. Measure and add sugar, salt and cinnamon. Beat again.
4. Add milk and rice. Mix together.
5. Pour slowly into baking dish. Dot with butter.
6. Place in oven and bake about $1\frac{1}{2}$ hours. (Use pot holders.)

MAKES 8 SERVINGS

Recipe

BREAD MODELING DOUGH

You Will Need:

2 slices day old white bread

2 tablespoons white household glue

2 drops glycerine

4 drops white vinegar

food coloring or poster paint

How To Make:
Remove crust and break bread into small pieces in a bowl. Add glue, glycerine, and vinegar. Mix with your hands until it isn't sticky. Divide dough and add a few drops of the desired color to each portion. Mix until blended.

How to Use:
Use hand lotion on your hands to keep dough from sticking. Make small objects such as jewelry or flowers. Allow to dry 1 to 2 days. Paint with a mixture of 1 tablespoon white glue and 1 tablespoon of water. Allow to dry, then apply one or two more coats. Bake at 225 degrees, for 4 minutes.

Cumulative Review/Test,

Give the letter for the correct answer.

1. Which number sentence is true?

    A 199 > 202   **C** 225 < 178
    B 211 > 189   **D** 194 < 149

2. Estimate the sum. First round both numbers to the nearest ten.

67 + 11

    A 70   **B** 90   **C** 80   **D** 60

3. Add.

$$\begin{array}{r} 38 \\ +17 \\ \hline \end{array}$$

    A 45
    B 41
    C 55
    D 51

4. Add.

$$\begin{array}{r} 473 \\ +\ 56 \\ \hline \end{array}$$

    A 439
    B 519
    C 429
    D 529

5. Add.

$$\begin{array}{r} 5,914 \\ +\ \ 265 \\ \hline \end{array}$$

    A 5,179
    B 5,779
    C 6,179
    D 6,279

6. Estimate the difference. First round both numbers to the nearest ten.

48 − 36

    A 10   **B** 20   **C** 30   **D** 0

7. Subtract.

$$\begin{array}{r} 682 \\ -\ 38 \\ \hline \end{array}$$

    A 654
    B 644
    C 554
    D 656

8. Subtract.

$$\begin{array}{r} 963 \\ -272 \\ \hline \end{array}$$

    A 791
    B 711
    C 611
    D 691

9. Subtract.

$$\begin{array}{r} 4,208 \\ -1,343 \\ \hline \end{array}$$

    A 2,965
    B 2,165
    C 2,865
    D 3,965

10. Which number sentence should be used to solve the problem?

Mark had 26 pennies. He spent 17 of them. How many pennies did he have left?

    A 26 + 19 = ▦
    B 17 − 15 = ▦
    C 17 + 15 = ▦
    D 26 − 17 = ▦

11. What time is shown on this clock?

    A 9:30
    B 6:45
    C 6:15
    D 7:45

12. Choose the most sensible unit of measure.

Length of a ladder

A Centimeters **C** Kilometers
B Meters **D** Square meters

13. Multiply.

$$\begin{array}{r} 6 \\ \times 5 \\ \hline \end{array}$$

A 11
B 30
C 35
D 25

14. Multiply.

$$\begin{array}{r} 7 \\ \times 9 \\ \hline \end{array}$$

A 63
B 56
C 64
D 16

15. Multiply.

$$\begin{array}{r} 8 \\ \times 6 \\ \hline \end{array}$$

A 64
B 48
C 56
D 42

16. Multiply.

$$\begin{array}{r} 7 \\ \times 7 \\ \hline \end{array}$$

A 81
B 35
C 49
D 45

Solve Problems 17–19.

17. Marta wrote 2 letters. Each was 6 pages long. How many pages did she write in all?

A 10 **B** 16 **C** 6 **D** 12

18. There are 8 chairs around a table. Each chair has 4 legs. How many legs are there in all?

A 32 **B** 24 **C** 12 **D** 36

19. Beth, Carl, Joy, and Rick have backpacks. One is blue, one red, one green, and one orange. Neither Joy nor Carl has the green backpack. Rick's backpack is blue. Joy's backpack is not orange. Who has the orange backpack?

A Beth **B** Carl **C** Joy **D** Rick

Read the problem below. Then answer the question.

A computer instruction book has 5 parts. Each part has 88 pages. How many pages in all are there?

20. Which number sentence would you choose to solve the problem?

A 88 + 5 = ▦
B 88 − 5 = ▦
C 88 × 5 = ▦
D 88 + 88 = ▦

Geometry and Measurement

Did You Know: Food companies usually put the "net weight" on their packages. The "net weight" is the weight of just the contents without the container.

Ketchup

NET WT. 14 OZ. – 397 GRAMS

Bread

ENRICHED BREAD

NET WT. 12 OZ.

Number-Sense Project

Estimate
Estimate the total weight in ounces of each item. Remember that some containers weigh more than others.

Gather Data
Look at containers of different types of food. Find the net weight of each when full. Then estimate the total weight with the container.

Analyze and Report
Make a poster with drawings or cut outs of different items. List the net weight under each item.

ONE HALF GALLON (1.89 *L*)

MILK

CORN FLAKES

PEANUT BUTTER

PEANUT BUT

NET WT. 16 OZ. (1 LB.)

NET WT.
18 OZ. (1 LB. 2 OZ.)
510 g

253

Solid Figures

Build Understanding

A. Shape Up!
Materials: Old magazines and newspapers, scissors, glue, large piece of paper
Groups: Partners

The pictures show solid shapes. They show cylinders, cubes, spheres, and rectangular prisms.

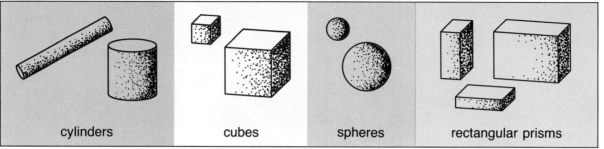

| cylinders | cubes | spheres | rectangular prisms |

a. Look through old magazines and newspapers. Cut out three or four pictures of objects that match each solid shape.

b. Fold a large piece of paper in half. Then fold the paper in half again. Unfold the paper. Write the names of the solid shapes in the 4 sections as shown.

c. Glue each magazine picture in the proper section.

d. Which of the 4 shapes was the hardest to find?

e. Which shape was easiest to find?

f. Why do you think there is more of one shape than another?

B. How many *surfaces,* or sides, does a rectangular prism have?

A rectangular prism has 6 surfaces. Each surface is called a *face.*

When two surfaces meet, they form an *edge.* How many edges does the rectangular prism have?

When three edges meet, they form a *corner.* How many corners does the rectangular prism have?

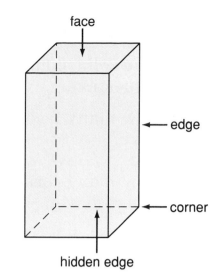

face
edge
corner
hidden edge

■ **Talk About Math**   Which solid shapes have curved or rounded surfaces? Which have only flat surfaces? Which have both flat and curved surfaces?

Check Understanding

Name the shape of each object.
Write *cylinder, cube, sphere,*
or *rectangular prism*.

1.

2.

3.

4.

Practice

Use the solid shapes at the right to answer each question.

5. How many faces does a cube have?

6. How many corners does a sphere have?

7. How many corners does a cylinder have?

8. How many corners does a cube have?

Answer each question.

9. What shape is a baseball?

10. What shape is a brick?

11. What shape is a soup can?

12. What shape is a nickel?

13. What shape is a box of crayons?

14. What shape is a child's block?

15. What shape has only two edges?

16. What shape has only one surface?

Do the pictures show two different views of the same object? Explain your answers.

17.

18.

Problem Solving

Cut out figures like those below. Fold along the dotted lines and try to make solid shapes. Tell which figures can be folded into solid shapes.

19.

20.

21.

22.

23.

Choose a ——— Strategy

City Needs New Tower
Four solid shapes are needed to build the new city tower. A cylinder, a rectangular prism, a sphere, and a cube are needed.

24. Use all four clues below to draw a picture of the new tower.

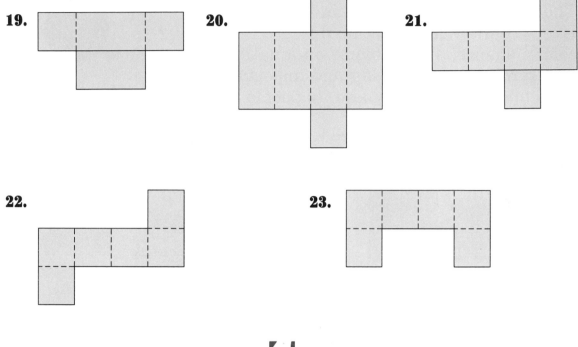

a. The cylinder will not touch the ground.

b. The rectangular prism is not between the cube and the sphere.

c. The cube is under the cylinder and above the rectangular prism.

d. The sphere is above the cylinder.

Geometric Figures

Build Understanding

There are many different kinds of flags. Every country has a national flag. The colors, shapes, and emblems on a national flag symbolize interesting and important facts about the country and its people.

A. Examine these national flags.

circle

triangle

square

rectangle

Haiti

Japan

pentagon

Puerto Rico

Peru

hexagon

a. Name the flags that use the following *geometric figures.*
- a triangle
- a circle

- a rectangle

octagon

b. John designed his own flag using geometric figures. Can you identify the figures that John used?

B. Geometric figures are made of **_curves_** or **_line segments._** Two **_sides,_** or segments, meet at a **_corner_** of a figure.

curves

a. Which geometric figure has no corners?

b. For each geometric figure shown on page 258, count the number of sides. Then count the number of corners.

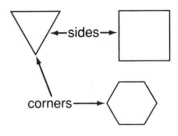

line segments

c. Compare the number of sides to the number of corners for each geometric figure. What do you notice?

■ **Write About Math** Segments and curves can be used to make all kinds of shapes. Draw a shape using only segments, using only curves, using segments and curves.

←sides→

corners→

Check Understanding

For another example, see Set A, pages 288–289.

Use the pictures of the flags to answer Exercises 1–3.

1. What figure is each stripe on the flag of Niger? How many sides and corners does this figure have?

2. What figure is the white part on the flag of the Philippines?

3. What other geometric figure do you see on the flag of Niger?

4. What is the difference between squares and other rectangles?

5. Which has more sides, a pentagon or an octagon?

Niger

Philippines

Give the name of each geometric figure.
Then give the number of sides and corners
each figure has.

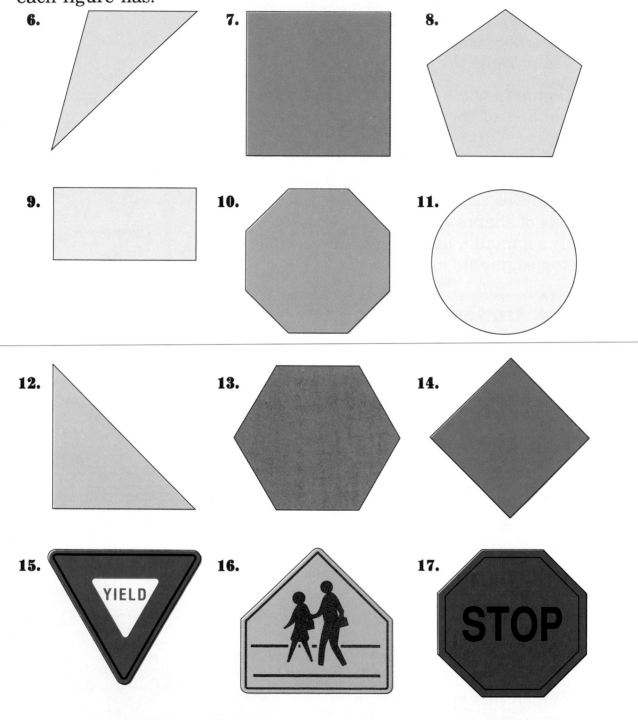

6.

7.

8.

9.

10.

11.

12.

13.

14.

15.

YIELD

16.

17.

STOP

Problem Solving

Make 3 squares. Fold one square to make two triangles. Cut on the fold.

Fold another square to make two rectangles. Cut on the fold. Do not cut the third square.

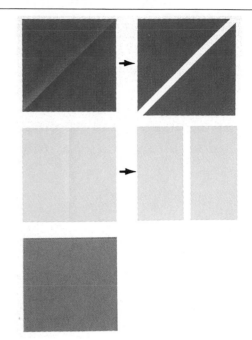

Put two or more figures together to answer Problems 18–21. Be sure to match sides that are the same length.

18. What is the largest triangle you can make?

19. What is the largest square you can make?

20. What is the largest rectangle, not square, you can make?

21. What other geometric figures can you make using any combination of the five figures? Record your work by drawing the new figures on paper.

22. Using your figures from above, create your own flag. You may wish to draw and include geometric figures from page 258.

23. **Use Data** Name the geometric figures that you see in Exercises 4–6 on page 169.

The joined circles of the international Olympic flag represent the people from Africa, Asia, Australia, Europe, and North and South America. The flag of every nation competing in the games has at least one of these colors.

Angles

Build Understanding

A. Two sides of a geometric figure that meet at a corner form an *angle.* The pictures below show angle R, angle S, and angle T.

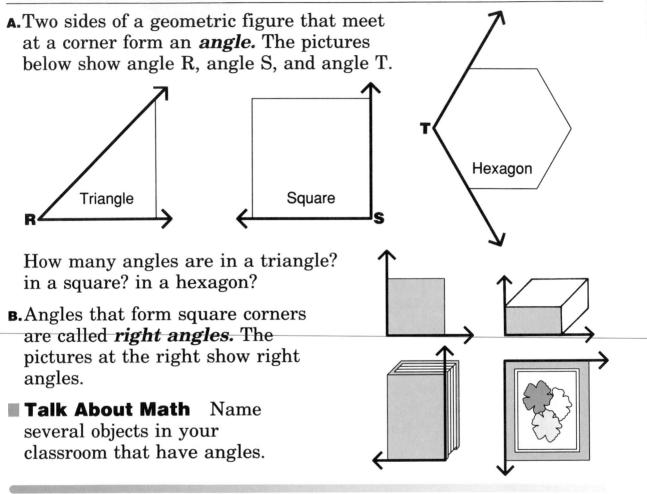

Triangle

Square

T

Hexagon

R

S

How many angles are in a triangle? in a square? in a hexagon?

B. Angles that form square corners are called *right angles.* The pictures at the right show right angles.

■ **Talk About Math** Name several objects in your classroom that have angles.

Check Understanding

For another example, see Set B, pages 288–289.

Can you find an angle on each object? Write *yes* or *no*. Then tell which angles are right angles.

1.   **2.**   **3.**   **4.**

Practice

For More Practice, see Set B, pages 290–291.

How many angles are in each figure? Are
they right angles? Write *yes* or *no*.

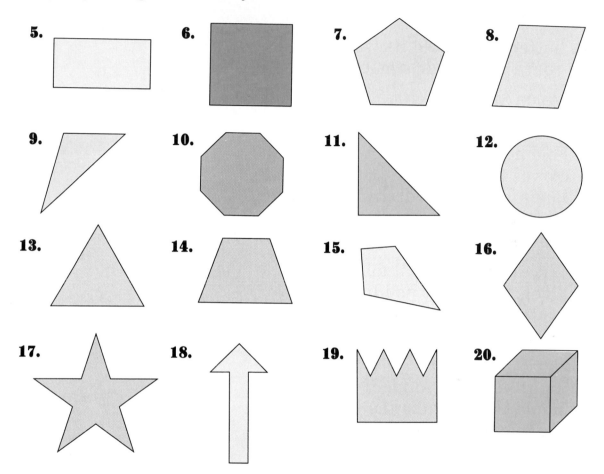

5. **6.** **7.** **8.**

9. **10.** **11.** **12.**

13. **14.** **15.** **16.**

17. **18.** **19.** **20.**

Problem Solving

21. Visual Thinking Name a
time when the hands of a
clock form a right angle.

23. Mental Math Tell two
ways to find the perimeter
of the figure at the right.

22. Draw a figure with 7 angles
and 7 corners.

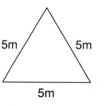

5m 5m

5m

Symmetry

Build Understanding

A butterfly can fold its wings so that the two parts match.

A. Match Making

Materials: Paper, markers, scissors

a. Fold a piece of paper in half. Draw curves to look like a butterfly wing. Begin and end your drawing at the fold. Your paper might look like the one at the right.

b. With the paper still folded, cut along the curves and unfold. Have you made a butterfly with two matching wings?

B. A figure is *symmetric* if you can fold it and make the two parts match. The fold line is the *line of symmetry.*

Make another symmetric figure by folding and cutting.

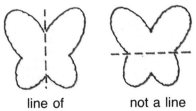

line of
symmetry

not a line
of symmetry

c. Some figures, such as the one at the right, do not have a line of symmetry. Draw a figure that has no line of symmetry.

■ **Talk About Math** How can you tell that the figure in Example C does not have a line of symmetry?

Check Understanding

For another example, see Set C, pages 288–289.

Which line, the red one or the blue one,
shows the line of symmetry? If there is no
line of symmetry, write *none*.

1.   2.   3.

Practice

For More Practice, see Set C, pages 290–291.

Does each figure look symmetric? Write *yes* or *no*.

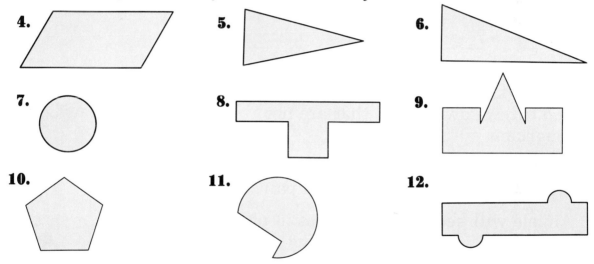

4.   5.   6.

7.   8.   9.

10.   11.   12.

Problem Solving

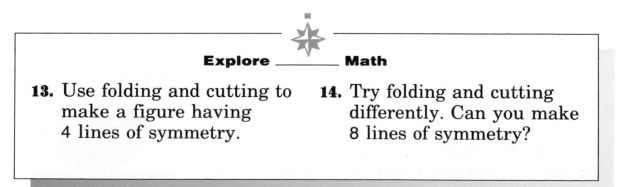

Explore ———— Math

13. Use folding and cutting to
make a figure having
4 lines of symmetry.

14. Try folding and cutting
differently. Can you make
8 lines of symmetry?

Congruence

Build Understanding

A. Angelo's job in the pillow factory is to inspect the pillow pieces. The top and bottom pieces must be exactly the same size and shape.

Figures that have the same size and shape are ***congruent.***

    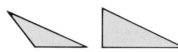

Congruent   Not congruent

B. Angelo keeps pairs of congruent pieces and throws away pairs that are not congruent.

a.

Look at the pairs of pieces in *a*, *b*, and *c*. What will Angelo do with each pair?

Angelo will keep the two pieces in pair *a*. The pieces are the same size and shape. They are congruent.

b.

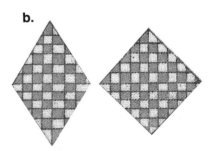

Angelo will throw away the pieces in pair *b*. They are not congruent because they are not the same size and shape.

Angelo will keep the pair of pieces in *c*. They are congruent.

c.

■ **Write About Math** Describe how you can tell that the pieces in *c* are congruent. Describe two ways you can tell that figures are not congruent.

Check Understanding

For another example, see Set D, pages 288–289.

Are the figures congruent? Write *yes* or *no*. Explain.

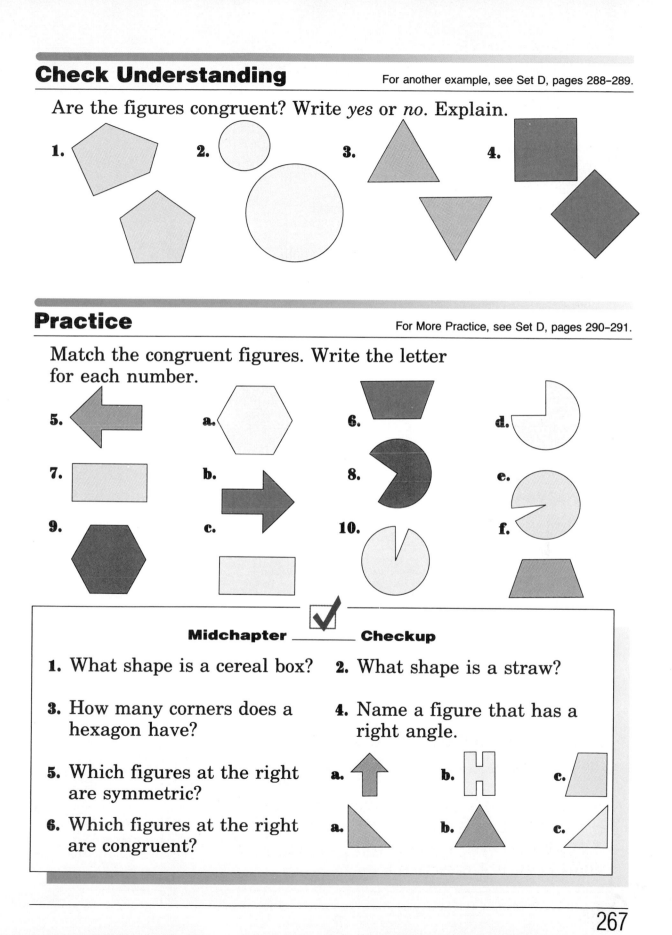

1.

2.

3.

4.

Practice

For More Practice, see Set D, pages 290–291.

Match the congruent figures. Write the letter
for each number.

5.   **a.**   **6.**   **d.**

7.   **b.**   **8.**   **e.**

9.   **c.**   **10.**   **f.**

✓ Midchapter ____ Checkup

1. What shape is a cereal box?   **2.** What shape is a straw?

3. How many corners does a
hexagon have?

4. Name a figure that has a
right angle.

5. Which figures at the right
are symmetric?

a.   **b.**   **c.**

6. Which figures at the right
are congruent?

a.   **b.**   **c.**

Problem Solving WORKSHOP

Explore as a Team

1. Use squares to see how many shapes you can make with 5 squares. They can be called *pentominoes*.
Rule: Squares must share at least one full side with another square.

These are pentominoes.

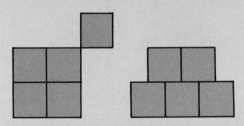

These are not pentominoes.

If one pentomino can fit exactly on another, they are the same.

is the same as

2. Record the pentominoes your group made on grid paper.

3. Guess which pentominoes can be folded into an open box. Check your guess by cutting and folding.

Visual Thinking Activity

The pattern can be folded into the cube shown. Which color is on the bottom?

Number-Sense Project

Look back at pages 252-253.

1. Estimate the net weight of each of the following.

Item	Total Weight	Net Weight
a. Box of cereal	20 oz.	
b. Loaf of bread	25 oz.	
c. Glass jar of strawberry jam	16 oz.	
d. Box of instant gelatin	8 oz.	

2. In writing, tell how total weight is different from net weight.

Explore with a Computer

Use the *Geometry Workshop Project* for this activity. At the computer, you will make lines of symmetry with the figures.

1. Slide, flip, and turn one of the figures. Then move the two figures so the sides that touch make a line of symmetry.

2. How many different ways can you do this?

269

Use Data from a Graph

Build Understanding

The graph tells about the favorite books of Mrs. Gordon's students. Compare Adventure Books and Fairy Tales. How many more students chose Adventure Books?

Understand QUESTION How many more students chose Adventure Books than Fairy Tales?

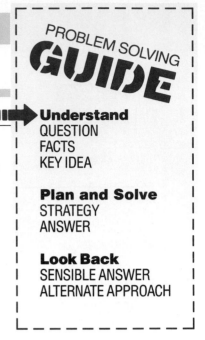

PROBLEM SOLVING
GUIDE

Understand
QUESTION
FACTS
KEY IDEA

Plan and Solve
STRATEGY
ANSWER

Look Back
SENSIBLE ANSWER
ALTERNATE APPROACH

We LOVE to Read!

Frog and Toad Books	📖 📖 📖 📖 📖 📖 📖
Little House Books	📖 📖
Fairy Tales	📖 📖 📖 📖 📖 📖
Mystery Books	📖 📖 📖 📖
Adventure Books	📖 📖 📖 📖 📖 📖 📖 📖 📖

Each 📖 equals one vote

FACTS The right column of the graph tells how many students chose a certain type of book as their favorite. 6 students chose Fairy Tales. 9 children chose Adventure Books.

KEY IDEA The graph shows number information that you can use to compare students' favorite kinds of books.

Plan and Solve Subtract to find how many more.

9 − 6 = 3

3 more students chose Adventure Books as their favorite.

Look Back Did you look in the correct rows to find the numbers?

■ **Talk About Math**   Explain how you can find the number of children in the class if each child had one vote shown on the graph.

Check Understanding

1. How many children liked Mystery Books best?

2. What kind of book was the most popular?

3. Did more students like Frog and Toad Books or Fairy Tales?

4. How many more students chose Fairy Tales than Mystery Books?

Practice

The graph at the right shows how many books some children read for a library contest.

How Many Books Read?								
Shauna	📖	📖	📖	📖	📖			
John	📖	📖	📖	📖				
Lisa	📖	📖						
Karl	📖	📖	📖	📖	📖	📖	📖	📖
Pam	📖	📖						

Each 📖 equals one book.

5. Who read the most books?

6. How many more books did Shauna read than John?

7. Who read 4 more books than John?

8. Which two people read the same number of books?

9. Which children read more books than Lisa?

Choose a 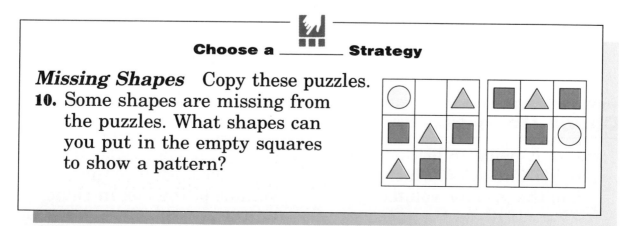 **Strategy**

Missing Shapes   Copy these puzzles.
10. Some shapes are missing from the puzzles. What shapes can you put in the empty squares to show a pattern?

Counting Cubes to Find Volume

Build Understanding

Fill It Up!
Materials: Unit cubes, chalkboard erasers or crayon boxes, empty boxes of various sizes
Groups: 4 students

A. Fill a box with chalkboard erasers or small crayon boxes. Record how many erasers or small boxes you use.

B. The box in the picture holds 2 layers of cubes. Each layer has 6 cubes. The box holds 12 cubes. It holds 12 cubic units.

The number of cubic units something holds is its *volume.* You can say the box has a volume of 12 cubic units.

___
1 Unit   1 Square unit   1 Cubic unit   12 Cubic units

Use unit cubes to show different shapes with a volume of 12 cubic units.

■ **Talk About Math** If you use cubes to measure the volume of the box in Example A, would you need more cubes or more erasers?

Check Understanding

1. Box A holds 16 bricks. Box B holds 12 bricks. Which box has the greater volume?

2. If a box holds exactly 5 rows of 4 cubes, what is the volume of the box in cubic units?

Practice

Find the volume of each solid shape in cubic units.
Remember to watch out for hidden cubes.

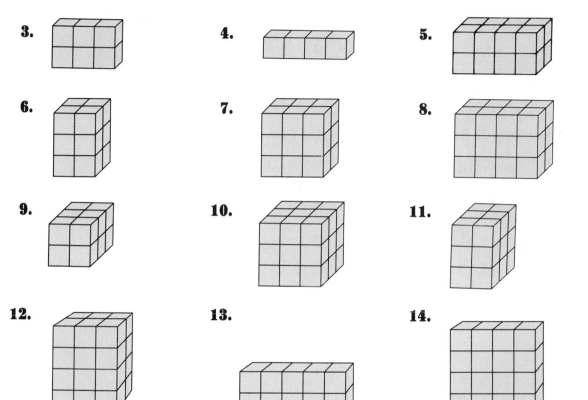

3.

4.

5.

6.

7.

8.

9.

10.

11.

12.

13.

14.

Problem Solving

15. Use cubes to build stacks. The first
layer has 4 cubes. How many cubes
are in a 2-layer stack? a 3-layer
stack? a 7-layer stack?

1 layer   2 layers   3 layers

Use cubes to build shapes like those below.
What is the volume of each?

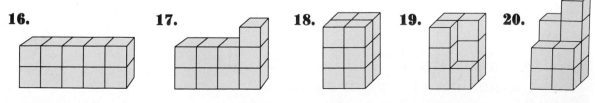

16.   **17.**   **18.**   **19.**   **20.**

Customary Units of Capacity

Build Understanding

Jorge is a baker. To make a cake, he measures liquids. Customary units for measuring liquids are the **cup** (c), the **pint** (pt), the **quart** (qt), and the **gallon** (gal).

Customary units for liquids tell how much liquid a container will hold.

A.

A gallon is 4 quarts.
1 gal = 4 qt

B.

A quart is 2 pints.
1 qt = 2 pt

C.

A pint is 2 cups.
1 pt = 2 c

D.

A drinking glass can hold about 1 cup.

■ **Write About Math**   Tell how you could find the number of cups in a gallon.

Check Understanding

For another example, see Set E, pages 288–289.

Choose the unit of measure you would use
to find how much the container holds.

1. Cereal bowl
cup   quart

2. Bathtub
quart   gallon

3. Watering can
cup   gallon

Choose the more sensible liquid measure
for the container.

4. Sand pail
2 qt   2 gal

5. Auto fuel tank
15 pt   15 gal

6. Flower vase
2 c   2 gal

Practice

For More Practice, see Set E, pages 290–291.

Estimation   Choose the more sensible
customary measure for each.

7. Drinking glass
quart   cup

8. Jug of cider
cup   gallon

9. Cat's water bowl
cup   quart

10. Wading pool
25 pt   25 gal

11. Juice pitcher
2 pt   2 gal

12. Baby bottle
1 c   1 qt

Write *cups*, *pints*, *quarts*, or *gallons* to tell which
you would use to measure how much each holds.

13. Can of soup

14. Washing machine

15. Thermos bottle

Problem Solving

Solve each problem.

16. Jorge needs 6 gallons of
milk. He has 3 one-gallon
containers, 8 one-quart
containers, and 8 one-pint
containers of milk. Does
he need to buy more milk?
Explain.

17. Critical Thinking   You
have 2 empty jars. One jar
holds 8 cups and the other
jar holds 3 cups. How can
you use these jars to
measure 5 cups of water?

Metric Units of Capacity

Build Understanding

Metric units used for measuring liquids are
the *milliliter* (mL) and the *liter* (L).

A. This small spoon holds
about 5 milliliters.

B. This bottle holds
about 1 liter.
A liter is
1,000 milliliters.
1 L = 1,000 mL

■ **Talk About Math**   Which is more, 750 mL
or 750 L? Explain why.

Check Understanding

For another example, see Set F, pages 288–289.

Choose the unit of measure you would use
to find how much the container holds.

1. Bucket

milliliter   liter

2. Water cup in bird cage

milliliter   liter

Choose the more sensible liquid measure
for the container.

3. Flower vase

1 mL   1 L

4. Paper cup

200 mL   200 L

5. Tea kettle

2 mL   2 L

6. Number Sense   Write these liquid measurements
in order from least to greatest.

50 L   5 mL   5 L   50 mL

Practice

For More Practice, see Set F, pages 290–291.

Estimation Choose the more sensible metric measure for each.

7. Wading pool

100 mL   100 L

8. Kitchen sink

20 mL   20 L

9. Thermos jug

3 mL   3 L

10. Liquid soap bottle

80 mL   80 L

11. Fish tank

15 mL   15 L

12. Medicine dropper

1 mL   1 L

Write *liter* or *milliliter* to tell which you would use to measure how much each holds.

13. Bathtub

14. Juice glass

15. Water tower

16. Oil barrel

17. Bottle cap

18. Doll's bottle

19. Swimming pool

20. Soup bowl

21. Gas tank

Reading ———— Math

Vocabulary In each sentence, one word has some missing letters. Copy each of these words and write one letter for each __?__ to complete the word. Use the Glossary at the back of the book if you need help with spelling.

1. The __?__ __?__ r __?__ m e t __?__ r of a figure is the distance around the figure.

2. The number of square units that cover a figure is the __?__ r __?__ a.

3. The number of cubic units that a shape can hold is its __?__ o __?__ um __?__ .

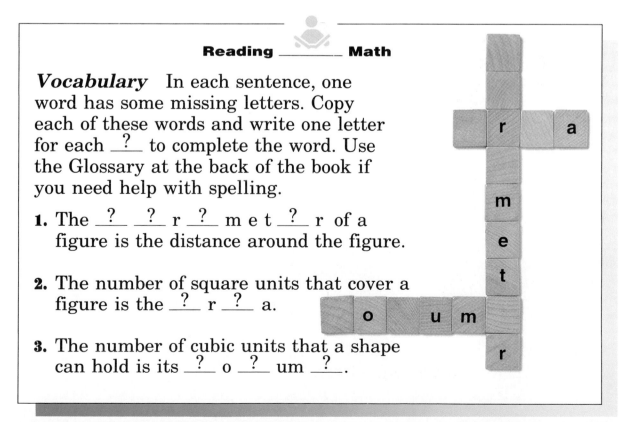

277

Customary Units of Weight

Build Understanding

Mrs. Kennedy is ordering cheese at the deli counter of a grocery store. She tells the clerk how much she needs, and the clerk weighs the cheese. The customary units for measuring weight are the **ounce** (oz) and the **pound** (lb).

A. This slice of cheese for a sandwich weighs about 1 ounce.

B. This loaf of bread weighs about 1 pound. A pound is 16 ounces. 1 lb = 16 oz

■ **Talk About Math** Which is more, 15 ounces or 15 pounds? Explain why.

Check Understanding

For another example, see Set G, pages 288–289.

Should each amount of food pictured be weighed in *ounces* or *pounds*? Write your answer.

1. **2.** **3.** **4.**

Practice

For More Practice, see Set G, pages 290–291.

Estimation Choose the more sensible customary measure for each.

5. Pair of socks

   6 oz   6 lb

6. Football player

   200 oz   200 lb

7. Baby's teddy bear

   8 oz   8 lb

8. Large dog

   70 oz   70 lb

9. Newborn baby

   9 oz   9 lb

10. Bag of potatoes

    5 oz   5 lb

Write *ounces* or *pounds* to tell which you would use to measure how much each weighs.

11. 10 dimes

12. Bookcase

13. 5 dictionaries

14. Pencil

15. 4 nails

16. Bar of soap

Mixed Practice Use the chart at the right to tell which customary measures a store uses to sell each product.

Customary Measures	
Capacity	Weight
Cup Pint Quart Gallon	Ounce Pound

17. Largest container of milk

18. Whole turkey

19. Sliced ham for sandwiches

20. Small drinks of lemonade

21. Frozen Yogurt

Problem Solving

Solve each problem.

22. Frances bought 9 ounces of peanuts and 6 ounces of walnuts. How can you tell if she has enough to make a pound?

23. **Calculator** Mary wants 2 pounds of sliced turkey. The scale reads 17 ounces. How many more ounces does she need?

Metric Units of Mass

Build Understanding

Metric units used for measuring mass are the **gram** (g) and the **kilogram** (kg).

A. A dollar bill has a mass of about 1 gram.

B. A baseball bat has a mass of about 1 kilogram. A kilogram is 1,000 grams.
1 kg = 1,000 g

■ **Talk About Math**   About how many five-dollar bills would it take for your money to weigh 1 kilogram? Explain why.

Check Understanding

For another example, see Set H, pages 288–289.

Should the object in the picture be measured in grams or kilograms?

1.

2.

3.

4.

Practice

For More Practice, see Set H, pages 290–291.

Estimation   Choose the more sensible metric measure for each.

5. Ballpoint pen

    2 g   2 kg

6. Piano

    400 g   400 kg

7. Typewriter

    15 g   15 kg

Write *grams* or *kilograms* to tell which you
would use to measure how much each weighs.

8. Slice of bread

9. Letter

10. Watermelon

11. School bus

12. Bicycle

13. Spoon

14. Toothpicks

15. Car tire

16. 10 grapes

Problem Solving

Number Sense   Solve each problem.

17. Would 2,000 dollar bills weigh more or
less than 1 kilogram?

18. The label on a can of soup shows
251 grams. How many cans could
make 1 kilogram? Tell how you found
your answer.

TIPS FOR
PROBLEM SOLVERS

**Share your thinking
with others.** Explaining
your ideas helps you think
better.

Skills Review   pages 168–169

For Exercises 1–3, tell whether you would use mental math
or paper and pencil. Then find each perimeter.

1. 9 in. / 6 in. / 6 in. / 9 in.

2. 2 m / 3 m / 3 m / 4 m / 4 m / 2 m / 2 m / 10 m

3. 7 ft / 3 ft / 3 ft / 5 ft / 9 ft

Too Little Information

Build Understanding

Katie is making salad for a holiday picnic. She needs to make enough for 16 servings. How many apples should she buy?

IIII➤ **Understand** QUESTION How many apples should she buy?

FACTS The recipe tells you how many cups of diced apples Katie needs for 8 servings.

KEY IDEA If you know the amount for 8 servings, you need to double it for 16 servings.

Plan and Solve Multiply everything in the recipe by 2 to double it.

ANSWER You need 8 cups of diced apples for 16 servings, but you still cannot tell how many apples to buy. The problem does not give you enough information to find out.

Look Back The missing information is the number of cups of diced apples you get from one apple.

■ **Talk About Math** What happens if you don't have enough information to solve a problem?

IIII➤

PROBLEM SOLVING GUIDE

Understand
QUESTION
FACTS
KEY IDEA

Plan and Solve
STRATEGY
ANSWER

Look Back
SENSIBLE ANSWER
ALTERNATE APPROACH

PICNIC APPLE SALAD

4 cups of diced apples

2 cups of plain yogurt

1 teaspoon of lemon juice

1 tablespoon of honey

Mix everything together.
Chill
Makes 8 servings

Check Understanding

Use the recipe for Oh Jay Drink
to answer the following questions.

1. Is there enough information
to make this recipe?

2. What information do you
need?

3. Why are units of measure important?

Practice

Tell how you solve each problem. If there is missing
information, tell where you could find it.

4. Emily wants to make tuna
salad. She needs 18 ounces of
tuna for her recipe. How
many cans should she buy?

5. Tyrone wants to take
16 packages of fruit juice to
the picnic. How many
3-packs of juice should he
buy?

6. Tanya asked the deli clerk
for 3 pounds of potato salad.
The clerk gave her four
8-ounce containers and one
16-ounce container. Did
Tanya get the right amount?

7. Mr. Gomez plans to serve
baked ham at a family party.
The recipe says to bake
1 pound of ham for each
diner. If he buys one ham,
will there be enough for him
and 15 guests?

Estimating Weights and Volumes

Build Understanding

A. About how many cubes do you think it will take to fill the carton?

It takes 10 cubes to fill the carton.
The volume is 10 cubic units.

B. The carrot weighs about 4 ounces. How many carrots do you think it will take to make one pound?

Remember that 16 oz = 1 lb.

4 oz + 4 oz + 4 oz + 4 oz = 16 oz = 1 lb

It will take about 4 carrots to make a pound.

■ **Talk About Math**   Explain what is the same and what is different about estimating volume and estimating weight.

Check Understanding

1. Which is the correct volume for the box, 4 cubic units or 12 cubic units?

2. The banana weighs 8 ounces. About how many bananas will it take to make a pound?

Practice

Is the correct volume shown for each picture? Write *yes* or *no*.

3.

less than 5 cubic units

4.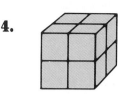

more than 6 cubic units

5.

exactly 8 cubic units

6.

less than 8 cubic units

7.

more than 8 cubic units

8.

exactly 10 cubic units

9.

less than 10 cubic units

10.

exactly 12 cubic units

Tell how many of each object would make about 1 pound.

11. 1-ounce cracker

12. 2-ounce hot dog

13. 8-ounce bunch of grapes

14. 5-ounce tomato

Skills Review

Give the name for each shape. Use *cylinder*, *rectangular prism*, *square*, or *triangle*.

1. Refrigerator

2.

3. How many right angles are in the figure in Exercise 2?

4. Is the figure in Exercise 2 symmetric?

5. Which two figures are congruent?

a.   b.   c.

6. Find the volume in cubic units.

Choose the more sensible measure for each.

7. Juice glass
   1 c   1 qt

8. Juice jug
   4 mL   4 L

9. Bunch of bananas
   2 oz   2 lb

10. Bag of dog food
   4 g   4 kg

11. How many dog biscuits would make about 1 pound?

1 oz

Problem-Solving Review

Solve each problem.

12. Jason built a tower in the shape of a rectangular prism. It was 3 layers high with 4 cubes in the bottom layer. How many cubes did the tower have?

13. Which solid shape has 6 congruent faces?

14. Tell which letters of the alphabet are made with only line segments. Then tell which ones are symmetric.

15. How many cups are in 2 pints?

16. Luke traced the bottoms of several cans. Were the figures he drew congruent? Why or why not?

17. **Data File** Use data from pages 402–403. How many more grams of fat are in cream cheese than in the same amount of mozzarella cheese?

18. **Make a Data File** Find 4 items that come in at least 3 different sizes. Make a chart telling the items and the 3 sizes for each.

Write the family of facts for the numbers in each exercise.

1. 4, 8, 12   **2.** 6, 14, 8

Replace each ⬡ with < or >.

3. 6,129 ⬡ 5,346

4. 5,578 ⬡ 5,780

5. 417 ⬡ 1,741

Find each sum or difference mentally.

6. 49 + 38   **7.** 55 + 26

8. 74 + 17   **9.** 46 − 20

10. 61 − 49   **11.** 53 − 28

12. Would you use inches, feet, or miles to measure the distance between your classroom door and the door to the office?

13. Find the perimeter.

14. Find the area in square centimeters.

Find each product.

15. 2	**16.** 9	**17.** 3
$\times 8$	$\times 2$	$\times 4$

18. 4	**19.** 8	**20.** 7
$\times 5$	$\times 8$	$\times 8$

21. 9	**22.** 3	**23.** 6
$\times 6$	$\times 3$	$\times 8$

Write two ways to find each product.

24. 3 × 6   **25.** 7 × 5

Answer each question. Use *sphere, rectangular prism, cylinder, triangle, hexagon,* or *octagon.*

26. What shape is your math book?

27. What shape has two surfaces that are circles?

28. What figure has 8 corners?

29. What figure has 6 sides?

Write *grams* or *kilograms* to tell which you would use to measure how much each weighs.

30. Elephant   **31.** Piece of paper

32. Crayon   **33.** Television set

Reteaching

Set A   pages 258–261

This stop sign is an octagon.

It has 8 corners and 8 sides.

Remember that geometric figures have curves or line segments as sides. Give the number of sides and corners.

1.   **2.**

Set B   pages 262–263

When two sides of a figure meet, they form an angle.

This hexagon has six angles, because it has six corners.

Remember that right angles form square corners. How many angles are there in each figure? Are they right angles?

1.   **2.**

Set C   pages 264–265

You can fold a square and make the two parts match. The dashed line is the fold line, or line of symmetry.

line of symmetry   no line of symmetry

Remember that some figures have more than one line of symmetry. Does each figure look symmetric? Write yes or no.

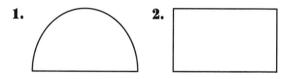

1.   **2.**

Set D   pages 266–267

Congruent figures have the same size and shape.

The triangles are congruent.

The squares are not congruent.

Remember that figures are congruent if you can place one on the other and they match.

Tell which is congruent to the figure at the right.

a.   **b.**

Set E   pages 274–275

John knows these facts:

A glass of water is about 1 cup.
Two cups make 1 pint.
Two pints make 1 quart.
Four quarts make 1 gallon.

He knew that the water in a fish tank is measured in gallons.

Remember that customary units for liquids tell how much liquid a container will hold.

Choose the more sensible customary measure for each.

1. Gas tank
   pint   gallon

2. Flower vase
   pint   gallon

Set F   pages 276–277

Amy knows these facts:

5 milliliters is about 1 teaspoon.
1 liter is 1,000 milliliters.

Knowing this, she knew that the water in the fish bowl is measured in liters.

Remember that milliliters are used when very small amounts of liquid are involved.

Write liter or milliliter to tell which you would use to measure how much each holds.

1.   **2.**

Set G   pages 278–279

José knows these facts:

A thin slice of bread weighs about 1 ounce.
A loaf of bread weighs about 1 pound.

José's dog could weigh 15 pounds, but not 15 ounces.

Remember that ounces are used to measure "dry" items and fluid ounces are used to measure liquid items.

Write ounces or pounds to tell which you would use to measure

1. a couch.   **2.** an eraser.

Set H   pages 280–281

Loo knows these facts:

A dollar bill has a mass of about 1 gram.
A baseball bat has a mass of about 1 kilogram.

She knew that the mass of an insect was measured in grams.

Remember that grams are used when very small amounts of mass are involved.

Write grams or kilograms to tell which you would use to measure

1. a medicine pill.   **2.** a truck.

More Practice

Give the name of each shape. Then give the
number of sides and corners each shape has.

1.   **2.**   **3.**

How many angles are there in each figure?
Are they right angles? Write *yes* or *no*.

1.   **2.**   **3.**   **4.**

Does each figure look symmetric? Write *yes*
or *no*.

1.   **2.**   **3.**   **4.**

Match the congruent figures. Write the letter
for each number.

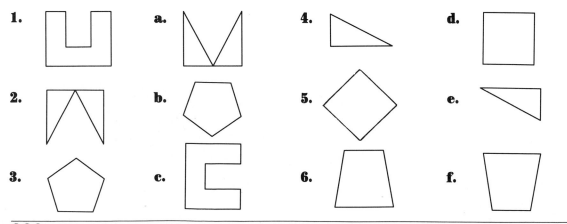

1.   **a.**   **4.**   **d.**

2.   **b.**   **5.**   **e.**

3.   **c.**   **6.**   **f.**

Independent Study **MORE PRACTICE**

Set E   pages 274–275

Estimation   Choose the more sensible customary measure for each.

1.

2 c   2 gal

2.

1 c   1 qt

3.

1 qt   1 gal

Set F   pages 276–277

Estimation   Choose the more sensible metric measure for each.

1. 10 mL   10 L

2. 4 mL   4 L

3. 250 L   250 mL

Set G   pages 278–279

Estimation   Choose the more sensible customary measure for each.

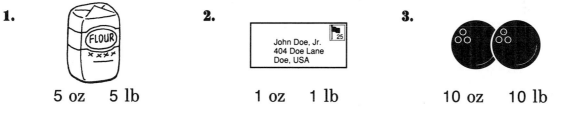

1. 5 oz   5 lb

2. 1 oz   1 lb

3. 10 oz   10 lb

Set H   pages 280–281

Estimation   Choose the more sensible metric unit for each.

1. 2 g   2 kg

2. 100 g   100 kg

3. 40 g   40 kg

Enrichment

Angles of Geometric Figures

Two line segments that meet form an angle. The sides of many geometric figures are line segments. When two sides meet at a corner, they form an angle. How many angles does a triangle have?

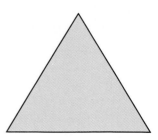

There are three angles, one at each corner of the triangle. Angle 1 is formed by sides CA and BA. The sides meet at corner A. This angle is named angle CAB or angle BAC. Is angle CAB the same as angle BAC? Every angle has two names made of three letters. The middle letter tells the corner where the angle is.

1. Write two names for angle 2.

2. What are two names for angle 3?

3. How many angles are in this square?

4. Name the angles. Give two names for each angle.

5. How many angles can you find in this rectangle? Write two names for each angle.

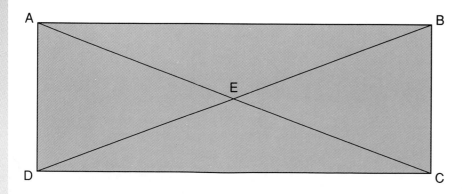

Chapter 8 Review/Test

Give the name for each shape. Use *sphere, cube, square,* or *hexagon.*

1.   **2.**

3. Is this angle a right angle?

4. Is the broken line a line of symmetry?

5. Which two figures are congruent?

a.   **b.**   **c.**

6. Find the volume in cubic units.

Choose the more sensible measure for each.

7. Can of tomato soup

cup   quart

8. Perfume bottle

milliliter   liter

9. Weight of a giraffe

ounce   pound

10. Mass of a ruler

gram   kilogram

11. Mass of a chair

gram   kilogram

12. Write how many 4-ounce peaches would make about 1 *pound.*

Winners of Weekly Spell-off	
Erin	X X X
Jacob	X X
André	X X X X
Elena	X X X
X = 1 spell-off won	

13. Which problem can be solved with data from the graph?

   a. How many words did Erin spell correctly?

   b. How many more times did André win than Jacob?

   c. How many children did not win a spell-off?

14. Solve the problem you chose in Exercise 13.

15. ■ **Write About Math**
Explain your reason for your answer to Exercise 4.

293

Division Concepts

9

Did You Know: In 1977, Peter Dowdeswell set a record for eating pancakes by eating 62 buttered pancakes with syrup in just under 7 minutes.

Number-Sense Project

Estimate
How many in
your family would
like to have some of
these pancakes?

Gather Data
In your family, if
these 18 pancakes
were divided equally,
how many would
each person get?

Analyze and Report
Compare your
results with other
students.

Sharing

Build Understanding

Deal Out the Daisies
Materials: Small objects
Groups: 3–5 students

A. Suppose you work at your aunt's flower shop. She hands you 15 flowers and 5 vases. You must put the same number of flowers in each vase. How many should go in each vase?

a. Use 15 small objects.

b. Show a place on your desk for each group.

c. Start by putting 1 object in each group.

d. Do you have enough to put 1 more in each group? Try.

e. Keep going until you do not have enough objects to put 1 in each group.

When you put the same number of objects into groups this way, you are ***sharing*** the objects equally among the groups.

You would put 3 flowers in each vase.

B. On another day you have 5 baskets to fill.

   a. If you have 10 flowers, how many go in each basket?

   b. If you have 20 flowers, how many go in each basket?

   c. If you have 25 flowers, how many go in each basket?

C. You have 24 tulips. Your aunt wants you to put the same amount into each vase.

   a. If you have 3 vases, how many flowers go in each vase?

   b. If you have 6 vases, how many go in each vase?

   c. If you have 8 vases, how many go in each vase?

■ **Talk About Math** In Example C, when you have more than 8 vases, will you put more or fewer flowers in each vase? How can you tell?

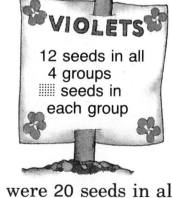

Check Understanding

For another example, see Set A, pages 322–323.

Look at the box at the right. Then answer the questions.

1. If you had 12 flower seeds, what would you do first to find how many seeds there would be in each group?

2. What would you do next?

3. How many would be in each group?

VIOLETS
12 seeds in all
4 groups
▥ seeds in each group

4. If there were 20 seeds in all, how many would be in each group?

Practice

For More Practice, see Set A, pages 324–325.

For each exercise use small objects or draw pictures to find the answer.

5. 16 in all
4 equal groups
How many in
each group?

6. 9 in all
3 equal groups
How many in
each group?

7. 12 in all
3 equal groups
How many in
each group?

8. 10 in all
2 equal groups
How many in
each group?

9. 25 in all
5 equal groups
How many in
each group?

10. 18 in all
2 equal groups
How many in
each group?

11. 14 in all
7 equal groups
How many in
each group?

12. 15 in all
3 equal groups
How many in
each group?

13. 12 in all
4 equal groups
How many in
each group?

14. 10 in all
5 equal groups
How many in
each group?

15. 8 in all
2 equal groups
How many in
each group?

16. 18 in all
6 equal groups
How many in
each group?

Problem Solving

Solve each problem.

17. A flower arrangement has 36 flowers. The same number of flowers are on each side of a candle. How many flowers are on each side?

18. All 36 flowers in the arrangement are roses or daisies. There are twice as many roses as daisies. How many roses are in the arrangement? How many daisies?

Tell the shape of each object in Exercises 1–8.
Use the pictures to help you.

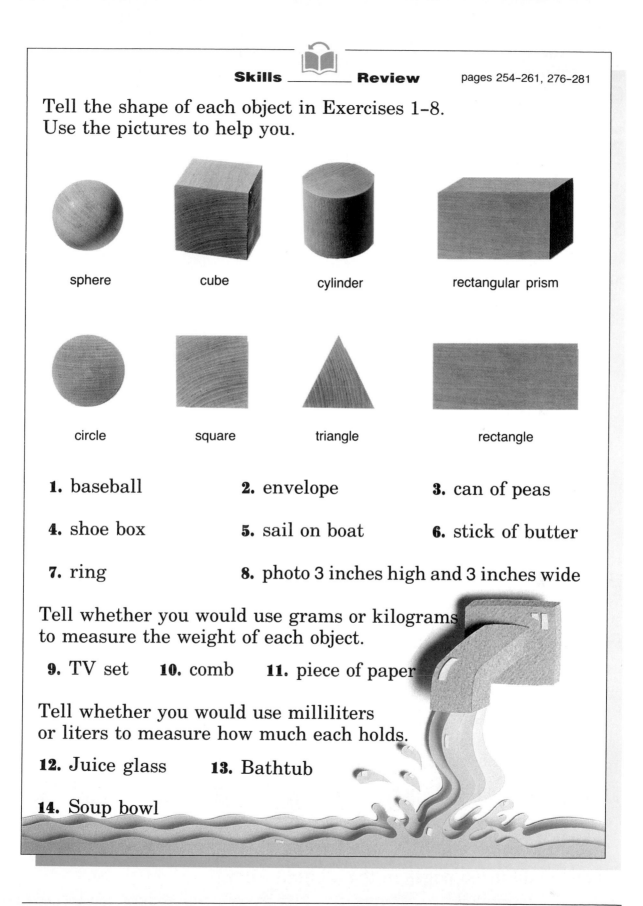

sphere   cube   cylinder   rectangular prism

circle   square   triangle   rectangle

1. baseball   **2.** envelope   **3.** can of peas

4. shoe box   **5.** sail on boat   **6.** stick of butter

7. ring   **8.** photo 3 inches high and 3 inches wide

Tell whether you would use grams or kilograms
to measure the weight of each object.

9. TV set   **10.** comb   **11.** piece of paper

Tell whether you would use milliliters
or liters to measure how much each holds.

12. Juice glass   **13.** Bathtub

14. Soup bowl

Grouping

Build Understanding

Gerbil Family Photos
Materials: Small objects
Groups: 3–5 students

A. Your class has been raising gerbils as a science project. Last week Geraldine and Billy Gerbil had babies. The teacher picked you to take pictures of them. Now you have 20 photos to put in the class album. If you want 4 photos on each page, how many pages will you use?

a. Count out 20 small objects. You will make a group for each page.

b. Start by making 1 group of 4.

c. Are there enough to make another group of 4? Try.

Each year people spend over 4 billion dollars on photo finishing.

d. Keep going until you do not have enough objects to make another group of 4. When you put objects together this way, you are **grouping** the objects.

You would use 5 pages in the album.

B. You have more album pages to fill. Put 4 photos on each page.

a. If you have 12 field trip photos, how many pages will you fill?

b. If you have 24 class play photos, how many pages will you fill?

c. If you have 28 school picnic photos, how many pages will you fill?

c. You took 24 photos of your science project for your album.

a. How many pages will you fill if you put 3 photos on a page?

b. How many pages will you fill if you put 6 photos on a page?

c. How many pages will you fill if you put 8 photos on a page?

■ **Talk About Math** In Example C, the total number of photos stays the same but the number of photos on a page changes. What can you say about the number of pages?

Check Understanding

For another example, see Set B, pages 322–323.

Use the numbers to write a story problem about gerbils. Find the answer.

1. 27 in all, 3 in each group

2. 15 in all, 3 in each group

Use small objects or draw pictures to find each answer.

3. 14 in all
2 in each group
How many groups?

4. 18 in all
9 in each group
How many groups?

Practice

For More Practice, see Set B, pages 324–325.

Use small objects or draw pictures to find each answer.

5. 12 in all
4 in each group
How many
groups?

6. 18 in all
3 in each group
How many
groups?

7. 30 in all
5 in each group
How many
groups?

8. 8 in all
4 in each group
How many
groups?

9. 15 in all
3 in each group
How many
groups?

10. 12 in all
2 in each group
How many
groups?

11. 10 in all
2 in each group
How many
groups?

12. 16 in all
4 in each group
How many
groups?

13. 24 in all
6 in each group
How many
groups?

Mixed Practice Use small objects or draw
pictures to find each answer.

14. 3 groups
3 in each group
How many
in all?

15. 18 in all
6 equal groups
How many in
each group?

16. 3 groups
8 in each group
How many
in all?

Number Sense Suppose you
have 20 objects. You want to make
equal groups with no objects left
over. Can you have equal groups of

17. 7 objects? **18.** 6 objects?

19. 5 objects? **20.** 4 objects?

21. 3 objects? **22.** 2 objects?

Problem Solving

Solve each problem.

23. The class had 9 goldfish. They put 3 fish in each bowl. How many bowls did they use?

TIPS FOR PROBLEM SOLVERS

Don't give up. Some problems take longer than others.

24. Mr. Hughes has 63 science books for his third graders. If he orders 49 more books, how many will he have?

25. For his project, Steve planted 3 rows of seeds. Each row had 25 seeds. How many seeds did he plant?

Explore ———— Math

■ Calculator You want to put 28 objects into groups of 7 each. You can use repeated subtraction to find the number of groups.

Press:	You see:	Make a ✔ each time you subtract.
28 (−) 7 (=)	*21*	✔
(−) 7 (=)	*14*	✔
(−) 7 (=)	*7*	✔
(−) 7 (=)	*0*	✔

Count how many 7s you subtracted from 28. There are 4 groups of 7 in 28.

Do repeated subtraction on your calculator to find the number of groups.

26. 16 in all, 2 in each group

27. 21 in all, 3 in each group

28. 10 in all, 5 in each group

29. 24 in all, 6 in each group

Meaning of Division

Build Understanding

A. During story hour, 6 children will read 12 pages orally. How many pages will each child read if each reads an equal number of pages?

Say: 12 pages divided equally among 6 children is 2 pages for each child. 12 divided by 6 is 2.

Write: **12 ÷ 6 = 2**

B. There are 18 books in a book case, 9 books on each shelf. How many shelves are there?

Say: 18 books divided by putting 9 on each shelf is 2 shelves. 18 divided by 9 is 2.

Write: **18 ÷ 9 = 2**

■ **Talk About Math**   Look at Examples A and B. Which shows sharing? Which shows grouping?

Check Understanding

For another example, see Set C, pages 322–323.

A▸ Use the picture to help answer
L
G each question.
E
B
R
A

1. How many books are on the table?

2. How many groups of 2 books could you make?
Complete: 12 ÷ 2 = ▦

3. If you make 6 equal groups, how many would be in each group?
Complete: 12 ÷ 6 = ▦

Practice

For More Practice, see Set C, pages 324–325.

ALGEBRA ▶ Write the division sentence for each exercise. Use the pictures to help you.

4.

▦ in all
3 bowls
▦ ÷ 3 = △

5.

▦ in all
3 boxes
▦ ÷ 3 = △

6.

▦ in all
5 in each box
▦ ÷ 5 = △

7.

▦ in all
△ bowls
▦ ÷ △ = ◈

8.

▦ in all
△ in each stack
▦ ÷ △ = ◈

9.

▦ in all
△ groups
▦ ÷ △ = ◈

Write the division sentence for each exercise.
Draw pictures to help you.

10. 28 in all
4 in each group
▦ groups
28 ÷ 4 = ▦

11. 21 in all
3 groups
▦ in each group
21 ÷ 3 = ▦

12. 16 in all
2 in each group
▦ groups
16 ÷ 2 = ▦

13. 36 in all
6 in each group
▦ groups
36 ÷ 6 = ▦

14. 24 in all
3 groups
▦ in each group
24 ÷ 3 = ▦

15. 12 in all
2 in each group
▦ groups
12 ÷ 2 = ▦

Dividing by Two and Three

Build Understanding

The P. E. teacher says biking is a healthy exercise. Her bike club has 18 bikers. If there are 3 bikers on a team, how many teams are there?

You can use repeated subtraction to help you find the number of groups. How many times can 3 be subtracted from 18? 6 times.

$$18 - 3 = 15$$
$$15 - 3 = 12$$
$$12 - 3 = 9$$
$$9 - 3 = 6$$
$$6 - 3 = 3$$
$$3 - 3 = 0$$

18 ÷ 3 = 6

There are 6 teams.

■ Talk About Math

How many teams would there be if there were 9 bikers on a team?

Where have you ridden a bicycle?

Check Understanding

For another example, see Set D, pages 322–323.

For Exercises 1–4, tell how you can use counting by 2s or 3s to help find the answer. Then write each answer.

1. 16 ÷ 2   **2.** 9 ÷ 3   **3.** 10 ÷ 2   **4.** 6 ÷ 3

5. Use repeated subtraction to find 24 ÷ 3.

Practice

For More Practice, see Set D, pages 324–325.

Write each answer. **Remember** to
draw pictures to help you.

6. 18 ÷ 2   **7.** 15 ÷ 3   **8.** 6 ÷ 2   **9.** 9 ÷ 3

10. 14 ÷ 2   **11.** 4 ÷ 2   **12.** 21 ÷ 3   **13.** 6 ÷ 3

14. 27 ÷ 3   **15.** 18 ÷ 3   **16.** 16 ÷ 2   **17.** 8 ÷ 2

18. 24 ÷ 3   **19.** 12 ÷ 3   **20.** 10 ÷ 2   **21.** 12 ÷ 2

Problem Solving

Solve each problem.

22. Critical Thinking In the example on page 306, how could you use addition or multiplication to find the answer?

23. Your school volleyball club has 14 players. The coach wants to make 2 equal teams. How many children will be on each team?

24. There are 12 members on the skating team. 4 of them started skating this year. How many started before this year?

25. The hiking club has 7 teams with 3 members in each team. How many members are there in all?

26. Estimation Carl has 23 decorations for the soccer team party. He wants to put them in 3 rooms. If he divided them as evenly as possible, about how many will be in each room?

Dividing by Four

Build Understanding

A. Candles are used in celebrations all around the world. In India, the autumn holiday *Divali* is celebrated by lighting candles. Sita has 12 candles. She wants to place the same number of candles on each of 4 windowsills. How many candles should she put on each windowsill?

You can use multiplication facts to help find the number on each windowsill.

Think: 4 times what number is 12?

$4 \times$ ▦ $= 12$
$4 \times 3 = 12$

$12 \div 4 = 3$

The Divali festival lasts for five days.

Sita should put 3 candles on each windowsill.

B. You can write $12 \div 4 = 3$ another way.

■ **Talk About Math** In the division fact, 12 is called the dividend. What is 12 called in the multiplication fact? What are 4 and 3 called in the multiplication fact?

Check Understanding

For another example, see Set E, pages 322–323.

Copy each exercise. Then write each quotient.

1. $8 \div 4$ **2.** $12 \div 4$ **3.** $4\overline{)28}$ **4.** $4\overline{)16}$

5. Circle each quotient in Exercises 1–4.

6. Put a box around each divisor in Exercises 1–4.

308

Practice

For More Practice, see Set E, pages 324–325.

Find each quotient.

7. 20 ÷ 4　　　　**8.** 16 ÷ 4　　　　**9.** 12 ÷ 4　　　　**10.** 8 ÷ 4

11. 28 ÷ 4　　　**12.** 24 ÷ 4　　　**13.** 32 ÷ 4　　　**14.** 4 ÷ 4

15. 4)‾32　　　　**16.** 4)‾16　　　　**17.** 4)‾20　　　　**18.** 4)‾36

Mental Math　Find each answer.

19. 42 + 7　　**20.** 12 ÷ 2　　**21.** 3 × 4　　**22.** 16 − 4　　**23.** 12 ÷ 3

24. 25 − 14　　**25.** 9 ÷ 3　　**26.** 18 + 6　　**27.** 5 × 7　　**28.** 20 − 8

Problem Solving

Solve each problem.

29. Tao and 3 friends made 16 lanterns. If each child made the same number of lanterns how many did each child make?

30. In China, people hang lanterns to welcome in the new year. Ming's family hung 5 strings of lanterns. Each string held 7 lanterns. How many lanterns were there altogether?

Paper lanterns are being made for the Moon Cake Festival in Kuala Lampur, Malaysia.

Midchapter ✓ **Checkup**

Write each answer.
1. 14 in all
7 equal groups
How many in each group?

2. 24 in all
3 in each group
How many groups?

Find each quotient.　　**3.** 24 ÷ 4　**4.** 15 ÷ 3　**5.** 6 ÷ 2

Problem-Solving Workshop

Number-Sense Project

Food	How many would like some?	Would each get an equal amount?	How many would I get?
15 pancakes	5	no	6
12 apples	4	no	1
8 slices of pizza	5	no	2
10 biscuits	5	no	3
15 strawberries	3	yes	5

Look back at pages 294-295.
Allan thought about how different foods would be divided in his family. He recorded the information above.

Would Allan get more or less of these items if they were divided equally in his family of five?

1. Pancakes   **2.** Biscuits

3. Apples   **4.** Strawberries

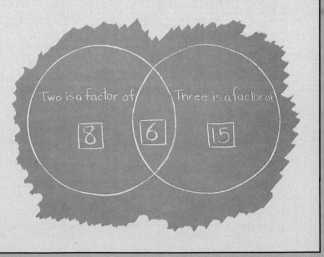

Critical Thinking Activity

Copy the two loops. Write the numbers in the correct loop or loops.

Real-Life Decision Making

You need to buy some new pencils. Two stores near your home are having a sale. How many pencils would you buy? Where would you buy them? Why? How much would they cost?

SALE
2 PENCILS FOR 18¢

15¢ each

15¢ each

SALE
All PENCILS 5¢ OFF

Math-at-Home Activity

Write the numbers 2, 2, 3, 3, 4, 4, 5, 5, 6, 7, 8, and 9 on individual pieces of paper and put them in a bag. Each member of your family should draw out 3 numbers. (Put in extra 2s, 3s, 4s, and 5s if you need them so everyone can have 3 numbers.)

You must look for items around your home that come in multiples of the numbers you have drawn. When everyone has found their items, make a list. Which multiple was easiest to find items for? Which was the hardest?

Try and Check

Build Understanding

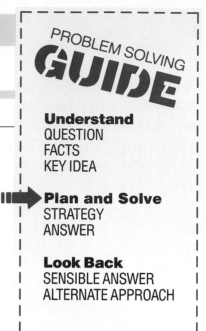

PROBLEM SOLVING

GUIDE

Understand
QUESTION
FACTS
KEY IDEA

Plan and Solve
STRATEGY
ANSWER

Look Back
SENSIBLE ANSWER
ALTERNATE APPROACH

Brian's father weighs 100 pounds more than Brian. Together they weigh 240 pounds. How much does Brian weigh?

Understand   Brian's father weighs 100 pounds more than Brian. The sum of their weights is 240 pounds.

Plan and Solve   STRATEGY   Guess Brian's weight. Add 100 pounds to find his father's weight. Check to see if those weights total 240 pounds.

If Brian weighs 60 pounds, then Brian's father weighs 60 + 100 or 160 pounds. Their total weight is 60 + 160 or 220 pounds. That is too small.

Try other weights. Make a table to help you.

	Brian	Father	Total	
Try 60 pounds.	60	160	220	too small
Try 80 pounds.	80	180	260	too large
Try 70 pounds.	70	170	240	correct

ANSWER   Brian weighs 70 pounds.

Look Back   Is the computation correct? Does Brian's father weigh 100 pounds more than Brian? Do the two weights total 240 pounds?

■ **Talk About Math** Can you think of another way to figure out Brian's weight?

Check Understanding

Solve the problem by answering Questions 1–5.

Ann and Amy are twins. Bob and Bill are twins. The girls are 2 years older than the boys. The sum of all four ages is 40. How old are they?

1. If Ann and Amy are 9 years old, how old are Bob and Bill?

2. If Ann and Amy are 9 years old, what is the sum of all four ages?

3. Are Ann and Amy older or younger than 9 years old?

4. What number could you try next for the age of Ann and Amy?

5. Try different numbers for the ages of Ann and Amy. Find the ages of Bob and Bill. Do this until you find four ages which total 40.

Practice

Solve each problem.

6. There are 100 math and science books on a shelf. There are 20 more math books than science books. How many of each kind are there?

7. There are 16 cans of either corn or peas in the cupboard. There are 3 times as many cans of corn as there are peas. How many cans of each are there?

8. John has 18 more tapes than his sister Cindy. Cindy has 24 tapes. How many tapes does John have?

9. Noreen has 2 dozen eggs. She has 4 fewer white eggs than brown eggs. How many eggs of each color are there?

313

Dividing by Five

Build Understanding

A. You can get a nickel for 5 pennies. How many groups of 5 pennies can be made from 35 pennies?

35 ÷ 5 = 7   5 × 7 = 35

You can get 7 nickels for 35 pennies.

B. If you divide the 35 pennies equally among 5 people, how many pennies would each person get?

35 ÷ 5 = 7

Remember: You can write division in two ways.

$$35 \div 5 = 7 \qquad 5\overline{)35}$$

Quotient ⟶ 7

Divisor

Dividend

Each person would get 7 pennies.

■ **Talk About Math**   Explain how you can use multiplication to check division.

Check Understanding

For another example, see Set F, pages 322–323.

Match each picture to a division sentence.

1.   **2.**   **3.**

a. 25 ÷ 5 = 5   **b.** 20 ÷ 5 = 4   **c.** 15 ÷ 5 = 3

Practice

For More Practice, see Set F, pages 324–325.

Write each quotient.

4. $30 \div 5$ **5.** $45 \div 5$ **6.** $10 \div 5$ **7.** $20 \div 5$

8. $35 \div 5$ **9.** $40 \div 5$ **10.** $15 \div 5$ **11.** $25 \div 5$

12. $5\overline{)30}$ **13.** $5\overline{)40}$ **14.** $5\overline{)35}$ **15.** $5\overline{)45}$

For each multiplication fact, write a division fact with 5 as the divisor.

16. $2 \times 5 = 10$ **17.** $6 \times 5 = 30$ **18.** $9 \times 5 = 45$ **19.** $7 \times 5 = 35$

Mixed Practice   Use mental math or paper and pencil to find each answer. Tell which method you used.

20. 6×5 **21.** $24 \div 4$ **22.** $18 + 209$ **23.** $20 \div 5$ **24.** $37 - 29$

25. $30 \div 5$ **26.** $16 \div 2$ **27.** $153 - 94$ **28.** $27 \div 3$ **29.** 4×9

30. 3×8 **31.** $16 \div 4$ **32.** $259 + 467$ **33.** $36 \div 4$ **34.** $520 - 195$

Problem Solving

Solve each problem.

35. Deanne has 40 cents. All of the coins are nickels. How many nickels does she have?

36. Su Lin has 7 nickels in his pocket. How much money is that?

37. Sasha has 9 nickels. He wants stickers that cost 55 cents. Does he have enough money?

38. Kelly has 15 cents in nickels in one hand and 6 nickels in her other hand. How many nickels does she have in all?

A
L
G
E
B
R
A

Write a Number Sentence

Build Understanding

T. J. is buying tapes at a store in the mall. Each package has 3 tapes. How many packages should T. J. buy to have 15 tapes in all?

Understand   You know how many in all. You know how many in each group. You need to find how many groups.

Plan and Solve   STRATEGY   You can use a number sentence to show how the parts of a problem are related.

Write the numbers and math signs for the words.

▦ packages	of 3 tapes each	is 15 tapes.
↓	↓	↓
▦	× 3	= 15

To find the missing number, think of the division fact.

$$15 \div 3 = ▦ \qquad 15 \div 3 = 5$$

ANSWER   T. J. needs to buy 5 packages of tapes.

Look Back   Read the question again. Does the answer make sense?

■ **Write About Math**   Explain how you could use objects to solve T. J.'s problem.

PROBLEM SOLVING
GUIDE

Understand
QUESTION
FACTS
KEY IDEA

▸ **Plan and Solve**
STRATEGY
ANSWER

Look Back
SENSIBLE ANSWER
ALTERNATE APPROACH

316

Check Understanding

Solve the problem by answering Questions 1–4.

Angie has to buy muffin pans. Each muffin pan will hold 6 muffins. How many muffin pans should Angie buy to bake 24 muffins?

1. What are you asked to find? **2.** What facts are you given?

3. Which number sentence can help solve this problem?
  a. 24 − 6 = ▦   **b.** ▦ + 6 = 24   **c.** ▦ × 6 = 24

4. Write the answer to the problem in a complete sentence.

Practice

Write a number sentence for each problem. Then solve the problems.

5. The mall has parking space for 1,280 cars in the north lot and 975 cars in the east lot. How many parking spaces are there in the two lots?

6. Brienne's Card Shop ordered 560 greeting cards in May. They ordered 435 cards in June. How many more cards did they order in May?

7. Cari wants to buy 12 pairs of socks. The socks are sold 3 pairs to a package. How many packages should Cari buy?

8. At the book store, a display shelf holds 8 books. There are 4 display shelves. How many books can be displayed?

Choose a ▦ Strategy

9. There are 5 children and 2 adults in each van. There are 40 children in all. How many vans are there? What is the total number of adults?

317

Families of Facts

Build Understanding

A. You can write
2 multiplication sentences
about the poster.

2 × 3 = 6
3 × 2 = 6

You also can write 2 division
sentences about the poster.

6 ÷ 2 = 3
6 ÷ 3 = 2

These four sentences are a
family of facts.

B. This family of facts has only
2 number sentences.

4 × 4 = 16
16 ÷ 4 = 4

■ **Talk About Math** What can you say about the
numbers that make up a family of facts?

Check Understanding

For another example, see Set G, pages 322–323.

1. Write two number sentences
to complete this family of
facts.

2 × 5 = 10   10 ÷ 5 = 2

2. Choose a multiplication fact.
Draw a picture for it. Write
the family of facts for it.

Practice

For More Practice, see Set G, pages 324–325.

Write the number sentences to complete
each family of facts. Write each answer.

3. $4 \times 5 = $ ▦   **4.** $3 \times 4 = $ ▦   **5.** $4 \times 2 = $ ▦   **6.** $5 \times 5 = $ ▦

$20 \div 4 = $ ▦ $12 \div 4 = $ ▦ $2 \times 4 = $ ▦

Write the family of facts using the given numbers.

7. 3, 5, 15   **8.** 2, 2, 4   **9.** 2, 5, 10   **10.** 4, 4, 16

11. 3, 8, 24   **12.** 5, 7, 35   **13.** 2, 6, 12   **14.** 4, 5, 20

Problem Solving

Solve each problem.

15. Choose one family of facts from Exercises 3–5. Write a word problem for each fact.

16. Use Data Will the families of facts for Exercises 3–24 on page 227 have 2 or 4 sentences? Why?

17. Critical Thinking Write 4 facts for the picture. You may use addition, subtraction, multiplication, and division.

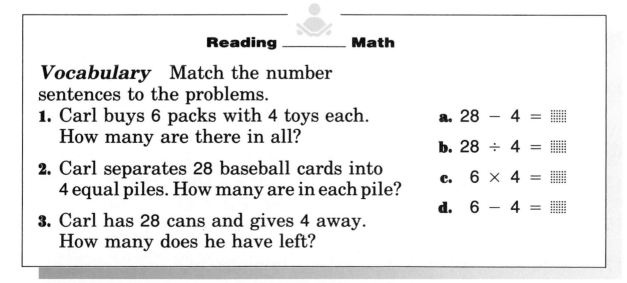

Reading ———— **Math**

Vocabulary Match the number
sentences to the problems.

1. Carl buys 6 packs with 4 toys each. How many are there in all?

2. Carl separates 28 baseball cards into 4 equal piles. How many are in each pile?

3. Carl has 28 cans and gives 4 away. How many does he have left?

a. $28 - 4 = $ ▦

b. $28 \div 4 = $ ▦

c. $6 \times 4 = $ ▦

d. $6 - 4 = $ ▦

319

Skills Review

Find each answer.

1. 15 in all
3 equal groups
How many in each group?

2. 12 in all
6 in each group
How many groups?

Write the division sentence for each exercise.

3. 27 in all
3 in each group
▦ groups
27 ÷ 3 = ▦

4. 18 in all
6 in each group
▦ ÷ 6 = ▵

Find each quotient.

5. 8 ÷ 2   **6.** 18 ÷ 2

7. 15 ÷ 3   **8.** 24 ÷ 3

9. 32 ÷ 4   **10.** 16 ÷ 4

11. 25 ÷ 5   **12.** 40 ÷ 5

Write the family of facts using the given numbers.

13. 4, 6, 24   **14.** 3, 3, 9

15. 2, 6, 12   **16.** 4, 5, 20

17. 4, 4, 16   **18.** 4, 3, 12

Problem-Solving Review

Solve each problem.

19. Dan bought 3 packages of ground beef. Each package weighed between 2 and 3 pounds. Could he have 7 pounds? 10 pounds? Explain.

20. Delia has 17 pairs of socks in 4 colors. There are 3 pairs more of blue than pink socks. She has 5 pairs of white socks and 1 pair of red. How many pairs of blue socks does Delia have?

21. Marta and Chuck each bought 18 books. Marta's bookcase has 3 shelves. Chuck's bookcase has 2 shelves. Who has more books on a shelf if the books are shared equally on the shelves? How many more?

22. **Data File** Use data from pages 402–403. Bonita can toast 4 slices of bread at one time. How many sets of toast will she make if she uses the entire loaf?

23. **Make a Data File** Find the number of players on 5 different team sports. Make a table to show your findings.

Write in order from least to greatest.

1. 568   92   342   216

2. 706   760   423   421

3. 1,456   2,901   1,546   2,109

Estimate each answer.

4. 69 − 35   **5.** 43 + 28

6. 55 + 37   **7.** 81 − 52

8. 68 + 42   **9.** 94 − 75

Find each sum or difference.

10.   473   **11.**   831   **12.**   687
       + 294   + 139   + 242

13.   312   **14.**   406   **15.**   511
       − 153   − 319   − 222

16.   7,009   **17.**   6,200
       − 3,127   − 4,396

18. 9 + 42 + 28 + 14

Find each product.

19.   3   **20.**   9   **21.**   0
       × 8   × 4   × 6

22.   8   **23.**   9   **24.**   6
       × 1   × 8   × 9

25.   7   **26.**   8   **27.**   8
       × 6   × 7   × 6

Give the name of each geometric figure.

28.   **29.**

30. Which two figures are congruent?

a.   b.   c.

31. Find the volume in cubic units.

Choose the more sensible measure for each.

32. Water jug
2 c   2 gal

33. Soup can
200 mL   200 L

34. How many apples would make about 1 pound?
3 oz

Find each quotient.

35. 12 ÷ 2   **36.** 18 ÷ 3

37. 21 ÷ 3   **38.** 16 ÷ 4

39. 28 ÷ 4   **40.** 35 ÷ 5

41. 20 ÷ 5   **42.** 45 ÷ 5

Reteaching

Set A   pages 296–298

There are 3 students in each art class group. Your group was given 27 crayons to share equally. How many will each student receive?

This picture shows that each student will receive 9 crayons.

Remember that you are sharing when you find how many objects are in each group.

For each exercise, use small objects or draw pictures to find each answer.

1. 16 in all
8 equal groups
How many in each group?

2. 12 in all
4 equal groups
How many in each group?

Set B   pages 300–303

Tony has 30 stamps to put in his stamp book. Each page will hold 6 stamps. How many pages will the stamps fill?

xx xx xx	xx xx xx	xx xx xx	xx xx xx	xx xx xx

The stamps will fill 5 pages.

Remember that the number of pages will be less if you put more stamps on each page.

Use small objects or draw pictures to find each answer.

1. 9 in all
3 in each group
▦ groups

2. 21 in all
7 in each group
▦ groups

Set C   pages 304–305

There are 4 students in each science class group. Amy's group has to collect 24 leaves for a science project. How many leaves will each student have to collect?

Say: 24 leaves divided equally among 4 students is 6 leaves for each student. 24 divided by 4 is 6.

Write: 24 ÷ 4 = 6

Remember that to divide means to share objects equally or to group objects equally.

Write the division sentence for each exercise. Draw pictures to help you.

1. 27 in all
9 in each group
▦ groups

2. 24 in all
3 groups
▦ in each group

Set D pages 306–307

The hiking club has 12 members. Each team has 2 people. How many teams are in the club?

Count the	$12 - 2 = 10$
number of	$10 - 2 = 8$
times you can	$8 - 2 = 6$
subtract 2	$6 - 2 = 4$
from 12.	$4 - 2 = 2$
	$2 - 2 = 0$

$12 \div 2 = 6$ There are 6 teams.

Remember that you can use counting by 2s to divide by 2, and counting by 3s to divide by 3.

Write each answer.

1. $10 \div 2$ **2.** $12 \div 3$

3. $16 \div 2$ **4.** $15 \div 3$

5. $14 \div 2$ **6.** $21 \div 3$

Set E pages 308–309

You can use multiplication facts to find $24 \div 4$.

Think: 4 times what number is 24?

$$4 \times \text{▦} = 24$$
$$4 \times 6 = 24$$
$$24 \div 4 = 6$$

Remember that the quotient is the answer to a division problem.

Find each quotient.

1. $28 \div 4$ **2.** $16 \div 4$

3. $4\overline{)12}$ **4.** $4\overline{)28}$

Set F pages 314–315

Each row in the plane has 5 seats. How many rows will 35 people fill? Find $35 \div 5$.

Think: $5 \times \text{▦} = 35$
 $5 \times 7 = 35$
 $35 \div 5 = 7$ It will take 7 rows.

Remember that you can write a division problem by using $\div$ or $\overline{)}$. Write each quotient.

1. $20 \div 5$ **2.** $30 \div 5$ **3.** $5\overline{)25}$

Set G pages 318–319

You can write a family of facts about this picture.

□ □ □
□ □ □
□ □ □
□ □ □

$3 \times 4 = 12$
$4 \times 3 = 12$
$12 \div 3 = 4$
$12 \div 4 = 3$

Remember that a family of facts for some numbers has only two number sentences.

Write the number sentences to complete each family of facts.

1. $4 \times 6 = 24$ **2.** $3 \times 5 = 15$
 $24 \div 6 = 4$

More Practice
Set A   pages 296–298

For each exercise use small objects or draw pictures to find each answer.

1. 18 in all
3 equal groups
How many in
each group?

2. 15 in all
3 equal groups
How many in
each group?

3. 12 in all
2 equal groups
How many in
each group?

4. 10 in all
5 equal groups
How many in
each group?

5. 21 in all
7 equal groups
How many in
each group?

6. 18 in all
6 equal groups
How many in
each group?

Set B   pages 300–303

Use small objects or draw pictures to find
each answer.

1. 10 in all
5 in each group
How many groups?

2. 12 in all
3 in each group
How many groups?

3. 18 in all
6 in each group
How many groups?

4. 24 in all
8 in each group
How many groups?

5. 16 in all
2 in each group
How many groups?

6. 30 in all
6 in each group
How many groups?

Set C   pages 304–305

Write the division sentence for each exercise.
Draw pictures to help you.

1. 24 in all
4 groups
▦ in each group
24 ÷ 4 = ▦

2. 15 in all
3 in each group
▦ groups
15 ÷ 3 = ▦

3. 25 in all
5 in each group
▦ groups
25 ÷ 5 = ▦

4. 9 in all
3 groups
▦ in each group
9 ÷ 3 = ▦

5. 20 in all
5 in each group
▦ groups
20 ÷ 5 = ▦

6. 16 in all
4 groups
▦ in each group
16 ÷ 4 = ▦

Set D pages 306–307

Write each answer.

1. 10 ÷ 2 **2.** 24 ÷ 3 **3.** 9 ÷ 3 **4.** 14 ÷ 2 **5.** 18 ÷ 3

6. 8 ÷ 2 **7.** 18 ÷ 2 **8.** 21 ÷ 3 **9.** 27 ÷ 3 **10.** 24 ÷ 2

Set E pages 308–309

Find each quotient.

1. 28 ÷ 4 **2.** 16 ÷ 4 **3.** 32 ÷ 8 **4.** 12 ÷ 4 **5.** 36 ÷ 4

6. $4\overline{)12}$ **7.** $4\overline{)8}$ **8.** $4\overline{)20}$ **9.** $4\overline{)32}$ **10.** $4\overline{)24}$

Mental Math Find each answer.

11. 31 + 8 **12.** 3 × 5 **13.** 15 − 3 **14.** 18 ÷ 2 **15.** 19 + 7

16. 5 × 8 **17.** 26 − 15 **18.** 15 ÷ 3 **19.** 4 × 7 **20.** 30 − 9

Set F pages 314–315

Write each quotient.

1. 40 ÷ 5 **2.** 35 ÷ 5 **3.** 45 ÷ 5 **4.** 30 ÷ 5

5. $5\overline{)20}$ **6.** $5\overline{)25}$ **7.** $5\overline{)10}$ **8.** $5\overline{)15}$

Mixed Practice Use mental math or paper and pencil
to find each answer. Tell which method you used.

9. 4 × 6 **10.** 40 ÷ 5 **11.** 16 + 107 **12.** 48 − 19

13. 24 ÷ 3 **14.** 15 ÷ 3 **15.** 136 − 87 **16.** 7 × 4

Set G pages 318–319

Copy the number sentences and write each answer.
Write the number sentences to complete each family of facts.

1. 3 × 6 = ▦ **2.** 4 × 9 = ▦ **3.** 5 × 2 = ▦ **4.** 3 × 3 = ▦
    18 ÷ 3 = ▦   36 ÷ 4 = ▦   2 × 5 = ▦

Write the family of facts using the given numbers.
5. 2, 4, 8 **6.** 5, 5, 25 **7.** 4, 5, 20 **8.** 4, 6, 24

Enrichment

Using Place Value to Divide

You can use place value to help you divide large numbers.

Find $26 \div 2$.

You can break the greater number into its expanded form.

26 = 20 + 6

Divide 20 by 2. Divide 6 by 2.

You can count by 2 to find how many twos are in 20.

2, 4, 6, 8, 10, 12, 14, 16, 18, 20
There are 10 twos in 20.

You can use division to find how many twos are in 6. There are 3 twos in 6.

Add the number of twos in 20 and the number of twos in 6.

10 + 3 = 13

26 ÷ 2 = 13

If there are 10 twos in 20, how many will be in

1. 40?　　　　　　　　**2.** 60?　　　　　　　　**3.** 80?

If there are 10 threes in 30, how many will be in

4. 60?　　　　　　　　**5.** 90?

Find each quotient.

6. 68 ÷ 2　　　　**7.** 46 ÷ 2　　　　**8.** 84 ÷ 2　　　　**9.** 22 ÷ 2

10. 39 ÷ 3　　　**11.** 63 ÷ 3　　　**12.** 36 ÷ 3　　　**13.** 93 ÷ 3

Chapter 9 Review/Test

The art class has 9 tables with 1 cup on each table.

1. If you have 27 markers, how many go in each cup?

2. If you have 18 markers, how many go in each cup?

The art class has 30 students.

3. If the students work in groups of 6, how many groups will there be?

4. If the students work in groups of 10, how many groups will there be?

5. Complete.

▦ in all

4 cups

▦ ÷ 4 = ▦

Write each quotient.

6. 14 ÷ 2   **7.** 9 ÷ 3

8. 16 ÷ 4   **9.** 45 ÷ 5

10. 2)‾12‾   **11.** 3)‾27‾

12. 4)‾32‾   **13.** 5)‾25‾

Complete each number sentence. Then write three more sentences to make a family of facts.

14. 3 × 8 = ▦   **15.** 5 × 9 = ▦

16. 4 × 7 = ▦   **17.** 2 × 6 = ▦

18. The school library has 500 books. There are 10 more books in the fiction section than in the nonfiction section. How many books of each kind are there?

Read this problem. Then answer the questions below.

Chin needs 25 invitations for his party. Each package has 5 invitations. How many packages should he buy?

19. What does the underlined statement mean?

   a. Chin must find a package with 25 invitations.

   b. Chin must buy more than one package.

   c. Chin can only invite 5 people.

20. Solve the problem above.

21. ■ **Write About Math** How can you use multiplication to help find a quotient?

Division Facts

Estimate
Predict which necklace design will be the most popular.

Gather Data
Ask 3 people who are not in your class which necklace they like the best. Tally the results.

Analyze and Report
Share your results with other students. Was your prediction of the most popular necklace correct?

Did You Know: People like different shapes and different colors. The most popular color in the U.S. is blue.

Dividing by Six

Build Understanding

Arrays on Display
Materials: Small objects
Groups: 4 students

A. Amy is a window dresser. She wants to display 18 mannequins. She wants to put the same number of mannequins in each row. If she puts 6 in each row, how many rows will she make?

a. Count out 18 objects.

b. Make a row with 6 objects.

c. Make as many more rows of 6 as you can.

d. How many rows could you make?

18 ÷ 6 = 3

Amy will make 3 rows with 6 mannequins in each row.

B. Make an array with 24 objects. Put 6 in each row. How many rows are there?

■ **Talk About Math** What multiplication facts could you write for the arrays you made?

Check Understanding

For another example, see Set A, pages 352–353.

Make or draw an array for each fact. Write the related multiplication fact for each.

1. 36 ÷ 6   **2.** 30 ÷ 6   **3.** 12 ÷ 6   **4.** 42 ÷ 6   **5.** 54 ÷ 6

Practice

For More Practice, see Set A, pages 354–355.

Write each quotient. **Remember** to make or draw arrays to help you.

6. $12 \div 6$ **7.** $24 \div 6$ **8.** $54 \div 6$ **9.** $48 \div 6$

10. $42 \div 6$ **11.** $30 \div 6$ **12.** $18 \div 6$ **13.** $36 \div 6$

14. $6\overline{)30}$ **15.** $6\overline{)42}$ **16.** $6\overline{)36}$ **17.** $6\overline{)18}$

18. $6\overline{)54}$ **19.** $6\overline{)48}$ **20.** $6\overline{)24}$ **21.** $6\overline{)12}$

Mixed Practice   Find each answer.

22. $42 \div 6$ **23.** $30 \div 6$ **24.** $24 \div 4$ **25.** $43 - 29$

26. $25 \div 5$ **27.** 8×5 **28.** $90 - 13$ **29.** $18 \div 2$

30. 9×8 **31.** $54 \div 6$ **32.** $28 + 64$ **33.** $28 \div 4$

34. $77 - 49$ **35.** $45 \div 5$ **36.** $36 + 48$ **37.** $32 \div 4$

38. $30 \div 5$ **39.** $54 + 27$ **40.** $48 \div 6$ **41.** $63 - 38$

Problem Solving

Solve each problem.

42. Millie displayed 6 of 27 outfits in one window. How many outfits are left to display?

43. If 6 mannequins fill 1 window, how many are needed to fill 5 windows?

44. Suppose David must move 48 mannequins. If 6 fit in the elevator with him, how many trips will he have to make?

45. Critical Thinking Suppose you begin with 72. Predict how many times you would need to subtract 6 to reach 0. Check your prediction.

Dividing by Seven

Build Understanding

Beth collects buttons from around the world. She has 56 buttons to put in 7 rows of a display box. If she wants the same number of buttons in each row, how many buttons will go in each row?

You can use multiplication to help you with division.

$7 \times \blacksquare = 56$

$7 \times 8 = 56$ So $56 \div 7 = 8$.

She can place 8 buttons in each row.

■ **Talk About Math**   Explain how you can use multiplication to check division. Then tell how you might use division to check multiplication.

Check Understanding

For another example, see Set B, pages 352–353.

Write two division sentences for each picture.

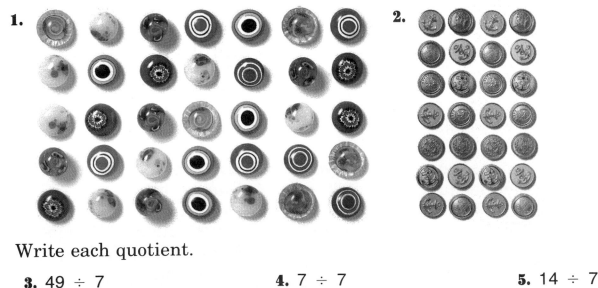

1.

2.

Write each quotient.

3. 49 ÷ 7   **4.** 7 ÷ 7   **5.** 14 ÷ 7

Practice

For More Practice, see Set B, pages 354–355.

Use each multiplication sentence to write
two division sentences.

6. 5 × 7 = 35   **7.** 9 × 7 = 63

Write each quotient.

8. 21 ÷ 7   **9.** 42 ÷ 7   **10.** 63 ÷ 7   **11.** 56 ÷ 7

12. 49 ÷ 7   **13.** 14 ÷ 7   **14.** 28 ÷ 7   **15.** 35 ÷ 7

16. 7)‾63‾   **17.** 7)‾28‾   **18.** 7)‾49‾

Mental Math   Find each answer.

19. 46 + 53   **20.** 24 ÷ 6   **21.** 41 − 11

22. 32 ÷ 4   **23.** 8 × 7   **24.** 38 − 21

25. 27 ÷ 3   **26.** 15 + 16   **27.** 49 ÷ 7

28. 9 × 4   **29.** 5 × 6   **30.** 56 ÷ 7

Buttons from Nepal are made
of bone or wood.

Problem Solving

Solve each problem.

31. Crystal has 14 embroidered
buttons from India, 7
buttons from France, and
7 Japanese buttons. How
many buttons does Crystal
have?

32. Last year, Laketa had 85
buttons in her collection.
Now she has 117 buttons.
How many buttons did
she add to her collection?

33. Andy has 28 buttons from
Nepal. If he displays 4
buttons in each tray, how
many trays will he need?

Dividing by Eight

Build Understanding

Nicole is helping her science teacher set up 40 microscopes. She will place 8 microscopes on each table. How many tables will Nicole be able to fill?

40 ÷ 8 = 5   since 5 × 8 = 40

■ **Talk About Math**   Explain how you could draw an array to show that 40 ÷ 8 = 5.

What kinds of things can you look at under a microscope?

Check Understanding

For another example, see Set C, pages 352–353.

A L G E B R A ▶ Write two division sentences for each picture.

1.
2.

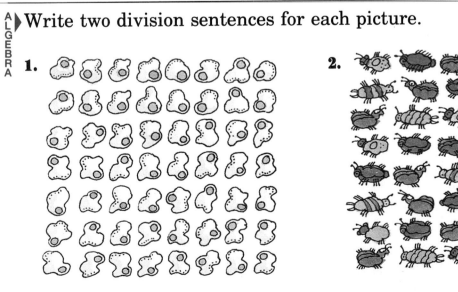

Write a multiplication sentence that would help you find each quotient; then write each quotient.

3. 64 ÷ 8   **4.** 72 ÷ 8   **5.** 16 ÷ 8   **6.** 48 ÷ 8

Practice

For More Practice, see Set C, pages 354–355.

Write each quotient.

7. 40 ÷ 8   **8.** 72 ÷ 8   **9.** 16 ÷ 8   **10.** 48 ÷ 8

11. 24 ÷ 8   **12.** 56 ÷ 8   **13.** 32 ÷ 8   **14.** 64 ÷ 8

15. 8$\overline{)32}$ **16.** 8$\overline{)56}$ **17.** 8$\overline{)16}$ **18.** 8$\overline{)64}$

19. 8$\overline{)72}$ **20.** 8$\overline{)24}$ **21.** 8$\overline{)48}$ **22.** 8$\overline{)40}$

Mixed Practice Use mental math or paper and pencil to do each exercise. Tell which method you used.

23. 24 ÷ 8   **24.** 410 − 26   **25.** 56 ÷ 8   **26.** 99 + 37

27. 7 × 7   **28.** 189 + 72   **29.** 24 ÷ 3   **30.** 66 − 57

31. 56 ÷ 7   **32.** 40 ÷ 5   **33.** 28 + 32   **34.** 6 × 4

35. 336 − 124   **36.** 64 ÷ 8   **37.** 227 + 567   **38.** 8 × 9

Problem Solving

39. Number Sense Find each quotient. Then write the next two facts of the pattern.
16 ÷ 8, 24 ÷ 8, 32 ÷ 8, ___?___, ___?___

40. Write the multiplication fact you could use to check each division fact in Exercises 7–14.

TIPS FOR PROBLEM SOLVERS

Take risks. Try your hunches. They often work.

Skills _____ Review   pages 274–275

Choose the more sensible measure for each container.
1. Soup bowl   **2.** Teakettle   **3.** Kitchen sink

   1 cup   1 quart   2 quarts   2 gallons   20 pints   20 gallons

Dividing by Nine

Build Understanding

Stickers	Price
Hearts	6¢ each
Stars	7¢ each
Ducks	8¢ each
Bears	9¢ each

Stephanie wants to buy some bear stickers. How many bear stickers can she buy for 54 cents?

$54 \div 9 = 6$ since $6 \times 9 = 54$

Stephanie can buy 6 bear stickers.

■ **Write About Math**   Draw two arrays to show that $54 \div 9 = 6$ and $54 \div 6 = 9$.

Check Understanding

For another example, see Set D, pages 352–353.

Write two division sentences for each picture.

1.

2.

Write a multiplication sentence that would help you find each quotient; then write each quotient.

3. $81 \div 9$ **4.** $54 \div 9$ **5.** $18 \div 9$ **6.** $72 \div 9$

Practice

For More Practice, see Set D, pages 354–355.

Write each quotient.

7. $45 \div 9$ **8.** $54 \div 9$ **9.** $81 \div 9$ **10.** $27 \div 9$

11. $72 \div 9$ **12.** $18 \div 9$ **13.** $36 \div 9$ **14.** $63 \div 9$

15. $9\overline{)54}$ **16.** $9\overline{)27}$ **17.** $9\overline{)72}$ **18.** $9\overline{)36}$

Mixed Practice   Use mental math, paper and pencil, or a calculator to find each answer. Tell which method you used.

19. $35 \div 5$ **20.** $100 - 26$ **21.** $81 \div 9$ **22.** $25 + 13$

23. 7×7 **24.** $2{,}118 - 243$ **25.** 8×4 **26.** $28 \div 4$

27. $54 \div 6$ **28.** $42 \div 7$ **29.** 9×4 **30.** $3{,}045 + 933$

Problem Solving

Use the chart on page 336 to solve Problems 31–33.

31. How many heart stickers could you buy for 48 cents?

32. Dante bought 5 bear and 7 star stickers. How much did he spend?

33. David spent 54 cents to buy some heart and some duck stickers. How many of each did he buy?

34. ▦ **Calculator**   If $63 \div 9 = 7$, what is $6{,}300 \div 9$? $6{,}300 \div 90$? $6{,}300 \div 900$?

35. **Estimation**   Carrie needed 52 stickers. One package has 6 stickers. She thought: Since $6 \times 8 = 48$ and $6 \times 9 = 54$, I should get 9 packages. Use Carrie's process to find how many packages of 8 stickers you would buy to get at least 47 stickers.

Families of Facts

Build Understanding

A. There are two multiplication sentences that describe this picture.

$3 \times 7 = 21$
$7 \times 3 = 21$

There are also two division sentences that describe this picture.

$21 \div 3 = 7$
$21 \div 7 = 3$

These four sentences form a family of facts.

B. This family of facts has only two number sentences.

$4 \times 4 = 16$
$16 \div 4 = 4$

■ **Talk About Math** How does knowing fact families help you remember basic facts?

Check Understanding

For another example, see Set E, pages 352–353.

1. Write a family of facts for this picture.

2. Complete this family of facts.
$5 \times 8 = 40 \quad 40 \div 8 = 5$

3. Write a family of facts that has only two number sentences.

Practice

For More Practice, see Set E, pages 354–355.

Write the family of facts for each picture.

4.   **5.**   **6.**

Copy. Then write each answer. Write number sentences to complete each family of facts.

7. $6 \times 9 =$ ▦   **8.** $7 \times 5 =$ ▦   **9.** $8 \times 8 =$ ▦   **10.** $9 \times 4 =$ ▦

　　$54 \div 9 =$ ▦   　　$35 \div 7 =$ ▦   　　　　　　　　$36 \div 9 =$ ▦

11. $4 \times 7 =$ ▦   **12.** $7 \times 7 =$ ▦   **13.** $8 \times 9 =$ ▦   **14.** $6 \times 3 =$ ▦

15. $5 \times 6 =$ ▦   **16.** $3 \times 4 =$ ▦   **17.** $9 \times 2 =$ ▦   **18.** $5 \times 5 =$ ▦

Mixed Practice Find each answer.

19. 7×9 **20.** $56 \div 8$ **21.** $40 \div 8$ **22.** $81 \div 9$

23. 6×7 **24.** 8×3 **25.** $54 \div 6$ **26.** 4×4

27. $12 \div 6$ **28.** 3×7 **29.** $49 \div 7$ **30.** $45 \div 9$

31. $42 \div 7$ **32.** $30 \div 6$ **33.** 5×9 **34.** 9×3

Midchapter ✓ Checkup

For each exercise, draw an array and write the family of facts.

1. $18 \div 9$ **2.** $64 \div 8$ **3.** $14 \div 7$

Find each quotient.

4. $72 \div 9$ **5.** $64 \div 8$ **6.** $49 \div 7$ **7.** $36 \div 6$

8. $9\overline{)81}$ **9.** $7\overline{)63}$ **10.** $8\overline{)48}$ **11.** $6\overline{)42}$

Number-Sense Project

Look back at pages 328-329.

1. How many of this necklace can Delia make if she has these beads on hand?

2. Delia also likes the third necklace in the picture on pages 328-329. How many of these necklaces can she make with the beads she has?

Type of Bead	Number on Hand
	40
	24
	18

Critical Thinking Activity

1 is the first odd number.
3 is the second odd number.
What is the tenth odd number?

Real-Life Decision Making

The teacher asks you to find enough helpers to carry 30 math books from the book room to your classroom. You and your helpers need to carefully bring all 30 books in one trip. How many helpers do you need?

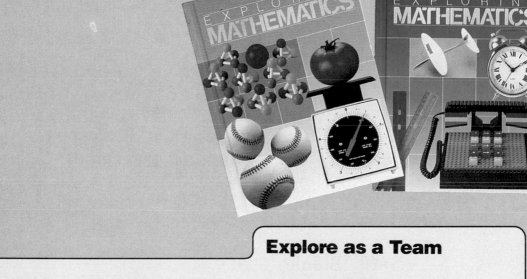

Explore as a Team

1. Without counting past 10, estimate how many squares are shaded.

2. Write about the method your group used to solve the problem.

TIPS FOR WORKING TOGETHER
Be a good tutor. Make up similar problems or easier ones to help someone understand.

Choose an Operation

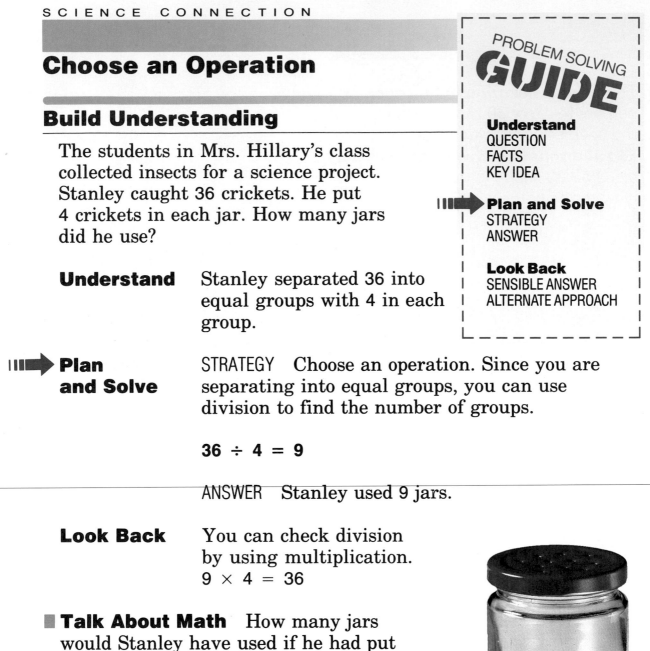

Build Understanding

The students in Mrs. Hillary's class collected insects for a science project. Stanley caught 36 crickets. He put 4 crickets in each jar. How many jars did he use?

Understand   Stanley separated 36 into equal groups with 4 in each group.

➤ **Plan and Solve**   STRATEGY   Choose an operation. Since you are separating into equal groups, you can use division to find the number of groups.

36 ÷ 4 = 9

ANSWER   Stanley used 9 jars.

Look Back   You can check division by using multiplication. 9 × 4 = 36

■ **Talk About Math**   How many jars would Stanley have used if he had put 6 crickets in each jar?

Check Understanding

Solve this problem by answering Questions 1–5.

Matt caught 15 grasshoppers. He used 8 of them for his project and let the rest go. How many grasshoppers did he let go?

1. What are you asked to find?

2. List the facts you need.

3. Should you add, subtract, multiply, or divide to solve this problem?

4. How did you decide which operation you should use?

5. How many grasshoppers did Matt let go?

Practice

Tell whether you should *add, subtract, multiply,* or *divide.* Then find each answer.

6. Teresita arranged her insects in a box. She made 7 rows with 7 in each row. How many insects did Teresita have in all?

7. The class caught 8 moths. They caught 6 more butterflies than moths. How many butterflies did they catch?

8. Jamie caught 7 June bugs, 8 dragonflies, and 4 fireflies. How many insects did he catch in all?

9. Of the 14 butterflies caught, 9 were monarchs. The rest were swallowtails. How many were swallowtails?

10. If 4 butterfly nets were shared equally by 24 students, how many students used each net?

Choose a _____ Strategy

What a Difference!

11. Think of 2 one-digit numbers. Their difference is double their quotient. What are the numbers?

12. Think of a two-digit number. If you add the digits together and then subtract 1, the difference is 2. What is the number?

PROBLEM SOLVING
STRATEGIES

Choose an Operation
Find a Pattern
Use Logical Reasoning
Make a Table
Draw a Picture
Try and Check
Write a Number Sentence

Zero and One in Division

Build Understanding

A. Tasha has 5 zinnia plants in a flat. How many groups of 5 does she have?

B. Tasha put 1 plant in each of 5 different pots. How many groups of 1 did she make?

$$5 \div 5 = 1$$

$$5 \div 1 = 5$$

C. The flat has no plants in it now. How many groups of 5 are there?

D. Tasha bought 5 more plants. How many groups of 0 are there?

$$0 \div 5 = 0$$

$$5 \div 0 = ?$$

More than 250,000 species of flowering plants exist.

We would not use any of the plants if we made groups of 0. So this question doesn't make sense.

■ **Talk About Math** What is the family of facts for Example A?

Check Understanding

For another example, see Set F, pages 352–353.

Write each quotient.

1. 4 ÷ 4   **2.** 8 ÷ 1   **3.** 0 ÷ 2   **4.** 9 ÷ 9   **5.** 7 ÷ 1

6. What is the quotient when any number is divided by itself? by 1?

7. What is the quotient when 0 is divided by any nonzero number?

Practice

For More Practice, see Set F, pages 354–355.

Write each quotient.

8. 9 ÷ 1   **9.** 0 ÷ 3   **10.** 7 ÷ 7   **11.** 6 ÷ 1   **12.** 8 ÷ 8

13. 0 ÷ 5   **14.** 4 ÷ 1   **15.** 3 ÷ 3   **16.** 0 ÷ 6   **17.** 2 ÷ 2

18. 0 ÷ 4   **19.** 2 ÷ 1   **20.** 0 ÷ 7   **21.** 1 ÷ 1   **22.** 0 ÷ 8

23. 0 ÷ 1   **24.** 8 ÷ 1   **25.** 35 ÷ 35   **26.** 67 ÷ 1   **27.** 0 ÷ 93

Mixed Practice   Find each answer.

28. 63 ÷ 9   **29.** 31 + 29   **30.** 5 × 8   **31.** 48 ÷ 8   **32.** 24 ÷ 4

33. 0 ÷ 6   **34.** 3 × 5   **35.** 72 ÷ 9   **36.** 7 × 8   **37.** 97 − 59

Problem Solving

Critical Thinking   Write a multiplication/ division family of facts in which

38. all of the numbers in the number sentences are the same.

39. one of the factors is 1.

40. **Use Data**   Draw an array and write the family of facts for one of Exercises 9–24 on page 203.

Remainders

Build Understanding

Button Up Your Socks
Materials: 27 small objects
Groups: Partners

A. Have you ever made a puppet out of a sock?

Teddy makes hand puppets. For each one he uses 6 buttons—4 for the puppet's shirt and 2 for the eyes. If Teddy has 27 buttons, how many hand puppets can he make?

a. Use 27 small objects.

b. Make groups of 6.

c. How many groups of 6 did you make? Are there any left over?

27 divided by 6 is 4 with a ***remainder*** of 3.

B. Divide 14 into 4 equal groups.

a. Show 14 objects.

b. Divide them equally into 4 groups.

c. Tell how many are in each group. Tell how many are left over.

What is 14 divided by 4? What is the remainder?

■ **Talk About Math** How could you write the answers for the problems in Examples A and B?

Check Understanding

For another example, see Set G, pages 352–353.

Use small objects to help you with each exercise.

1. Show 20 in all. Make groups of 3. How many groups? What is the remainder?

2. 8 ÷ 3   **3.** 9 ÷ 4   **4.** 7 ÷ 2   **5.** 10 ÷ 6   **6.** 15 ÷ 9

Practice

For More Practice, see Set G, pages 354–355.

Use small objects to help you with each exercise.
Remember to tell the remainder.

7. 17 ÷ 3   **8.** 11 ÷ 2   **9.** 14 ÷ 4   **10.** 15 ÷ 8   **11.** 13 ÷ 6

12. 19 ÷ 4   **13.** 16 ÷ 5   **14.** 14 ÷ 6   **15.** 10 ÷ 7   **16.** 20 ÷ 5

17. 21 ÷ 5   **18.** 22 ÷ 5   **19.** 23 ÷ 5   **20.** 24 ÷ 5   **21.** 25 ÷ 5

22. 26 ÷ 6   **23.** 27 ÷ 8   **24.** 12 ÷ 5   **25.** 16 ÷ 6   **26.** 15 ÷ 4

27. 28 ÷ 6   **28.** 9 ÷ 4   **29.** 20 ÷ 6   **30.** 14 ÷ 3   **31.** 7 ÷ 2

32. 30 ÷ 7   **33.** 29 ÷ 3   **34.** 34 ÷ 6   **35.** 19 ÷ 5   **36.** 42 ÷ 7

Problem Solving

Explore ———— Math

37. If you make 7 groups, what is the greatest number that could be left over?

38. If you make groups of 3 objects, could 3 objects be left over?

39. Compare the remainder with the divisor in each of Exercises 7–36. Which is always greater, the divisor or the remainder?

Interpret the Remainder

PROBLEM SOLVING
GUIDE

Understand
QUESTION
FACTS
KEY IDEA

Plan and Solve
STRATEGY
ANSWER

Look Back
SENSIBLE ANSWER
ALTERNATE APPROACH

Build Understanding

A class of 28 students is going to the history museum. A car can carry 5 students. How many cars are needed for the trip?

Understand   They need enough cars to carry all 28 students, even if it means one car will have some empty seats.

Plan and Solve   STRATEGY   Draw 28 Xs. Circle groups of 5.

ANSWER   There are 5 groups of 5 with 3 left over.

Five cars could carry only 25 students. So 6 cars are needed for the 28 students.

Look Back   SENSIBLE ANSWER $6 \times 5 = 30$. So 6 cars will be enough to carry 28 students.

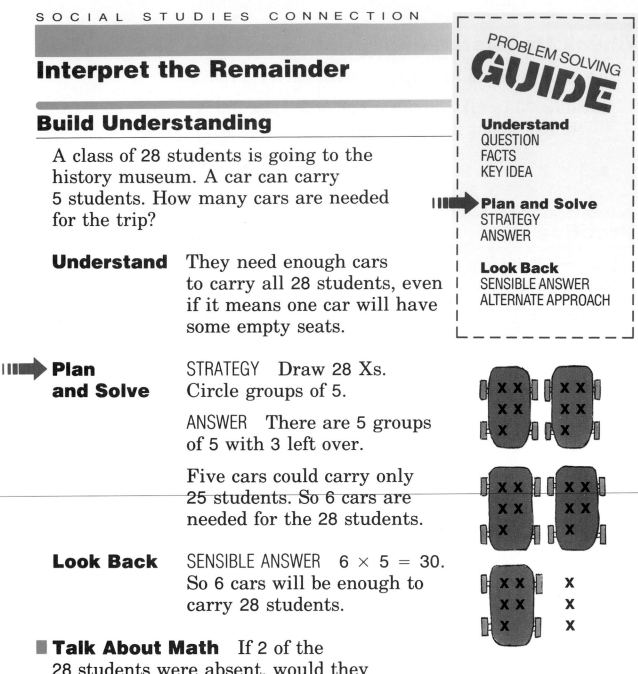

■ **Talk About Math**   If 2 of the 28 students were absent, would they still need 6 cars? Why?

Check Understanding

Solve this problem by answering Questions 1–4.

Daniel has 55 cents. He wants to spend it on stickers in the gift shop. If each sticker costs 7 cents, how many could he buy?

1. What do you need to divide?

2. How many Xs should you draw? How many Xs will you put in each group?

3. How many groups did you make? How many Xs were left over?

4. How many stickers can Daniel buy? Will he have money left? How much?

Practice

Draw a picture to help you solve each problem.

5. The class has 15 pictures of the trip to put on 4 poster boards. They put the same number of pictures on each board. How many pictures were not used?

6. Mr. Chang's class needs 3 vans to go to the museum. Each van holds 9 students. What is the greatest number of students who can go to the museum from Mr. Chang's class?

7. There are 50 people going into the museum lunchroom. Only 6 people can sit at each table. How many tables are needed to seat the people?

8. The gift shop sells lava rocks. Each bag holds 3 rocks. How many bags can Nicky fill if she has 19 rocks?

Reading ———— Math

Main Idea Tell which phrase best describes the remainder in Exercise 7.

a. The number of people who will sit at a table that is not full

b. The number of people who do not get to eat

c. The number of tables that are needed

Skills Review

Write each quotient.

1. 18 ÷ 6   2. 45 ÷ 9

3. 14 ÷ 7   4. 24 ÷ 8

5. 18 ÷ 9   6. 36 ÷ 6

7. 32 ÷ 8   8. 21 ÷ 7

9. 45 ÷ 9   10. 64 ÷ 8

11. 0 ÷ 6   12. 3 ÷ 3

13. 40 ÷ 8   14. 27 ÷ 9

15. 63 ÷ 7   16. 30 ÷ 6

17. 9 ÷ 1   18. 35 ÷ 7

19. 48 ÷ 6   20. 56 ÷ 8

21. 7)‾42‾   22. 6)‾48‾

23. 8)‾72‾   24. 9)‾81‾

Write the family of facts.

25. 8 × 7 = 56   26. 30 ÷ 5 = 6

27. 72 ÷ 8 = 9   28. 4 × 7 = 28

Divide. Write each quotient and remainder.

29. 18 ÷ 5   30. 13 ÷ 2

31. 25 ÷ 6   32. 22 ÷ 7

Problem-Solving Review

Solve each problem.

33. What am I? I make cars shine. All symmetric are the 3 letters of mine.

34. Mica has 3 cats. Each cat eats 3 meals a day. A box of cat food has 8 meal-sized packets. Does Mica need more than 1 box a day?

35. Mr. Lewis started making a wooden puzzle by cutting an 8-inch by 9-inch board into 1-inch squares. How many puzzle pieces were there?

36. Jessica took 24 photos with one roll of film and 36 photos with another. How many photos did she take?

37. **Data File** Use data from pages 402–403. To make one decoration Victor needs 6 stars, 8 pine branches, and 7 snowflakes. How many decorations can he make if he has one bag of each?

38. **Make a Data File** Look at the information on the labels of 5 types of food. List the number of grams of carbohydrates, fat, and protein there is in one serving.

Write the family of addition and subtraction facts for the numbers in each exercise.

1. 4, 8, 12   **2.** 7, 0, 7

Write the number in standard form.

3. four thousand, thirty-six

4. eight hundred two thousand, forty-nine

Find each sum or difference.

5. 42	**6.** 67	**7.** 81
+ 38	+ 17	− 56

8. 1,302	**9.** 2,471	**10.** 482
+ 798	+ 2,569	− 356

Measure the line segment to the nearest

11. half inch.   **12.** centimeter.

Find each product.

13. 5	**14.** 8	**15.** 2
× 4	× 5	× 6

16. 7	**17.** 8	**18.** 9
× 6	× 8	× 4

19. Is the angle a right angle? Write *yes* or *no*.

20. Does the figure look symmetric? Write *yes* or *no*.

21. Find the volume of the solid shape in cubic units.

22. Would you use grams or kilograms to measure how much a cat weighs?

Find each quotient.

23. 18 ÷ 2   **24.** 24 ÷ 4

25. 21 ÷ 3   **26.** 30 ÷ 5

27. 36 ÷ 6   **28.** 28 ÷ 4

29. 24 ÷ 3   **30.** 16 ÷ 2

31. 45 ÷ 5   **32.** 35 ÷ 7

33. 6 ÷ 1   **34.** 63 ÷ 9

35. 48 ÷ 8   **36.** 0 ÷ 7

Divide. Write each quotient and remainder.

37. 26 ÷ 4   **38.** 21 ÷ 5

39. 17 ÷ 3   **40.** 25 ÷ 8

Reteaching

Set A   pages 330–331

If you have 12 objects, you can make an array that has 6 objects in each row.

x x x x x x
x x x x x x

You can make 2 rows with 6 objects in each row.

12 ÷ 6 = 2

Remember that the quotient is the answer to a division problem.

Write each quotient.

1. 18 ÷ 6   **2.** 36 ÷ 6

3. 6)‾24   **4.** 6)‾54

Set B   pages 332–333

Allen has collected 42 model cars. He wants to display them on 7 shelves. If he places the same number of cars on each shelf, how many cars will he place on each?

You can use multiplication to help you with division.

7 × ▦ = 42
7 × 6 = 42
So   42 ÷ 7 = 6

He can place 6 cars on each shelf.

Remember that if the product of the quotient and the divisor is the dividend, the quotient is correct.

Write each quotient.

1. 49 ÷ 7   **2.** 14 ÷ 7

3. 7 ÷ 7   **4.** 28 ÷ 7

5. 7)‾42   **6.** 7)‾21

7. 7)‾14   **8.** 7)‾35

Set C   pages 334–335

This array shows two division sentences.

x x x x x x x x
x x x x x x x x
x x x x x x x x
x x x x x x x x
x x x x x x x x
x x x x x x x x

48 ÷ 6 = 8   48 ÷ 8 = 6

Remember that you can use multiplication to help you find a quotient. Write each quotient.

1. 56 ÷ 8   **2.** 16 ÷ 8

3. 24 ÷ 8   **4.** 64 ÷ 8

5. 8)‾32   **6.** 8)‾48

7. 8)‾24   **8.** 8)‾40

352

Set D pages 336–337

These arrays show divisions.

$36 \div 4 = 9$ $36 \div 9 = 4$

Remember that the dividend is the number being separated into groups. Write each quotient.

1. $27 \div 9$ **2.** $45 \div 9$ **3.** $54 \div 9$

4. $9\overline{)81}$ **5.** $9\overline{)63}$ **6.** $9\overline{)45}$

Set E pages 338–339

This family of facts describes this array.

x x x x x x $4 \times 6 = 24$
x x x x x x $6 \times 4 = 24$
x x x x x x $24 \div 6 = 4$
x x x x x x $24 \div 4 = 6$

Remember that you can use one multiplication or division fact to help you write a family of facts.

1. Write the family of facts for this picture.

x x x x x x x x x
x x x x x x x x x

Set F pages 344–345

This array shows that $4 \div 4 = 1$.

| x | x | x | x |

Knowing this division fact, you can write a family of facts.

$4 \div 1 = 4$
$4 \times 1 = 4$
$1 \times 4 = 4$

Remember that dividing a number by 0 makes no sense.

Write each quotient.

1. $9 \div 9$ **2.** $8 \div 1$

3. $6 \div 1$ **4.** $0 \div 5$

5. $86 \div 86$ **6.** $92 \div 1$

Set G pages 346–347

Divide 13 into groups of 4.

| x x x x | | x x x x | | x x x x | x

You can divide 13 into 3 groups of 4 with 1 left over. So $13 \div 4$ is 3 with a remainder of 1.

Remember that the remainder should be less than the divisor.

Use small objects to help you answer each exercise.

1. $9 \div 2$ **2.** $14 \div 3$

3. $17 \div 5$ **4.** $16 \div 4$

5. $22 \div 4$ **6.** $13 \div 5$

More Practice

Set A pages 330–331

Write each quotient.

1. 18 ÷ 6	**2.** 12 ÷ 6	**3.** 36 ÷ 6	**4.** 42 ÷ 6
5. 6⟌12	**6.** 6⟌48	**7.** 6⟌54	**8.** 6⟌24

Mixed Practice Find each answer.

9. 7 × 5	**10.** 36 ÷ 4	**11.** 36 − 27	**12.** 42 ÷ 6
13. 57 + 38	**14.** 8 × 7	**15.** 45 ÷ 5	**16.** 24 ÷ 4
17. 21 ÷ 3	**18.** 70 − 39	**19.** 24 ÷ 6	**20.** 16 ÷ 2

Set B pages 332–333

Write each quotient.

1. 14 ÷ 7	**2.** 35 ÷ 7	**3.** 49 ÷ 7	**4.** 56 ÷ 7
5. 7⟌42	**6.** 7⟌28	**7.** 7⟌21	**8.** 7⟌35

Mental Math Find each answer.

9. 8 × 4	**10.** 17 + 26	**11.** 46 − 13	**12.** 24 ÷ 3
13. 36 ÷ 4	**14.** 42 ÷ 6	**15.** 42 ÷ 7	**16.** 9 × 6

Set C pages 334–335

Write each quotient.

1. 16 ÷ 8	**2.** 64 ÷ 8	**3.** 24 ÷ 8	**4.** 72 ÷ 8
5. 8⟌24	**6.** 8⟌40	**7.** 8⟌32	**8.** 8⟌48

Mixed Practice Use mental math or paper and pencil to do each exercise. Tell which method you used.

9. 27 ÷ 3	**10.** 620 − 48	**11.** 87 + 29	**12.** 6 × 7
13. 17 + 33	**14.** 84 − 37	**15.** 35 ÷ 5	**16.** 8 × 8
17. 42 ÷ 6	**18.** 8 × 4	**19.** 7 × 4	**20.** 23 + 39

Set D   pages 336–337

Write each quotient.

1. 27 ÷ 9   **2.** 72 ÷ 9   **3.** 36 ÷ 9   **4.** 63 ÷ 9

5. 9$\overline{)45}$ **6.** 9$\overline{)18}$ **7.** 9$\overline{)63}$ **8.** 9$\overline{)81}$

Mixed Practice   Use mental math, paper
and pencil, or a calculator to find each
answer. Tell which method you used.

9. 45 ÷ 5   **10.** 90 − 36   **11.** 6 × 6   **12.** 4,088 + 811

Set E   pages 338–339

Write the family of facts for each picture.

1. X X X X X X
   X X X X X X
   X X X X X X

2. X X X X X X X
   X X X X X X X
   X X X X X X X
   X X X X X X X

3. X X X X X X X X X X
   X X X X X X X X X X

Copy and complete each sentence. Write number
sentences to complete each family of facts.

4. 7 × 8 = ▦   **5.** 9 × 3 = ▦   **6.** 8 × 4 = ▦   **7.** 9 × 9 = ▦
   56 ÷ 8 = ▦   27 ÷ 9 = ▦   32 ÷ 8 = ▦

8. 3 × 8 = ▦   **9.** 6 × 9 = ▦   **10.** 7 × 3 = ▦   **11.** 6 × 7 = ▦

Set F   pages 344–345

Write each quotient.

1. 4 ÷ 4   **2.** 8 ÷ 1   **3.** 0 ÷ 5   **4.** 1 ÷ 1

5. 0 ÷ 182   **6.** 47 ÷ 47   **7.** 103 ÷ 1   **8.** 94 ÷ 94

Set G   pages 346–347

Use small objects to help you answer each exercise.

1. 7 ÷ 2   **2.** 11 ÷ 3   **3.** 14 ÷ 5   **4.** 21 ÷ 3

5. 23 ÷ 4   **6.** 17 ÷ 8   **7.** 21 ÷ 6   **8.** 12 ÷ 7

Enrichment

Missing Factors and More

When you divide, you are looking for a *missing factor.*

40 ÷ 8 = ▦ is the same as **8 × ▦ = 40.**

Complete each number sentence.

1. 6 × ▦ = 54   **2.** 35 ÷ ▦ = 5

3. ▦ × 7 = 42   **4.** 24 ÷ ▦ = 8

5. 4 × ▦ = 16   **6.** 9 × ▦ = 63

7. 8 × ▦ = 72   **8.** ▦ × 2 = 14

9. 27 ÷ ▦ = 3   **10.** ▦ ÷ 5 = 6

Divide. Then decide if you should replace the ▦ with >, <, or = .

11. 48 ÷ 8 ▦ 56 ÷ 7   **12.** 72 ÷ 8 ▦ 27 ÷ 3

13. 18 ÷ 3 ▦ 14 ÷ 2   **14.** 42 ÷ 6 ▦ 81 ÷ 9

15. 30 ÷ 5 ▦ 36 ÷ 6   **16.** 18 ÷ 2 ▦ 36 ÷ 9

Which of the numbers 1 to 9 will make each sentence true? Each exercise may have more than one answer.

17. 54 ÷ 6 < 3 × ▦   **18.** 4 × ▦ > 40 ÷ 5

19. 3 × ▦ > 36 ÷ 9   **20.** 24 ÷ ▦ < 35 ÷ 7

21. 6 × 6 > 8 × ▦   **22.** 16 ÷ 4 < 2 × ▦

Chapter 10 Review/Test

Write each quotient.

1. 48 ÷ 6   **2.** 3 ÷ 1

3. 36 ÷ 9   **4.** 40 ÷ 8

5. 0 ÷ 2   **6.** 42 ÷ 7

7. 6)‾2‾4‾   **8.** 7)‾6‾3‾

9. 8)‾5‾6‾   **10.** 9)‾5‾4‾

Copy and write each answer. Circle the fact that does not belong to the family of facts.

11. 24 ÷ 3   **12.** 16 ÷ 8
    3 × 8   4 × 4
  24 ÷ 4   16 ÷ 4
    8 × 3
  24 ÷ 8

Divide. Write each quotient and remainder.

13. 17 ÷ 8   **14.** 32 ÷ 6

15. 61 ÷ 7   **16.** 85 ÷ 9

Tell whether you would add, subtract, multiply, or divide to solve each problem.

17. Of the 32 cans on the shelf, 8 are soup cans. How many are not soup cans?

18. If each car can carry 5 children, how many cars are needed for 15 children?

19. Susie's cat book has 42 pages. Her horse book is 15 pages longer. How many pages does the horse book have?

20. Solve Problem 18.

Pablo has 36 photographs. He will put 8 on each page of his album.

21. Choose the most sensible answer for the number of pages Pablo needs for his pictures.

  a. 4 pages   **c.** 28 pages
  b. 44 pages   **d.** 5 pages

22. If all the album pages are empty at first, how many pictures will Pablo put on the last page he uses?

23. ■ **Write About Math** In Exercise 12, tell why the fact you chose does not belong to that family.

Fractions and Decimals

11

Did You Know: Apatosaurus (Brontosaurus) was 70 feet long and weighed over 60,000 pounds. It lived in what is now Colorado, Oklahoma, Utah, and Wyoming.

USA 25 Stegosaurus

USA 25 Brontosaurus

USA 25 Tyrannosaurus

Number-Sense Project

Estimate
Predict which dinosaur is the best known.

Gather Data
Show 4 people pictures of 4 dinosaurs and have them try to name each one. Record which ones they could name.

Analyze and Report
Was your prediction correct? Compare your results with other students. Did everyone come up with the same answer?

USA
25 *Pteranodon*

Fractions: Part of a Whole

Build Understanding

A. Fraction Cut-ups
Materials: Unlined paper, red crayon, tracing paper, scissors

Lee is helping to make 4 clown costumes for the school play. How can he cut a piece of cloth into 4 equal parts? Equal parts are all the same size. You can use a piece of paper to show how to make 4 equal parts.

a. Fold a piece of paper in two. Then fold it again.

b. Open the paper. Cut along each fold. Are the parts equal?

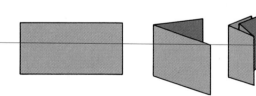

B. How many equal parts of the whole does each picture show?

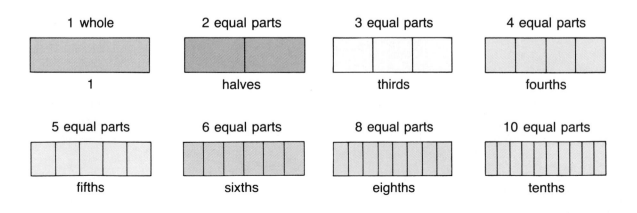

1 whole	2 equal parts	3 equal parts	4 equal parts
1	halves	thirds	fourths

5 equal parts	6 equal parts	8 equal parts	10 equal parts
fifths	sixths	eighths	tenths

c. This figure is divided into sixths.

a. Trace the figure and cut it out. Then cut it apart along the lines.

b. Pick up one part. This part is one sixth of the whole figure. *Fractions* name equal parts of a whole, so one sixth is a fraction.

You write one sixth as $\frac{1}{6}$.

numerator ⟶ 1 ⟵ number of parts set aside
denominator ⟶ 6 ⟵ number of equal parts in all

c. Pick up the parts of the figure to show two sixths, three sixths, four sixths, and five sixths.

■ **Talk About Math** Is each part of this circle one third of the whole circle? Explain.

Check Understanding

For another example, see Set A, pages 396–397.

Write the fractions.

1.

2. Two thirds

3.

Number Sense Answer each question.

4. In Exercises 1–3, what is the denominator of each fraction?

5. What does the denominator of a fraction stand for?

6. In Exercises 1–3, what is the numerator of each fraction?

7. What does the numerator of a fraction stand for?

Practice

For More Practice, see Set A, pages 398–399.

Copy and complete the table.

8.

Equal parts	2	3	4	5	6	7	8	9	10	12
Name	Halves									

Which fraction names the shaded part?

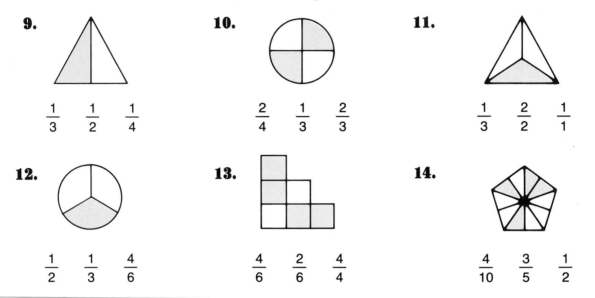

9. $\dfrac{1}{3}$ $\dfrac{1}{2}$ $\dfrac{1}{4}$

10. $\dfrac{2}{4}$ $\dfrac{1}{3}$ $\dfrac{2}{3}$

11. $\dfrac{1}{3}$ $\dfrac{2}{2}$ $\dfrac{1}{1}$

12. $\dfrac{1}{2}$ $\dfrac{1}{3}$ $\dfrac{4}{6}$

13. $\dfrac{4}{6}$ $\dfrac{2}{6}$ $\dfrac{4}{4}$

14. $\dfrac{4}{10}$ $\dfrac{3}{5}$ $\dfrac{1}{2}$

Which picture is shaded to show the fraction?

15. Two thirds

a.   b.

16. Three eighths

a.   b.

17. Six tenths

a.   b.

18. One half

a.   b.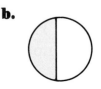

Write a fraction to name the shaded part.
Write the fraction as a number and with words.

19.   **20.**   **21.**

Problem Solving

Solve each problem.

22. Kim, Chaz, and Rob cut a ribbon into 3 equal parts. Each took 1 part. What part of the whole ribbon did each get?

23. Mikey cut a piece of cloth into 6 equal pieces. How can he cut the cloth again to get 12 equal pieces?

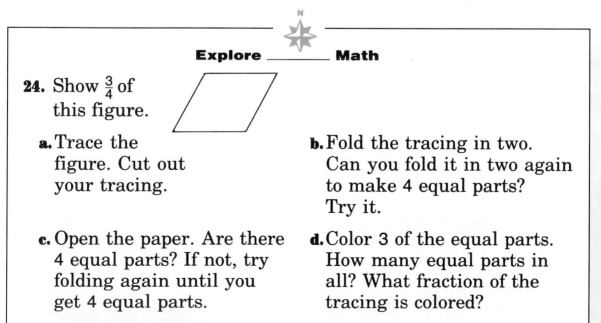

Explore ———— Math

24. Show $\frac{3}{4}$ of this figure.

a. Trace the figure. Cut out your tracing.

b. Fold the tracing in two. Can you fold it in two again to make 4 equal parts? Try it.

c. Open the paper. Are there 4 equal parts? If not, try folding again until you get 4 equal parts.

d. Color 3 of the equal parts. How many equal parts in all? What fraction of the tracing is colored?

Fractions: Part of a Set

Build Understanding

People around the world like to dance.

Indian dancers tell stories by moving their arms, hands, feet, and fingers.

Polynesian dancers perform at festivals, swaying their hips and waving their arms. The dances tell stories and describe the beautiful scenery of the islands.

Folk dances, such as the Mexican hat dance, are part of Mexican fiestas.

A. Out of 15 students in Maria's class, 7 are participating in a dance festival.

$$\frac{\text{number of dancers} \longrightarrow 7}{\text{number of students in all} \longrightarrow 15}$$

The fraction $\frac{7}{15}$ shows what part of the class are dancers.

B. Three of the dancers wear hats when they dance.

$$\frac{\text{number of dancers who wear hats} \longrightarrow 3}{\text{number of dancers} \longrightarrow 7}$$

The fraction $\frac{3}{7}$ shows what part of the dancers wear hats.

■ **Talk About Math** Explain how to write a fraction showing how many students in Maria's class are not dancers.

Check Understanding

For another example, see Set B, pages 396–397.

1. What fraction describes Maria's whole class?

2. What fraction of the dancers are wearing leis?

3. What fraction of the dancers do not wear hats?

4. The dancers with hats make up what fraction of the class?

Practice

For More Practice, see Set B, pages 398–399.

What fraction stands for the blue part of each group?
Write the letter.　**a.** $\frac{1}{6}$　**b.** $\frac{5}{8}$　**c.** $\frac{3}{4}$　**d.** $\frac{4}{6}$　**e.** $\frac{3}{5}$　**f.** $\frac{1}{2}$　**g.** $\frac{1}{3}$

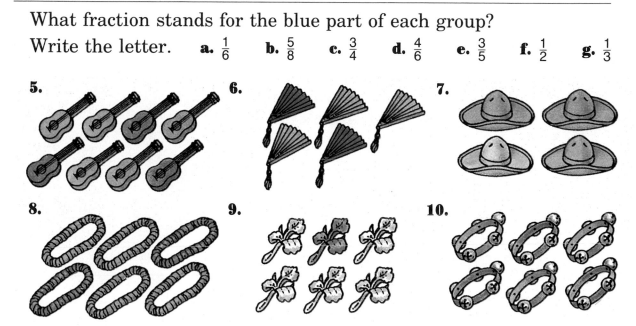

5.

6.

7.

8.

9.

10.

Problem Solving

What fraction of the dance books have

11. blue covers?

12. covers that are not blue?

13. the word *dancing* in the titles?

14. the word *dances* in the titles?

Solve.

15. Maria has 3 of the dance books. Two of them are blue. The other book has *dancing* in the title. Name a dance book Maria does **not** have.

Equal Fractions

Build Understanding

The Jackson twins are making cards.
They use a sheet of construction paper to
make each card.

Jackie folded her pink paper in half. Julie
folded her paper in fourths. Then the
twins opened their papers.

Jackie saw that one half of her paper was
the same as two fourths of Julie's paper.

The fractions $\frac{1}{2}$ and $\frac{2}{4}$ are equal.

■ **Talk About Math**   Suppose a
friend of the twins folded the paper
in sixths. Do you think $\frac{3}{6}$ is the same
as $\frac{1}{2}$ and $\frac{2}{4}$? Why or why not?

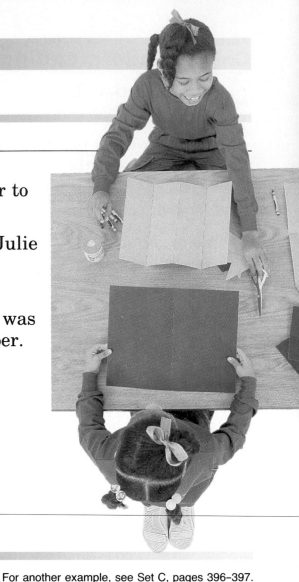

Check Understanding

For another example, see Set C, pages 396–397.

Julie wants to make yellow cutouts, all the
same size, to paste on the green card. She
begins by folding a sheet of yellow
construction paper.

1. How many equal parts are there?

2. How many of these parts make up one half of the sheet?

3. How many of these parts make up one fourth of the sheet?

How many eighths are there in

4. one half?   **5.** one fourth?   **6.** one whole?

For More Practice, see Set C, pages 398–399.

Complete each number sentence to show equal fractions.

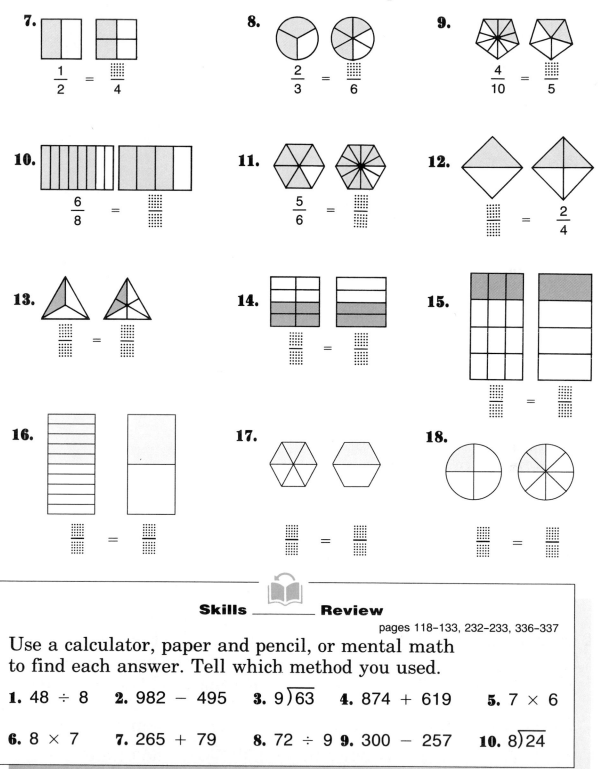

7. $\dfrac{1}{2} = \dfrac{}{4}$

8. $\dfrac{2}{3} = \dfrac{}{6}$

9. $\dfrac{4}{10} = \dfrac{}{5}$

10. $\dfrac{6}{8} = \dfrac{}{}$

11. $\dfrac{5}{6} = \dfrac{}{}$

12. $\dfrac{}{} = \dfrac{2}{4}$

13. $\dfrac{}{} = \dfrac{}{}$

14. $\dfrac{}{} = \dfrac{}{}$

15. $\dfrac{}{} = \dfrac{}{}$

16. $\dfrac{}{} = \dfrac{}{}$

17. $\dfrac{}{} = \dfrac{}{}$

18. $\dfrac{}{} = \dfrac{}{}$

Skills Review

pages 118–133, 232–233, 336–337

Use a calculator, paper and pencil, or mental math
to find each answer. Tell which method you used.

1. $48 \div 8$ **2.** $982 - 495$ **3.** $9\overline{)63}$ **4.** $874 + 619$ **5.** 7×6

6. 8×7 **7.** $265 + 79$ **8.** $72 \div 9$ **9.** $300 - 257$ **10.** $8\overline{)24}$

Finding Fractional Parts

Build Understanding

Keegan has 18 rabbits for his magic act. If $\frac{1}{3}$ of the rabbits are brown, how many rabbits are brown?

A. Think of dividing the whole set of rabbits into 3 equal groups. How many rabbits will be in each group?

There are six brown rabbits.

B. Suppose Keegan puts bow ties on $\frac{1}{2}$ of the rabbits. How many rabbits wear bow ties?

To find $\frac{1}{2}$ of a number, you can divide the number by 2. Find $\frac{1}{2}$ of 18.

■ Mental Math

Think: $18 \div 2 = 9$
So $\frac{1}{2}$ of $18 = 9$.

There are 9 rabbits wearing bow ties.

■ **Talk About Math** What division fact could you use to answer the question in Example A? Do you prefer to divide a set into equal groups or use division to find the answer? Why?

Check Understanding

For another example, see Set D, pages 396–397.

Answer questions 1–4 about the picture to solve this problem.

If $\frac{1}{2}$ of the hats have red bands, how many hats have red bands?

1. How many hats are there?

2. What number will you find $\frac{1}{2}$ of?

3. Which division fact can help you solve the problem?

4. How many hats have red bands?

Practice

For More Practice, see Set D, pages 398–399.

Find each number.

5. $\frac{1}{6}$ of 12

6. $\frac{1}{3}$ of 9

7. $\frac{1}{4}$ of 16

8. $\frac{1}{5}$ of 10

9. $\frac{1}{8}$ of 32

10. $\frac{1}{5}$ of 5

11. $\frac{1}{4}$ of 24

12. $\frac{1}{6}$ of 48

13. $\frac{1}{9}$ of 36

14. $\frac{1}{5}$ of 25

15. $\frac{1}{2}$ of 14

16. $\frac{1}{8}$ of 64

17. $\frac{1}{4}$ of 20

18. $\frac{1}{8}$ of 48

19. $\frac{1}{3}$ of 21

20. $\frac{1}{5}$ of 35

21. $\frac{1}{6}$ of 36

22. $\frac{1}{9}$ of 45

23. $\frac{1}{7}$ of 42

24. $\frac{1}{3}$ of 33

25. **Calculator** Use your calculator to find $\frac{1}{16}$ of 288.

Problem Solving

Solve each problem.

26. A magician has 6 magic wands. Three of the wands are broken. What fraction are broken?

27. Draw 12 top hats. Color $\frac{1}{3}$ of the hats red. Color $\frac{1}{2}$ of the hats black.

369

Try and Check

Build Understanding

Sarah saw 7 clowns in the circus. Each clown was on a bicycle or tricycle. Sarah counted 16 wheels in all. How many clowns were on bicycles?

Understand Sarah needs to know how many clowns rode bicycles. She knows each clown was on a bicycle or tricycle. Sarah also knows that there were 16 wheels. The sum of the bicycle wheels and the tricycle wheels must equal 16.

 Plan and Solve STRATEGY Sarah can make a guess and then check to see if she is correct.

Number of Bicycles	Number of Tricycles	Bicycle Wheels	Tricycle Wheels	Total Wheels
4	3	8	9	17
6	1	12	3	15
5	2	10	6	16

too many wheels

too few wheels

correct

Look Back Is Sarah's computation correct? Is the number of bicycles and tricycles equal to 7? Is the number of wheels equal to 16?

■ **Write About Math** How could you draw a picture to help find the answer?

PROBLEM SOLVING
GUIDE

Understand
QUESTION
FACTS
KEY IDEA

Plan and Solve
STRATEGY
ANSWER

Look Back
SENSIBLE ANSWER
ALTERNATE APPROACH

Check Understanding

Solve this problem by answering questions 1–4.

The 7 clowns had 27 pompons on their clown suits. Some suits had 5 pompons, and some suits had 3 pompons. How many suits had 5 pompons each?

1. What is the total number of pompons on the clown suits?

2. How many pompons could be on one clown suit?

3. If only one clown had 5 pompons, how many pompons would there be in all?

4. Try different numbers until you get 27 pompons on 7 suits. How many clowns had 5 pompons?

Practice

Solve each problem.

5. The circus charges $2 for each child under 12 and $5 for each child over 12. Sarah gave the cashier $18 for 6 children. How many were under 12? How many were over 12?

6. In a parade, there are dogs in clown shoes and people in clown shoes. In all, there are 24 shoes. One half of the clowns are people. How many are dogs?

7. Four clowns lined up for the parade. Gruffy was in front of Rosey and behind Yo. Buzzy was at the end of the line. Which clown was first in line?

8. In one act, the clowns wear red or blue. Twice as many clowns wear blue as red. If 33 clowns are in the act, how many are wearing blue? How many are wearing red?

Comparing Fractions

Build Understanding

A. Kelly is making salad dressing. His recipe calls for $\frac{1}{2}$ cup of yogurt and $\frac{1}{3}$ cup of oil. Does he need more yogurt or oil?

You can see that $\frac{1}{2}$ cup is more than $\frac{1}{3}$ cup.

So $\frac{1}{2}$ is greater than $\frac{1}{3}$.

$\frac{1}{2} > \frac{1}{3}$

You can see that $\frac{1}{3}$ cup is less than $\frac{1}{2}$ cup.

$\frac{1}{3} < \frac{1}{2}$

B. Which is greater, $\frac{1}{3}$ cup or $\frac{2}{3}$ cup?

You can see that $\frac{2}{3}$ cup is more than $\frac{1}{3}$ cup.

So $\frac{2}{3}$ is greater than $\frac{1}{3}$.

$\frac{2}{3} > \frac{1}{3}$

Also, $\frac{1}{3}$ cup is less than $\frac{2}{3}$ cup.

So $\frac{1}{3}$ is less than $\frac{2}{3}$.

$\frac{1}{3} < \frac{2}{3}$

What types of foods do you like to cook?

■ **Talk About Math** Suppose there are two pizzas of equal size. One is divided into 6 equal parts. The other is divided into 7 equal parts. Which pizza has larger pieces? Explain.

Check Understanding

Use < or > to complete each number sentence.

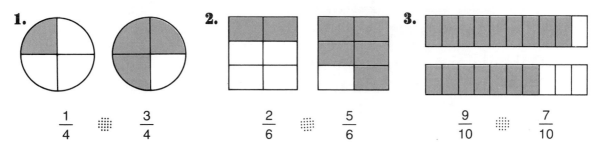

1. $\frac{1}{4}$ ▦ $\frac{3}{4}$

2. $\frac{2}{6}$ ▦ $\frac{5}{6}$

3. $\frac{9}{10}$ ▦ $\frac{7}{10}$

4. In Example A the two fractions have the same numerator but different denominators. Explain how to tell which is larger.

5. In Example B the two fractions have the same denominator but different numerators. Explain how to tell which is larger.

Practice

Write each number sentence using <, >, or =.

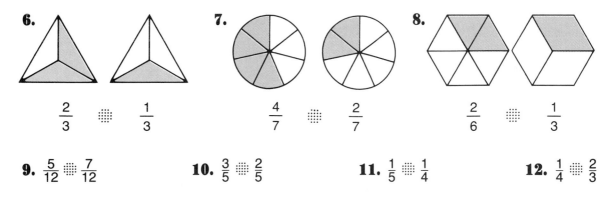

6. $\frac{2}{3}$ ▦ $\frac{1}{3}$

7. $\frac{4}{7}$ ▦ $\frac{2}{7}$

8. $\frac{2}{6}$ ▦ $\frac{1}{3}$

9. $\frac{5}{12}$ ▦ $\frac{7}{12}$

10. $\frac{3}{5}$ ▦ $\frac{2}{5}$

11. $\frac{1}{5}$ ▦ $\frac{1}{4}$

12. $\frac{1}{4}$ ▦ $\frac{2}{3}$

Problem Solving

Write a fraction for each of the following problems.

13. Four of the 6 cooking club members are from Ms. Barr's class.

14. Two of the six cooking club members are from Mr. Lane's class.

15. Use > or < to compare the fractions.

Ordering Fractions

Build Understanding

A. In Oakdale, many children walk to school. Stella walks $\frac{1}{3}$ mile. CJ walks $\frac{1}{2}$ mile. Lou walks $\frac{1}{4}$ mile. Who has the longest walk? Who has the shortest?

The fraction strips on page 375 can help you find the answers.

You can see that $\frac{1}{3} < \frac{1}{2}$. The fraction strips show that $\frac{1}{4} < \frac{1}{2}$ and $\frac{1}{4} < \frac{1}{3}$. From least to greatest the order of the fractions is $\frac{1}{4}, \frac{1}{3}, \frac{1}{2}$.

CJ's $\frac{1}{2}$-mile walk is the longest. Lou's $\frac{1}{4}$-mile walk is the shortest.

B. Write $\frac{1}{3}, \frac{4}{6}$, and $\frac{2}{8}$ in order from greatest to least. Use the fraction strips.

Find the strip for thirds. $\frac{1}{3}$ is one section. Draw a line on your paper to show how long this is.
Find the strip for sixths. $\frac{4}{6}$ is four sections. Draw a line to show how long this is.
Find the strip for eighths. $\frac{2}{8}$ is two sections. Draw a line to show how long this is.
From greatest to least the order of the fractions is

$\frac{4}{6}, \frac{1}{3}, \frac{2}{8}$.

■ **Talk About Math** Explain how comparing fractions is related to ordering fractions.

$\frac{1}{2}$	$\frac{1}{2}$

$\frac{1}{3}$	$\frac{1}{3}$	$\frac{1}{3}$

$\frac{1}{4}$	$\frac{1}{4}$	$\frac{1}{4}$	$\frac{1}{4}$

$\frac{1}{5}$	$\frac{1}{5}$	$\frac{1}{5}$	$\frac{1}{5}$	$\frac{1}{5}$

$\frac{1}{6}$	$\frac{1}{6}$	$\frac{1}{6}$	$\frac{1}{6}$	$\frac{1}{6}$	$\frac{1}{6}$

$\frac{1}{8}$	$\frac{1}{8}$	$\frac{1}{8}$	$\frac{1}{8}$	$\frac{1}{8}$	$\frac{1}{8}$	$\frac{1}{8}$	$\frac{1}{8}$

$\frac{1}{10}$	$\frac{1}{10}$	$\frac{1}{10}$	$\frac{1}{10}$	$\frac{1}{10}$	$\frac{1}{10}$	$\frac{1}{10}$	$\frac{1}{10}$	$\frac{1}{10}$	$\frac{1}{10}$

Check Understanding

For another example, see Set E, pages 396–397.

Read the problem. Then use the fraction strips to answer the questions below and solve the problem.

From least to greatest, what is the order of these fractions? $\frac{7}{8}, \frac{3}{4}, \frac{5}{6}$

1. Which two fraction strips will you look at first?

2. What will those strips tell you?

3. Which two fraction strips will you look at next?

4. What will those strips tell you?

5. Which two fraction strips will you look at last?

6. Write the fractions in order from least to greatest.

Practice

For More Practice, see Set E, pages 398–399.

Write the fractions in order from least to greatest.
Remember you can use the fraction strips on page 375.

7. $\frac{1}{4}, \frac{1}{6}, \frac{5}{6}$ **8.** $\frac{2}{3}, \frac{2}{5}, \frac{1}{3}$ **9.** $\frac{5}{8}, \frac{5}{6}, \frac{4}{5}$ **10.** $\frac{2}{5}, \frac{2}{3}, \frac{3}{8}$

11. $\frac{4}{10}, \frac{4}{5}, \frac{8}{8}$ **12.** $\frac{6}{10}, \frac{2}{3}, \frac{3}{9}$ **13.** $\frac{2}{5}, \frac{5}{8}, \frac{3}{5}, \frac{1}{2}$ **14.** $\frac{1}{4}, \frac{7}{8}, \frac{1}{2}, \frac{3}{5}$

Use the fraction strips to find a fraction
between the two that are given.

15. $\frac{1}{5}$ and $\frac{1}{3}$ **16.** $\frac{1}{2}$ and $\frac{3}{4}$ **17.** $\frac{3}{5}$ and $\frac{2}{3}$ **18.** $\frac{3}{10}$ and $\frac{2}{5}$

Problem Solving

Explore ———— **Math**

Mary used fraction strips
to make a number line.

For 3 feet, the unit is feet.
You can think of a fraction
as a unit.

For 3 fourths, the unit is fourths.

19. Look at Mary's number
line and count by fourths.
How many units are there
from 0 to 1 *fourth?* 0 to
2 *fourths?* 0 to 3 *fourths?*
0 to 1?

20. Keep counting by fourths.
The next number is 1 and
1 *fourth.* You write this as
$1\frac{1}{4}$. How would you write
1 and 2 *fourths?*

21. Copy Mary's number line.
Fill in the numbers
between 1 and 2. What
number did you write for
1 and 3 *fourths?*

22. A whole number and a
fraction is a ***mixed
number.*** What are the
mixed numbers on your
number line?

Write a fraction that names the shaded part.

1. **2.** **3.** **4.**

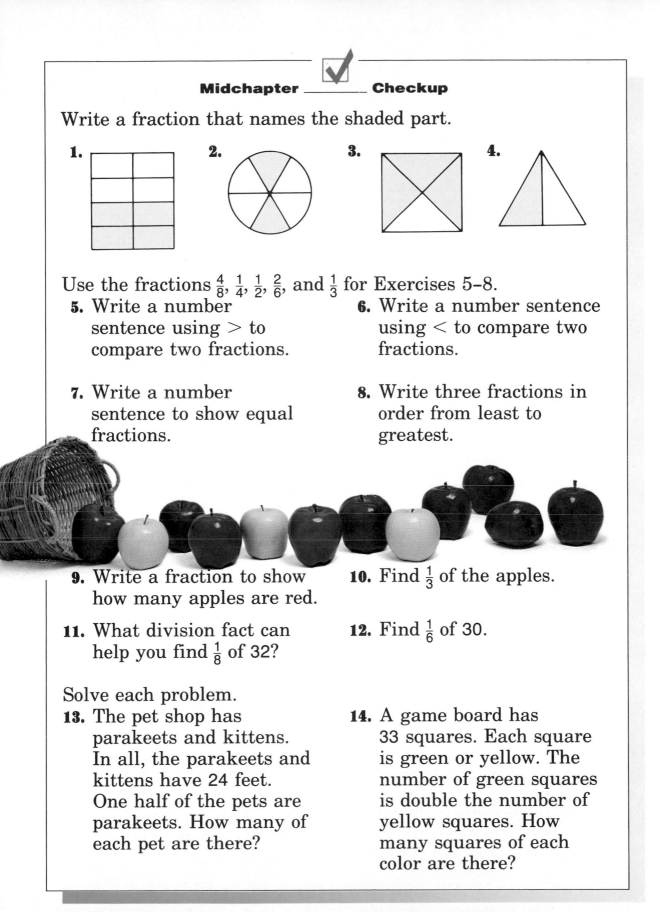

Use the fractions $\frac{4}{8}$, $\frac{1}{4}$, $\frac{1}{2}$, $\frac{2}{6}$, and $\frac{1}{3}$ for Exercises 5–8.

5. Write a number sentence using $>$ to compare two fractions.

6. Write a number sentence using $<$ to compare two fractions.

7. Write a number sentence to show equal fractions.

8. Write three fractions in order from least to greatest.

9. Write a fraction to show how many apples are red.

10. Find $\frac{1}{3}$ of the apples.

11. What division fact can help you find $\frac{1}{8}$ of 32?

12. Find $\frac{1}{6}$ of 30.

Solve each problem.

13. The pet shop has parakeets and kittens. In all, the parakeets and kittens have 24 feet. One half of the pets are parakeets. How many of each pet are there?

14. A game board has 33 squares. Each square is green or yellow. The number of green squares is double the number of yellow squares. How many squares of each color are there?

Number-Sense Project

Look back at pages 358-359.
One class collected this information

AGE	Number surveyed	Dinosaurs Correctly Named			
		Tyrannosaurus	Apatosaurus (Brontosaurus)	Pterandon	Stegosaurus
Preteen	30	20	15	6	10
Teenage	24	18	6	4	12
Adult	40	10	5	2	4

1. How many preteens were asked to identify the dinosaurs?

2. What fraction of the preteens could correctly name Apatosaurus?

3. If 100 preteens, instead of 30, were asked to identify Apatosaurus, how many do you think would be able to do it?

MATH
laugh

If your clock strikes 13, what time is it?

ANSWER: Time to get a new clock.

Problem Solving WORKSHOP

Explore with a Computer

Use the *Fractions Workshop Project* for this activity.

Aunt Sophia cut a pumpkin pie into 6 equal pieces and a blueberry pie into 12 equal pieces to serve at a party. After the party some of each pie was not eaten.

1. At the computer, shade the first unit to show that 2 pieces of pumpkin pie were left. Write the amount as a fraction.

2. Shade the second unit to show that 4 pieces of blueberry pie were left. Write the amount as a fraction.

3. Compare the two pies. Which pie has more left over?

Real-Life Decision Making

Answer these questions. Explain your thinking.

1. You are very hungry. Would you rather have $\frac{1}{4}$ or $\frac{1}{8}$ of a small pizza?

2. Your feet are very tired. Would you rather walk $\frac{1}{3}$ mile or $\frac{1}{4}$ mile to get home?

3. Would you rather wait in line for a movie $\frac{1}{2}$ hour or $\frac{1}{4}$ hour?

Critical-Thinking Activity

- Bonnie lives on the top floor.
- Carole lives below Donna.
- Ann lives above Donna.

  Who lives on the second floor?

Tenths

Build Understanding

ACTIVITY

Cover It Up!

Materials: Decimal models

A. a. Cover one whole with tenths.

b. How many tenths cover one whole?

You can write the fraction $\frac{1}{10}$ as the **decimal** 0.1. You read both $\frac{1}{10}$ and 0.1 as "one **tenth**."

B. a. Show 1 whole and 3 tenths.

b. What is the fraction and the decimal for these models?

You read $1\frac{3}{10}$ and 1.3 as "one and three tenths."

c. What number does this model show?

$\frac{10}{10}$ or 1.0

■ **Talk About Math** How are decimals and fractions alike?

Check Understanding

Use decimal models for Exercises 1 and 2.
Place 3 tenths on top of 1 whole.

1. Write the fraction and the decimal for the part of the whole that is covered.

2. Write the fraction and the decimal for the part of the whole that is *not* covered.

Practice

Show the fraction with a decimal model. Write the decimal.

3. $\frac{4}{10}$ **4.** one tenth   **5.** $\frac{6}{10}$ **6.** two tenths   **7.** $\frac{10}{10}$

8. $\frac{7}{10}$ **9.** five tenths   **10.** $\frac{3}{10}$ **11.** nine tenths   **12.** $\frac{8}{10}$

Write the decimal and the fraction for the shaded parts.

13.   **14.**   **15.**

16.   **17.**   **18.**

Write the decimal.

19. three tenths   **20.** $\frac{4}{10}$ **21.** seven tenths   **22.** $\frac{9}{10}$

23. eight tenths   **24.** $\frac{2}{10}$ **25.** six tenths   **26.** $\frac{5}{10}$

27. four tenths   **28.** $\frac{1}{10}$ **29.** $\frac{3}{10}$ **30.** ten tenths

Mixed Practice Write the fractions in order from least to greatest. Use the fraction strips on page 375 if you need help.

31. $\frac{1}{10}, \frac{5}{10}, \frac{3}{10}$ **32.** $\frac{2}{5}, \frac{2}{10}, \frac{2}{3}$ **33.** $\frac{4}{5}, \frac{4}{8}, \frac{4}{10}$ **34.** $\frac{6}{10}, \frac{1}{2}, \frac{1}{4}$

35. $\frac{7}{10}, \frac{4}{10}, \frac{9}{10}$ **36.** $\frac{1}{3}, \frac{4}{6}, \frac{3}{3}$ **37.** $\frac{6}{8}, \frac{1}{4}, \frac{2}{4}$ **38.** $\frac{7}{8}, \frac{1}{2}, \frac{6}{10}$

39. ▓ **Calculator** Find a decimal for $\frac{8}{10}$.   **Press:** 8 ⊘ 10 ⊜
Write the decimal.

Decimal Place Value

Build Understanding

How do you read the digits on a digital thermometer?

Lee took his temperature with a thermometer. His body temperature was normal.

The digits in the place-value box show how many degrees Fahrenheit Lee's temperature was.

Tens	Ones	Tenths
9	**8**	**6**
tens digit	ones digit	tenths digit
9 tens	8 ones	6 tenths
90	8	$\frac{6}{10}$

98.6 ← standard form

The decimal point separates ones from tenths.

Lee's temperature was 98.6°F. You read 98.6 as "ninety-eight and six tenths."

A decimal can also be written as a fraction. The decimal 98.6 is the same as the fraction $98\frac{6}{10}$.

■ **Talk About Math** How is place value with decimals like place value with whole numbers?

Write each number as a decimal and as a fraction.

1.

Ones	Tenths
3	2

2.

Ones	Tenths
1	6

3.

Ones	Tenths
0	3

4. Lee wrote the number fourteen in a place-value box. Did he write it correctly? If not, show how it should be written.

Tens	Ones	Tenths
0	1	4

5. Lee wrote the number one and seven tenths in a place-value box. Write the number correctly if you think Lee is wrong.

Tens	Ones	Tenths
1	7	0

Practice

For More Practice, see Set F, pages 398–399.

Copy each exercise. Underline the tenths digit.

6. 28.1   **7.** 13.9   **8.** 96.8   **9.** 72.7   **10.** 65.8

11. 76.7   **12.** 43.2   **13.** 10.6   **14.** 58.5   **15.** 34.0

Tell what place the 4 is in for each exercise.

16. 47.5   **17.** 4.5   **18.** 87.4   **19.** 14.8   **20.** 36.4

Write the decimals in words.

21. 53.9   **22.** 37.3   **23.** 25.1   **24.** 73.8   **25.** 16.7

Mixed Practice   Find each number.

26. $\frac{1}{10}$ of 40   **27.** $\frac{1}{10}$ of 70   **28.** $\frac{1}{10}$ of 60   **29.** $\frac{1}{10}$ of 30   **30.** $\frac{1}{10}$ of 90

31. $\frac{1}{4}$ of 36   **32.** $\frac{1}{6}$ of 42   **33.** $\frac{1}{5}$ of 45   **34.** $\frac{1}{8}$ of 48   **35.** $\frac{1}{7}$ of 49

36. $\frac{1}{2}$ of 10   **37.** $\frac{1}{8}$ of 64   **38.** $\frac{1}{6}$ of 54   **39.** $\frac{1}{3}$ of 21   **40.** $\frac{1}{9}$ of 36

Hundredths

Build Understanding

Count the Squares
Materials: Decimal models

A. a. Cover 1 tenth with hundredths. How many hundredths cover 1 tenth?

b. Cover 1 whole with tenths. Since 10 hundredths cover 1 tenth, you can count by tens to find the total number of hundredths in 1 whole. How many hundredths are in 1 whole?

c. What part of 1 whole is one hundredth?

You can write $\frac{1}{100}$ as 0.01.

You read both $\frac{1}{100}$ and 0.01 as "one **hundredth**."

Ones	Tenths	Hundredths
0	0	1

B. a. Show 1 whole, 3 tenths, and 6 hundredths.

b. What number do these models show? You read $1\frac{36}{100}$ and 1.36 as "one and thirty-six hundredths."

Ones	Tenths	Hundredths
1	3	6

c. What number does this place-value box show?

Ones	Tenths	Hundredths
1	0	0

$\frac{100}{100}$ or 1.00

■ **Talk About Math** Tell what the 0 in 3.07 means. Is 3.07 the same as 3.7? Explain.

Check Understanding

Write the fraction and the decimal.

1.

2.

Use decimal models to show the numbers.

3. 0.03   **4.** $1\frac{45}{100}$ **5.** two and sixteen hundredths

Number Sense Write the fraction and the decimal for each model.

6.

7.

8. Tell whether each pair of models in Exercises 6 and 7 names the same number or different numbers.

Practice

Use decimal models. Write the decimals.

9. $\frac{9}{100}$ **10.** $\frac{66}{100}$ **11.** $1\frac{84}{100}$ **12.** two and three hundredths

Tell whether each pair names the same number.

13. $\frac{50}{100}, \frac{5}{10}$ **14.** $8\frac{2}{100}, 8.02$ **15.** $9\frac{47}{100}, 94.7$ **16.** $\frac{37}{100}, 3.7$

Mixed Practice   Answer each question.

17. In 62.5, what digit is in the tenths place?

18. In 3.27, in what place is the 7?

19. In 2.05, in what place is the 0?

20. In 8.97, what digit is in the tenths place?

21. Write the decimal for $\frac{7}{10}$.

22. Write the decimal for $4\frac{63}{100}$.

23. What fraction does the model show?

24. What decimal does the model show?

25. Write a decimal that has 6 in the tenths place.

26. Write a decimal that has 6 in the hundredths place.

27. What fraction does the model show?

28. Write the decimal shown by the models.

Problem Solving

Solve each problem.

29. Of the 100 students at the amusement park, 56 rode on the roller coaster. Write a decimal for the part of the group that did not ride.

30. Twenty-nine of the students were third graders. Write a decimal for the part of the group made up of third graders.

31. Critical Thinking You can write 25¢ as $0.25. How can you write these amounts?
39¢   56¢   4¢

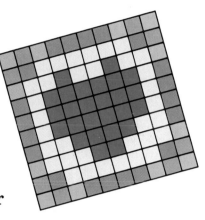

32. Use a sheet of 10 × 10 grid paper. Color each square to make a design. Use five to eight different colors in the design. Then write a decimal for each color to show what part of the grid paper has that color.

Choose a 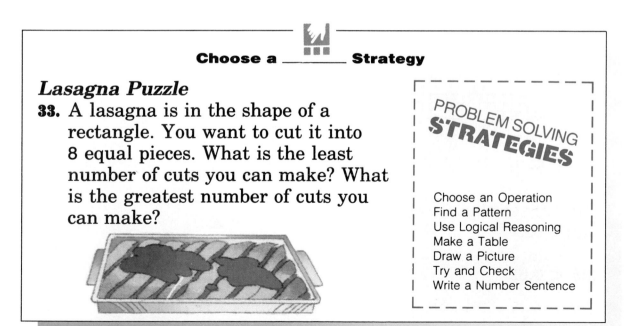 **Strategy**

Lasagna Puzzle

33. A lasagna is in the shape of a rectangle. You want to cut it into 8 equal pieces. What is the least number of cuts you can make? What is the greatest number of cuts you can make?

> **PROBLEM SOLVING STRATEGIES**
>
> Choose an Operation
> Find a Pattern
> Use Logical Reasoning
> Make a Table
> Draw a Picture
> Try and Check
> Write a Number Sentence

Comparing Decimals

Build Understanding

A. Mrs. Lopez has 10 dogs in puppy training class. Out of the 10 puppies, 0.4 are collies and 0.6 are not collies. Are more of the puppies collies or are more not collies?

You can see that 0.6 is greater than 0.4.

0.6 > 0.4

More dogs are not collies.

B. Which is less, 0.62 or 0.25?

You can see that 0.25 is less than 0.62.

0.25 < 0.62

So 0.25 is less than 0.62.

How many breeds of dogs can you name?

■ **Talk About Math** How is comparing decimals like comparing whole numbers?

Check Understanding

For another example, see Set G, pages 396–397.

Write each number sentence using < or >.

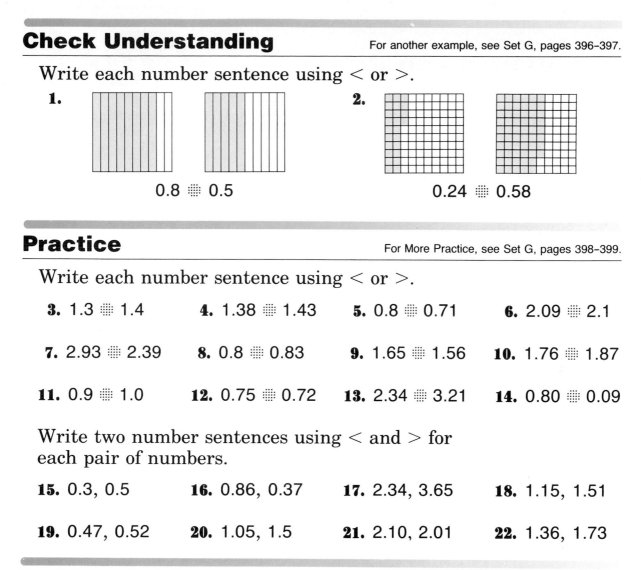

1.   0.8 ⬚ 0.5

2.   0.24 ⬚ 0.58

Practice

For More Practice, see Set G, pages 398–399.

Write each number sentence using < or >.

3. 1.3 ⬚ 1.4 **4.** 1.38 ⬚ 1.43 **5.** 0.8 ⬚ 0.71 **6.** 2.09 ⬚ 2.1

7. 2.93 ⬚ 2.39 **8.** 0.8 ⬚ 0.83 **9.** 1.65 ⬚ 1.56 **10.** 1.76 ⬚ 1.87

11. 0.9 ⬚ 1.0 **12.** 0.75 ⬚ 0.72 **13.** 2.34 ⬚ 3.21 **14.** 0.80 ⬚ 0.09

Write two number sentences using < and > for each pair of numbers.

15. 0.3, 0.5 **16.** 0.86, 0.37 **17.** 2.34, 3.65 **18.** 1.15, 1.51

19. 0.47, 0.52 **20.** 1.05, 1.5 **21.** 2.10, 2.01 **22.** 1.36, 1.73

Problem Solving

Answer each question.
Out of 20 dogs in a class,

23. 8 learned to sit on Monday. How many dogs did not learn to sit?

24. there are 14 females. How many are males?

Number Sense   Answer each riddle.

25. I am a decimal in hundredths. I am less than 0.4. I am greater than 0.35. The sum of my digits is 10. Who am I?

26. I am a decimal in tenths. I am greater than 0.38. I am less than 0.44. Who am I?

389

Use Alternate Strategies

Build Understanding

Kim cut a tamale pie into 10 pieces. Her family ate 0.3 of the pie. Her guests ate 0.5 of the pieces. What part of the pie is left?

PROBLEM SOLVING
GUIDE

Understand
QUESTION
FACTS
KEY IDEA

➤ **Plan and Solve**
STRATEGY
ANSWER

Look Back
SENSIBLE ANSWER
ALTERNATE APPROACH

Understand You need to find what part of the pie was not eaten. There were 10 pieces in all, and 0.3 and 0.5 were eaten. Think of 0.3 and 0.5 as $\frac{3}{10}$ and $\frac{5}{10}$.

The sum of 3, 5, and the pieces left must equal 10 because $\frac{10}{10}$ equals one whole.

➤ **Plan and Solve**

STRATEGY Draw a picture by shading a decimal model.

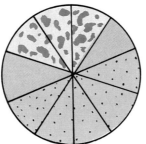

ANSWER The part left is 0.2, or 2 pieces of pie.

STRATEGY Try adding different numbers to 3 and 5. Then check the answer.

$3 + 5 + 4 = 12$ too much
$3 + 5 + 1 = 9$ too small
$3 + 5 + 2 = 10$ correct

ANSWER Two pieces are left. Two pieces are $\frac{2}{10}$, or 0.2 of the pie.

Look Back Which strategy do you like better? Explain.

■ **Talk About Math** Can you think of 0.3 and 0.5 as whole numbers in this problem? Explain.

Check Understanding

1. What part of the pie is 1 piece? Write the decimal.

2. How do you know how many pieces of pie 0.3 and 0.5 are?

3. If 0.2 and 0.4 were eaten, what part would be left?

4. Write a number sentence for Exercise 3 using pieces of pie.

Practice

Write two strategies you could use to solve each problem. Use both ways to find the answer.

5. How many slices of pizza will be on the next tray?

6. Kim cut French bread into 10 equal pieces. She used half the pieces for lunch. She used 0.2 of the pieces for dinner. What part of the bread is left?

7. On one side of the table, Bob is sitting in the middle. Willa is to the left of Greg and to the right of Bob. Rea is to the left of Yuri. In what order are they sitting?

8. Kim has 100 paper plates. She put 0.7 of them at Table A, 0.26 at Table B, and the rest at Table C. How many plates are at each table?

TIPS FOR PROBLEM SOLVERS

Share your thinking with others. Explaining your ideas helps you think better.

Using Decimals

Build Understanding

A. Kate has 2 one-dollar bills, 3 dimes, and 9 pennies. How much money does Kate have?

Ones	Tenths	Hundredths
2	**3**	**9**
2 dollars	3 dimes	9 pennies
200 cents	30 cents	9 cents
$\frac{200}{100}$	$\frac{30}{100}$	$\frac{9}{100}$

Kate has $2.39.

B. Decimals can be used in many ways. Write each decimal and think about how it is used.

1.09

7.5

103.5

Decimals can be used to count.

Decimals can be used to measure.

Decimals can be used to tell order.

C. Estimation You can estimate using decimals. About how long is the stick to the nearest centimeter?

When a centimeter is separated into ten equal parts, you can measure in tenths of a centimeter.

The stick is 4.3 centimeters long. You can see that 4.3 centimeters is closer to 4 centimeters than to 5 centimeters.

The stick is about 4 centimeters long.

■ **Talk About Math** Where else are decimals used?

Check Understanding

For another example, see Set H, pages 396–397.

Write a decimal and a fraction to answer each question. What part of a dollar is

1. 1 penny? **2.** 1 nickel? **3.** 1 dime? **4.** 1 quarter?

Practice

For More Practice, see Set H, pages 398–399.

Write what the meter will show when the car travels another tenth of a mile.

5.

| 0 | 0 | 1 | 1 . | 4 |

6.

| 0 | 0 | 2 | 7 . | 6 |

7. Estimation About how long is the sausage, to the nearest centimeter?

Problem Solving

Calculator You can use a calculator to find a decimal for a fraction.

For $\frac{1}{4}$, press: 1 $\div$ 4 $=$ The display shows *0.25*.

Use a calculator to solve each problem. For Exercises 8–13, write each fraction as a decimal.

8. $\frac{1}{5}$ **9.** $\frac{2}{8}$ **10.** $\frac{9}{12}$ **11.** $\frac{12}{16}$ **12.** $10\frac{1}{4}$ pounds **13.** $14\frac{1}{2}$ inches

14. Critical Thinking I am a mixed number between 5 and 6. The sum of my numerator and my denominator is 9. My numerator is 1 less than my denominator. Write me as a mixed number and as a decimal.

15. Use Data Use your calculator to help you find the decimals for the fractions in Exercises 19–21 on page 363.

Skills Review

1. Which picture is shaded to show one fourth?

   a.   b.

2. What fraction of the stars are shaded?

3. Complete the number sentence to show equal fractions.

   $\frac{1}{2} = \frac{}{4}$

Find each number.

4. $\frac{1}{5}$ of 10   5. $\frac{1}{9}$ of 27

Replace ▦ with < or >.

6. $\frac{4}{9}$ ▦ $\frac{2}{9}$ 7. 1.24 ▦ 1.35

8. Write $\frac{1}{4}$, $\frac{1}{8}$, and $\frac{5}{8}$ in order from least to greatest. Use fraction pieces to help.

Write the decimal.

9. four tenths   10. $\frac{7}{10}$ 11. $\frac{17}{100}$

Tell what place the 6 is in.

12. 8.6   13. 16.5

14. What decimal part of a dollar is 2 dimes?

Problem-Solving Review

Solve each problem.

15. Jordan peeled an orange and pulled apart the sections. There were 9 sections. If the sections were exactly equal, what fraction would each section represent?

16. A box of 27 dog treats is shared equally among 3 dogs. How many treats will each dog get?

17. Fifty-seven of 100 students answer a survey. Write a decimal to show what part of the students answered it.

18. Of the 24 bulbs Dan planted, $\frac{1}{8}$ did not make flowers. How many made flowers?

19. **Data File** Use data from pages 402–403. Find the number of loaves of bread Jon will get if he buys $\frac{1}{4}$ of the wheat loaves and $\frac{1}{2}$ of the raisin loaves.

20. **Make a Data File** Use a cookbook. Make a list of 10 ingredients using fractions such as $\frac{1}{2}$, $\frac{1}{3}$, $\frac{1}{4}$, $\frac{1}{8}$, $\frac{2}{3}$, and $\frac{3}{4}$. Write each fraction, label, and ingredient.

1. Put in alphabetical order: tree, flower, weed, garden

Write these numbers in order from least to greatest.

2. 415   92   142   95

3. 794   915   749   905

Estimate each answer.

4. 95 − 69   **5.** 52 + 28

Find each answer.

6. 638   **7.** 506   **8.** 760
     +281   −319   −592

9. What time is shown on the clock?

Find each product.

10. 7   **11.** 0   **12.** 8
      ×4   ×5   ×1

13. 6   **14.** 9   **15.** 8
      ×8   ×8   ×7

16. Is this a sphere or a cylinder?

17. Give the name of this figure.

18. Find the volume in cubic units.

19. Tell how many 8-oz grapefruits would make about 1 pound.

8 oz

Find each quotient.

20. 16 ÷ 2   **21.** 24 ÷ 3

22. 36 ÷ 4   **23.** 30 ÷ 5

24. 24 ÷ 6   **25.** 28 ÷ 7

26. 32 ÷ 8   **27.** 45 ÷ 9

28. 7 ÷ 7   **29.** 0 ÷ 4

Write the other multiplication and division sentences in the family of facts.

30. 9 ÷ 3 = 3   **31.** 6 × 7 = 42

Complete the number sentence.

32.   **33.**

$\frac{1}{4} = \frac{\text{▨}}{8}$ $\frac{1}{2} = \frac{\text{▨}}{8}$

Find each number.

34. $\frac{1}{3}$ of 15   **35.** $\frac{1}{6}$ of 12

Replace ▦ with <, > or =.

36. $\frac{5}{6}$ ▦ $\frac{3}{6}$ **37.** $\frac{3}{4}$ ▦ $\frac{6}{8}$

38. 2.34 ▦ 2.43   **39.** 1.2 ▦ 0.2

Reteaching

Set A pages 360–363

Fractions name equal parts of a whole. This figure is divided into 4 equal parts. So each part is one fourth of the whole figure.

You write one fourth as $\frac{1}{4}$.

Remember that the denominator tells you the number of equal parts. Which fraction names the shaded part?

1. $\frac{2}{5}$ $\frac{3}{5}$ $\frac{1}{2}$ 2. $\frac{1}{4}$ $\frac{1}{3}$ $\frac{3}{4}$

Set B pages 364–365

There are 16 students in the school band. Five of the students play the trumpet. This can be shown as a fraction.

$$\frac{\text{number of trumpet players}}{\text{number of students in all}} = \frac{5}{16}$$

Remember that fractions name parts of a set of objects.

What fraction stands for the blue part of this group?

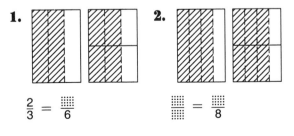

a. $\frac{2}{5}$ **b.** $\frac{3}{5}$

Set C pages 366–367

Fold a sheet of paper in half. Shade one part.

Fold the paper into 4 equal parts.

So $\frac{1}{2}$ and $\frac{2}{4}$ are equal.

Remember that the paper must be folded into equal parts.

Complete each number sentence to show equal fractions.

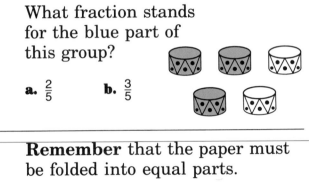

1. $\frac{2}{3} = \frac{}{6}$ 2. $\frac{}{} = \frac{}{8}$

Set D pages 368–369

Find $\frac{1}{5}$ of 30.
To find $\frac{1}{5}$ of a number you can divide the number by 5. Think:
$30 \div 5 = 6$ So $\frac{1}{5}$ of 30 is 6.

Remember that the denominator of the fraction is the divisor. Answer each question.

1. Find $\frac{1}{6}$ of 30.   **2.** Find $\frac{1}{8}$ of 24.

Independent Study RETEACHING

Set E   pages 374–377

Use the fraction strips on page 375 to help you write these fractions in order from greatest to least.

$\frac{1}{3}, \frac{2}{5}, \frac{3}{8}$

The order is: $\frac{2}{5}, \frac{3}{8}, \frac{1}{3}$

Remember that the inequality symbol always points to the smaller number.

Write the fractions in order from least to greatest.

1. $\frac{1}{4}, \frac{1}{5}, \frac{1}{8}$ **2.** $\frac{2}{5}, \frac{2}{6}, \frac{2}{3}$ **3.** $\frac{1}{3}, \frac{5}{8}, \frac{2}{4}$

Set F   pages 382–383

Randy ran the distance in 45.6 seconds.

Tens	Ones	Tenths
4	5	6

Read 45.6 as "forty-five and six tenths."

Remember that you read the decimal point as "and."

Tell what place the 3 is in for each exercise.

1. 36.9   **2.** 80.3

3. 73.1   **4.** 46.3

Set G   pages 388–389

Compare 0.53 and 0.35.

You can see that 0.53 is greater than 0.35.   0.53 > 0.35

Remember that > means "greater than" and < means "less than."

Write each number sentence using < or >.

1. 2.4 ⊞ 2.5   **2.** 1.26 ⊞ 1.3

3. 0.7 ⊞ 0.6   **4.** 0.62 ⊞ 0.53

Set H   pages 392–393

Decimals are used in many ways. This scale at the supermarket shows two ways.

2.6 lb	$6.35
weight	money

Remember that the decimal point separates ones from tenths.

Write what the meter reading will show when the car travels another tenth of a mile.

More Practice

Set A pages 360–363

Which fraction names the shaded part?

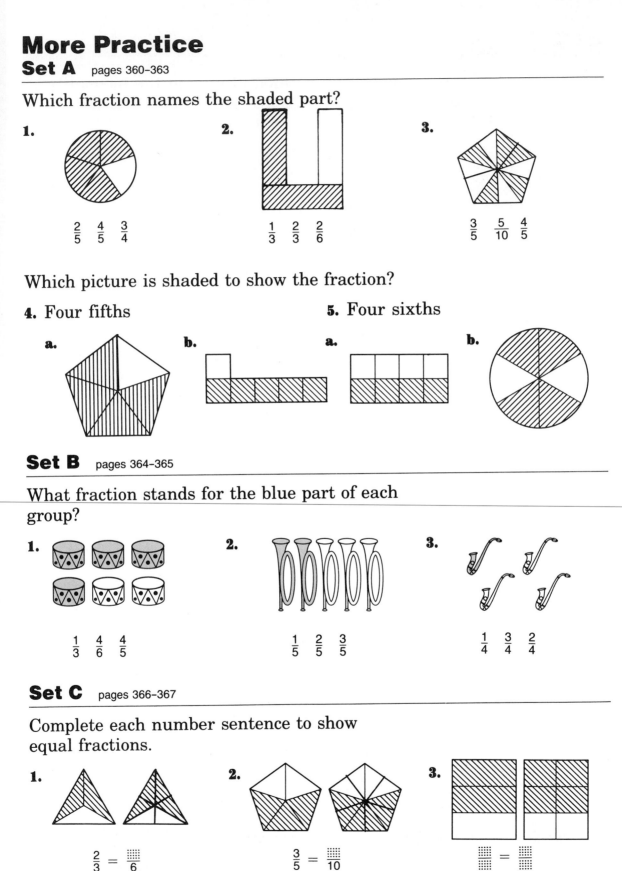

1.

$\frac{2}{5}$ $\frac{4}{5}$ $\frac{3}{4}$

2.

$\frac{1}{3}$ $\frac{2}{3}$ $\frac{2}{6}$

3.

$\frac{3}{5}$ $\frac{5}{10}$ $\frac{4}{5}$

Which picture is shaded to show the fraction?

4. Four fifths

a. b.

5. Four sixths

a. b.

Set B pages 364–365

What fraction stands for the blue part of each group?

1.

$\frac{1}{3}$ $\frac{4}{6}$ $\frac{4}{5}$

2.

$\frac{1}{5}$ $\frac{2}{5}$ $\frac{3}{5}$

3.

$\frac{1}{4}$ $\frac{3}{4}$ $\frac{2}{4}$

Set C pages 366–367

Complete each number sentence to show equal fractions.

1.

$\frac{2}{3} = \frac{}{6}$

2.

$\frac{3}{5} = \frac{}{10}$

3.

$\frac{}{} = \frac{}{}$

398

Set D pages 368–369

Find each number.

1. $\frac{1}{3}$ of 12   2. $\frac{1}{8}$ of 24   3. $\frac{1}{3}$ of 27   4. $\frac{1}{7}$ of 35

5. $\frac{1}{4}$ of 28   6. $\frac{1}{6}$ of 30   7. $\frac{1}{4}$ of 32   8. $\frac{1}{8}$ of 64

Set E pages 374–377

Use the fraction strips on page 375 to help you write the fractions in order from least to greatest.

1. $\frac{2}{6}, \frac{2}{3}, \frac{2}{10}$ 2. $\frac{1}{3}, \frac{2}{8}, \frac{2}{4}$ 3. $\frac{3}{8}, \frac{3}{4}, \frac{4}{6}$ 4. $\frac{6}{10}, \frac{6}{8}, \frac{5}{6}$

Set F pages 382–383

Copy each exercise. Underline the tens digit.

1. 36.5   2. 81.9   3. 27.3   4. 59.7   5. 91.8

Tell what place the 5 is in for each exercise.

6. 35.9   7. 56.4   8. 68.5   9. 57.3   10. 91.5

11. Write the decimals in Exercises 1–5 in words.

Set G pages 388–389

Write each number sentence using < or >.

1. 1.8 ▦ 1.7   2. 1.83 ▦ 1.96   3. 0.6 ▦ 0.52   4. 3.02 ▦ 3.2

Write two number sentences using < and > for each pair of numbers.

5. 0.6, 0.7   6. 0.72, 0.27   7. 3.48, 3.52   8. 2.1, 2.01

Set H pages 392–393

Write what the meter reading will show when the car travels another tenth of a mile.

1. `|   |   |   |   | 7 | 6 . 2 |`   2. `|   |   |   |   | 5 | 8 . 8 |`

399

Enrichment

Number Sense with Fractions

Here is a number line showing fractions
between the whole numbers 0 and 1. Fractions
between any two whole numbers are exactly
the same as these.

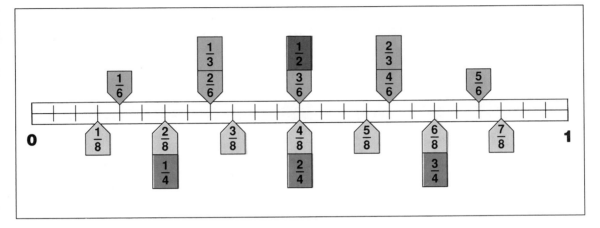

Use the number line. Tell whether the fraction
is closer to 0 or to 1.

1. $\frac{4}{6}$ **2.** $\frac{3}{4}$ **3.** $\frac{1}{6}$ **4.** $\frac{5}{8}$ **5.** $\frac{7}{8}$

6. Between which two whole numbers does $9\frac{1}{8}$ lie?

7. To which number is $9\frac{1}{8}$ closer, 9 or 10?

8. To which number is $5\frac{2}{3}$ closer, 5 or 6?

9. To which number is $1\frac{5}{6}$ closer, 1 or 2?

10. To which number is $10\frac{1}{4}$ closer, 10 or 11?

For each exercise, tell what whole number is closest.

11. $7\frac{4}{6}$ **12.** $26\frac{5}{6}$ **13.** $99\frac{1}{3}$ **14.** $47\frac{2}{8}$ **15.** $1\frac{1}{4}$

16. $3\frac{2}{3}$ **17.** $11\frac{7}{8}$ **18.** $9\frac{1}{4}$ **19.** $23\frac{6}{8}$ **20.** $321\frac{1}{8}$

Chapter 11 Review/Test

1. What fraction names the shaded part?

2. What fraction of the balls are yellow?

3. Complete the number sentence to show equal fractions.

$$\frac{3}{4} = \frac{}{}$$

4. Find $\frac{1}{2}$ of 10.

Replace each ▦ with < or >.

5. 0.7 ▦ 0.4

6. 0.27 ▦ 0.3

7. $\frac{3}{6}$ ▦ $\frac{1}{6}$

8. Write $\frac{3}{5}$, $\frac{7}{10}$, $\frac{1}{10}$ in order from least to greatest.

Write each decimal.

9. 5 tenths

10. 8 tenths

11. thirty-seven hundredths

For each decimal, tell what place the 6 is in.

12. 26.5

13. 11.6

14. 67.4

15. What decimal part of a dollar is 1 dime?

Read this problem. Then answer the questions below.

Five friends had a race. Ann finished behind Roy and ahead of Lew. <u>Pam finished ahead of Roy</u>, but Pam did not win the race. Tim raced in his new sneakers. What was the order of finish?

16. What does the underlined statement mean?

   a. Pam was behind Roy at the end of the race.

   b. Roy came in last in the race.

   c. Pam got to the finish line before Roy.

17. Solve the problem above.

18. ■ **Write About Math**
Describe a second strategy you could use to solve the problem above.

Data File

1. Bar Graph
The graph shows grams of fat in different kinds of cheese.

2. Picture Graph
This shows the number of loaves of bread baked daily.

3. Product Label
The label tells the weight and the number of slices in the loaf of bread.

4. Product Labels
These materials are for making crafts.

5. List
This is Ian's weekly shopping list.

1. Fats in Cheese

Bar graph: Grams of fat per 1 ounce serving

Cheese	Grams of fat
Cream	10
Mozzarella	7
Swiss	8
American	9
Feta	6

Sunshine Bakery
Daily Production Report (Bread)

Wheat	🍞🍞🍞🍞🍞🍞🍞🍞🍞
Rye	🍞🍞🍞🍞
White	🍞🍞
Raisin	🍞🍞🍞🍞🍞🍞
Pumpernickel	🍞🍞🍞🍞

Each 🍞 is 1 loaf of bread

2. Bread Baking

3. Bread Loaf

Romel's
Wheat Bread
Sandwich Loaf
16 ounces 24 slices

402

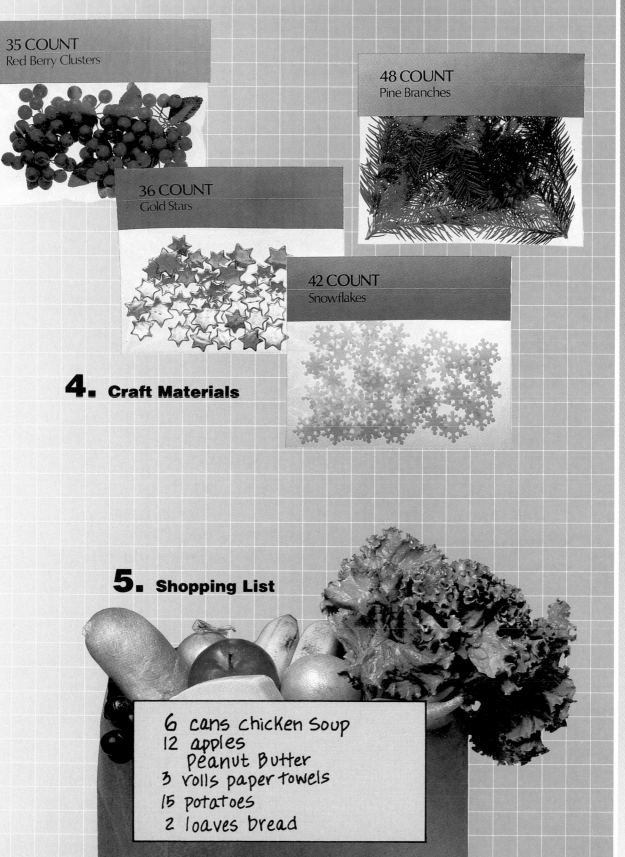

35 COUNT
Red Berry Clusters

48 COUNT
Pine Branches

36 COUNT
Gold Stars

42 COUNT
Snowflakes

4. Craft Materials

5. Shopping List

6 cans chicken Soup
12 apples
   Peanut Butter
3 rolls paper towels
15 potatoes
2 loaves bread

Give the letter for the correct answer.

1. Add.

134	**A** 156
51	**B** 346
+261	**C** 456
	D 446

2. Subtract.

	A 768
	B 762
886	**C** 758
−128	**D** 752

3. What time is shown?

A 3:07
B 3:35
C 4:07
D 4:35

4. What is the length of this line segment to the nearest centimeter?

A 4 cm   **C** 6 cm
B 5 cm   **D** 3 cm

5. Find the perimeter.

10 ft
4 ft   4 ft
10 ft

A 14 feet   **C** 40 feet
B 6 feet   **D** 28 feet

6. Tell whether you *add*, *subtract*, or *multiply*. Then find the answer.

Marge made 2 leather bracelets each week for 3 weeks. How many bracelets did Marge make in all?

A Add or multiply; 6
B Subtract; 1
C Add; 5
D Multiply; 9

7. Multiply.

6
×7

A 13
B 1
C 36
D 42

8. Multiply.

7
×8

A 15
B 56
C 1
D 64

9. Which is a right angle?

A   C
B   D

10. Which of the following should be measured in milliliters?

A a raindrop
B the water in a bathtub
C the water in a lake
D the fuel in a car's tank

11. Try and check to solve the problem.

John and his sister Sarah have 35 tapes. Sarah has 15 more tapes than John. How many tapes does each child have?

A Sarah has 10. John has 25.
B Sarah has 30. John has 15.
C Sarah has 25. John has 10.
D Sarah has 15. John has 20.

12. Divide.

$4\overline{)36}$

A 12
B 6
C 8
D 9

13. Divide.

$36 \div 9$

A 27
B 4
C 45
D 8

14. Divide.

$5 \div 5$

A 2
B 1
C 10
D 0

15. Divide.

$33 \div 6$

A 6 Remainder 2
B 27 Remainder 1
C 5 Remainder 3
D 14 Remainder 5

16. Solve the problem.

Lance collected 48 rocks. He divided them into 6 equal piles. How many rocks did he put in each pile?

A 288 **B** 8 **C** 42 **D** 54

17. What fraction names the shaded part?

A $\frac{3}{5}$ **C** $\frac{5}{7}$
B $\frac{3}{8}$ **D** $\frac{5}{8}$

18. Which decimal means the same as $\frac{57}{100}$?

A 57.0 **C** 0.57
B 5.7 **D** 0.0057

19. Which number sentence is true?

A 1.5 < 1.05
B 0.5 < 0.3
C 2.09 > 2.1
D 0.75 > 0.37

Read the problem below. Then answer the question.

Ruth did 63 extra math problems in 7 days. She did the same number of problems each day. How many problems did she do each day?

20. Which number sentence would you use to solve the problem?

A 63 + 7 = ▦ **C** 63 × 7 = ▦
B 63 − 7 = ▦ **D** 63 ÷ 7 = ▦

Time and Money

12

Did You Know: When our country was first being settled, coins were scarce. To make more coins, dollars were cut into 8 bits. Two bits equaled 25¢, four bits equaled 50¢, six bits equaled 75¢, and eight bits equaled $1.

Number-Sense Project

Estimate
Predict the year that will appear most often on pennies people have.

Gather Data
Tally the year of each penny you have at home (up to 100). Tally those in banks, in purses, etc. Do not tally pennies in coin collections.

Analyze and Report
Find the total number of pennies for each year. Compare your results with other students.

Minutes Before the Hour

Build Understanding

A. Before and After
Materials: Clock with movable hands, worksheet with clock faces

What did you do at
10 minutes before 9:00 today?

a. Show 8:00 on your clock.

b. Show 8:15. You say:
   "15 minutes *after* 8."

c. Show 8:30. You say:
   "30 minutes *after* 8."

d. Show 8:50. You say:
   "50 minutes *after* 8."

e. Start at the number 12 on your clock.
Count by fives as you move backward to
the minute hand. You also say:
"10 minutes *before* 9" for 8:50.

At 30 minutes after the hour, you can
begin counting minutes before the next
hour.

B. 3:35
   or
   35 minutes after 3:00
   or
   25 minutes before 4:00

c. Estimation   What could you do in
   1 minute? in 5 minutes? in 10 minutes?

■ **Write About Math**   Write about what might be
happening at the time shown in Example B.

Check Understanding
For another example, see Set A, pages 432–433.

Copy and complete each time.

1. ▦ minutes after ▦

▦ : ▦

2. ▦ minutes after ▦

▦ minutes before ▦

▦ : ▦

3. Why are there three ways to tell the time
shown on the clock in Exercise 2 and only
two ways to tell the time shown on the
clock in Exercise 1?

Practice
For More Practice, see Set A, pages 434–435.

Write each time as minutes before the hour.

4.   5.   6.   7.

Estimation   Answer the questions.

8. How many times can you
write your name in 1 minute?

9. How long does it take you to
get dressed in the morning?

Show each time on your clock. On your worksheet, draw the hands on a clock.

10. 10 minutes before 6

11. 15 minutes after 2

12. 6 minutes after 9

13. 23 minutes before 12

Write the letter for the most reasonable time.

14. wake up for school

a. 10 minutes before 3:00

15. leave school

b. 15 minutes before 12:00

16. eat lunch

c. 20 minutes before 7:00

Problem Solving

Write the time as minutes before the hour.
Use your clock to help you.

17. It was 25 minutes before 2:00 when Aki began looking for his money to buy a snack. It took Aki 5 minutes to find his money. What time was it when Aki found his money?

18. Suki's mother was supposed to pick her up at 2:30. Her mother was 10 minutes late. What time was it when Suki's mother picked her up?

Use Data Write the time as minutes before the hour. Use the bus schedule on page 414.

19. The bus arrived at Orange Street 15 minutes late. What time did the bus arrive at Orange Street?

20. The bus left school at 3:30 instead of 3:00. What time did it arrive at Apple Street?

Reading ———— Math

Vocabulary Copy and complete the paragraph using the words below to fill in the blanks. Each word may be used more than once.

before   **after**

Suppose you look at your watch and see that the time is 6:40. The time is forty minutes __?__ six. You could also say the time is twenty minutes __?__ seven. In thirty minutes, the time will be ten minutes __?__ seven. Thirty-five minutes after that, the time will be fifteen minutes __?__ eight or forty-five minutes __?__ seven.

411

Calendar: Year

Build Understanding

JANUARY						
S	M	T	W	Th	F	S
						1
2	3	4	5	6	7	8
9	10	11	12	13	14	15
16	17	18	19	20	21	22
23/30 24/31	25	26	27	28	29	

FEBRUARY						
S	M	T	W	Th	F	S
		1	2	3	4	5
6	7	8	9	10	11	12
13	14	15	16	17	18	19
20	21	22	23	24	25	26
27	28					

MARCH						
S	M	T	W	Th	F	S
		1	2	3	4	5
6	7	8	9	10	11	12
13	14	15	16	17	18	19
20	21	22	23	24	25	26
27	28	29	30	31		

APRIL						
S	M	T	W	Th	F	S
					1	2
3	4	5	6	7	8	9
10	11	12	13	14	15	16
17	18	19	20	21	22	23
24	25	26	27	28	29	30

MAY						
S	M	T	W	Th	F	S
1	2	3	4	5	6	7
8	9	10	11	12	13	14
15	16	17	18	19	20	21
22	23	24	25	26	27	28
29	30	31				

JUNE						
S	M	T	W	Th	F	S
			1	2	3	4
5	6	7	8	9	10	11
12	13	14	15	16	17	18
19	20	21	22	23	24	25
26	27	28	29	30		

JULY						
S	M	T	W	Th	F	S
					1	2
3	4	5	6	7	8	9
10	11	12	13	14	15	16
17	18	19	20	21	22	23
24/31	25	26	27	28	29	30

AUGUST						
S	M	T	W	Th	F	S
	1	2	3	4	5	6
7	8	9	10	11	12	13
14	15	16	17	18	19	20
21	22	23	24	25	26	27
28	29	30	31			

SEPTEMBER						
S	M	T	W	Th	F	S
				1	2	3
4	5	6	7	8	9	10
11	12	13	14	15	16	17
18	19	20	21	22	23	24
25	26	27	28	29	30	

OCTOBER						
S	M	T	W	Th	F	S
						1
2	3	4	5	6	7	8
9	10	11	12	13	14	15
16	17	18	19	20	21	22
23/30 24/31	25	26	27	28	29	

NOVEMBER						
S	M	T	W	Th	F	S
		1	2	3	4	5
6	7	8	9	10	11	12
13	14	15	16	17	18	19
20	21	22	23	24	25	26
27	28	29	30			

DECEMBER						
S	M	T	W	Th	F	S
				1	2	3
4	5	6	7	8	9	10
11	12	13	14	15	16	17
18	19	20	21	22	23	24
25	26	27	28	29	30	31

A. Chile celebrates its birthday, or Independence Day, on September 18. People dress in Spanish costumes and folk dancers perform the national dance, the *cueca*. What day of the week is that on the calendar?

B. June has 30 days. In the Philippines, Independence Day is celebrated on June 12. In Greece, Independence Day is celebrated on March 25. How many days does March have?

■ **Talk About Math** Does your birthday fall on the same day of the week each year? Explain.

Check Understanding

For another example, see Set B, pages 432–433.

Use the calendar on page 412 to answer Exercises 1–4.

1. What day of the week is June 16?

2. What is the date of the last Friday in September?

3. Which months have 30 days?

4. How many months have more than 30 days?

Practice

For More Practice, see Set B, pages 434–435.

Use the calendar on page 412. Write the day of the week of each Independence Day.

5. Bolivia, August 6

6. Togo, April 27

7. Honduras, September 15

8. United States, July 4

Write the date.

9. Jamaica celebrates Independence Day on the first Monday in August.

10. Venezuela celebrates Independence Day the day after the United States Independence Day.

Bolivia celebrates Independence Day with parades. It is also celebrated in this way in the United States.

Problem Solving

Use the calendar on page 412 to solve each problem.

11. Independence Day in Nigeria is October 1. In Turkey it is four weeks later. What is the date of Independence Day in Turkey?

12. **Calculator** Use a calculator to find the number of days in a year.

13. How many weeks are there in a year?

Multiple-Step Problems

Build Understanding

Ann rides the 3:00 bus from school to Lemon Drive. It then takes Ann 15 minutes to walk home from Lemon Drive. What time does Ann get home?

Understand
QUESTION
FACTS
KEY IDEA

Plan and Solve
STRATEGY
ANSWER

Look Back
SENSIBLE ANSWER
ALTERNATE APPROACH

Understand   QUESTION   What time does Ann get home?

FACTS   The schedule shows that the bus stops at Lemon Drive at 3:25. Then Ann walks for 15 minutes.

KEY IDEA   You want to find out what time it is 15 minutes after 3:25.

Plan and Solve   Count by fives to add 15 minutes to 3:25. Ann gets home at 3:40, or 20 minutes before 4:00.

Look Back   Check again that the bus arrives at 3:25. Add 25 and 15 to find how many minutes after 3:00 Ann arrives home.

Bus Schedule Sunflower School	
Leave School:	3:00
Arrive	Time
Apple Street	3:10
Peach Lane	3:15
Lemon Drive	3:25
Cherry Avenue	3:30
Orange Street	3:35
Raisin Lane	3:55
Banana Square	4:00

■ **Talk About Math**   Suppose Ann stopped twice on her walk home. What else would you need to know to solve the problem?

Check Understanding

Shirley rides the bus from school to Peach Lane. She walks from Peach Lane to her house in 10 minutes.

Use the schedule on page 414 to answer each question.

1. How long does it take Shirley to ride from school to Peach Lane?

2. How long does it take Shirley to get home from school?

Practice

Answer each question.

3. Paco rides from school to Orange Street. Then he walks 10 minutes to his home. When does he get home?

4. Paco also walks 5 minutes from his classroom to the school bus. How long does it take him to get home?

5. You can ride the bus from Peach Lane to Raisin Lane or from Apple Street to Orange Street. Which ride takes more time? How much more time?

6. Luis gets home at 3:30. Julie gets off the bus at Banana Square and walks home in 12 minutes. How much longer does it take Julie to get home than Luis?

Choose a _____ Strategy

Fun at Camp Waterfall Chris goes to Camp Waterfall. She jogs from 8:15 until 8:30. She swims from 8:45 until 9:20.

7. How much time does Chris spend swimming? How much time does she spend jogging?

8. What is the difference between these two times?

Identifying Coins and Bills

Build Understanding

What are the values of different coins and bills?

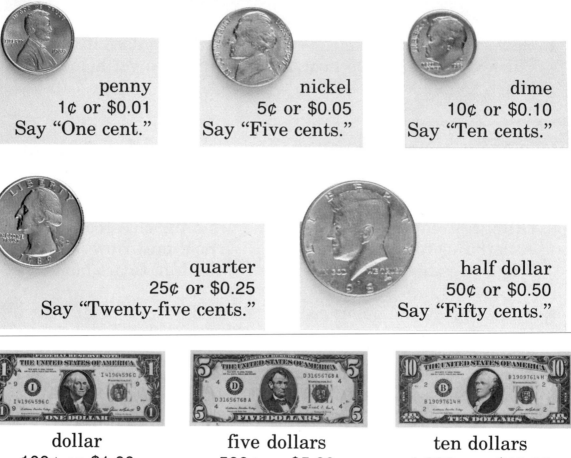

penny	nickel	dime
1¢ or $0.01	5¢ or $0.05	10¢ or $0.10
Say "One cent."	Say "Five cents."	Say "Ten cents."

quarter	half dollar
25¢ or $0.25	50¢ or $0.50
Say "Twenty-five cents."	Say "Fifty cents."

dollar	five dollars	ten dollars
100¢ or $1.00	500¢ or $5.00	1,000¢ or $10.00
Say "One dollar."	Say "Five dollars."	Say "Ten dollars."

■ **Write About Math** How would you write
one dollar, one dime, and one penny together,
using a dollar sign and a decimal point?

Check Understanding

For another example, see Set C, pages 432–433.

Tell how many of each it takes to make one dollar.

1. penny   **2.** dime   **3.** nickel   **4.** quarter   **5.** half dollar

Practice

For More Practice, see Set C, pages 434–435.

Write two letters to name each coin or bill.
Use each letter only once.

6. **7.** **8.** **9.**

10. **11.** **12.** **13.**

a. 25¢   **e.** 5¢   **i.** 25 cents   **m.** 10¢
b. 1¢   **f.** half dollar   **j.** 5 cents   **n.** five dollars
c. $10.00   **g.** $1.00   **k.** $5.00   **o.** $0.10
d. fifty cents **h.** ten dollars   **l.** one dollar   **p.** $0.01

Problem Solving

For Problems 14–16, write the name of the coin or bill.

14. I am the coin worth the least.

15. I am made out of paper and am worth four quarters.

16. I am worth more than 10 cents but less than 50 cents.

17. Critical Thinking   Mari has twice as much money as Pete. Pete has twice as much money as Jon. Jon has 10¢. How much money does Mari have?

Midchapter ✓ Checkup

1. What coin is the same as $0.05?

2. How many months are in one year?

3. Write 6:45 in words using minutes before the hour.

4. Al reads 1 hour in the morning and 1 hour at night. How many hours does he read in 5 days?

Problem-Solving Workshop

Number-Sense Project

Look back at pages 406-407.

Candice found these pennies at home.

Year	Number of Pennies
1990	15
1989	3
1988	2
1987	4
1986	1
1985	
1984	2
1983	9
1982	4
1981	6
1980	
1979	4

1. In what year do you think Candice collected this information?

2. What was the oldest penny Candice found?

3. Candice recorded the dates of 50 pennies. If she had recorded 100 pennies, how many do you think she would have found dated 1990? 1988? 1979?

Math-at-Home Activity

Play this game with someone at home. Put 16 pennies in rows like this.

Take turns taking away 1, 2, or 3 pennies. You may take the pennies from only one row during a turn. The player who takes the last penny is the winner.

Real-Life Decision Making

You are at the carnival. You have 20 minutes to use your last 3 ride tickets.

1. Besides the number of minutes each ride takes, what are some other things to consider that will use up time?

2. Decide if you can take 3 rides and which they will be.

Carnival Rides	
Ride	**Minutes**
Ferris Wheel	5
Merry-Go-Round	4
Roller Coaster	7
Tilt and Spin	7
Roll and Splash	8

Critical Thinking Activity

Clues

a. Danielle has 38¢

b. She has at least one penny, nickel, and dime.

c. She has more pennies than dimes.

d. She has the same number of nickels as pennies.

e. She has 8 coins. How many coins of each type does Danielle have?

Hint: Real or play coins can help you.

Counting Money

Build Understanding

Working for Peanuts
Materials: Play money
Groups: Partners

Peanuts For Sale

Joanne helps the Pep Club sell peanuts at school games. How much money does she have right now?

a. Joanne has two one-dollar bills, one half dollar, three quarters, four dimes, three nickels, and six pennies. Show this with play money.

b. Count the bills first. Then count the coins. Look for combinations that equal one dollar.

These coins equal one dollar.

Joanne has $3.86. She has three dollars and eighty-six cents.

Each American eats about $6\frac{1}{3}$ pounds of peanuts in one year.

■ **Write About Math** What is the least number of coins and bills you could have and still have $3.86?

Check Understanding

For another example, see Set D, pages 432–433.

Write the amount of money shown.

1.

2.

Practice

For More Practice, see Set D, pages 434–435.

Use play money to complete Exercises 3–12.
For Exercises 3–6, write each amount in words.

3. $5.62   **4.** $3.73   **5.** $7.82   **6.** $2.36

For Exercises 7–12, write the amount of money.
Remember to use a $ and . in your answers.

7. 1 quarter, 1 dime

8. 2 dimes, 3 pennies

9. 6 dimes, 4 pennies, 1 nickel

10. 1 quarter, 3 nickels, 4 pennies

11. 1 half dollar, 1 penny, 1 dime, 1 quarter, 1 nickel, 2 dollars

12. 3 dollars, 2 quarters, 3 nickels, 2 dimes, 1 penny

Problem Solving

Solve each problem. Use play money if needed.

13. Critical Thinking Suppose you have 8 quarters, 5 dimes, 5 nickels, and 5 pennies. Explain why $2.81 is not a reasonable total for the value of all the coins.

14. Juan has 2 quarters and 3 nickels in his pocket. He has 6 dimes and 10 pennies in his desk. Does he have more money in his pocket or his desk? How much more?

CONSUMER CONNECTION

Adding and Subtracting Money

Build Understanding

A. Cameron had $5.38. Then he got $7.50 for his birthday. How much does he have now?

Think:

$5.38	538	Line up the decimal points. Place $ and . in your answer.
+ 7.50	+750	
$12.88	1288	

Cameron has $12.88.

"COMPACT DISC SALE"

$9.97

B. Cameron wants a compact disc that is on sale for $9.97. How much money will Cameron have left from his $12.88 if he buys the disc?

Paper and Pencil

$12.88	Line up the decimal points.
− 9.97	Place $ and . in your answer.
$ 2.91	

▦ Calculator

Press: 12.88 ⊟ 9.97 ⊟

Display: *2.91*

Cameron has $2.91 left.

■ **Write About Math** How is adding and subtracting money different from adding and subtracting whole numbers?

Check Understanding

For another example, see Set E, pages 432–433.

Write the letter for the correct answer.

1. $7.06
   +4.98

2. $6.42
   − 3.68

3. $10.19
   + 2.21

a. $12.40
b. $12.04
c. $2.74

4. ▦ **Calculator** On a calculator, add $0.25 and $0.25. Explain why there is no 0 after the 5.

Practice

For More Practice, see Set E, pages 434–435.

Add or subtract. **Remember** to line up the decimal
points and place $ and . in your answers.

5. $1.19 +0.79	**6.** $3.72 +5.25	**7.** $3.00 −2.98	**8.** $7.88 +9.45	**9.** $7.20 −4.50
10. $9.35 −3.28	**11.** $10.05 + 3.99	**12.** $40.76 −30.50	**13.** $82.34 − 9.99	**14.** $26.73 +66.78
15. $36.78 +17.98	**16.** $54.90 −27.18	**17.** $29.37 +63.12	**18.** $99.43 −53.08	**19.** $56.60 + 4.19

Mixed Practice   Choose mental math, paper
and pencil, or a calculator to solve each problem.
Tell which method you used.

20. $36.11 − $23.09   **21.** 7×8 **22.** $49 \div 7$ **23.** $53.51 + $3.51

24. $42.90 − $27.88   **25.** 9×7 **26.** $54 \div 6$ **27.** $62.09 + $17.43

Problem Solving

Solve each problem.

28. Carlisle sold two compact discs, one for
$9.75 and one for $9.50. How much
money did he receive?

29. Sarah wants to buy a compact disc
that costs $14.98. She has $12.39. How
much more money does she need?

Compare problems
to help you relate new
problems to ones you've
solved before.

Skills ____ **Review**   pages 388–389

Copy each sentence and complete with >, <, or = .
1. 0.23 ⬤ 0.30   **2.** 0.8 ⬤ 0.18   **3.** 0.5 ⬤ 0.50   **4.** 5.76 ⬤ 5.09

Making Change

Build Understanding

A. Quick Change Artist
Materials: Play money
Groups: Work with a partner or small group. Take turns being the clerk and customers.

How much change does the clerk give a customer who pays 2 one-dollar bills for a set of jacks that costs $1.68?

a. Is there any one coin that you can add to $1.68 and get $2.00?

b. What coins could the clerk add to $1.68 to make the total end in 0 or 5?

c. What coins could the clerk then add to $1.70 to make $2.00?

d. Show the correct change using the fewest coins possible.

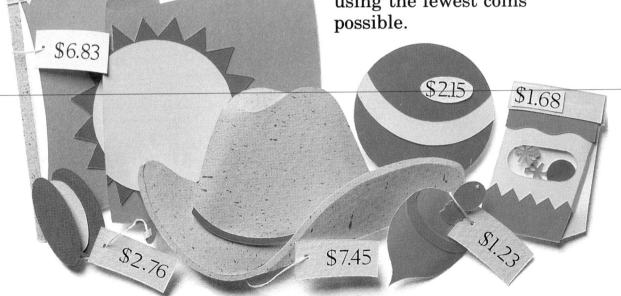

$6.83
$2.15
$1.68
$2.76
$7.45
$1.23

B. You can also subtract to find out how much change to give a customer.

The customer receives 32 cents.

$$\begin{array}{r} \$2.00 \\ -1.68 \\ \hline \$0.32 \end{array}$$

■ **Talk About Math** Which way of making change do you like better? Why?

Check Understanding

For another example, see Set F, pages 432–433.

Mental Math   Choose the letter for the correct amount of change.

1. You gave the clerk $5.00 for a game that costs $3.50.

   a. $1.00   **b.** $1.25   **c.** $1.50

2. You gave the clerk $3.00 for markers that cost $2.25.

   a. $0.50   **b.** $0.75   **c.** $0.85

Practice

For More Practice, see Set F, pages 434–435.

Use the prices on page 424 to answer each question.

What is the change from $3.00 for each of these?

What is the change from $10.00 for each of these?

3. ball   4. yo yo   5. top

6. flag   7. ball   8. hat

What are the fewest coins that will make:

9. $0.25?   10. $0.52?   11. $0.12?

12. $0.88?   13. $0.33?   14. $0.41?

15. $0.76?   16. $0.45?   17. $0.97?

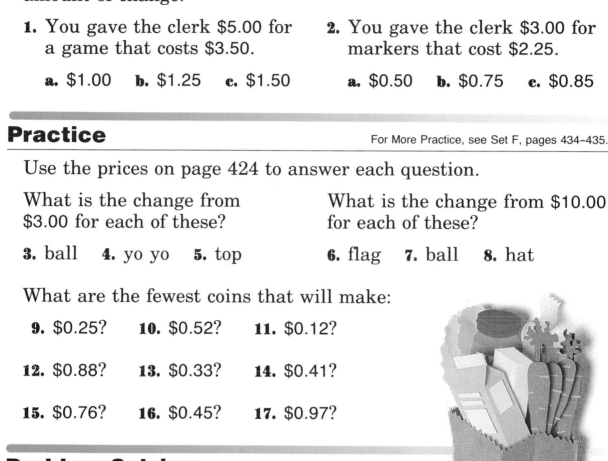

Problem Solving

18. **Number Sense**   Why would you give the clerk $24.02 for groceries that cost $23.52? Use play money to find your change.

Explore ———— Math

Penny put a half dollar in the change machine and got back 6 coins.

19. In what way(s) could the machine have given Penny 6 coins for a half dollar?

20. What coins could Penny get if her change had been 5 coins? 7 coins?

Work Backward

Build Understanding

Hank exercised this morning. He lifted weights for 30 minutes. Then he jogged for 20 minutes. Hank finished exercising at 7:30. What time did he begin exercising?

Understand   You want to know when Hank began exercising. You know he finished at 7:30 and spent 20 minutes and 30 minutes exercising.

Plan and Solve   STRATEGY   You can work backward, step by step, to find when Hank began each activity.

What is 20 minutes before 7:30? What is 30 minutes before that?

ANSWER   Hank began jogging 20 minutes before 7:30, so he began jogging at 7:10. He began lifting weights 30 minutes before that, so he began exercising at 6:40.

Look Back   Add 30 minutes and 20 minutes to 6:40 to check that your answer is sensible.

■ **Write About Math**   Explain how you could use a clock to make sure your answer is correct.

PROBLEM SOLVING
GUIDE

Understand
QUESTION
FACTS
KEY IDEA

▶ **Plan and Solve**
STRATEGY
ANSWER

Look Back
SENSIBLE ANSWER
ALTERNATE APPROACH

426

Check Understanding

Hank had soup, a sandwich, and dessert for lunch. Hank spent $3.25.

1. What was the cost of the lunch without soup?

2. What was the cost without a sandwich and soup?

3. What was the cost of the dessert?

Practice

Choose mental math, paper and pencil, or calculator to solve each problem.

4. Lisa is 5 years older than Jon. The gym teacher is 22 years older than Lisa. The teacher is 44 years old. How old is Jon?

5. Two weeks ago Lisa spent $15. This week she spent $4. She has $18 left. How much money did she have at first?

6. Jon had 12 peppers. He had 2 more red peppers than green ones. How many green peppers did he have?

7. Jon did some sit-ups. Then he did 16 leg-lifts and 10 bicycles. In all, he did 51 exercises. How many sit-ups did Jon do?

Choose a _____ Strategy

Snazzy Sneakers Solve the problem.

8. Karen spent $41.00 for 2 pairs of sneakers. One pair cost $3.00 more than the other. How much did each pair cost?

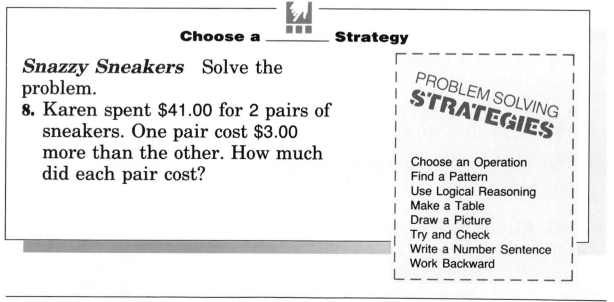

PROBLEM SOLVING
STRATEGIES

Choose an Operation
Find a Pattern
Use Logical Reasoning
Make a Table
Draw a Picture
Try and Check
Write a Number Sentence
Work Backward

Estimation and Money

Build Understanding

Nick has $6. He wants to buy cereal for $2.33, bananas for $1.86, and milk for $1.20. Does Nick have enough money for all three items?

A. You can estimate amounts to the nearest dollar.

Is cereal closer to $2 or $3?   cereal $2
Are bananas closer to $1 or $2?   bananas $2
Is milk closer to $1 or $2?   milk $1
                                                   $5

Nick has $6. He has enough money.

B. Sometimes it is better to estimate a higher amount.

Estimate $1.19 + $1.32 + $2.36 as you did in Example A.

Is your estimate higher or lower than the actual total? Suppose you have $4.00. Does this estimate tell you whether $4.00 is enough?

To get a better answer, estimate to the next higher ten cents.

$0.19 + $0.32 + $0.36 is about
$0.20 + $0.40 + $0.40 = $1.00.

$5.00 is a better estimate of the total than $4.00.

■ **Talk About Math** How is estimating useful when you are shopping?

What types of stores are in your neighborhood?

Check Understanding

For another example, see Set G, pages 432–433.

Use the register tape to estimate to the nearest dollar.

1. What would you estimate for meat? for milk? for soup?

2. **Number Sense** If you wanted to make sure you had enough money, would you estimate $3 or $4 for the last item on the tape? Why?

3. What is the estimated total of the groceries?

4.68 Meat

2.26 Milk

1.73 Soup

3.50 Produce

Practice

For More Practice, see Set G, pages 434–435.

Estimate to the nearest dollar.
Then use a calculator to find the actual sum.

4. $1.43 + $0.81 + $3.22

5. $6.88 + $4.39 + $0.93

6. $5.22 + $1.44 + $1.91

7. $1.36 + $4.47 + $2.29

8. $31.19 + $12.75 + $19.43

9. $5.62 + $2.16 + $9.99

10. $17.89 + $13.45 + $16.09

11. $21.17 + $35.63 + $19.54

12. $41.11 + $13.98 + $9.62

13. $15.45 + $12.83 + $21.46

14. $15.61 + $4.37 + $20.78 + $2.11

Problem Solving

Solve each problem.

15. Cal wants to buy items for $5.67, $3.18, $9.82, and $2.45. He has $21. Estimate the total. Do you think Cal has enough money?

16. **Critical Thinking** Why is it unwise to think you have enough money if your estimated total is the same as the money you have?

Skills Review

1. Write the time as minutes before the hour.

Use the calendar on page 412. Write the day of the week.

2. August 15   3. May 6

4. What coin is the same as $0.10?

5. What coin is the same as 5 cents?

Write the amount of money.

6. 1 quarter, 1 nickel, 3 pennies

7. 2 dollars, 2 quarters, 2 dimes

Add or subtract.

8. $2.19
    + 3.28

9. $4.78
    − 2.99

10. $30.25
    − 20.55

11. $36.46
    +   8.75

Write the change from $10.00 for a

12. $5.75 meal.   13. 99¢ pen.

Estimate to the nearest dollar.

14. $2.64 + $0.91 + $4.25

15. $15.56 + $3.77 + $21.48

Problem-Solving Review

Solve each problem.

16. Lou's bread must bake for 45 to 55 minutes. If Lou put the bread in the oven at 10:35 A.M., what is the earliest time it will be done?

17. Draw a square. Draw diagonal lines to connect the opposite corners. Shade one part. Tell what fraction of the square it is.

18. Six photos fit on a page of a photo album. How many pages will 54 photos fill?

19. Two teams were working on a set of math problems. The Red team had finished $\frac{5}{8}$ of the set. The Blue team had $\frac{7}{8}$ of the set finished. Which team had finished more problems?

20. **Data File** Use data from pages 532–533. Jim has $4.50 to spend on dinner and a beverage. What can he order and still have enough money to pay the bill?

21. **Make a Data File** Make a list of the admission cost to 5 different types of entertainment.

Write the number in standard form.

1. four hundred thirty-nine

2. five thousand, two hundred

3. six hundred ten thousand, one hundred fourteen

Find each answer mentally.

4. 46 + 39   **5.** 78 − 32

Find each answer.

6. 1,403
   + 2,678

7. 9,060
   − 7,921

8. $6.79
   + 3.45

9. $12.02
   − 9.15

10. 5
   ×4

11. 3
   ×5

12. 8
   ×3

Use blocks or multiplication to find each product.

13. 4 × 3 × 2   **14.** 2 × 4 × 2

Choose the more sensible unit of measure.

15. Distance to Mars
    foot   mile

16. Capacity of a bath tub
    cup   gallon

17. Weight of a slice of bread
    gram   kilogram

Find each quotient.

18. 18 ÷ 2   **19.** 15 ÷ 3

20. 20 ÷ 4   **21.** 40 ÷ 5

22. 36 ÷ 6   **23.** 42 ÷ 7

24. 56 ÷ 8   **25.** 81 ÷ 9

Find each number.

26. $\frac{1}{4}$ of 24   **27.** $\frac{1}{9}$ of 27

28. Write $\frac{3}{4}$, $\frac{1}{2}$, and $\frac{3}{8}$ in order from least to greatest. Use fraction pieces to help.

Tell what place the 7 is in.

29. 8.7   **30.** 27.9

31. Write $4\frac{37}{100}$ as a decimal.

32. Give the time as minutes before the hour.

33. What coin is worth 25¢?

34. How much money is 2 dimes and 2 quarters?

Write the change from $5.00 for a

35. $1.85 shake.   **36.** 69¢ drink.

37. Estimate $4.88 + $6.20 to the nearest dollar.

Reteaching

Set A pages 408–411

Amy got home from band practice at

      15 minutes before 5.

Show this time on your clock.

At 30 minutes after the hour you can begin counting minutes before the next hour.

15 minutes before 5 is the same as 45 minutes after 4.

Remember that you count backwards starting at 12 on your clock to find the number of minutes before the hour.

Write each time as minutes before the hour.

1.   **2.**

Set B pages 412–413

The Winkler family vacation began on the fourth Monday of August. Use the calendar on page 412 to write this date.

The fourth Monday is August 25.

When writing and speaking, the endings "st," "nd," "rd," and "th" are often added to the end of dates. You can write and say August 25 as

      "August twenty-fifth."

Remember that the months of the year do not have the same number of days.

Use the calendar on page 412 to write the date.

1. Father's Day, third Sunday in June

2. Memorial Day, fifth Friday in May

Set C pages 416–417

There is usually more than one way of using coins to show amounts of money.

Here are three ways to show 57¢.

   1 half-dollar, 1 nickel, 2 pennies
   2 quarters, 1 nickel, 2 pennies
   5 dimes, 1 nickel, 2 pennies

Remember that the penny is the coin that is worth the least.

Give two ways of using coins to show each amount.

1. $0.30   **2.** 55¢

3. 78¢   **4.** $0.90

Set D pages 420–421

You have the coins. How much money is this?

3 quarters   4 nickels
3 dimes   6 pennies

3 quarters + 2 dimes + 1 nickel = $1.

This leaves you with 1 dime, 3 nickels, and 6 pennies, or $0.31. You have a total of $1.31.

Remember to look for combinations of coins that equal one dollar when you count coins.

Write the amount of money. Remember to use $ and . in your answers.

1. 3 quarters, 1 nickel, 2 pennies

2. 1 quarter, 4 dimes, 1 nickel

Set E pages 422–423

Ellen spent $25.90 and $9.78. How much did she spend?

$25.90   Line up the decimal points.
+ 9.78   Place $ and . in your answer.
$35.68   Amount spent

Remember to line up the decimal points when you add or subtract. Add or subtract.

1. $8.03   **2.** $73.46
   + 1.98   − 9.87

Set F pages 424–425

Tony bought a hat for $7.56. He gave the clerk $8.00. How much change did he receive?

$8.00   Line up the decimal points.
− 7.56   Place $ and . in your answer.
$0.44

The clerk used the fewest coins possible: 1 quarter, 1 dime, 1 nickel, 4 pennies.

Remember to place $ and . in your answers when you add or subtract money.

What are the fewest coins possible that will make each amount?

1. $0.27   **2.** $0.75

3. $0.16   **4.** $0.90

Set G pages 428–429

Estimate $1.13 + $9.72 + $4.85 by rounding to the nearest dollar.

$1.13 ⟶ $ 1.00
9.72 ⟶ 10.00
4.85 ⟶ 5.00
       $16.00

Remember that estimating will help you decide if you have enough money.

Estimate the sum by rounding to the nearest dollar.

1. $3.55 + $0.92 + $6.25

More Practice

Set A pages 408–411

Write each time as minutes before the hour.

1.
2.
3.
4.

Estimation Answer each question.

5. How long does it take you to travel to school?

6. How long did it take you to do Exercises 1–4 above?

Show each time on your clock. On your worksheet, draw the hands on a clock.

7. 20 minutes before 8

8. 20 minutes after 8

9. 12 minutes after 11

10. 21 minutes before 2

Set B pages 412–413

Use the calendar on page 412. Write the day of the week.

1. Election Day, November 4

2. Halloween, October 31

3. Memorial Day, May 30

4. Groundhog Day, February 2

Write the date.

5. Abraham Lincoln's Birthday, second Wednesday in February

6. Washington's Birthday, third Monday in February

7. Armed Forces Day, third Saturday in May

8. Martin Luther King, Jr., Day, third Monday in January

Set C pages 416–417

Give two ways of using coins to show each amount.

1. $0.10

2. $0.22

3. $0.67

4. 75¢

5. $0.79

6. $0.18

7. 28¢

8. $0.35

9. $0.60

10. $0.99

Set D pages 420–421

Use play money to complete Exercises 1–9.
For Exercises 1–4, write each amount in words.

1. $4.83 **2.** $9.17 **3.** $8.64 **4.** $6.98

For Exercises 5–9, write the amount of money.

5. 1 quarter, 1 nickel **6.** 4 dimes, 3 nickels **7.** 2 quarters, 3 pennies

8. 4 dollars, 3 quarters, 2 dimes, 4 nickels, 7 pennies

Set E pages 422–423

Add or subtract.

1. $2.81	**2.** $8.44	**3.** $6.00	**4.** $7.01	**5.** $27.88
+ 0.38	+ 5.67	− 3.88	+ 3.89	+ 39.73

Mixed Practice Choose mental math, paper and pencil, or a calculator to solve each problem. Tell which method you used.

6. $49.36 − $11.04 **7.** 9 × 7 **8.** 54 ÷ 6 **9.** 10 × 9

Set F pages 424–425

Use the prices on page 424 to answer each exercise.

1. What is the change from $2.00 for each of these?
a. top **b.** jacks

2. What is the change from $8.00 for each of these?
a. hat **b.** flag

What are the fewest possible coins that will make each amount?

3. $0.21 **4.** $0.60 **5.** $0.49 **6.** $0.76

Set G pages 428–429

Estimate each amount by rounding to the nearest dollar, and find the estimated sum. Then use a calculator to find the actual sum.

1. $4.09 + $7.81 + $3.20 **2.** $5.91 + $8.42 + $9.64

3. $8.48 + $12.24 + $17.61 + $20.52

Enrichment

Patterns in the Calendar

Look at the red rectangle on the top calendar.

1. What is the sum of the numbers in the dotted ring?

2. What is the sum of the numbers in the solid ring?

3. What do you notice about the two sums?

4. Copy the calendar. Then draw a rectangle around four other numbers. Are the diagonal sums equal?

5. Does any rectangle have both sums equal to the number of days in a week?

Look at the rectangle drawn on the bottom calendar.

6. What is the sum of the numbers in the rectangle?

7. Add the middle number 3 times.

8. What do you notice about this sum and the sum of the numbers in the rectangle?

9. Copy the calendar. Then draw a rectangle around five numbers in a row. Find the sum of the numbers. Add the middle number 5 times. Compare the sums.

MAY

S	M	Tu	W	Th	F	S
		1	2	3	4	5
6	7	8	9	10	11	12
13	14	15	16	17	18	19
20	21	22	23	24	25	26
27	28	29	30	31		

JUNE

S	M	Tu	W	Th	F	S
					1	2
3	4	5	6	7	8	9
10	11	12	13	14	15	16
17	18	19	20	21	22	23
24	25	26	27	28	29	30

Chapter 12 Review/Test

Write each time as minutes before the hour.

1.   **2.**

MAY							JUNE						
S	M	T	W	Th	F	S	S	M	T	W	Th	F	S
					1	2	3	1	2	3	4	5	6	7
4	5	6	7	8	9	10	8	9	10	11	12	13	14
11	12	13	14	15	16	17	15	16	17	18	19	20	21
18	19	20	21	22	23	24	22	23	24	25	26	27	28
25	26	27	28	29	30	31	29	30					

3. Which day of the week is May 25?

4. What is the date of the second Wednesday in June?

Write the name of the coin or bill for each amount.

5. 100 pennies

6. 25 cents

Write the amount of money. Use a $ and . in your answers.

7. 3 dimes, 6 pennies

8. 1 dime, 1 half dollar, 2 nickels

Add or subtract.

9. $35.72
     − 8.49

10. $6.11
      + 0.59

Write the change from $5.00 for a

11. $3.80 ball.   **12.** 49¢ drink.

13. Which is the better estimate for $2.95 + $0.78?

    a. $4.00   **b.** $3.00

14. Janet is 5 years older than Bob. Bob is 2 years older than Pablo. If Janet is 18 years old, how old is Pablo?

Read this problem. Then answer the questions below.

Tim and Roy walked from the park to Roy's home in 25 minutes. Then Tim walked to his home in 20 minutes. If they left the park at 1:30, what time did Tim get home?

15. Which could be the *first step* in solving this problem?

    a. 25 − 20 = 5 minutes
    b. 25 + 20 = 45 minutes
    c. The time 25 minutes before 1:30 is 1:05.

16. Solve the problem above.

17. ■ **Write About Math** Write how many dimes it takes to make $2.00.

Multiplication Computation

13

Did You Know: The California Giant Sequoias shown at left are among the world's oldest and largest living things. Some are thousands of years old and 200 feet tall.

Number-Sense Project

Estimate
Predict how people would answer the question: "If you were going to be a tree, what kind of tree would you be?"

Gather Data
Ask people of different ages this question.

Analyze and Report
Look to see if a person's age made a difference in the tree they picked. Compare your results with other students.

Exploring Multiplication

Build Understanding

Stamp of Approval
Materials: Tens, hundreds
Groups: 4 students

A. A sheet of regular stamps has 100 stamps. How many stamps are in 4 sheets?

Show 4 hundreds.

There are 400 stamps in all.

B. Special stamps come 50 in a sheet. How many stamps are in 3 sheets?

Use tens to show 50. Now make 3 groups of 50.

3×5 tens $= 15$ tens

There are 15 tens or 150 stamps in all.

■ **Talk About Math**   Explain how you could count by tens to find the answer to Example B mentally.

Check Understanding

For another example, see Set A, pages 464–465.

Use the picture to help you find

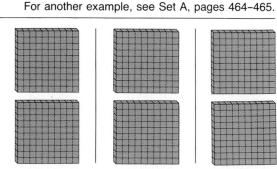

  1. how many groups.

  2. how many in each group.

  3. how many in all.

Give the standard form for each exercise.
Use tens and hundreds if you need them.

4. 5 tens

5. 18 tens

6. 10 tens

7. 4 hundreds

8. 12 hundreds

9. 10 hundreds

10. 2 forties

11. 2 thirties

12. 2 nineties

13. 7 hundreds

14. 9 tens

15. 3 sixties

16. 3 groups of 5 hundreds

17. 5 groups of 3 hundreds

18. 6 groups of twenty

19. 6 groups of 2 hundreds

20. 7 groups of forty

21. 4 groups of fifty

22. Mental Math How could you use mental math to find the answers in Exercises 4–21?

Problem Solving

Solve each problem.

23. Each page of Myrna's stamp book holds 20 stamps. How many stamps are on 8 full pages?

24. Myrna's brother Lee has 56 stamps. If there are 7 stamps on each page of his book, how many pages are in Lee's stamp book?

25. Myrna bought 3 sheets of stamps with 100 stamps on each sheet. She sold 53 stamps to Jules. How many stamps does she have left?

Multiples of 10 and 100: Mental Math

Build Understanding

A. Jennifer sells hand puppets to stores. There are 70 hand puppets in each box she sells. How many puppets are in 3 boxes?

The boxes all have the same number, so you can multiply.
Find 3 × 70.
Think: 70 is a multiple of 10, so 70 = 7 tens.

Show: 3 groups of 7 tens

Think about the largest puppet you have ever seen.

3 × 7 tens = 21 tens
3 × 70 = 210

There are 210 hand puppets in 3 boxes.

B. Find 2 × 500.

Think: 500 is a multiple of 100, so 500 is 5 hundreds.

Show: 2 groups of 5 hundreds

2 × 5 hundreds = 10 hundreds
2 × 500 = 1,000

■ **Talk About Math** How could you use addition to find the answers to Examples A and B?

442

Check Understanding

For another example, see Set B, pages 464–465.

Find each product.

1. 6 × 10   **2.** 6 × 100   **3.** 6 × 30   **4.** 6 × 300

5. Look at Exercises 1 and 2. Describe how they are alike and how they are different.

6. Look at Exercises 3 and 4. Do you see the same patterns that you found in Exercises 1 and 2? Explain your answer.

Practice

For More Practice, see Set B, pages 466–467.

Mental Math   Find each product mentally.

7. 4 × 10   **8.** 15 × 10   **9.** 26 × 10   **10.** 10 × 8

11. 6 × 100   **12.** 7 × 100   **13.** 100 × 36   **14.** 100 × 22

15. 8 × 20   **16.** 5 × 70   **17.** 40 × 4   **18.** 80 × 5

19. 4 × 900   **20.** 7 × 300   **21.** 600 × 8   **22.** 500 × 5

23. 6 × 200   **24.** 10 × 9   **25.** 400 × 4   **26.** 43 × 100

Problem Solving

Number Sense   Give each answer.

27. Look at Exercises 7–14. What rule can you give for multiplying by 10? by 100?

28. Look at Exercises 15–26. What rule can you give for multiplying by a multiple of 10? by a multiple of 100?

Critical Thinking   Use the information on page 442 to solve each problem.

29. How many boxes of puppets would the store manager buy if she needed 700 puppets?

30. How many boxes of puppets would the store manager buy if she needed 7,000 puppets?

Estimating Products

Build Understanding

School Bus

A. Mr. Banks drives a school bus. Each day, he drives 42 miles. Estimate the number of miles he drives his bus in 5 days.

Because Mr. Banks drives the same distance each day, you can multiply.

Estimate 5 × 42.
Round 42 to the nearest 10.
42 is closer to 40 than it is to 50.

5 × 40 = 200   5 × 4 = 20

Mr. Banks drives about 200 miles in 5 days.

B. Estimate 6 × 267.
Round 267 to the nearest hundred.
267 is closer to 300 than to 200.

6 × 300 = 1,800   6 × 3 = 18

■ **Talk About Math**   In Example A, does Mr. Banks drive more than or fewer than 200 miles in 5 days? Tell how you know.

Check Understanding

For another example, see Set C, pages 464–465.

1. Estimate 7 × 38.

2. Would 7 × 38 be greater than 7 × 40? Tell how you know.

3. Estimate 4 × 523.

4. Would 4 × 523 be greater or less than 4 × 500? Why?

Practice

For More Practice, see Set C, pages 466–467.

Estimate each product.

5. 4 × 17

6. 24 × 3

7. 62 × 7

8. 9 × 88

9. 8 × 382

10. 832 × 3

11. 5 × 741

12. 936 × 4

13. 8 × 26

14. 44 × 4

15. 430 × 4

16. 2 × 580

17. 9 × 347

18. 73 × 5

19. 8 × 92

20. 713 × 3

21. 37 × 6

22. 2 × 641

23. 5 × 275

24. 24 × 7

Mental Math   Find each product mentally.

25. 10 × 7

26. 16 × 10

27. 42 × 10

28. 50 × 5

29. 9 × 100

30. 21 × 100

31. 100 × 37

32. 100 × 61

Number Sense   Give each answer.

33. In which of Exercises 5–24 do you think your estimated product will be less than the actual product?

34. In which of Exercises 5–24 do you think your estimated product will be greater than the actual product?

35. How can you decide if the actual product will be greater or less than the estimate?

Skills _____ Review   pages 372–373

Which is greater?

1. $\frac{2}{3}$ or $\frac{1}{3}$

2. $\frac{3}{4}$ or $\frac{1}{4}$

3. $\frac{1}{5}$ or $\frac{1}{6}$

4. $\frac{3}{5}$ or $\frac{2}{5}$

Exploring Multiplication Further

Build Understanding

A Class Act
Materials: Tens and ones
Groups: 4 students

A. Parkview Elementary School has 3 classes of third graders. Each class has 32 students. In all, how many third-grade students attend Parkview Elementary School?

How many are there in 3 groups of 32?

You can use your tens and ones to find the answer.

a. Think: Make 3 groups of 32.

Show:

b. Think: Combine the 3 groups.

Show:

c. Think: Count the tens: 9 tens
Count the ones: 6 ones

Write the answer in standard form: **96**

There are 96 third-grade students in all.

B. Find four groups of 23. Use tens and ones.

a. Think: 4 groups of 23

Show: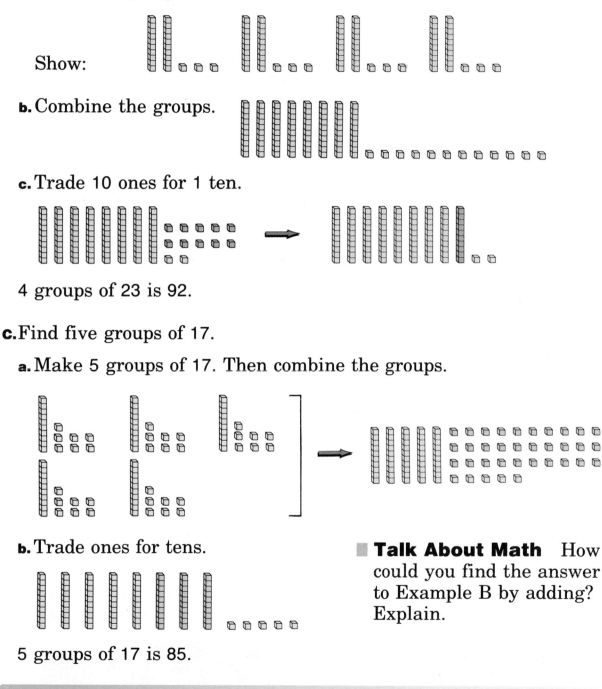

b. Combine the groups.

c. Trade 10 ones for 1 ten.

4 groups of 23 is 92.

C. Find five groups of 17.

a. Make 5 groups of 17. Then combine the groups.

b. Trade ones for tens.

5 groups of 17 is 85.

■ **Talk About Math**   How could you find the answer to Example B by adding? Explain.

Check Understanding

For another example, see Set D, pages 464–465.

Use tens and ones to help you find how many are in

1. 2 groups of 34.   **2.** 3 groups of 25.   **3.** 3 rows of 17.

Practice

For More Practice, see Set D, pages 466–467.

Use tens and ones to help you find how many are in

4. 2 groups of 24.

5. 4 groups of 12.

6. 5 rows of 11.

7. 3 rows of 31.

8. 4 groups of 19.

9. 3 groups of 26.

10. 5 rows of 18.

11. 2 rows of 48.

12. 6 groups of 16.

13. 2 groups of 33.

14. 3 rows of 62.

15. 4 rows of 22.

16. 6 rows of 14.

17. 3 groups of 27.

18. 5 groups of 13.

Estimation Estimate each product.

19. 8×27

20. 45×4

21. 739×5

22. 613×6

Problem Solving

Solve each problem.

23. At Parkview School, there are 3 fourth-grade classes. Each class has 22 fourth-grade students. How many fourth-grade students are there in all?

24. Parkview School has bike racks for 80 bikes. There are 67 bikes in the racks. How many more bikes can be put in the racks?

25. There are 26 players on the third-grade soccer team, 31 players on the fourth-grade team, and 39 players on the fifth-grade team. How many players in all are on the 3 teams?

26. Write a story problem about 3 × 24. Use tens and ones to solve your problem.

27. Show how you would solve Problem 23 using paper and pencil.

28. **Calculator** Write a story problem using 15 × 24. Solve your problem using a calculator.

Explore ———— Math

Calculator Each of the squares has been cut from a multiplication table like the one on page 246.

In each square, find the product of the numbers on each diagonal.

29.

2	3
4	6

30.

2	3	4
4	6	8
6	9	12

31.

3	6	9	12
4	8	12	16
5	10	15	20
6	12	18	24

$2 \times 6 = 12$
$3 \times 4 = $ ▦

$2 \times 6 \times 12 = $ ▦
$4 \times 6 \times 6 = $ ▦

32. Describe the pattern you see.

33. **Use Data** Do you think the pattern will be the same for a 5-by-5 square on the multiplication table? Choose a 5-by-5 square from the table on page 246. Find the products of the numbers on each of its diagonals to see if you are right.

Multiplication: Renaming Ones

Build Understanding

A video store has 4 shelves of cartoon videos. Each shelf has 18 cartoon videos. How many cartoon videos does the store have?

Since the rows are all the same size, you can multiply. Find 4 × 18.

Estimate the answer first:
18 is close to 20. So your answer should be close to 4 × 20, or 80.

With Place-Value Materials

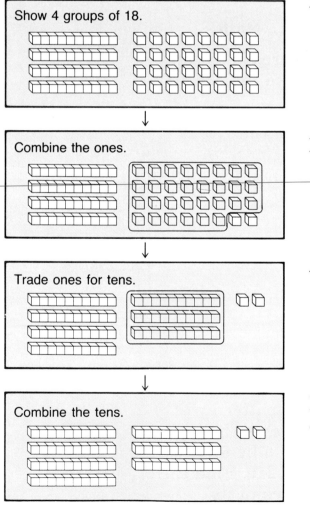

Show 4 groups of 18.

↓

Combine the ones.

↓

Trade ones for tens.

↓

Combine the tens.

With Paper and Pencil

Write the problem.

$$\begin{array}{r} 18 \\ \times\ 4 \\ \hline \end{array}$$

Multiply the ones.

$$\begin{array}{r} 18 \\ \times\ 4 \\ \hline \end{array}$$ 4 × 8 ones = 32 ones

Write the ones. Write the tens.

$$\begin{array}{r} {\scriptstyle 3} \\ 18 \\ \times\ 4 \\ \hline 2 \end{array}$$ 32 = 3 tens 2 ones

Multiply the tens. Add the extra tens. Write the tens.

$$\begin{array}{r} {\scriptstyle 3} \\ 18 \\ \times\ 4 \\ \hline 72 \end{array}$$ 4 × 1 ten = 4 tens
4 tens + 3 tens = 7 tens

There are 72 cartoon videos.

■ **Talk About Math** Explain how you can use an estimate to check if an answer is reasonable.

Check Understanding

For another example, see Set E, pages 464–465.

Multiply. **Remember** to estimate the product first.

1. 37 × 2	**2.** 26 × 5	**3.** 15 × 6	**4.** 32 × 4	**5.** 22 × 3

Practice

For More Practice, see Set E, pages 466–467.

Multiply. Use tens and ones if you need them.

6. 29 × 3	**7.** 24 × 4	**8.** 12 × 7	**9.** 18 × 5	**10.** 38 × 2
11. 19 × 5	**12.** 39 × 2	**13.** 12 × 8	**14.** 13 × 7	**15.** 36 × 2

16. 26 × 3   **17.** 47 × 2   **18.** 13 × 4   **19.** 16 × 2   **20.** 28 × 3

21. 17 × 5   **22.** 25 × 3   **23.** 37 × 2

24. 14 × 7   **25.** 23 × 4   **26.** 22 × 3

✓ **Midchapter** _____ **Checkup**

Find each answer.

1. How much is 27 tens? Give your answer in standard form.

2. How much is 11 hundreds? Give your answer in standard form.

3. **Mental Math** Find 10 × 6.

4. **Estimation** Estimate 4 × 96.

5. How many are in 6 groups of 12?

6. Find 3 × 26.

Explore as a Team

Estimate how many beans are on the grid paper.

1. A small jar of beans was emptied onto the grid paper. Choose one of the squares. Record how many beans are in that square.

2. Choose 3 other squares. Record how many beans are in each of these squares.

TIPS FOR **WORKING TOGETHER**

To make sure your group understands the task or solution, have each group member say it in his or her own words, summarize the steps, or give an example.

3. Decide how many beans are usually in a square.

4. Discuss how you could use the grid paper to estimate the number of beans in all. Compare your new estimates with your original estimates.

Visual Thinking Activity

1. How many cubes are in the bottom layer?

2. How many cubes are there in all?

Number-Sense Project

Look back at pages 438-439.
One class recorded these results.

AGE	Apple	Maple	Oak	Palm	Pine	Weeping Willow
Pre-Teen	4	6	10	4	18	10
Teen	8	8	10	14	6	4
Adult	8	8	20	4	9	1

Choice of Tree

1. How many adults in all were asked to make a choice?

2. If 100 adults were asked, how many would probably pick the oak tree?

3. Write a sentence telling how popular the oak tree was with the different age groups.

Real-Life Decision Making

You are helping to give a birthday party for your sister. The party will be from 2:00 to 4:00 P.M. on Saturday.

1. How much time is planned for the party?

2. How long should you plan for games?

3. About what time should you plan to eat?

4. About what time should your sister open the presents?

Too Much Information

Build Understanding

PROBLEM SOLVING

GUIDE

Understand
QUESTION
FACTS
KEY IDEA

Plan and Solve
STRATEGY
ANSWER

Look Back
SENSIBLE ANSWER
ALTERNATE APPROACH

There are 16 crayons in a box, in 2 rows of 8 each. A box is at each of 6 tables in the room. How many crayons are there in all?

Understand QUESTION What is the total number of crayons?

FACTS Each box has 16 crayons. There are 6 tables. Each table has a box. You do not need to know that there are 2 rows of 8 crayons in each box.

KEY IDEA You know there are 6 tables, so there must be 6 boxes. Since each box has the same number of crayons, you can multiply.

Plan and Solve

$$\begin{array}{r} \overset{3}{1}6 \\ \times\ \ 6 \\ \hline 9\,6 \end{array}$$

There are 96 crayons in all.

Look Back 16 is close to 20. $6 \times 20 = 120$ Because 16 is less than 20, 96 is a reasonable answer.

■ **Talk About Math** How could you solve the problem if you did not know the total number of crayons in each box?

Next time you use crayons, think about how many colors there are.

Check Understanding

Solve this problem by answering Questions 1–7.

Pencils come in packages of 10. Each pencil costs 9¢. How many pencils are in 7 packages?

1. What does the problem ask you to find?

2. What facts are you given?

3. What information is not needed?

4. How many groups of 10 pencils are there?

5. What operation would you use to solve the problem?

6. Solve the problem.

7. Is your answer to Problem 6 reasonable?

Practice

Solve each problem.

8. Construction paper comes in packages of 200 sheets. Each sheet costs 5¢. How many sheets are in 5 packages?

9. A large box of crayons has 4 sections. Each section has 2 rows of 8 crayons. How many crayons are in a box?

10. Mr. Garcia has 36 erasers. The erasers are 3 different colors. If 9 of his students share the erasers equally, how many erasers will each person get?

11. There are 24 students at 6 tables. On each table is 16 ounces of clay. How many ounces of clay are there in all?

Reading ———— Math

Identifying Unneeded Information   List the information that you did not need in order to solve Problems 8–11.

Multiplication: Renaming Ones and Tens

Build Understanding

Linda works on an automobile assembly line. The line puts together 34 cars every hour. How many cars can the line put together in 4 hours?

The same number of cars are put together every hour, so you can multiply. Find 4×34.

Estimation Estimate first. 34 is close to 30. Since $4 \times 30 = 120$, your answer should be close to 120.

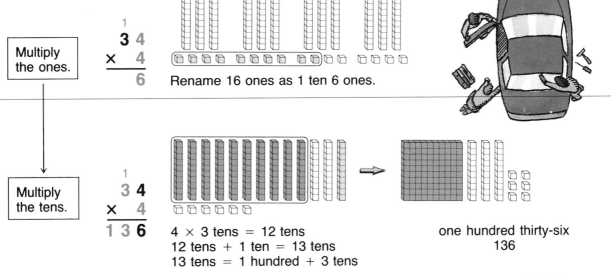

Multiply the ones.	$\begin{array}{r} 1 \\ 3\,4 \\ \times\ \ 4 \\ \hline 6 \end{array}$

Rename 16 ones as 1 ten 6 ones.

Multiply the tens.	$\begin{array}{r} 1 \\ 3\,4 \\ \times\ \ 4 \\ \hline 1\,3\,6 \end{array}$

4×3 tens = 12 tens
12 tens + 1 ten = 13 tens
13 tens = 1 hundred + 3 tens

one hundred thirty-six
136

Linda's assembly line puts together 136 cars in 4 hours.

■ **Talk About Math** How can you tell that your estimate in the example will be less than the actual answer?

Check Understanding

For another example, see Set F, pages 464–465.

For each exercise, tell whether you need to rename the ones. Then multiply.

1.	56	2.	24	3.	72	4.	61	5.	47
	× 3		× 2		× 5		× 9		× 8

Practice

For More Practice, see Set F, pages 466–467.

Multiply. **Remember** to estimate first.

6.	32	7.	53	8.	11	9.	46	10.	38
	× 4		× 7		× 3		× 6		× 7

11.	74	12.	91	13.	38	14.	52	15.	47
	× 9		× 8		× 5		× 2		× 3

16. 3×83 **17.** 4×71 **18.** 9×338 **19.** 6×47

20. 5×57 **21.** 8×62 **22.** 2×463 **23.** 7×287

Mixed Practice Use paper and pencil or mental math to find each answer. Tell which method you used.

24. 7×30 **25.** 98×2 **26.** $120 + 6$ **27.** $80 - 43$

28. $32 \div 8$ **29.** 39×4 **30.** 9×17 **31.** $52 + 9$

32. $87 - 49$ **33.** $56 \div 7$ **34.** $68 + 37$ **35.** 45×6

Problem Solving

Solve each problem.

36. If the assembly line for trucks can make 23 trucks in one hour, how many trucks can it make in an 8-hour shift?

37. The factory runs two 8-hour shifts each day. How many hours does it operate in a 5-day work week?

Choose an Operation

PROBLEM SOLVING
GUIDE

Understand
QUESTION
FACTS
KEY IDEA

Plan and Solve
STRATEGY
ANSWER

Look Back
SENSIBLE ANSWER
ALTERNATE APPROACH

Build Understanding

A *potlatch* has been an important ceremony of the Pacific Northwest Coast Indians for many years. It can take years to prepare for and every member of the clan participates. A potlatch is an expression of pride and unity. Years ago, blankets, canoes, shell necklaces, and coppers were given to show wealth and to honor each recipient.

Suppose 2,762 shell necklaces and 1,540 blankets were given away at one potlatch. How many more necklaces than blankets were given away?

Understand You need to find how many more necklaces than blankets were given away.

Plan and Solve STRATEGY Subtract the number of blankets from the number of necklaces.

$$\begin{array}{r} 2{,}7\,6\,2 \\ -\ 1{,}5\,4\,0 \\ \hline 1{,}2\,2\,2 \end{array}$$

ANSWER There were 1,222 more necklaces than blankets given away.

This Kwakiutl woman is holding a metal plaque called a *copper*. It is one of the most valuable gifts given at potlatches.

Look Back Estimate to see if your answer is reasonable.

Since 1,222 is close to 1,300, the answer is reasonable.

$$2{,}762 - 1{,}540$$
$$\downarrow \qquad\qquad \downarrow$$
$$2{,}800 - 1{,}500 = 1{,}300$$

■ **Talk About Math** How can you use addition to check your answer?

Check Understanding

Coppers were very valuable. One copper had a value of 4,500 blankets. Another copper had a value of 3,650 blankets. What was the total value of the two coppers?

1. What is the question?

2. What are the two key facts?

3. Which operation should you use to solve the problem?

4. What is the answer? How do you know it makes sense?

Practice

Tell whether you would *add, subtract, multiply,* or *divide.* Then find each answer.

5. *Kwanzaa* is an African American holiday that lasts for 7 days. Yolanda gave 3 handmade gifts each day. How many gifts did she give in all?

6. In Korea, a baby receives gifts on his or her hundredth day. Kim is 16 days old. How many days is it to his hundredth day?

7. Gifts are given on New Year's Day in the Netherlands. Peter bought his 3 sisters identical dolls. The total cost was $21. How much did each doll cost?

8. Use Data Look at the map on page 124. The Golds made a trip from Detroit to Independence and back for a family birthday party. How many miles did they travel?

Choose a ▬ **Strategy**

A Gift Puzzle

9. Jana made some gifts. She gave 1 to her teacher and 2 to each of 5 friends. She then had 2 gifts left. How many gifts did she have in the beginning?

Multiplication with Hundreds

Build Understanding

The third-grade class in Talbot School used 3 medium-sized boxes of building blocks to build a play area for their gerbils. How many blocks did they use in all?

Building Blocks		
Small Box	96 blocks	$ 6.95
Medium Box	152 blocks	$ 9.89
Large Box	328 blocks	$13.99

Since the 3 boxes have the same number of blocks, you can multiply. Find 3 × 152.

Estimation   You can find a range to estimate the answer. The product is between 300 and 600.

Round 152 down.
3 × 152
↓
$$3 \times 100 = 300$$

Round 152 up.
3 × 152
↓
$$3 \times 200 = 600$$

Multiply to find the actual answer.

| Multiply the ones.
3 × 2 ones = 6 ones |

$$\begin{array}{r} 1\ 5\ 2 \\ \times \qquad 3 \\ \hline 6 \end{array}$$

| Multiply the tens.
3 × 5 tens = 15 tens
Rename 15 tens as 1 hundred and 5 tens. |

$$\begin{array}{r} {\scriptstyle 1} \\ 1\ 5\ 2 \\ \times \qquad 3 \\ \hline 5\ 6 \end{array}$$

| Multiply the hundreds.
3 × 1 hundred = 3 hundreds
3 hundreds + 1 hundred = 4 hundreds |

$$\begin{array}{r} {\scriptstyle 1} \\ 1\ 5\ 2 \\ \times \qquad 3 \\ \hline 4\ 5\ 6 \end{array}$$

The students used 456 blocks.

■ **Talk About Math**   How do you know your answer is reasonable?

Check Understanding

For another example, see Set G, pages 464–465.

Find each product. In which exercise do you need
to rename ones as tens? tens as hundreds?

1. 142
    × 4

2. 308
    × 5

3. 417 × 2

4. 821 × 6

Practice

For More Practice, see Set G, pages 466–467.

Find each product. **Remember** to find an estimate first.

5. 119
    × 3

6. 351
    × 5

7. 115
    × 6

8. 106
    × 7

9. 454
    × 4

10. 2 × 239

11. 4 × 562

12. 5 × 250

13. 7 × 614

14. 6 × 338

15. 3 × 771

16. 8 × 197

17. 9 × 319

Mixed Practice   Use paper and pencil or mental math to find
each answer. Tell which method you used.

18. 34 + 50

19. 124 × 4

20. 198 − 49

21. 16 × 8

22. 49 × 8

23. 50 − 25

24. 128 + 220

25. 72 ÷ 9

Problem Solving

Use the chart on page 460 to solve Problems 26 and 27.

26. How many blocks would
you have if you had one box
of each size?

27. Estimation   How many
small boxes would have
about the same number of
blocks as in a large box?

■ **Calculator**   Solve each problem.

28. Arrange the digits 2, 5, 8,
and 9 to make a 3-digit and
a 1-digit number that will
give you the greatest
product when you multiply.

29. The product of a 1-digit
number and a 2-digit
number is 228. Their sum is
44. What are the two
numbers?

Skills Review

Give the standard form for each exercise.

1. 12 tens   **2.** 8 hundreds

3. 4 groups of 6 hundreds

4. 5 groups of fifty

Find each product mentally.

5. 6 × 10   **6.** 24 × 10

7. 100 × 9   **8.** 5 × 300

Estimate each product.

9. 6 × 18   **10.** 56 × 5

11. 749 × 3   **12.** 4 × 421

Use tens and ones to help you find how many are in

13. 4 groups of 15.

14. 3 rows of 24.

Multiply.

15. 17
× 6

16. 25
× 3

17. 58
× 5

18. 72
× 9

19. 195
× 2

20. 407
× 7

21. 8 × 64   **22.** 4 × 327

Problem-Solving Review

Solve each problem.

23. A package of paper plates holds 36 plates. How many plates are in 3 packages?

24. A one-way bus ticket is $56. A round-trip ticket is $98. How much is saved by buying a round-trip ticket instead of 2 one-way tickets?

25. How can you make a dollar from quarters and nickels using 12 coins in all?

26. Write a number with 4 in the tens place and tenths place.

27. If Marco types 62 words per minute, how many words can he type in 5 minutes?

28. **Data File** Use data from pages 532–533. Tell which trains go from San Francisco after 6:15 A.M. to get to Menlo Park by 9:00 A.M. How long is the trip?

29. **Make a Data File** Most flowers have petals in multiples of 3 or 5. Find at least two flowers with petals in multiples of 3, and two with petals in multiples of 5. Draw a picture of each and label.

Is each number odd or even?

1. 36   **2.** 47   **3.** 95

Round to the nearest hundred.

4. 865   **5.** 439   **6.** 52

Find each sum or difference.

7. $\begin{array}{r} 237 \\ +372 \end{array}$ **8.** $\begin{array}{r} 523 \\ -189 \end{array}$ **9.** $\begin{array}{r} 602 \\ -493 \end{array}$

10. Choose the most sensible temperature of cold milk.

    7°C   32°C   50°C

11. Which figure is a rectangle?

    a.   b.

Write the family of multiplication and division facts using the given numbers.

12. 6, 7, 42   **13.** 8, 8, 64

Find each quotient.

14. $18 \div 6$ **15.** $35 \div 7$

16. $56 \div 8$ **17.** $27 \div 9$

18. Complete the number sentence.

$\frac{1}{3} = \frac{}{6}$

Complete using $<$, $>$, or $=$.

19. $\frac{3}{5}$ ▦ $\frac{2}{5}$ **20.** 2.5 ▦ 2.7

21. What decimal part of a dollar is 4 dimes?

22. Give the time as minutes before the hour.

Write the amount of money.

23. 2 quarters, 2 nickels

24. 1 dollar, 3 dimes, 2 pennies

Write the change from $10.00 for a

25. $8.99 book.   **26.** $2.45 card.

Estimate to the nearest dollar.

27. $3.98 + $0.82 + $7.24

28. $17.57 + $53.72 + $9.35

Find each product mentally.

29. 100×7 **30.** 32×10

Multiply.

31. 5×9 **32.** 4×7

33. 33×8 **34.** 29×4

35. 5×57 **36.** 66×7

37. 3×135 **38.** 9×504

Reteaching

Set A   pages 440–441

Give the standard form for
4 forties.

$$4 \times 4 \text{ tens} = 16 \text{ tens} = 160$$

Show 160 with fewer pieces.
Replace 10 tens with a hundred.

1 hundred 6 tens $= 160 \leftarrow$ Standard form

Remember that a hundred
equals 10 tens.

Give the standard form for each
exercise. Use tens and hundreds
to help you.

1. 7 tens   **2.** 14 tens

3. 16 tens   **4.** 5 hundreds

5. 4 thirties   **6.** 3 sixties

Set B   pages 442–443

Find 3×300.
Think: 300 is a multiple of 100, so
         300 is 3 hundreds.
Show: 3 groups of 300.

$$3 \times 3 \text{ hundreds} = 9 \text{ hundreds}$$
$$3 \times 300 = 900$$

Remember that you can also use
addition to solve a multiplication
problem.

Mental Math   Find each
product mentally.

1. 6×10 **2.** 13×10

3. 25×10 **4.** 8×100

Set C   pages 444–445

Estimate 4×475. Round
475 to the nearest hundred.

475 is closer to 500 than 400.

To find 4×500,
think: $4 \times 5 = 20$
So $4 \times 500 = 2,000$.

Remember that the actual
product will be greater than the
estimate if you round down.
Estimate each product.

1. 5×18 **2.** 6×21

3. 8×72 **4.** 3×225

5. 9×512 **6.** 640×4

Set D pages 446–449

Find 3 groups of 34.
Make 3 groups of 34.

Combine the groups.
Trade 10 ones for 1 ten.

3 groups of 34 is 102.

Remember that you can find the answer to the example at the left by adding 3 groups of 34.

Use tens and hundreds to help you find how many are in

1. 2 groups of 31.

2. 4 groups of 14.

3. 5 groups of 12.

4. 6 groups of 17.

Set E pages 450–451

Find 6×14.

6×4 ones $= 24$ ones 6×1 ten $= 6$ tens

$$2 \longleftarrow 2 \text{ tens}$$
$$\begin{array}{r} 14 \\ \times\ 6 \\ \hline 4 \end{array} \longleftarrow 4 \text{ ones}$$

$$\begin{array}{r} 2 \\ 14 \\ \times\ 6 \\ \hline 84 \end{array} \quad 6 \text{ tens} + 2 \text{ tens}$$

Remember to add the extra tens after you multiply the tens.

Multiply.

1. $\begin{array}{r} 17 \\ \times\ 3 \\ \hline \end{array}$ **2.** $\begin{array}{r} 14 \\ \times\ 8 \\ \hline \end{array}$

Set F pages 456–457

Find 7×48.

7×8 ones $= 56$ ones 7×4 tens $= 28$ tens

$$5 \longleftarrow 5 \text{ tens}$$
$$\begin{array}{r} 48 \\ \times\ 7 \\ \hline 6 \end{array}$$

$$\begin{array}{r} 5 \\ 48 \\ \times\ 7 \\ \hline 336 \end{array} \quad 28 \text{ tens} + 5 \text{ tens}$$

Remember to estimate first in order to see if the answer is reasonable.

Multiply.

1. $\begin{array}{r} 37 \\ \times\ 6 \\ \hline \end{array}$ **2.** $\begin{array}{r} 43 \\ \times\ 5 \\ \hline \end{array}$

Set G pages 460–461

Find 4×176.

4×6 ones 4×7 tens 4×1 hundred

$$\begin{array}{r} 2 \\ 176 \\ \times\ 4 \\ \hline 4 \end{array} \qquad \begin{array}{r} 3\,2 \\ 176 \\ \times\ 4 \\ \hline 04 \end{array} \qquad \begin{array}{r} 3\,2 \\ 176 \\ \times\ 4 \\ \hline 704 \end{array}$$

Remember to add the extra hundreds after you multiply the hundreds. Find each product.

1. $\begin{array}{r} 271 \\ \times\ 5 \\ \hline \end{array}$ **2.** $\begin{array}{r} 318 \\ \times\ 8 \\ \hline \end{array}$

More Practice

Set A   pages 440–441

Give the standard form for each exercise. Use
tens and hundreds to help you.

1. 8 tens   **2.** 17 tens   **3.** 11 tens   **4.** 3 fifties   **5.** 11 hundreds

6. 3 groups of six hundreds   **7.** 4 groups of four hundreds

8. 5 groups of thirty   **9.** 5 groups of sixty

10. 6 groups of forty   **11.** 5 groups of two hundreds

Set B   pages 442–443

Mental Math   Find each product mentally.

1. 3×10 **2.** 12×10 **3.** 24×10 **4.** 10×9

5. 4×100 **6.** 8×100 **7.** 100×32 **8.** 100×41

9. 7×30 **10.** 4×60 **11.** 20×4 **12.** 70×6

13. 5×800 **14.** 9×300 **15.** 400×5 **16.** 600×6

Set C   pages 444–445

Estimate each product.

1. 3×11 **2.** 4×22 **3.** 59×6 **4.** 8×44

5. 7×412 **6.** 564×5 **7.** 8×390 **8.** 842×6

9. 9×32 **10.** 4×46 **11.** 687×3 **12.** 4×726

13. 5×639 **14.** 88×4 **15.** 7×68 **16.** 927×2

Number Sense   Give each answer.

17. In which of Exercises 1–16 do
you think your estimated
product will be less than the
actual product?

18. In which of Exercises 1–16 do
you think your estimated
product will be greater than
the actual product?

Set D pages 446–449

Use tens and ones to help you find how many are in

1. 2 groups of 26. **2.** 4 groups of 11. **3.** 5 groups of 21.

4. 4 rows of 42. **5.** 3 rows of 17. **6.** 4 groups of 34.

7. 6 rows of 18. **8.** 4 rows of 52. **9.** 2 groups of 49.

Set E pages 450–451

Find each product.

1. $\begin{array}{r} 23 \\ \times\ 3 \end{array}$ **2.** $\begin{array}{r} 26 \\ \times\ 5 \end{array}$ **3.** $\begin{array}{r} 12 \\ \times\ 8 \end{array}$ **4.** $\begin{array}{r} 19 \\ \times\ 4 \end{array}$ **5.** $\begin{array}{r} 37 \\ \times\ 2 \end{array}$

6. 18 × 6 **7.** 11 × 9 **8.** 14 × 7 **9.** 29 × 3 **10.** 38 × 2

11. 22 × 4 **12.** 15 × 5 **13.** 12 × 6 **14.** 17 × 3 **15.** 34 × 2

Set F pages 456–457

Multiply.

1. $\begin{array}{r} 23 \\ \times\ 5 \end{array}$ **2.** $\begin{array}{r} 34 \\ \times\ 3 \end{array}$ **3.** $\begin{array}{r} 55 \\ \times\ 6 \end{array}$ **4.** $\begin{array}{r} 92 \\ \times\ 2 \end{array}$ **5.** $\begin{array}{r} 47 \\ \times\ 4 \end{array}$

6. 54 × 7 **7.** 82 × 5 **8.** 38 × 6 **9.** 26 × 8

10. 9 × 42 **11.** 6 × 51 **12.** 7 × 35 **13.** 4 × 84

Mixed Practice Use paper and pencil or mental math to find each answer. Tell which method you used.

14. 150 + 9 **15.** 9 × 20 **16.** 62 − 34 **17.** 63 ÷ 7

Set G pages 460–461

Find each product.

1. $\begin{array}{r} 318 \\ \times\ 2 \end{array}$ **2.** $\begin{array}{r} 164 \\ \times\ 5 \end{array}$ **3.** $\begin{array}{r} 237 \\ \times\ 4 \end{array}$ **4.** $\begin{array}{r} 408 \\ \times\ 9 \end{array}$ **5.** $\begin{array}{r} 128 \\ \times\ 6 \end{array}$

6. 3 × 143 **7.** 6 × 350 **8.** 4 × 229 **9.** 8 × 508

Enrichment

Multiplication with Money

How could you find the cost of 5 pounds of apples at the Farmer's Market?

Find 5 × 43¢. Think of 43¢ as 43 ones.

Multiply the ones. Rename if needed.	Multiply the tens. Write the answer as dollars and cents.

$$\begin{array}{r} \overset{1}{4\ 3} \\ \times\ \ 5 \\ \hline 5 \end{array}$$

$$\begin{array}{r} \overset{1}{4\ 3} \\ \times\ \ 5 \\ \hline 2\ 1\ 5 \end{array}$$ **215¢**   215¢ is the same as $2.15.

Five pounds of apples cost $2.15.

Multiply. Write each answer as dollars and cents.

1. $27¢ \atop \times\ 5$
2. $81¢ \atop \times\ 5$
3. $33¢ \atop \times\ 6$
4. $60¢ \atop \times\ 5$
5. $23¢ \atop \times\ 4$

6. 4 × 74¢
7. 2 × 15¢
8. 36¢ × 7
9. 51¢ × 8

Find the cost of each of the following.

10. 3 pounds of pears
11. 4 pounds of oranges
12. 5 pounds of bananas
13. 6 kiwi fruit

Chapter 13 Review/Test

1. Give the standard form for 6 groups of 3 hundreds.

Find each product mentally.

2. 90 × 4   **3.** 60 × 5

Estimate each product.

4. 23 × 9   **5.** 4 × 492

6. Find how many are in 4 groups of 26.

▌▌::: ▌▌::: ▌▌::: ▌▌:::

Use Exercises A and B to answer Items 7–12. Draw pictures to help you.

A. 24   **B.** 37
    × 2   × 4
  ─────   ─────

In Exercise A, how many

7. ones will there be?

8. tens will there be?

9. In Exercise A, did you need to rename any ones as tens?

In Exercise B, how many

10. ones will there be?

11. tens will there be in all?

12. did you need to rename any ones as tens?

Draw pictures to help find each product.

13. 5 × 14   **14.** 6 × 23

15. 4 × 91   **16.** 7 × 302

17. Oranges come in bags of 12. Tomatoes come in boxes of 8. How many oranges are there in 6 bags?

Read this problem. Then answer the questions below.

Each of the 3 Thompson children went on 9 rides. How many rides did they take in all?

18. Would you add, subtract, multiply, or divide to solve the problem?

19. Pat got an answer of 6 for the problem. Does this answer make sense? Why or why not?

20. Solve the problem above.

21. ▪ **Write About Math** Is your estimate for Exercise 5 greater or less than the exact product? How do you know?

Statistics, Graphing, and Probability

14

Did You Know: Some large libraries receive as many as 10 different newspapers every day.

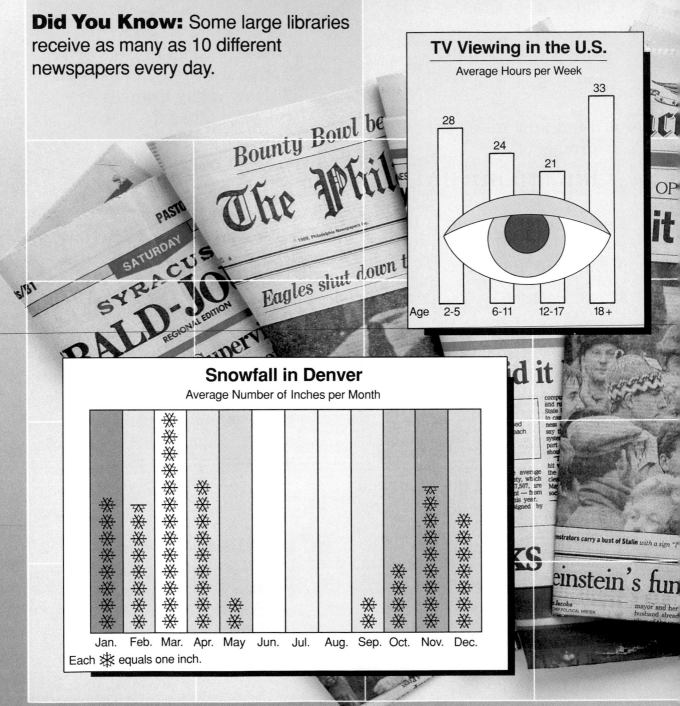

TV Viewing in the U.S.
Average Hours per Week

Age 2-5	6-11	12-17	18+
28	24	21	33

Snowfall in Denver
Average Number of Inches per Month

Jan. Feb. Mar. Apr. May Jun. Jul. Aug. Sep. Oct. Nov. Dec.

Each ❆ equals one inch.

Estimate
Predict how many graphs will appear in the newspaper the next 5 days.

Gather Data
Check the newspaper you selected and record the number of graphs which appear.

Analyze and Report
When people are done reading the newspaper, cut out the graphs. Group them into categories. Give each category a name. Compare your categories with other students.

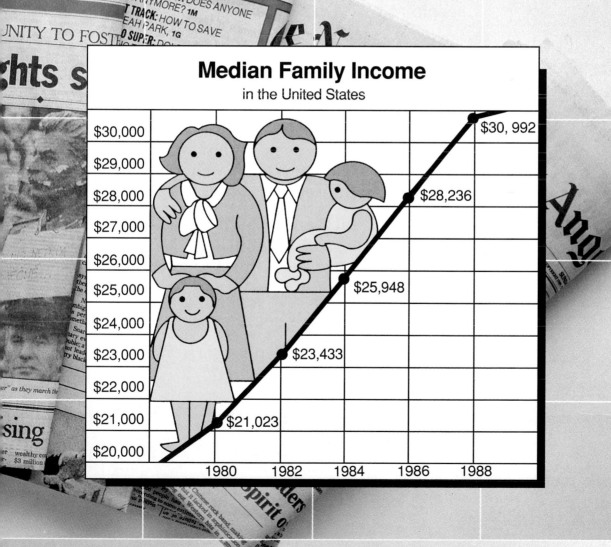

Median Family Income
in the United States

$30,000 — $30,992
$29,000
$28,000 — $28,236
$27,000
$26,000
$25,000 — $25,948
$24,000
$23,000 — $23,433
$22,000
$21,000 — $21,023
$20,000

1980   1982   1984   1986   1988

Collecting Data

Build Understanding

There will be 10 people at Brian's birthday picnic. Brian will serve either hot dogs or hamburgers. Which should he serve?

III➡ **Understand**
QUESTION
FACTS
KEY IDEA

Plan and Solve
STRATEGY
ANSWER

Look Back
SENSIBLE ANSWER
ALTERNATE APPROACH

PROBLEM SOLVING GUIDE

III➡ **Understand**   QUESTION   What food should Brian serve?

FACTS   There will be 10 people at the picnic.

KEY IDEA   Brian needs a way to find out which food his guests will like.

Plan and Solve   To get the information, or **data,** Brian could ask different kinds of questions.

- He could ask each guest, "What would you like to eat at the picnic?" Then he might get 10 different answers!

- He could ask each guest, "Which would you like, hot dogs or hamburgers?" Then he might get answers that would help him.

- Because Brian likes hot dogs better, he could just ask, "Do you like hot dogs?"

Brian decided to serve hamburgers. Which question do you think he asked?

Look Back   Could Brian have done something else to get an answer?

■ **Talk About Math**   What other questions could Brian have asked? Would the results always be the same?

472

Check Understanding

Do you need to collect data from several people to find out

1. which colors people like?

2. how plants grow?

3. if your friend can play with you?

4. how students travel to school?

5. If you answered *no* to any of Questions 1–4, tell how you might get the information to answer those questions.

Practice

Write at least two questions you could ask your classmates to help you answer each question below.

6. The class will take sandwiches on a trip. The lunchroom can make cheese, chicken, tuna, ham, and egg salad sandwiches. How many sandwiches of each kind should the class order?

7. You are ordering 4 pizzas for a class party. A pizza can have 1 topping or no toppings. A topping can be sausage, peppers, or mushrooms. How many pizzas should have toppings?

8. You ask classmates about their favorite animals. What kinds of animals do your friends like?

9. Which of your questions for Problems 6–8 do you think would give you more helpful data?

10. Estimation Helen brought paper plates on a picnic. She used 32 plates for sandwiches, 27 for salads, and 18 for desserts. She had 43 plates left. About how many plates did she bring in all?

Collecting and Organizing Data

Build Understanding

A. My Favorite Things
Materials: Tally charts
Groups: 3–6 students

Has anyone ever asked what
your favorite game is? Your
group is going to collect data
about things people like.

a. Decide whether your group will
collect data about favorite games,
colors, pets, or other things.

b. Decide what questions to ask to
get the data you need. Decide how
to record the data.

c. Gather Data   Each member of
your group asks the questions of
5 people outside your group.

B. Sara's group made this **tally
chart** to show some data they
collected.

Our Favorite Games		
Name of Game	Tally	Number
Jacks	////	4
Tag	//// ////	10
Marbles	//// /	6
Hopscotch	////	4
Checkers	//	2

■ **Talk About Math**   Did your
group get the information you
needed? Did you need to change
any questions?

474

Check Understanding

For another example, see Set A, pages 498–499.

In a tally chart what does

1. each / mean?

2. ////// mean?

3. What questions do you think Sara's group asked to get the results in the tally chart?

4. Can you tell from the tally chart how many children played tag last Saturday?

5. Make a tally chart to show the results of your questions.

Practice

For More Practice, see Set A, pages 500–501.

Record data about the dolls shown.
Copy and complete each tally chart.

6.

Scarf	Tallies	Number
yes		
no		

7.

Snow Shovel	Tallies	Number

8.

Color of snow-suit	Tallies	Number

9.

Color of mittens	Tallies	Number

10.

Pompon on hat	Tallies	Number

11.

Color of boots	Tallies	Number

Pictographs

Build Understanding

African foods differ from region to region. Corn, cassava (tapioca), yams, bananas, and plantains are common throughout.

Fu-fu is eaten in many African countries. It can be made from cassava, cornmeal, or rice. It is smooth and creamy like pudding.

Peanuts are called groundnuts in Africa and are used in stew.

Plantains are in the banana family. They are longer than bananas, and are fried or boiled before they are eaten.

A third-grade class held a taste test of African foods and recorded favorites on a tally chart. Students then worked in pairs to make pictographs from their data.

Each pair wrote a title at the top of their pictograph, and then listed the kinds of food. Partners used a face to stand for a certain number of children. They wrote that number at the bottom.

They drew faces in the graph for the numbers on the tally chart.

Type of Food	Tally	Number
Fu-fu	//	2
Fried plantain	//// ///	8
Boiled plantain	//// /	6
Groundnut stew	////	4

Favorite Foods of Children	
Fu-fu	
Fried plantain	
Boiled plantain	
Groundnut stew	
Each ☺ stands for 2 children.	

■ Talk About Math Look at the pictographs made by the third-grade class shown below. Talk about the different ways each group showed the same data.

Check Understanding

For another example, see Set B, pages 498–499.

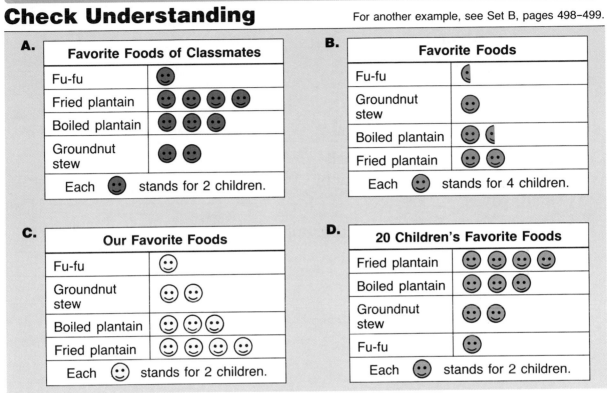

Look at Graphs A, B, C, and D to answer Exercises 1–2.

1. Do you think it matters in what order the food is listed? Why?

2. What does ☺ stand for in Graphs A, C, and D? Graph B?

For Exercises 3–7, suppose you used this tally chart to make a pictograph.

3. What title would you use?

4. How would you list the choices?

5. What picture would you use?

6. How many tally marks would each picture stand for?

7. How many pictures would you show in each row?

What is your favorite snack food?		
Snack	Tally	Number
Grapes	//// ////	10
Crackers	////	4
Raisins	//// ///	8

Practice

For More Practice, see Set B, pages 500–501.

In many countries in Africa there is a day called Market Day. Baskets, pottery, wood carvings, jewelry, and clothing to be sold are often displayed on straw mats on the ground.

Avi, a third-grader, asked her classmates what item they would like to buy if they went to a Market Day. The tally chart at the right shows the results of Avi's survey.

8. Copy and complete the pictograph using Avi's tally chart.

9. Describe what your graph shows without using numbers.

Items at Market Day		
Item	Tally	Number
food	////	5
pottery	//	2
baskets		0
jewelry	//// //	7
carvings	///	3
clothing	///	3

Items 3rd-Graders Buy	
food	★ ★ ⸝
pottery	
carvings	
baskets	
jewelry	
clothing	
Each ★ stands for 2 people.	

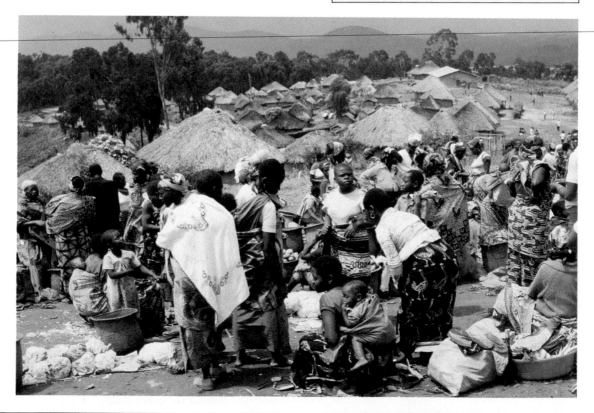

478

10. Musicians stroll through the crowds on Market Day. The graph at the right tells about the musicians. How many musicians play the drums?

11. A *kundi* is a guitar made from goat skin stretched over a wooden frame. How many musicians play a kundi?

Instruments Played at Market Day

Drums	🥁 🥁 🥁
Flutes	🎵 🎵 🎵 🎵 🎵
Kundis	🎸 🎸 🎸 🎸 🎸 🎸

Each instrument represents 3 musicians.

Use Data Make your own pictograph. Use the tally chart on page 474 and complete Exercises 12–16.

12. Write a title for your graph.

13. List the games at the left.

14. Decide what picture you will use to stand for people.

15. Decide how many people each picture will stand for.

16. Draw pictures in your graph next to each game.

Mixed Practice Study the pictograph at the right. Then answer the questions. Students at Smith School were asked to name their favorite school lunch.

Favorite School Lunch

Hamburger	☺ ☺ ☺
Spaghetti	☺ ☺ ☺ ☺
Pizza	☺ ☺
Taco	☺ ☺ ☺ ☺ ☺

Each ☺ stands for 16 people.

17. How many students like tacos?

18. How many students like spaghetti?

Problem Solving

Calculator Use the pictograph above to solve each problem.

19. If each student picked only one kind of food as a favorite, how many students were asked?

20. If the answer to Exercise 19 represents half of the students in Smith Elementary School, how many students in all attend the school?

Bar Graphs

Build Understanding

Mrs. Ruiz manages the Shirt Boutique. One of her jobs is to record the sales of different styles of clothing on a bar graph.

Sales of Shirts Week of April 3		
Type of Shirt	Tally	Number
No Sleeves	UHT UHT	10
Short Sleeves	UHT UHT UHT UHT	20
Long Sleeves	UHT	5
Tank Top	UHT	5

A. To help her draw the bar graph, Mrs. Ruiz first collected data using a tally chart.

B. Mrs. Ruiz wrote a title for her bar graph. Along the bottom of the graph, she wrote the name of each style of shirt. At the left, Mrs. Ruiz wrote the numbers that would help her draw the bars.

Sales of Shirts Week of April 3

c. In a different color, Mrs. Ruiz added to the bars on her graph for the week of April 10.

■ **Talk About Math** Why is the bar graph more useful to Mrs. Ruiz than just her weekly tallies?

Sales of Shirts
Weeks of April 3 and April 10

Check Understanding

For another example, see Set C, pages 498–499.

1. When Mrs. Ruiz orders T-shirts for May, which kind should she buy the most of?

2. If you were Mrs. Ruiz, would you order more tank tops for May? Why?

3. **Number Sense** Why did Mrs. Ruiz count by 5s on the side of her graph instead of by 2s?

4. Why does Mrs. Ruiz use a new color for each different week of sales?

5. How many shirts of each kind were sold the week of April 10?

Practice

For More Practice, see Set C, pages 500–501.

Mrs. Ruiz also keeps track of when her store is the busiest. Use the tally sheet and answer the questions to complete the graph.

6. Copy the unfinished graph on page 482 and write a title that explains the data it will show.

Number of People in Store		
Time	Tally	Number
9 to noon	�	20
noon to 3		80
3 to 6		30
6 to 9		40

481

7. Decide what numbers you will use and write them along the bottom of your graph.

9 to noon

noon to 3

3 to 6

6 to 9

8. Draw your bars in the graph. Your bars will go from left to right instead of bottom to top.

9. Write a summary of your finished graph without using numbers.

Problem Solving

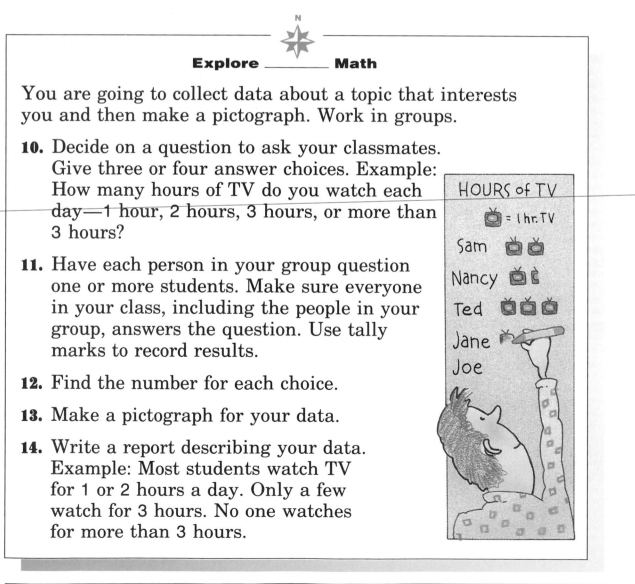

Explore ——— Math

You are going to collect data about a topic that interests you and then make a pictograph. Work in groups.

10. Decide on a question to ask your classmates. Give three or four answer choices. Example: How many hours of TV do you watch each day—1 hour, 2 hours, 3 hours, or more than 3 hours?

11. Have each person in your group question one or more students. Make sure everyone in your class, including the people in your group, answers the question. Use tally marks to record results.

12. Find the number for each choice.

13. Make a pictograph for your data.

14. Write a report describing your data. Example: Most students watch TV for 1 or 2 hours a day. Only a few watch for 3 hours. No one watches for more than 3 hours.

HOURS of TV

= 1 hr. TV

Sam

Nancy

Ted

Jane

Joe

1. Suppose you are planning to serve 7 people at a party. Which question would help you best to know what to buy? Why?

   a. What drink do you like best?
   b. Which drink do you like best—orange juice, lemonade, or grape juice?

2. A ____?____ is a way of recording data.

3. In recording data, how many does ||||| represent?

4. Study this tally chart made by the third graders at Zane School. Then complete the chart and make a pictograph from the data. **Remember** to decide how many people each picture should stand for.

Favorite Colors		
Color	Tally	Number
Blue	⊦⊦⊦⊦ ⊦⊦⊦⊦ //	▦
Green	⊦⊦⊦⊦ ⊦⊦⊦⊦	▦
Yellow	///	3
Red	⊦⊦⊦⊦ ⊦⊦⊦⊦ ⊦⊦⊦⊦	▦

Favorite Flowers		
Flower	Tally	Number
Lilac	⊦⊦⊦⊦ ⊦⊦⊦⊦	10
Tulip	⊦⊦⊦⊦ ⊦⊦⊦⊦ ⊦⊦⊦⊦	15
Buttercup	⊦⊦⊦⊦	5
Iris	⊦⊦⊦⊦ ⊦⊦⊦⊦	10

Use the tally chart at the left to answer Questions 5 and 6.

5. What flower was more popular than the iris?

6. Make a bar graph to show the data in the table.

Problem Solving WORKSHOP

Real-Life Decision Making

Do you need an increase in your allowance? How much is your present allowance? What do you use it for? How much of an increase do you need? List 3 reasons why you would need to have it increased.

Could this graph help you convince your parents? It shows the allowance for 42 eight-year-olds.

Number-Sense Project

Look back at pages 470-471.

1. How many pictographs do you see?

2. How many bar graphs do you see?

3. Tell how you could make a bar graph into a pictograph or a pictograph into a bar graph.

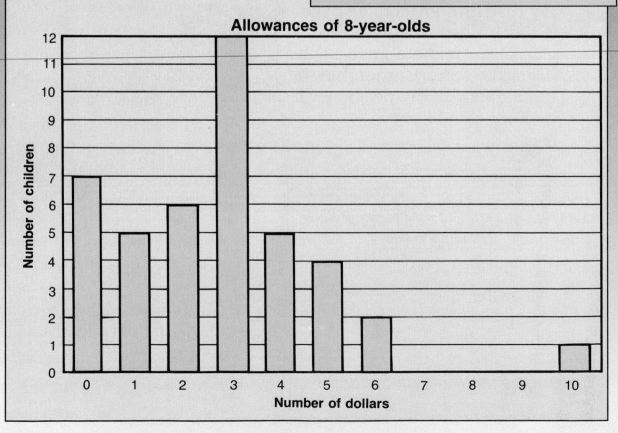

Allowances of 8-year-olds

Explore with a Computer

Use the *Graphing and Probability Workshop Project* for this activity.

1. At the computer, use the **Toss coin** option to do an experiment.

2. Toss 3 coins twenty times.

3. Record the results in the table.

4. View the data in the table as a **Bar graph**.

5. Repeat the experiment, tossing the coins 100 times.

6. Create your own experiment using up to 4 coins.

Math-at-Home Activity

Play *Odd or Even* with someone at home. Each player makes a fist. Put out 1-5 fingers on the count of *three*. One player calls *odd* or *even* just before the fingers are shown.

Odd or Even

	1	2	3	4	5	6	7	8	9	10
Match										
No match										

Number of times

If the sum of the number of fingers matches the *odd* or *even* called, you have a *match*. Predict how many times your call and finger sum will match if you do the activity 18 times. Record the results on a bar graph.

Make a Graph

Build Understanding

The slips of paper show the number of cans collected each week for recycling. The first class to collect 50 cans wins a prize. What is the best way to keep track of the contest?

Understand All the facts are on slips of paper. You can record data to see which class is winning.

Plan and Solve STRATEGY You could make a table.

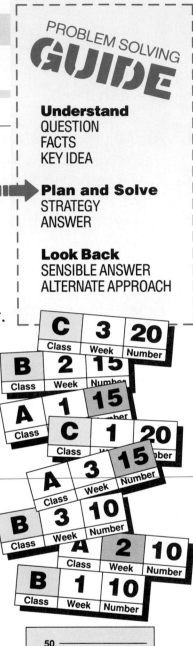

	Week 1	Week 2
Class A	15	10
Class B	10	15
Class C	20	10

Is it easy to see which class has collected the most cans?

A graph helps you compare data.

ANSWER You can make a bar graph to show the data.

Look Back Does the graph tell you at a glance which class is ahead? Could you use a pictograph to show the data?

■ **Talk About Math** Why is it better to use a graph than a table for the Example?

PROBLEM SOLVING GUIDE

Understand
QUESTION
FACTS
KEY IDEA

➤ **Plan and Solve**
STRATEGY
ANSWER

Look Back
SENSIBLE ANSWER
ALTERNATE APPROACH

Check Understanding

Use the slips of paper, table, and graph on
page 486 to help answer Problems 1–4.

1. Number Sense Why did
the person who made this
graph count by 5s?

2. When reading the graph, do
you need the numbers to know
which class is ahead? Why?

3. Do you need the numbers to
put data on the graph? Why?

4. Copy and complete the graph.
Use the data for Week 3.

Practice

The three third-grade classes in
Pia's school collected bottles for
recycling. The data at the right
show the numbers of bottles
collected for two weeks. Make a
table or a graph to help you
with each problem.

1	1	20
Class	Week	Number

1	2	20
Class	Week	Number

2	1	25
Class	Week	Number

2	2	15
Class	Week	Number

3	1	25
Class	Week	Number

3	2	20
Class	Week	Number

5. Which class collected the
most bottles?

6. Mental Math How many
bottles did Class 2 collect?

7. Which two classes collected
the same number of bottles?

8. Explain why you chose to
make a graph or a table.

Choose a ⬛ Strategy

Secret Square

9. Copy these shapes. Put them
together to make one large square.

PROBLEM SOLVING STRATEGIES

Choose an Operation
Find a Pattern
Use Logical Reasoning
Make a Table
Draw a Picture
Try and Check
Write a Number Sentence
Work Backward
Make a Graph

487

Locating Points on a Grid

Build Understanding

A. You can use *number pairs* to find places on a map. Use the numbers at the side and bottom. What will you find at (5, 2) on the map?

Begin at the star.

(5, 2)

Move 5 units to the right.   Move 2 units up.

The store is at (5, 2) on the map.

B. What number pair tells where the theater is on the map?

Start at the theater. Follow the street down to the number on the bottom. The theater is 4 units to the right of the star.

Now start at the theater and follow the street to the number on the side. The theater is 5 units up from the star.

The theater is at (4, 5) on the map.

Ⓐ Town Square   Ⓕ Stadium

Ⓑ Library   Ⓖ Store

Ⓒ Health Club   Ⓗ Park

Ⓓ Theater   Ⓘ Hospital

Ⓔ Museum

■ Write About Math
Explain how you could get to the library from the museum.

Check Understanding

For another example, see Set D, pages 498–499.

Locate the number pair (8, 3) on the map.

1. Where on the map do you begin?

2. How many units do you move to the right?

3. How many units do you move up?

4. What will you find at (8, 3)?

Practice

For More Practice, see Set D, pages 500-501.

Name the building located at each number pair.

5. (3, 8)   **6.** (1, 4)   **7.** (6, 6)   **8.** (2, 1)   **9.** (4, 5)

Write the number pair for each corner.

10. Lake Rd., Oak St.

11. Lake Rd., Fairview Rd.

12. Pen St., Delaware Ave.

13. Stadium Place, Poe St.

14. Beech Rd., Sunset Rd.

15. Robin Rd., Elm St.

16. Tulip Blvd., Oak St.

17. Park Ave., Main St.

18. Market St., Sun Lane

19. King St., Dove Place

Problem Solving

Use grid paper to solve the problem.

20. Mark a starting point. Then find a point for each number pair below. Connect the points in order. Name the figure.

(1, 2) (2, 3) (4, 3) (4, 1) (2, 1) (1, 2)

TIPS FOR PROBLEM SOLVERS

Visualize the problem in your mind to help you understand it better.

21. Critical Thinking Explain how all the number pairs on Sun Lane are alike. Explain how all the number pairs on Market St. are alike.

Skills _____ Review   pages 122-123

Tell whether you would use paper and pencil, mental math, or a calculator. Then find each answer.

1. 4 × 6   **2.** 12 + 10   **3.** 25 ÷ 5   **4.** 2 × 7

5. 69 − 39   **6.** 3,278 + 847   **7.** 400 + 125   **8.** 900 − 98

Probabilities

Build Understanding

AUGUST 15

71

78

80

82

"It will be sunny and 85 degrees tomorrow."

Do you know if it will snow tomorrow? What would a Kansas City weather forecaster say about the *chance* of snow on August 15?

Would he say he is *certain* it will snow? That snow is *possible?* That it is *impossible* to have snow on that date?

The forecaster does not even talk about a chance of snow on August 15. If asked, he would say snow is impossible because it is too warm.

In February, Kansas City often has snow. The chance, or **probability,** of snow is greater in February than in August.

■ **Talk About Math**   Have you ever heard a weather forecaster say, "There is a slight chance of rain"? What do you think this means?

Check Understanding

For another example, see Set E, pages 498–499.

1. Would you say it is certain, possible, or impossible for you to become a weather forecaster?

2. What kinds of weather is it possible for you to have tomorrow?

3. What kinds of weather would be impossible for you to have tomorrow?

4. Can you be certain about the weather you will have tomorrow? Explain.

Practice

For More Practice, see Set E, pages 500–501.

You can be a forecaster right now. Tell whether you think each event is *certain, possible,* or *impossible.*

5. You will grow taller during the next year.

6. When you phone a friend, the line will be busy.

7. You will grow to 100 feet tall.

8. Humans will travel to Mars.

9. You will watch TV tonight.

10. Tomorrow will have 24 hours.

Lila is 8 years old. She says, "I want to be a weather forecaster." Tell whether each statement is *certain, possible,* or *impossible.*

11. Lila will be a weather forecaster.

12. Lila will talk about the weather on television.

13. Lila will be 12 years old tomorrow.

14. Lila likes to look at maps.

Problem Solving

15. Gather Data Record the weather forecast and the actual weather for three days. Use a chart like the one shown. How many of the forecasts were correct?

Weather Forecast	Actual Weather
sunny	cloudy

Critical Thinking Answer each question. Then explain your reasoning for each answer.

16. Do you think that every student gave the same answers to Exercises 5–10?

17. If Exercises 5–10 have different answers, can all the answers be correct?

Outcomes

Build Understanding

What is your favorite animal?

Without looking, Alison picks one animal card from the box. What are the possible *outcomes?*

Alison could get an elephant card, a lion card, or a giraffe card.

Is Alison more likely to get an elephant card or a lion card?

It is *more likely* that Alison will get an elephant card. There are more elephant cards in the box.

Is Alison more likely to get a lion card or a giraffe card when she picks from the box? Why?

Alison has an equal chance of getting a lion or a giraffe card because there are two lion cards and two giraffe cards. Getting a lion card and getting a giraffe card are *equally likely.*

■ **Talk About Math**   What fraction of the cards have elephants? lions? giraffes?

Check Understanding

For another example, see Set F, pages 498–499.

1. Which is less likely, that Alison will pick an elephant card or a lion card from the box without looking?

2. How many more lion and giraffe cards would you put in the box to make all the outcomes equally likely?

Practice

For More Practice, see Set F, pages 500–501.

List all the possible outcomes.

3.   **4.**   **5.**

Use the pictures in Exercises 3–5 to answer Exercises 6–11.
Are the outcomes equally likely? If not, which is more likely?

6. To pick a green marble or to pick a blue marble

7. To pick a red marble or to pick a green marble

8. To spin a 1 or to spin a 5

9. To spin a 5 or to spin a 7

10. To pick a circle or to pick a triangle

11. To pick a square or to pick a triangle

Problem Solving

Critical Thinking   Solve the problem.

12. Explain how you could change the spinner in Exercise 3 so that it would be more likely to spin a 1 than a 3, 5, or 7.

Choose a _____ Strategy

Yellow, White, and Blue
13. Ramon has a bag of marbles. There are more yellow than white marbles. There are more white than blue marbles. If Ramon picks a marble without looking, is he less likely to pick a yellow or a blue marble?

Experiments

Build Understanding

Chances Are
Materials: Spinner, tally charts, colored paper, paper bags
Groups: Partners

a. Make a spinner like the one shown.

b. List all the possible outcomes. Which outcomes are equally likely? Is any outcome more likely than red? Is any outcome less likely than yellow?

c. Each partner predicts how often the spinner will land on red in 8 spins.

d. Do the experiment. Record the results.

e. Compare the results to your predictions.

■ **Talk About Math** Do you think you could predict the results better if the spinner were spun 40 or 100 times? Why or why not?

Check Understanding

For another example, see Set G, pages 498–499.

Do the experiment in the example 3 more times.
Record the results of the 4 experiments in 4 tally charts.

1. Did the spinner land on red the same number of times in each experiment?

2. In all 32 spins that you made, how many times did the spinner land on red?

3. If you spun 32 times in a row, how many times do you think the spinner would land on red?

4. Do 32 spins in a row. How many times did you get red? Was the result close to your prediction?

Practice

For More Practice, see Set G, pages 500–501.

Answer the following questions. You may want to do one of these activities with your partner.

Experiment A

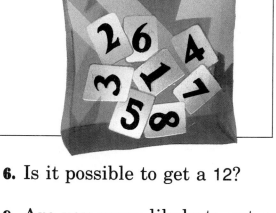

a. Pick one card from the bag without looking.

b. Record the number. Return the card to the bag.

---

5. Is it possible to get an 8?

6. Is it possible to get a 12?

7. Do you have an equal chance to get a 3 or a 5?

8. Are you more likely to get a 4 than an 8?

9. How many times do you think you would get a 6 in 8 picks?

10. How many times do you think you would get a 6 in 80 picks?

Experiment B

a. Pick a marble from the jar without looking.

b. Record the color. Return the marble to the jar.

---

11. Do you have an equal chance to get a blue or a red marble?

12. Are you more likely to get a green marble than a red one?

13. How many blue marbles do you think you would get in 8 picks?

14. How many blue marbles do you think you would get in 80 picks?

Skills Review

1. Complete the tally chart.

○○△△○□○△△△○△□□

Shape	Tally	Number
Circle		
Square		
Triangle		

Student Council Membership

| Girls | |
| Boys | |

Each ☺ or ☺ stands for 3 students.

Student Council Meetings

Sept.	
Oct.	
Nov.	

0 2 4 6 8

2. How many girls are in Student Council?

3. How many meetings were held in October?

4. What letter is at (1, 2)?

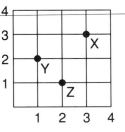

4
3
2
1
 1 2 3 4

X
Y
Z

5. Give the number pair for X.

6. Tell whether it is certain, possible, or impossible for you to grow 1 foot today.

7. List all the possible outcomes.

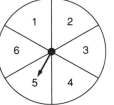

8. Are you more likely to spin a 3 than a 4?

Problem-Solving Review

Solve each problem.

9. Lined notebook paper comes in packages of 300 sheets. A package that usually costs $2.19 has been reduced to $1.49. How much will you save if you buy 2 packages?

10. I am a decimal in hundredths. I am greater than 0.6, but less than 0.65. The sum of my digits is 9. Who am I?

11. These are the answers some children gave when asked "What do you like to do best in the summer?" Make a tally chart to show the results.

SWIM
PICNIC
SWIMMING
BIKE RIDING
BOAT RIDE
BOATING
SWIMMING
BIKE RIDE
SWIM AT THE LAKE
GO SWIMMING
RIDE MY BIKE
PICNICS
SAIL ON MY BOAT

12. **Data File** Use data from pages 532–533. What day do people go to the movies most often? Which are the two least busy days?

13. **Make a Data File** Find 1 pictograph and 3 bar graphs in newspapers or magazines. Make a display and write a sentence about each graph.

Find each sum or difference.

1. 7,090
− 4,183

2. 5,600
− 1,890

3. $5.78
+ 3.76

4. $8.90
− 4.85

5. 68 + 49 + 17

6. 36 + 8 + 14

Estimate each product.

7. 7 × 28

8. 853 × 5

Find each answer.

9. 8
×5

10. 3
×6

11. 7
×4

12. 9
×9

13. 6
×7

14. 8
×9

15. 19 × 4

16. 42 × 5

17. 69 × 3

18. 6 × 93

19. 4 × 452

20. 5 × 309

21. 35 ÷ 5

22. 63 ÷ 7

23. $\frac{1}{6}$ of 24

24. $\frac{1}{8}$ of 40

Write the fractions in order from least to greatest.

25. $\frac{1}{4}, \frac{3}{4}, \frac{5}{8}$

26. $\frac{1}{2}, \frac{2}{5}, \frac{9}{10}$

27. Tell how many 8-ounce sausages would make about 1 pound.

28. Complete the tally chart.

Animal	Tally	Number
Dog		
Bird		
Turtle		

29. Tell whether it is certain, possible, or impossible that you will go to sleep tonight.

There are 5 white chips, 3 blue chips, and 3 red chips in a bag. Suppose you pick a chip without looking.

30. List all the possible outcomes.

31. Is it more likely to pick a blue than a white chip?

32. Is it equally likely to pick a blue or a red chip?

Give the number pair for each point.

33. A   **34.** B

Reteaching

You can use a tally chart to show how many leaves there are of each color. For each leaf, mark / in your chart next to its color. To be sure you record every leaf, you can work from left to right.

Remember that / in a tally chart means 1 and ⧸⧸⧸⧸ means 5.

1. The first 3 leaves from left to right are recorded in this chart. Copy and complete the chart.

Bill's Leaf Collection

Color	Tally	Number
Green	/	
Red		
Yellow	//	

You can make a pictograph from the data in this tally chart.

Favorite Fruits of Our Class

Fruit	Tally	Number
Apple	⧸⧸⧸⧸ ⧸⧸⧸⧸ ⧸⧸⧸⧸ ⧸⧸⧸⧸	20
Pear	⧸⧸⧸⧸	5
Peach	⧸⧸⧸⧸ ⧸⧸⧸⧸ ⧸⧸⧸⧸	15
Orange	⧸⧸⧸⧸ ⧸⧸⧸⧸	10

Let ☺ stand for 5 students.
4 × 5 = 20, so 4 faces will show the 20 students who like apples.

Remember that each picture in a pictograph stands for some number.

Let ☺ stand for 5 students.

1. How many faces will stand for the 10 students who like oranges?

2. Make a pictograph to show the data in the tally chart.

The bar graph at the right shows the data from Set B.

Remember that it doesn't matter whether the bars on a graph go up and down or from left to right.

Use the graph. Which fruit is

1. most popular?

2. least popular?

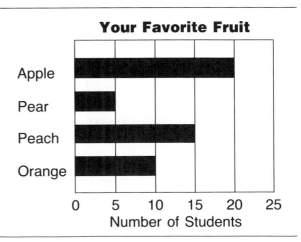

Your Favorite Fruit

498

Set D pages 488–489

On the graph, the number pair for the school is (4, 3).

Remember that the first number in a number pair is the number of units to the right of the star. Name the building located at

1. (5, 1).   **2.** (3, 5).

(graph with buildings: Library at (3,5), Movies at (1,4), School at (4,3), Mall at (2,2), Bank at (5,1); axes labeled 1–6, star at origin)

Set E pages 490–491

Some events are certain to happen. "The sun will rise in the east."

Some events are impossible. "It will snow in Hawaii."

Some events are possible. "The Cubs will win the pennant."

Remember that the chance of an event happening is called probability.

Do you think each event is certain, possible, or impossible?

1. You will sleep 8 hours tonight.

2. You will be 200 years old.

Set F pages 492–493

If you spin this spinner, the four possible outcomes are A, B, C, and D. **Remember** that outcomes are not always equally likely.

1. Are you more likely to spin an A or a C?

2. Are A and B equally likely?

3. Which outcomes are less likely than spinning a B?

Set G pages 494–495

On this spinner, there is an equal chance of getting any of the 5 numbers. However, there is a greater chance of getting an odd number than of getting an even number.

Remember that you can predict the results better the more times the spinner is spun.

1. Why is there a greater chance of getting an odd number than of getting an even number?

More Practice

Set A   pages 474–475

Record data about the figures shown.
Copy and complete each tally chart.

1.

Shape of Figures	Tallies	Number
Curved		
Not Curved		

2.

Color of Figures	Tallies	Number

3.

Number of Straight Sides	Tallies	Number

Set B   pages 476–479

For Exercises 1–3, suppose you used the tally chart to make a pictograph.

1. What title would you use?

2. How would you list the choices?

What is Your Favorite Hamburger?

Type	Tally	Number
Regular burger	//// //// //// ///	18
Cheeseburger	//// //// //	12
Pizzaburger	//// /	6

3. How many tally marks would each picture stand for?

Set C   pages 480–482

This tally sheet shows the sizes of shoes sold on Tuesday.

1. Copy the unfinished graph.

2. What numbers will you use? Write them below the graph.

3. Draw the bars in the graph.

Number of Shoes Sold

Size	Tally	Number
$5–5\frac{1}{2}$	//// //// //// ////	20
$6–6\frac{1}{2}$	//// //// //// //// //// //// //// //// //// //// //// ////	60
$7–7\frac{1}{2}$	//// //// //// //// //// //// //// ////	40
$8–8\frac{1}{2}$	//// //// //// //// //// //// //// //// //// ////	50

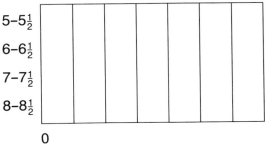

Number of Shoes Sold

$5–5\frac{1}{2}$
$6–6\frac{1}{2}$
$7–7\frac{1}{2}$
$8–8\frac{1}{2}$

0

Set D   pages 488–489

Name the building located at
each number pair.

1. (2, 2)   **2.** (1, 4)   **3.** (4, 1)

Write the number pair for each
corner.

4. Ash Rd., Oak St.   **5.** Elm St.,
                                          Red Rd.

Set E   pages 490–491

Tell whether you think each event is
certain, possible, or impossible.

1. The sun will set in the west.   **2.** You will grow to 6 feet tall.

3. It will snow in Chicago on   **4.** The sun will set in the east.
February 12.

Set F   pages 492–493

Use the spinner at the right.

1. List all the possible outcomes
for the spinner.

2. Are the outcomes equally likely?

Which is more likely,
3. to spin a 1 or a 2?   **4.** to spin a 3 or a 4?

Set G   pages 494–495

Use the spinner at the right.

1. Do you have an equal chance to
spin a 4 or a 2?

2. Are you more likely to spin a 3 than a 1?

3. How many times do you think
you would get a 4 in 8 spins?

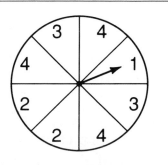

Enrichment

Number Cube Game

Each cube has the numbers from 1 to 6. Roll two number cubes like these. Add the numbers you get.

What is the least sum you could get? What is the greatest sum you could get?

If you rolled the cubes 40 times, what sum do you think you would get most often?

Do the experiment. Record the sums in a grid like the one shown. Every time you get a sum, put an X in a box above that number. This kind of graph is called a *line plot.*

1. What sum is shown most often in the line plot?

2. What sum is shown least often in the line plot?

3. What sums did you get most often in your 40 rolls?

Sums from Two Number Cubes

			X					
		X	X					
		X	X	X				
	X		X	X	X	X		
X	X	X	X	X	X	X	X	
X	X	X	X	X	X	X	X	X	X
X	X	X	X	X	X	X	X	X	X

Number of Times

2 3 4 5 6 7 8 9 10 11 12
Sums of Numbers

4. What sums did you get least often in your 40 rolls?

5. List all the combinations of numbers that could give a sum of 2.

6. List all the combinations of numbers that could give a sum of 7.

7. Explain why certain sums come up more often than others.

Chapter 14 Review/Test

Write two questions to help you gather the necessary data.

1. Your class is going on a roller-skating party. How many pairs of skates will the class need to rent?

Weather in April

Each picture means 3 days.

2. How many more sunny days than cloudy days were there in April?

Favorite Playground Activity

3. How many more children chose the swings than the sandbox as their favorite?

4. What letter is at (3, 2)?

5. Give the number pair for A.

6. Tell whether it is certain, possible, or impossible for you to be 25 years old next year.

7. A jar of nuts contains many more almonds than peanuts. Which outcome is more likely?

   a. To pick an almond

   b. To pick a peanut

   c. To pick a raisin

8. Suppose a jar has 5 pink plastic chips in it, 2 orange, and 7 purple. If you pick one chip, are you more likely to get a purple chip or an orange chip?

9. Make a tally chart for the information in Item 8.

10. Look at the graph in Item 3. The seesaw was the favorite activity of 4 other children. How could you show this on the graph?

   a. Change the numbers to read 0–16.

   b. Draw 4 seesaws.

   c. Add a bar for seesaw.

11. ■ **Write About Math**
Explain how you found the number pair for Item 5.

Division
Computation

15

Did You Know: The least crowded time to visit amusement parks is Tuesday through Friday, especially on cloudy and cool days.

Number-Sense Project

Estimate
Predict how many in your class would want to ride the Log Ride.

Gather Data
Take a poll in your class to see how many would like to ride the Log Ride.

Analyze and Report
Total the results. Then compare the results to your prediction.

Sharing Money

Build Understanding

Dividing It Up
Materials: Play money
Groups: 3–5 students

Frank, Juan, and Ted received $42. They want to share the money equally. How much money will each boy get?

Total Money Received
10 10 10 10 1 1

Frank	Juan	Ted	Left to share
10	10	10	10 1 1
10	10	10	1 1 1 1 1 1 1 1 1 1 1 1
10 1 1 1 1	10 1 1 1 1	10 1 1 1 1	

a. Use play money to show how much the boys received.

b. Put the ten-dollar bills into three groups.

c. How many ten-dollar bills are in each group? Are there any left over? Trade any leftover ten-dollar bills for one-dollar bills.

d. How many dollar bills are there to share? Divide the dollar bills among the three groups.

e. Count the money in each group. There are 4 dollar bills and 1 ten-dollar bill in each group.

Each boy will get $14.

■ **Talk About Math** Why is it necessary to trade the leftover ten-dollar bill for dollar bills?

Check Understanding

For another example, see Set A, pages 526–527.

Use play money to divide $48 into 4 equal groups.

1. How many $10 bills and $1 bills will you use?

2. How many equal groups will you make?

3. Divide the play money into equal groups. How much money is in each group?

4. Was a trade necessary to solve this problem? Why or why not?

Practice

For More Practice, see Set A, pages 528–529.

Use play money to divide each amount of money into equal groups. Draw a picture to show your answer. Then write how much is in each group.

5. $28 into 2 equal groups

6. $60 into 5 equal groups

7. $63 into 3 equal groups

8. $75 into 5 equal groups

9. $56 into 4 equal groups

10. $39 into 3 equal groups

11. $55 into 5 equal groups

12. $64 into 4 equal groups

13. $45 into 3 equal groups

14. $52 into 4 equal groups

15. $36 into 2 equal groups

16. $48 into 3 equal groups

17. $85 into 5 equal groups

18. $88 into 4 equal groups

Problem Solving

Solve each problem.

19. The 3 boys decided to buy a croquet set for $45. Each boy will pay the same amount. How much will each boy pay?

20. Together, the boys earned $14 on Monday, $12 on Thursday, and $25 on Saturday. How much did they earn in all?

Missing Factors

Build Understanding

The Fit-n-Fun Club is buying oranges. Each basket has 6 oranges. How many baskets must they buy to have 66 oranges?

Missing Factor	Factor	Product
▦	× **6**	= **66**
Baskets	Oranges in each basket	Oranges in all

Think about related multiplication and division sentences for ▦ × 6 = 66.

▦ × **6** = **66**   **66** ÷ ▦ = **6**

6 × ▦ = **66**   **66** ÷ **6** = ▦

Find 66 ÷ 6. You can use repeated subtraction to find the missing factor.

As each basket is put into the cart, you can subtract 6 from the number still needed.

$$66 - 6 = 60$$
$$60 - 6 = 54$$
$$54 - 6 = 48$$
$$48 - 6 = 42$$
$$42 - 6 = 36$$
$$36 - 6 = 30$$
$$30 - 6 = 24$$
$$24 - 6 = 18$$
$$18 - 6 = 12$$
$$12 - 6 = 6$$
$$6 - 6 = 0$$

Since you subtracted six 11 times, 11 is the missing factor.
$6 \times 11 = 66$ and
$66 \div 6 = 11$

The club should buy 11 baskets of oranges.

Oranges are grown in warm countries all over the world. They are the world's second leading fruit crop—apples are first!

■ **Talk About Math** Tell how you can use multiplication to check division.

Match each multiplication sentence with the
related division sentence. Then give each missing factor.

1. ▦ × 4 = 72   **2.** 6 × ▦ = 78

a. 78 ÷ 6 = 13   **b.** 72 ÷ 4 = 18

Practice

For More Practice, see Set B, pages 528–529.

Match each multiplication sentence with the related
division sentence. Then give the missing factor.

3. ▦ × 9 = 144   **4.** 4 × ▦ = 160

5. 5 × ▦ = 160   **6.** 3 × ▦ = 144

7. ▦ × 4 = 144   **8.** 2 × ▦ = 160

9. 7 × ▦ = 448   **10.** ▦ × 8 = 448

11. ▦ × 6 = 174   **12.** 8 × ▦ = 256

13. 9 × ▦ = 324   **14.** ▦ × 3 = 256

a. 144 ÷ 3 = 48	**b.** 144 ÷ 4 = 36
c. 144 ÷ 9 = 16	**d.** 324 ÷ 9 = 36
e. 256 ÷ 3 = 82	**f.** 160 ÷ 5 = 32
g. 448 ÷ 7 = 64	**h.** 448 ÷ 8 = 56
i. 256 ÷ 8 = 32	**j.** 160 ÷ 2 = 80
k. 160 ÷ 4 = 40	**l.** 174 ÷ 6 = 29

Problem Solving

Critical Thinking   Write related multiplication
and division sentences in which

15. one factor is a multiple of 10.

16. one factor is 10 times as great as
the other factor.

Solve the problem.

17. The club is going to spend $60 for jump
ropes. One kind costs $3, and another
kind costs $4. How many more $3 jump
ropes can they buy than $4 jump ropes?

TIPS FOR PROBLEM SOLVERS

Be flexible. If you get
stuck, try another idea.

Remainders When Sharing Money

Build Understanding

What's Left?
Materials: Play money
Groups: 3–5 students

Joy, Mary, and Barbara want to share $40 equally.
How much money should each receive?

Use play money to find $40 ÷ 3.

a. Divide the $10 bills.

b. Trade the leftover $10 bill for ten $1 bills.

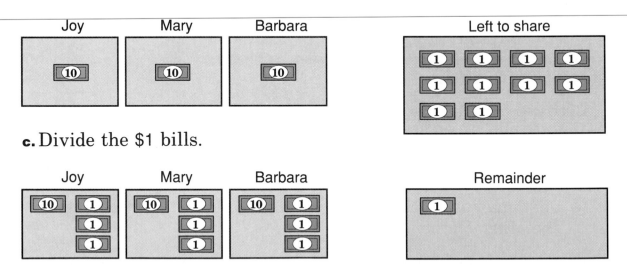

c. Divide the $1 bills.

Each girl should get $13. There is $1 left over.

■ **Talk About Math**   What might the girls do
with the leftover $1?

510

Check Understanding

For another example, see Set C, pages 526–527.

Find $59 ÷ 4. Use play money to help you.

1. How many $10 bills and $1 bills will you use?

2. How many equal groups will you make?

3. How many $10 bills will there be in each of the 4 groups?

4. Do you need to make a trade? Why or why not?

5. How many $1 bills will be in each of the 4 groups?

6. Do you have any $1 bills left over? If so, how many?

7. What answer did you record?

Practice

For More Practice, see Set C, pages 528–529.

Tell how much money is in each group and how much is left over. Use play money.

8. $46 into 4 equal groups

9. $35 into 3 equal groups

10. $68 into 6 equal groups

11. $33 into 2 equal groups

12. $56 into 5 equal groups

13. $52 into 4 equal groups

14. $53 into 4 equal groups

15. $54 into 4 equal groups

16. $55 into 4 equal groups

Problem Solving

Number Sense Find a pattern in the quotients and remainders for Exercises 13–16. Use the pattern to tell what the quotient and remainders will be.

17. 56 ÷ 4   **18.** 57 ÷ 4   **19.** 58 ÷ 4   **20.** 59 ÷ 4   **21.** 60 ÷ 4

22. Each of the 3 girls paid $15 to buy tickets to a professional baseball game. How much did they pay in all?

23. Critical Thinking Joy and Mary put some $1 bills into stacks of 2. How many dollar bills could they have left over?

Explore ———— Math

For each of Exercises 24–28, find the sum of the digits of each dollar amount.
24. $24   **25.** $75   **26.** $45   **27.** $78   **28.** $30

29. By what one number can you evenly divide each of the sums in Exercises 24–28?

30. Use your play money to divide each amount of money in Exercises 24–28 by the number you found in Exercise 29.

31. When the sum of the digits of a number can be divided evenly by 3, by what number can you divide the entire number?

Tell which numbers can be evenly divided by 3. Do not actually divide.
32. 174   **33.** 255   **34.** 93   **35.** 1,792   **36.** 455

37. 1,796   **38.** 1,782   **39.** 3,875   **40.** 4,944   **41.** 8,145

Find each answer. **Remember** to rename if necessary.

1. 41 × 5   **2.** 81 + 97   **3.** 64 ÷ 8   **4.** 28 − 19

5. 0 ÷ 3   **6.** 2,076 + 1,348   **7.** 160 − 74   **8.** 4 × 3

9. 12 × 5   **10.** 15 + 8   **11.** 101 − 40   **12.** 56 ÷ 7

13. 9 − 9   **14.** 35 × 2   **15.** 24 ÷ 3   **16.** 6,019 + 7,834

17. 182 − 97   **18.** 36 ÷ 4   **19.** 4 + 5   **20.** 1 × 38

Tell what fraction of the

21. birds are yellow.   **22.** plants have flowers.

23. cars are blue.   **24.** girls have red hair.

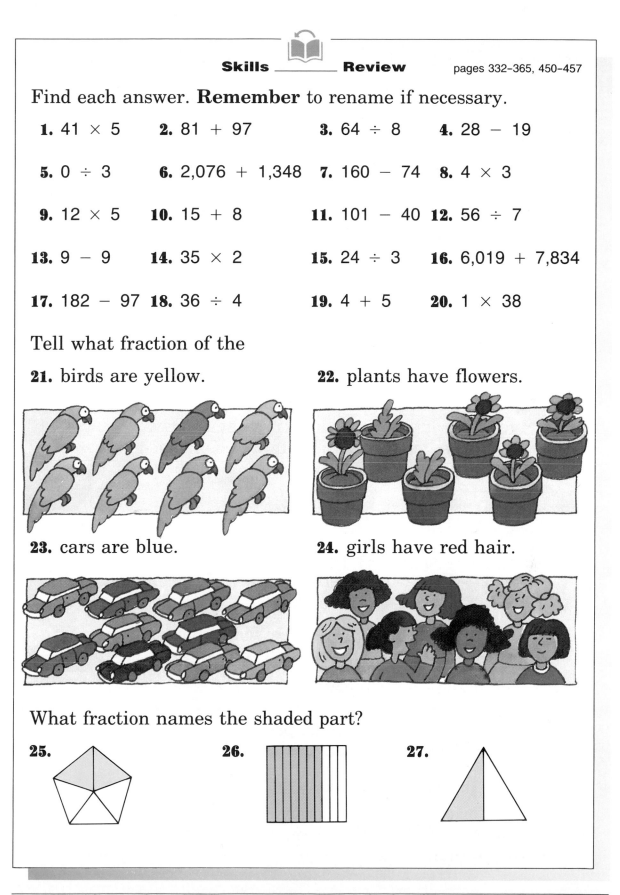

What fraction names the shaded part?

25.   **26.**   **27.**

Interpret the Remainder

Build Understanding

In Thailand, long-tailed boats called *hang yaos* are used to travel the rivers and canals. Each boat has many rows of seats, with room for 2 people in each row. Suppose that 25 people wish to travel on a *hang yaos*. How many rows of seats must one boat have for every person to sit down?

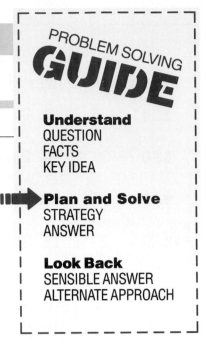

PROBLEM SOLVING
GUIDE

Understand
QUESTION
FACTS
KEY IDEA

➤ **Plan and Solve**
STRATEGY
ANSWER

Look Back
SENSIBLE ANSWER
ALTERNATE APPROACH

Understand Two people fill one row of seats.

 Plan and Solve STRATEGY Divide 25 by 2 by making groups of 2. If there is a remainder, one more row of seats will be needed.

There are 12 groups of 2 with a remainder of 1.
25 ÷ 2 = 12, remainder 1

ANSWER For every person to have a seat, there must be 13 rows of seats.

Look Back Use multiplication. $12 \times 2 = 24$
$13 \times 2 = 26$
Since there are 25 people,
13 rows of seats are needed.

■ **Talk About Math** Do you always use the remainder? For example, how many canoes can be rented for $37 if each canoe costs $5 to rent?
37 ÷ 5 = 7, remainder 2

Check Understanding

Use the fact 58 ÷ 4 = 14, remainder 2 to tell whether the answer is 14 or 15 for each problem. Explain why you chose the number you did.

1. A *samlor* is a 3-wheeled vehicle with pedals or a motor. How many 4-person *samlors* should 58 people rent?

2. Manit's father rents *samlors* to tourists for $4 each. How many can be rented for $58?

Practice

Solve each problem.

There is a network of canals in Thailand called *klongs*. They are used for traveling from place to place, for floating markets, and for sightseeing tours.

3. There is one guide for every 7 tourists traveling the *klong*. How many guides are there for 93 tourists?

4. A tour costs $6 per person. Can 13 people tour the *klongs* for $75?

5. There are 8 boats that are used for tours. Each boat seats 7 people. How many people can tour at one time if all boats and seats are being used?

6. In the fall, boat races are held in Thailand. If one boat has 27 oarsmen and another has 26, how many oarsmen in all are racing?

Midchapter ✓ Checkup

Draw pictures to help you find each answer.
1. 22 ÷ 2   **2.** 42 ÷ 3   **3.** 31 ÷ 2   **4.** 34 ÷ 3

Mental Math   Use the chart to help find each missing factor.
5. ▦ × 4 = 64   **6.** 5 × ▦ = 50 | **a.** 64 ÷ 4 = 16   **b.** 50 ÷ 5 = 10 |

Solve the problem.
7. How many $4 books can Leigh buy for $62?
[62 ÷ 4 = 15, remainder 2]

Math-at-Home Activity

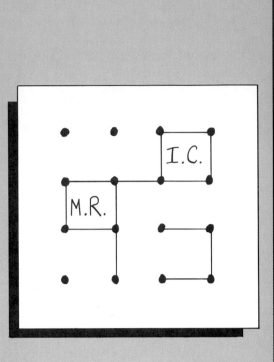

Play *Complete the Most Squares* with someone at home. Draw 16 dots; 4 rows with 4 dots in each row. The first player connects two dots drawing straight up or across. Take turns drawing a line segment to connect two dots.

When your line segment completes a square, write your initials in the square.

After all line segments have been drawn, count your initialed squares. The winner is the player who completes the most squares.

Math Laugh

Math Laugh

If you take 3 apples from 12 apples what do you have?

ANSWER: You have three apples.

Problem Solving WORKSHOP

Number-Sense Project

Look back at pages 504-505.
A book of ride tickets costs $40.00. A class of students bought 6 books.

1. How much did 6 books cost?

2. If 5 students shared one book equally, how much did each student pay?

3. If there were 40 tickets in each book, how much did each ticket cost? On how many rides could each student go?

4. How many students were in the class?

Explore as a Team

1. Make a rectangle with 24 squares.

2. How many rectangles can you make with an area of 24 squares? Record them on square grid paper.

3. Is the perimeter always the same?

Remember: Perimeter is the distance around.

TIPS FOR
WORKING TOGETHER

Involve your whole group.
Help everyone to participate.

Recording Division

Build Understanding

Planning Purchases
Materials: Play money
Groups: 3–5 students

A. Todd wants to spend the same amount of money for each of 3 birthday presents. He has saved $42. How much can he spend for each present? Divide 42 into 3 equal groups.

a. Divide the $10 bills.

Left to share

b. Record what you did.

$10 bills | $1 bills

```
      1 |
  3)4 | 2
```
1 $10 bill each

$10 bills | $1 bills

```
      1 |
  3)4 | 2
  - 3 |
```
3 $10 bills shared

$10 bills | $1 bills

```
      1 |
  3)4 | 2
  - 3 |
    1
```
1 $10 bill left

c. Trade the leftover $10 bill for ten $1 bills and record.

Left to share

$10 bills | $1 bills

```
      1 |
  3)4 | 2
  - 3 |
    1 | 2
```
12 $1 bills to share

518

d. Divide the $1 bills.

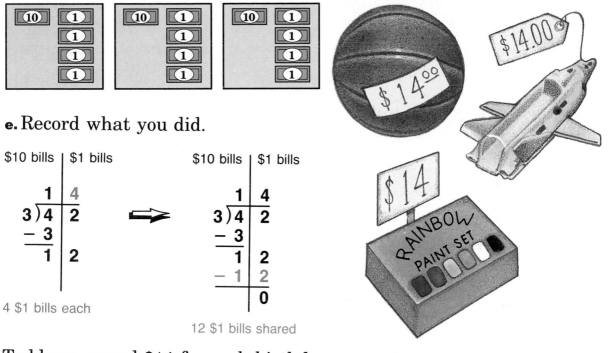

e. Record what you did.

$10 bills	$1 bills
1	4

$$3 \overline{)4}\ \ 2$$
$$\underline{-3}$$
$$\ \ 1\ \ 2$$

4 $1 bills each

$10 bills	$1 bills
1	4

$$3 \overline{)4}\ \ 2$$
$$\underline{-3}$$
$$\ \ 1\ \ 2$$
$$\underline{-1\ \ 2}$$
$$\ \ \ \ \ \ 0$$

12 $1 bills shared

Todd can spend $14 for each birthday present.

B. Use play money to divide 51 into 4 equal groups and record.

Remainder

a. Divide the $10 bills.

b. Trade the leftover $10 bill.

c. Divide the $1 bills.

d. Tell the number of $1 bills left over.

$10 bills	$1 bills
1	2

$$4 \overline{)5}\ \ 1$$
$$\underline{-4}$$
$$\ \ 1\ \ 1$$
$$\underline{-0\ \ 8}$$
$$\ \ \ \ \ \ 3$$

12 in each group, remainder 3

■ **Talk About Math** When you divide a two-digit number by a one-digit number, how can you tell if your quotient will be less than or greater than $10?

Check Understanding

For another example, see Set D, pages 526–527.

Find $72 ÷ 3. You can use play money. Record each step.

1. How many $10 bills and $1 bills will you use?

2. How many equal groups will you make?

3. How many $10 bills will there be in each of the 3 groups?

4. Do you need to make a trade before you can find how many $1 bills will be in each of the 3 groups? Explain.

5. How many $1 bills will be in each of the 3 groups?

6. What answer did you record?

Practice

For More Practice, see Set D, pages 528–529.

Use play money to divide each amount of money into equal groups. Record your work.

7. $34 into 3 equal groups

8. $52 into 4 equal groups

9. $56 into 4 equal groups

10. $56 into 5 equal groups

11. $66 into 3 equal groups

12. $66 into 4 equal groups

13. $75 ÷ 5

14. $43 ÷ 2

15. $78 ÷ 6

16. $82 ÷ 7

17. $41 ÷ 5

18. $91 ÷ 7

19. $54 ÷ 2

20. $83 ÷ 4

21. $72 ÷ 6

22. $67 ÷ 5

23. $92 ÷ 4

24. $25 ÷ 2

25. $58 ÷ 4

26. $62 ÷ 5

27. $81 ÷ 3

28. $96 ÷ 5

Mixed Practice   Use paper and pencil or mental math to find each answer. Tell which method you used.

29. 3 × 9

30. 53 ÷ 6

31. 16 × 8

32. 18 ÷ 3

33. 22 ÷ 4

34. 12 ÷ 2

35. 7 × 48

36. 22 ÷ 5

37. 3 × 27

38. 72 ÷ 8

Problem Solving

Solve each problem.

39. Sela spent an equal amount of money on each of 4 presents. She had $92 to spend. How much money did she spend for each present?

40. **Calculator** Suppose you went to the bank to get quarters for 375 pennies. How many quarters would you get?

41. Critical Thinking Find amounts less than $20 that cannot be shared equally among 4 students. Describe the pattern you see.

42. Estimation Look at Exercises 17–24. Without dividing, how can you tell when a quotient will be greater than 10?

43. Ms. Sarat can pay for a $60 dress in equal monthly payments. How much will Ms. Sarat have to pay each month if she wants to pay it off in 2 months? 3 months? 4 months? 5 months? 6 months?

44. Use Data Look at Exercises 9 and 10 on page 204. Write two division sentences for each array.

Reading ———— Math

Numbers and Symbols Match the number sentence with its description.

1. The divisor is 7 and the dividend is 28.

2. One factor is 4 and the product is 28.

3. One addend is 7 and the sum is 28.

a. $7 + 21 = 28$	
b. $7 \times 4 = 28$	
c. $28 - 7 = 21$	
d. $28 \div 7 = 4$	

Choose an Operation

Build Understanding

Ramona gave $64 to the
4 workers who did her gardening.
They shared the money equally.
How much did each worker get?

PROBLEM SOLVING GUIDE

Understand
QUESTION
FACTS
KEY IDEA

⮞ **Plan and Solve**
STRATEGY
ANSWER

Look Back
SENSIBLE ANSWER
ALTERNATE APPROACH

Understand The workers needed to divide the money into 4 equal groups.

⮞ **Plan and Solve** STRATEGY Divide 64 by 4.

$10 bills	$1 bills
1	6

$$4)\overline{64}$$
$$\underline{-\ 4}$$
$$2\ \ 4$$
$$\underline{-\ 2\ \ 4}$$
$$0$$

ANSWER Each worker received $16.

Look Back 4 × 16 = 64, so 64 ÷ 4 = 16. $16 is correct.

■ **Talk About Math** How could drawing a picture help you decide whether to use addition, subtraction, multiplication, or division?

What would you grow in a garden?

Check Understanding

Solve this problem by answering Questions 1–4.

The workers were paid $64 each week for 5 weeks. How much did they earn in all?

1. How much do the workers make each week?

2. How many weeks did they work?

3. What operation helps you find how much they made in all?

4. How much did the workers make in 5 weeks?

Practice

Tell whether you should *add, subtract, multiply,* or *divide.* Then find the answer.

5. The workers made $64 in 2 hours. How much were they paid for each hour?

6. If 54 flowers were planted equally in 6 beds, how many were planted in each bed?

7. Of 32 bushes, the workers were able to trim 16 of them on Monday. How many were left to trim?

8. Ramona paid $3.49 for each of 3 rose bushes and $7.98 for each of 2 lilac bushes. How much did she pay in all?

Choose a 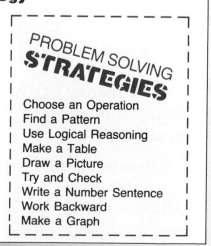 Strategy

9. *Baseball Puzzler* Fred gave Tom half of his baseball cards. Tom gave Nan half of the cards that he got from Fred. Nan gave Sam half of the cards that she got from Tom. Sam got 6 cards. How many cards did Fred have at the start?

PROBLEM SOLVING
STRATEGIES

Choose an Operation
Find a Pattern
Use Logical Reasoning
Make a Table
Draw a Picture
Try and Check
Write a Number Sentence
Work Backward
Make a Graph

Skills Review

Use play money to divide $33 into 3 equal groups.

1. How many $10 bills and $1 bills will you use?

2. How much money is in each group?

Choose the division sentence for each multiplication sentence. Then give the missing factor.

3. 3 × ▦ = 48
   a. 48 ÷ 4 = 12
   b. 48 ÷ 3 = 16

4. ▦ × 6 = 132
   a. 132 ÷ 6 = 22
   b. 132 ÷ 3 = 44

Tell how much money is in each group and how much is left over. Use play money.

5. $53 into 5 equal groups

6. $45 into 2 equal groups

7. $74 into 6 equal groups

Use play money to divide each amount of money into equal groups.

8. $79 into 6 equal groups

9. $62 ÷ 4   **10.** $95 ÷ 8

11. $86 ÷ 7   **12.** $48 ÷ 5

Problem-Solving Review

Solve each problem.

13. If you have 2 blue pencils and 2 red pencils in a drawer, do you have an equal chance of getting either color if you grab one without looking?

14. At Kay's Gift Shop, pins cost $2, hats cost $5, and T-shirts cost $13. Find the cost of 2 hats, 3 pins, and 1 T-shirt.

15. Each rack holds 100 items. There are 13 racks. How many items are there in all?

16. A teacher hid 75 items. Nine students took part in the search. About how many items would each student be expected to find?

17. **Data File** Use data from pages 532–533. Karen wants to make half of the party cocoa recipe. Find the number of cups of milk and the number of marshmallows she needs.

18. **Make a Data File** Find 5 different types of numerical data about a newspaper, such as cost, number of sections, year it was founded, date of issue, and so on.

Replace each ▒ with < or >.

1. 745 ▒ 754

2. 4,130 ▒ 1,340

Estimate each answer.

3. 89 − 46   **4.** 44 + 33

Find each sum or difference.

5. 631 + 394   **6.** 312 − 191

Measure the length of your pencil to the nearest

7. half inch.   **8.** centimeter.

9. Is this a cylinder or sphere?

Write the other multiplication and division sentences in each family of facts.

10. 9 × 4 = 36   **11.** 72 ÷ 9 = 8

Divide. Write each quotient and remainder.

12. 22 ÷ 5   **13.** 35 ÷ 8

14. Write the decimal and fraction for the shaded part.

15. Give the time as minutes before the hour.

16. Write the amount of money for 1 quarter and 2 dimes.

17. Write the change from $10.00 for a $6.50 movie.

18. Give the standard form for 14 tens.

Multiply.

19. 73 × 6   **20.** 168 × 7

21. How many fish were sold?

22. How many cats were sold?

Pet Shop Sales

Cats Dogs Birds Fish

Tell whether it is certain, possible, or impossible that

23. it will rain tomorrow.

24. it will be 180°F outside.

25. Match the multiplication sentence with the related division sentence. Then give the missing factor.

     8 × ▒ = 144   **a.** 144 ÷ 9 = 16
                   b. 144 ÷ 8 = 18

Use play money to divide each amount into equal groups.

26. $45 ÷ 4   **27.** $95 ÷ 7

28. $63 ÷ 6   **29.** $76 ÷ 5

Reteaching

Set A pages 506–507

Divide $45 into 3 equal groups.

| $10 | $10 | $1 | $1 | $1 |

| $10 | $10 | $1 | $1 |

Put the ten-dollar bills into
3 groups.

| $10 | $10 | $10 | Left over: | $10 |

Trade the leftover $10 for
10 one-dollar bills. There are
now 15 dollar bills to share.
Divide the dollar bills among the
3 groups.

$10	$1		$10	$1		$10	$1
$1			$1			$1
$1			$1			$1
$1			$1			$1
$1			$1			$1

There is $15 in each group.

Remember that sharing money
means dividing the money into
equal groups.

Use play money to divide each
amount of money into equal
groups. Draw a picture to show
your answer. Then write how
much is in each group.

1. $26 into 2 equal groups

2. $40 into 5 equal groups

3. $65 into 5 equal groups

4. $48 into 4 equal groups

5. $36 into 3 equal groups

Set B pages 508–509

Find the missing factor.

$$\text{▦} \times 8 = 48$$

Think about related division
and multiplication sentences.

$$\text{▦} \times 8 = 48 \qquad 48 \div \text{▦} = 8$$
$$8 \times \text{▦} = 48 \qquad 48 \div 8 = \text{▦}$$

Find $48 \div 8$. To find the missing
factor use repeated subtraction.

$$48 - 8 = 40 \qquad 24 - 8 = 16$$
$$40 - 8 = 32 \qquad 16 - 8 = 8$$
$$32 - 8 = 24 \qquad 8 - 8 = 0$$

You subtracted 6 times. So 6 is
the missing factor.

$$6 \times 8 = 48 \text{ and } 48 \div 8 = 6.$$

Remember that you can use
repeated subtraction to solve a
division problem.

Match each multiplication with
the related division sentence.
Then give the missing factor.

1. $\text{▦} \times 8 = 120$ | **a.** $144 \div 6 = 24$

2. $\text{▦} \times 6 = 144$ | **b.** $144 \div 8 = 18$

3. $5 \times \text{▦} = 120$ | **c.** $120 \div 6 = 20$

4. $6 \times \text{▦} = 120$ | **d.** $120 \div 5 = 24$

5. $\text{▦} \times 8 = 144$ | **e.** $120 \div 8 = 15$

Set C pages 510–512

Find $50 ÷ 4.
Divide $50 into 4 equal groups.

a. Divide the $10 bills.

| $10 | $10 | $10 | $10 | Left: | $10 |

b. Trade the leftover $10 bill for ten $1 bills.

$10→ [$1] [$1] [$1] [$1] [$1]
    [$1] [$1] [$1] [$1] [$1]

c. Divide the $1 bills among the 4 groups.

[$10][$1] [$10][$1] [$10][$1] [$10][$1]
    [$1]   [$1]   [$1]   [$1]
                Remainder: [$1][$1]

Each group has $12. There is $2 left over.

Remember that you can trade a $1 bill for ten dimes or 100 pennies.

Tell how many in each group and how many left over. Use play money.

1. $34 into 3 equal groups

2. $38 into 3 equal groups

3. $34 into 2 equal groups

4. $38 into 2 equal groups

5. $43 into 4 equal groups

6. $43 into 3 equal groups

Set D pages 518–521

Divide $41 into 3 equal groups and record.

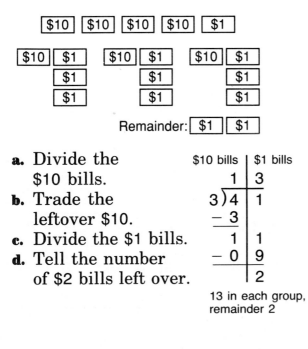

[$10] [$10] [$10] [$10] [$1]

[$10][$1] [$10][$1] [$10][$1]
    [$1]   [$1]   [$1]
    [$1]   [$1]   [$1]

Remainder: [$1] [$1]

a. Divide the $10 bills.
b. Trade the leftover $10.
c. Divide the $1 bills.
d. Tell the number of $2 bills left over.

	$10 bills	$1 bills
	1	3
3)‾	4	1
	− 3	
	1	1
	− 0	9
		2

13 in each group, remainder 2

Remember that if the first digit of the dividend is greater than the divisor, the quotient will be greater than $10.

Use play money to divide each amount of money into equal groups.

1. $48 into 4 equal groups

2. $48 into 5 equal groups

3. $48 into 7 equal groups

4. $55 ÷ 5   **5.** $25 ÷ 2

6. $25 ÷ 3   **7.** $72 ÷ 8

8. $61 ÷ 5   **9.** $73 ÷ 4

More Practice

Set A pages 506–507

Use play money to divide each amount of money into equal groups. Draw a picture to show your answer. Then write how much in each group.

1. $24 into 2 equal groups

2. $24 into 3 equal groups

3. $24 into 4 equal groups

4. $24 into 6 equal groups

5. $21 into 3 equal groups

6. $21 into 7 equal groups

7. $70 into 5 equal groups

8. $36 into 4 equal groups

9. $36 into 3 equal groups

10. $48 into 3 equal groups

11. $48 into 4 equal groups

12. $48 into 6 equal groups

13. $60 into 4 equal groups

14. $60 into 6 equal groups

Set B pages 508–509

Match each multiplication with the related division sentence. Then give the missing factor. Match Exercises 1–8 with a–h. Match Exercises 9–14 with i–n.

1. $\text{▦} \times 9 = 180$

2. $5 \times \text{▦} = 180$

3. $4 \times \text{▦} = 156$

4. $\text{▦} \times 6 = 156$

5. $6 \times \text{▦} = 180$

6. $\text{▦} \times 4 = 180$

7. $3 \times \text{▦} = 156$

8. $2 \times \text{▦} = 156$

a. $180 \div 6 = 30$ **b.** $180 \div 4 = 45$

c. $156 \div 3 = 52$ **d.** $180 \div 9 = 20$

e. $156 \div 4 = 39$ **f.** $156 \div 2 = 78$

g. $180 \div 5 = 36$ **h.** $156 \div 6 = 26$

9. $\text{▦} \times 6 = 216$

10. $2 \times \text{▦} = 180$

11. $3 \times \text{▦} = 180$

12. $3 \times \text{▦} = 216$

13. $\text{▦} \times 4 = 216$

14. $\text{▦} \times 8 = 216$

i. $180 \div 3 = 60$ **j.** $216 \div 3 = 72$

k. $216 \div 6 = 36$ **l.** $180 \div 2 = 90$

m. $216 \div 8 = 27$ **n.** $216 \div 4 = 54$

Set C   pages 510–512

Tell how many in each group and how many
left over. Use play money.

1. $32 into 3 equal groups

2. $37 into 3 equal groups

3. $37 into 2 equal groups

4. $64 into 6 equal groups

5. $59 into 5 equal groups

6. $59 into 4 equal groups

7. $57 into 4 equal groups

8. $64 into 5 equal groups

9. $63 into 5 equal groups

10. $23 into 2 equal groups

11. $47 into 3 equal groups

12. $46 into 5 equal groups

13. $39 into 2 equal groups

14. $31 into 6 equal groups

15. $64 into 5 equal groups

16. $28 into 3 equal groups

17. $52 into 3 equal groups

18. $69 into 6 equal groups

Set D   pages 518–521

Use play money to divide each amount of
money into equal groups.

1. $52 into 4 equal groups

2. $52 into 5 equal groups

3. $63 into 3 equal groups

4. $63 into 4 equal groups

5. $65 ÷ 5   **6.** $31 ÷ 2   **7.** $72 ÷ 6   **8.** $78 ÷ 7

9. $65 ÷ 4   **10.** $47 ÷ 5   **11.** $97 ÷ 7   **12.** $87 ÷ 4

Mixed Practice   Use paper and pencil or
mental math to find each answer. Tell which
method you used.

13. 4 × 7   **14.** 44 ÷ 7   **15.** 15 × 9   **16.** 42 ÷ 6   **17.** 31 ÷ 5

18. 18 ÷ 3   **19.** 8 × 43   **20.** 27 ÷ 4   **21.** 4 × 29   **22.** 63 ÷ 9

Enrichment

Riddle Rhyme

Riddle 1
Less than sixty pennies
I have in all.
They are in 5 piles
That are equally tall.
I can trade in one pile
And get less than a dime.
But more than a nickel
All of the time.
If I now made 7 piles
They would be equally tall.
Tell me how many pennies
Do I really have in all?

Riddle 2
How many nickels
Do I have in all
If they are in 2 piles
That are equally tall?
I would get less than 5 dimes
If I traded both piles
And more than 1 dime
For 1 pile—and 1 smile!
If I made 3 piles
They would be equally tall.
Tell me how many nickels
Do I have in all?

Answer Questions 1–4 to find the solution
to Riddle 1.

1. Read the first four lines of
the riddle. Which amounts of
money are possible?

2. Which amounts of money can
you eliminate after reading
the fifth and sixth lines?

3. Which amounts of money can
you eliminate after reading
the seventh and eighth lines?

4. Read the rest of the lines
and solve the riddle. Give
your answer.

5. Use a similar procedure to solve
Riddle 2. Give your answer.

Chapter 15 Review/Test

Draw a picture to show how to divide.

1. $36 into 3 equal groups

2. $50 into 5 equal groups

Choose the division sentence for each multiplication sentence. Then give the missing factor.

3. $7 \times \blacksquare = 84$
  a. $84 \div 6 = 14$
  b. $84 \div 7 = 12$

4. $\blacksquare \times 32 = 96$
  a. $96 \div 3 = 32$
  b. $96 \div 6 = 13$

5. $8 \times \blacksquare = 128$
  a. $128 \div 8 = 16$
  b. $128 \div 4 = 32$

Tell how many are in each group and how many are left over. Draw pictures to help you.

6. $80 into 7 equal groups

7. $74 into 4 equal groups

8. $57 into 2 equal groups

9. Each ride at the carnival uses 4 tickets. A ticket book has 50 tickets. How many rides can the Lee family take with 1 book of tickets?

Use this exercise to answer Items 10–13. Draw pictures to help you.

$10 bills	$1 bills

$6 \overline{)9 \;\;|\; 3}$

When $93 is divided into 6 equal groups, how many

10. $10 bills will there be?

11. $1 bills will there be?

12. $1 bills will be left over?

13. Did you need to trade any $10 bills for $1 bills?

14. Draw pictures to divide $75 into 3 equal groups.

Read this problem. Then answer the questions below.

Stan collected 18 tree leaves. He mounted 2 leaves on each page of an album. How many pages did he use?

15. Would you multiply or divide to solve the problem?

16. Solve the problem.

17. ■ **Write About Math** Explain what it means to divide.

1. Train Schedule
Find the city in which you start. Look across the row to find the time you want to leave. Look down that column to find the time the train arrives at the station you want.

2. Menu
This is the children's menu.

3. Bar Graph
The graph shows how many people attend the movies each day.

4. Recipe
Be careful when using the stove.

5. Toll Charges
The chart tells how long each toll road is and the cost to travel on each.

	Train 022	Train 026	Train 028	Train 034	Train 036
	AM	AM	AM	AM	AM
San Francisco	4:50	6:00	6:30	8:00	10:00
San Bruno	5:11	6:21	6:51	8:21	10:19
Broadway	5:18	6:28	6:58	8:28	10:26
Hillsdale	5:30	6:39	7:09	8:39	10:37
Redwood City	5:39	6:49	7:19	8:49	10:47
Menlo Park	5:46	6:57	7:26	8:56	10:53
Sunnyvale	6:02	7:13	7:43	9:12	11:09
San Jose	6:18	7:30	8:00	9:28	11:25

1. Train Schedule

2. Restaurant Menu

MENU

BURGER
Served with fries.
$3.50

GRILLED CHEESE
Served with fries.
$2.95

SPAGHETTI
Served with bread.
$2.95

CHICKEN FINGERS
Served with fries.
$4.50

JR. TURKEY OR HAM SANDWICH
Served with fries.
$3.65

JR. SALAD
$2.95

ROAST CHICKEN
Served with veggies and fries.
$4.50

BBQ RIBS
Served with veggies and fries.
$4.50

A bakery treat will be served with each meal, as well.

BEVERAGES 50¢

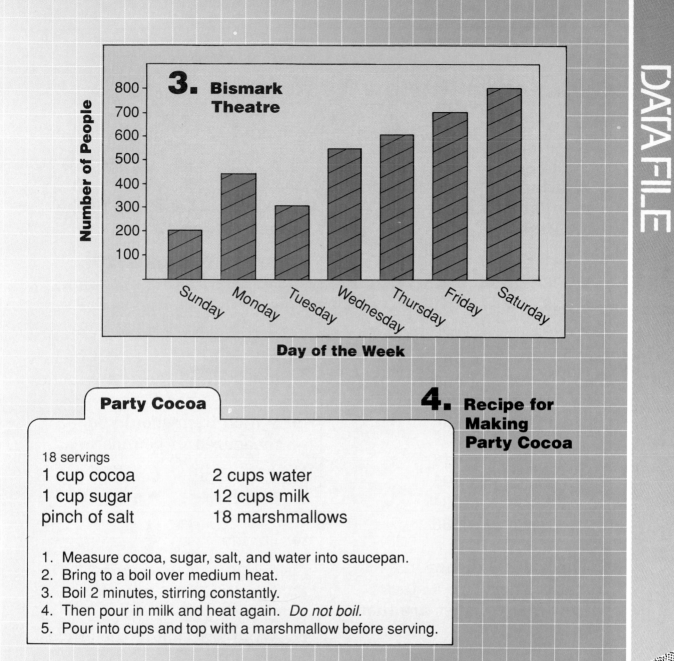

3. Bismark Theatre

Number of People (y-axis): 100, 200, 300, 400, 500, 600, 700, 800

Day of the Week (x-axis): Sunday, Monday, Tuesday, Wednesday, Thursday, Friday, Saturday

Party Cocoa

4. Recipe for Making Party Cocoa

18 servings

1 cup cocoa	2 cups water
1 cup sugar	12 cups milk
pinch of salt	18 marshmallows

1. Measure cocoa, sugar, salt, and water into saucepan.
2. Bring to a boil over medium heat.
3. Boil 2 minutes, stirring constantly.
4. Then pour in milk and heat again. *Do not boil.*
5. Pour into cups and top with a marshmallow before serving.

5. Kentucky Toll Road Information

Road Name	Miles	Auto Toll	Auto with Trailer
Audubon Parkway	23	$0.50	$1.10
Blue Grass Parkway	72	$1.30	$2.90
Cumberland Parkway	88.2	$2.00	$4.00
Daniel Boone Parkway	59.4	$1.40	$2.80
Green River Parkway	69.7	$1.50	$3.00
Pennyrile Parkway	60	$1.00	$2.30
Purchase Parkway	49	$0.90	$2.00

Cumulative Review/Test, Chapters 1–15

Give the letter for the correct answer.

1. Which numbers are written in order from least to greatest?

A 641   629   758

B 732   758   629

C 629   641   732

D 758   732   641

2. Add.

$$672 + 187$$

A 759
B 859
C 869
D 485

3. Subtract.

$$725 - 139$$

A 616
B 696
C 694
D 586

4. There are 8 dishes in each stack. There are 4 stacks. How many dishes are there in all?

A 4   **B** 12   **C** 23   **D** 32

5. Multiply.

$$13 \times 5$$

A 55
B 65
C 18
D 63

6. Multiply.

$$137 \times 3$$

A 391
B 140
C 411
D 311

7. Round 73 to the nearest ten.

A 70   **B** 80   **C** 75   **D** 60

8. What is the length to the nearest inch?

A 1 inch   **C** 3 inches
B 4 inches   **D** 2 inches

9. Which item should be measured in pounds?

A a pencil   **C** a dog
B a flower   **D** a spoon

10. Divide.

$$20 \div 5$$

A 7
B 15
C 25
D 4

11. What fraction of the circles are shaded?

A $\frac{2}{5}$ **B** $\frac{2}{3}$ **C** $\frac{3}{5}$ **D** $\frac{3}{6}$

12. Which decimal means the same as $\frac{39}{100}$?

A 0.039   **C** 0.39
B 39.0   **D** 3.9

13. What time is shown?

A 20 minutes after 8
B 20 minutes after 9
C 20 minutes before 8
D 20 minutes before 9

14. Find the amount of money.

2 quarters, 3 dimes, 6 pennies.

A $0.56   **C** $0.71
B $0.86   **D** $1.36

Study the graph. Then answer the question.

State Flowers

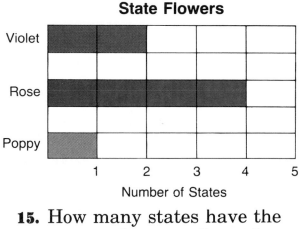

Number of States

15. How many states have the rose as the state flower?
A 1   **B** 2   **C** 3   **D** 4

16. How many 3-packs of tickets should Trina buy if she needs 47 tickets?

A 15   **B** 16   **C** 14   **D** 17

17. Decide whether you should *add, subtract, multiply,* or *divide.* Then find the answer.

Gardeners made $93 in 3 weeks. How much were they paid for each week?

A Add; $96
B Subtract; $90
C Multiply; $279
D Divide; $31

Read the problem. Then answer the question.

There are 20 students at 5 tables. On each table there are 10 pounds of clay. How many pounds of clay are there in all?

18. What is the key idea?

A There are 20 students at 5 tables, so you can divide.

B There are 10 pounds of clay on each of the 5 tables, so you can multiply.

C There are 10 pounds of clay for 20 students, so you can divide.

D There is a greater number of students than pounds of clay, so you can subtract.

Ordinal Numbers

Review

> *Ordinal numbers* tell order and position.
>
> **A.** Tell the position of B in ABLE. Use an ordinal number.
>
> B is the 2nd letter in ABLE.
>
> **B.** Ten people are in line ahead of Kaye. Use an ordinal number to tell Kaye's position in line.
>
> Kaye is 11th in line.

Practice

Tell the position of the given letter in each word. Use an ordinal number.

1. E in END   **2.** M in ARM   **3.** I in MILK

4. B in NUMBER   **5.** H in MONTH   **6.** T in COMPUTER

Tell the position of the given letter in the alphabet. Use an ordinal number.

7. C   **8.** G   **9.** H   **10.** L   **11.** M   **12.** X

13. P   **14.** Z   **15.** U   **16.** A   **17.** R   **18.** T

19. D   **20.** N

Tell Ed's position in line. Use an ordinal number.

21. There are 3 people ahead of Ed.

22. There are 6 people ahead of Ed.

23. There are 9 people ahead of Ed.

24. There are 13 people ahead of Ed.

Addition Basic Facts

Review

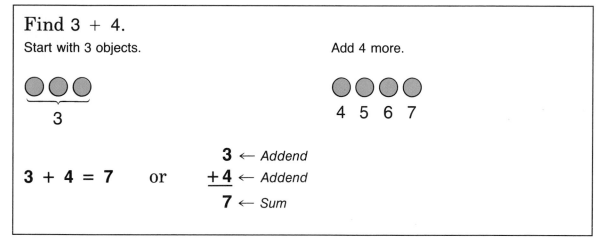

Find 3 + 4.

Start with 3 objects.

3

Add 4 more.

4 5 6 7

3 + 4 = 7   or

3 ← Addend
+4 ← Addend
7 ← Sum

Practice

Add.

1. 8 +2	**2.** 5 +1	**3.** 5 +8	**4.** 7 +5	**5.** 9 +6	**6.** 6 +0
7. 2 +7	**8.** 6 +8	**9.** 7 +6	**10.** 4 +6	**11.** 4 +4	**12.** 9 +2
13. 3 +9	**14.** 8 +8	**15.** 1 +3	**16.** 6 +3	**17.** 7 +8	**18.** 8 +4

19. 6 + 5

20. 7 + 4

21. 3 + 5

22. 6 + 1

23. 9 + 4

24. 7 + 9

25. 2 + 4

26. 4 + 0

27. 5 + 2

28. 6 + 6

29. 5 + 6

30. 2 + 8

31. 7 + 5

32. 3 + 6

33. 1 + 4

34. 3 + 7

35. 6 + 7

36. 8 + 7

37. 3 + 7

38. 9 + 7

Subtraction Basic Facts

Review

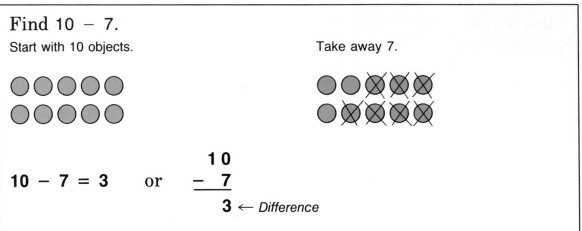

Find 10 − 7.

Start with 10 objects.　　　　　　　　　　Take away 7.

$$10 - 7 = 3 \quad \text{or} \quad \begin{array}{r} 10 \\ -\ 7 \\ \hline 3 \end{array} \leftarrow \textit{Difference}$$

Practice

Subtract.

1. $\begin{array}{r} 7 \\ -6 \\ \hline \end{array}$	**2.** $\begin{array}{r} 9 \\ -3 \\ \hline \end{array}$	**3.** $\begin{array}{r} 14 \\ -\ 7 \\ \hline \end{array}$	**4.** $\begin{array}{r} 12 \\ -\ 4 \\ \hline \end{array}$	**5.** $\begin{array}{r} 11 \\ -\ 6 \\ \hline \end{array}$	**6.** $\begin{array}{r} 5 \\ -3 \\ \hline \end{array}$
7. $\begin{array}{r} 6 \\ -5 \\ \hline \end{array}$	**8.** $\begin{array}{r} 9 \\ -4 \\ \hline \end{array}$	**9.** $\begin{array}{r} 10 \\ -\ 8 \\ \hline \end{array}$	**10.** $\begin{array}{r} 18 \\ -\ 9 \\ \hline \end{array}$	**11.** $\begin{array}{r} 11 \\ -\ 6 \\ \hline \end{array}$	**12.** $\begin{array}{r} 16 \\ -\ 7 \\ \hline \end{array}$
13. $\begin{array}{r} 10 \\ -\ 2 \\ \hline \end{array}$	**14.** $\begin{array}{r} 9 \\ -8 \\ \hline \end{array}$	**15.** $\begin{array}{r} 8 \\ -0 \\ \hline \end{array}$	**16.** $\begin{array}{r} 10 \\ -\ 9 \\ \hline \end{array}$	**17.** $\begin{array}{r} 6 \\ -6 \\ \hline \end{array}$	**18.** $\begin{array}{r} 12 \\ -\ 7 \\ \hline \end{array}$

19. 11 − 4　　　　**20.** 11 − 7　　　　**21.** 5 − 2　　　　**22.** 10 − 1

23. 12 − 9　　　　**24.** 7 − 7　　　　**25.** 12 − 3　　　　**26.** 13 − 6

27. 8 − 5　　　　**28.** 9 − 1　　　　**29.** 9 − 5　　　　**30.** 8 − 6

31. 6 − 0　　　　**32.** 10 − 4　　　　**33.** 17 − 8　　　　**34.** 15 − 9

35. 9 − 8　　　　**36.** 4 − 4　　　　**37.** 9 − 7　　　　**38.** 16 − 9

Whole Numbers Through Hundreds

Review

The standard form of the number three hundred fifty-seven is 357. The number has 3 digits.

hundreds	tens	ones
3	**5**	**7**
↑	↑	↑
3 is the hundreds digit.	5 is the tens digit.	7 is the ones digit.

Practice

Write each number in standard form.

1. ninety-two

2. fourteen

3. forty-one

4. eighty-five

5. seven hundred twenty

6. four hundred fifty-six

7. one hundred sixty-three

8. five hundred fifty

Tell which digit is the hundreds digit.

9. 473   **10.** 216   **11.** 500   **12.** 795   **13.** 340   **14.** 827

15. 122   **16.** 601   **17.** 230   **18.** 961   **19.** 134   **20.** 785

Tell which digit is the tens digit.

21. 367   **22.** 710   **23.** 925   **24.** 846   **25.** 691   **26.** 182

Tell which digit is the ones digit.

27. 831   **28.** 547   **29.** 268   **30.** 674   **31.** 492   **32.** 920

Comparing Two-Digit Numbers

Review

A. Which number is greater, 27 or 46?
To compare two-digit numbers, first look at the tens digits.

27   The tens digit is 2.
46   The tens digit is 4.

4 tens is more than 2 tens, so 46 is greater than 27.

B. Compare 84 and 81. Use $>$ or $<$.

The tens digits are the same, so look at the ones digits.

84   The ones digit is 4.
81   The ones digit is 1.

Write 84 $>$ 81   84 **is greater than** 81.
     or 81 $<$ 84   81 **is less than** 84.

Practice

Tell which is the greater number.

1. 35, 61   **2.** 52, 12   **3.** 44, 47   **4.** 17, 71

Tell which number is less.

5. 53, 13   **6.** 8, 32   **7.** 97, 90   **8.** 25, 30

Replace ∷ with $<$ or $>$.

9. 79 ∷ 46   **10.** 88 ∷ 98   **11.** 61 ∷ 8   **12.** 40 ∷ 45

13. 6 ∷ 2   **14.** 77 ∷ 33   **15.** 14 ∷ 19   **16.** 12 ∷ 25

Ordering Two-Digit Numbers

Review

Write 69, 35, 42, and 67 in order from least to greatest.
First look at the tens digits.

3 tens	4 tens	6 tens
3 5	**4** 2	**6** 9
		6 7

The tens digits are the same in 69 and 67.
So compare the ones.

9 > 7   so   **6 9 > 6 7**.

The numbers in order from least to greatest
are 35, 42, 67, and 69.

Practice

Write these numbers in order from least to greatest.

1. 37   31   45   **2.** 68   59   65   **3.** 72   23   95

4. 53   37   56   **5.** 49   33   11   **6.** 36   92   97

7. 23   12   26   **8.** 46   51   15   **9.** 89   33   45

Write these numbers in order from greatest to least.

10. 56   52   63   **11.** 68   59   65   **12.** 10   97   89

13. 47   61   68   **14.** 72   96   93   **15.** 64   13   95

16. 70   94   21   **17.** 88   77   71   **18.** 58   28   32

Two-Digit Addition

Review

Find 57 + 26.

How many ones?   13 ones   Make a ten.

Record
1 ten and 3 ones.   How many tens?

$$\begin{array}{r} 57 \\ +26 \\ \hline \end{array}$$

$$\begin{array}{r} {\scriptstyle 1} \\ 57 \\ +26 \\ \hline 3 \end{array}$$

$$\begin{array}{r} {\scriptstyle 1} \\ 57 \\ +26 \\ \hline 83 \end{array}$$

Practice

Add.

1. $\begin{array}{r} 13 \\ +59 \\ \hline \end{array}$
2. $\begin{array}{r} 64 \\ +27 \\ \hline \end{array}$
3. $\begin{array}{r} 22 \\ +68 \\ \hline \end{array}$
4. $\begin{array}{r} 71 \\ +\ 3 \\ \hline \end{array}$
5. $\begin{array}{r} 50 \\ +44 \\ \hline \end{array}$

6. $\begin{array}{r} 25 \\ +37 \\ \hline \end{array}$
7. $\begin{array}{r} 42 \\ +19 \\ \hline \end{array}$
8. $\begin{array}{r} 31 \\ +66 \\ \hline \end{array}$
9. $\begin{array}{r} 87 \\ +\ 7 \\ \hline \end{array}$
10. $\begin{array}{r} 18 \\ +\ 6 \\ \hline \end{array}$

11. $\begin{array}{r} 77 \\ +19 \\ \hline \end{array}$
12. $\begin{array}{r} 53 \\ +40 \\ \hline \end{array}$
13. $\begin{array}{r} 94 \\ +\ 2 \\ \hline \end{array}$
14. $\begin{array}{r} 68 \\ +17 \\ \hline \end{array}$
15. $\begin{array}{r} 55 \\ +33 \\ \hline \end{array}$

16. $\begin{array}{r} 73 \\ +17 \\ \hline \end{array}$
17. $\begin{array}{r} 42 \\ +51 \\ \hline \end{array}$
18. $\begin{array}{r} 31 \\ +60 \\ \hline \end{array}$
19. $\begin{array}{r} 75 \\ +21 \\ \hline \end{array}$
20. $\begin{array}{r} 69 \\ +29 \\ \hline \end{array}$

21. 36 + 25
22. 67 + 31
23. 82 + 8
24. 19 + 15

25. 6 + 18
26. 88 + 9
27. 48 + 43
28. 5 + 15

29. 22 + 71
30. 51 + 30
31. 64 + 26
32. 43 + 39

33. 63 + 17
34. 74 + 8
35. 4 + 34
36. 57 + 34

Three Addends

Review

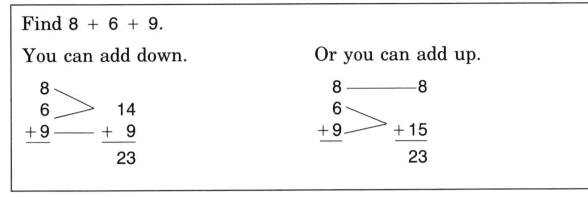

Find 8 + 6 + 9.

You can add down.

8	
6	14
+9	+ 9
	23

Or you can add up.

8	8
6	
+9	+15
	23

Practice

Find these sums.

1. 9	**2.** 8	**3.** 7	**4.** 6	**5.** 9	**6.** 5
7	4	3	8	1	6
+1	+9	+5	+9	+4	+7

7. 2	**8.** 4	**9.** 3	**10.** 5	**11.** 9	**12.** 8
7	5	7	2	4	6
+6	+9	+8	+6	+3	+5

13. 4 + 5 + 3   **14.** 6 + 7 + 2   **15.** 9 + 7 + 5

16. 3 + 9 + 2   **17.** 7 + 3 + 5   **18.** 6 + 5 + 6

19. 8 + 4 + 5   **20.** 5 + 7 + 8   **21.** 4 + 5 + 9

22. 9 + 6 + 5   **23.** 5 + 6 + 5   **24.** 7 + 2 + 8

25. 4 + 8 + 3   **26.** 8 + 6 + 1   **27.** 8 + 9 + 8

28. 2 + 7 + 7   **29.** 5 + 1 + 9   **30.** 4 + 9 + 7

31. 3 + 6 + 7   **32.** 7 + 4 + 8   **33.** 2 + 8 + 7

Two-Digit Subtraction

Review

Find 54 − 28.

Think: Are there
enough ones in 54? No.

Trade a ten for
10 more ones.

Rename 54.
Subtract the ones.
Subtract the tens.

$$\begin{array}{r} 5\,4 \\ -2\,8 \\ \hline \end{array}$$

$$\begin{array}{r} {}^{4}\,{}^{14} \\ \cancel{5}\,\cancel{4} \\ -2\,8 \\ \hline 26 \end{array}$$

Practice

Find each difference.

1. 46 − 28	**2.** 31 − 3	**3.** 57 − 39	**4.** 62 − 38	**5.** 81 − 29
6. 50 − 37	**7.** 92 − 76	**8.** 95 − 48	**9.** 54 − 49	**10.** 44 − 8
11. 71 − 68	**12.** 83 − 76	**13.** 52 − 26	**14.** 91 − 34	**15.** 63 − 9
16. 62 − 57	**17.** 80 − 31	**18.** 72 − 49	**19.** 75 − 69	**20.** 81 − 39

21. 75 − 29   **22.** 82 − 57   **23.** 45 − 17   **24.** 90 − 77

25. 62 − 14   **26.** 83 − 24   **27.** 75 − 48   **28.** 98 − 59

29. 72 − 6   **30.** 52 − 39   **31.** 96 − 18   **32.** 33 − 17

33. 20 − 14   **34.** 66 − 29   **35.** 53 − 5   **36.** 63 − 46

Time: Hour and Half-Hour

Review

A. One hour is 60 minutes. The **hour hand** on a clock moves from one number to the next in 60 minutes or 1 hour.

The **minute hand** moves from one small mark to the next in 1 minute.

2:00 or 2 o'clock

B. A half-hour is 30 minutes. The minute hand on a clock moves through 30 small marks in a half-hour.

2:30 or
30 minutes after 2

Practice

Write the time in two ways.

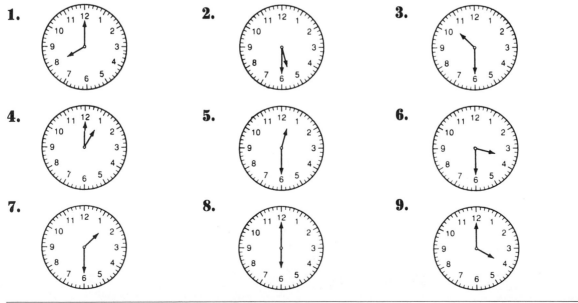

1.

2.

3.

4.

5.

6.

7.

8.

9.

Time: Quarter Hour

Review

A quarter of an hour is 15 minutes. The
minute hand on a clock moves through
15 small marks in a quarter of an hour.

Write each time in two ways.

A.

9:15
or
15 minutes after 9

B.

9:45
or
45 minutes after 9

Practice

Write each time in two ways.

1.

2.

3.

4. 6:15

5. 10:45

6.

7.

8.

9.

Measuring to the Nearest Inch

Review

A. Measure the line segment to the nearest inch.

The end of the line segment is closer to 1 inch than 2 inches.
The length to the nearest inch is 1 inch.

B. Measure the length of the pencil to the nearest inch.

The end of the pencil is closer to 3 inches than 2 inches.
The length to the nearest inch is 3 inches.

Practice

Measure each line segment to the nearest inch.

1. ————————————   **2.** ————————————————

3. ——————————————————————————

4. ————————————————————

5. ——————————————————————————————

6. ———————————————

7. ————————————————————————————

Measuring to the Nearest Centimeter

Review

A. Measure the line segment to the nearest centimeter.

The end of the line segment is closer to 6 centimeters than 7 centimeters.
The length to the nearest centimeter is 6 centimeters.

B. Measure the line segment to the nearest centimeter.

The end of the line segment is closer to 5 centimeters than 4 centimeters.
The length to the nearest centimeter is 5 centimeters.

Practice

Measure each line segment to the nearest centimeter.

1. _____

2. _____

3. _____

4. _____

5. _____

6. _____

7. _____

Counting to $0.99

Review

Write the amount of money.

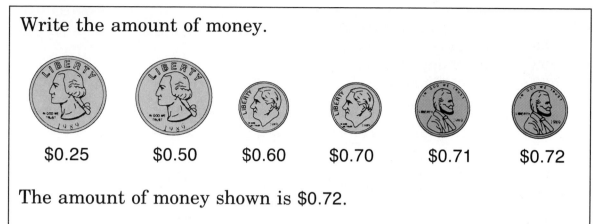

$0.25 $0.50 $0.60 $0.70 $0.71 $0.72

The amount of money shown is $0.72.

Practice

Use $ and . to write each amount of money.

1.

2.

3.

4.

5.

6.

7.

8.

9.

10.

11.

12.

Independent Study Handbook

Contents

How to Use a Calculator

Calculators are used in everyday life at home and at work. They are useful tools when computing with large numbers or when computations involve many numbers. *Remember*:

- ▸ **Do** estimate to check whether you pushed the correct buttons.

- ▸ **Don't** use a calculator when paper and pencil or mental math is faster.

Calculator displays

- ▸ **Number of digits** What is the greatest number you can display on your calculator? If you press 99,999 × 99,999, you get a number with more digits than the calculator display can show. Most calculators will show some kind of an "error" message.

- ▸ **Unnecessary zeros** If you add $2.10 and $3.20, you do not enter the "$" on your calculator. Most calculators will display 5.3 for the answer. Calculators usually drop unnecessary zeros. You write the answer as $5.30. A zero always precedes a decimal less than one.

Calculator keys

Display
Shows the number that is being used in a calculation or the solution of a calculation.

Memory Recall
Displays what is in memory. Push it twice to clear the memory.

Memory Minus
Subtracts the display from what is in the memory.

Memory Plus
Adds the display to what is in the memory.

On-Off, Clear
Turns the calculator on. Press it once to clear the last number entered. Press it twice to clear everything.

Divide

Multiply

Subtract

Add

Equals

Decimal point

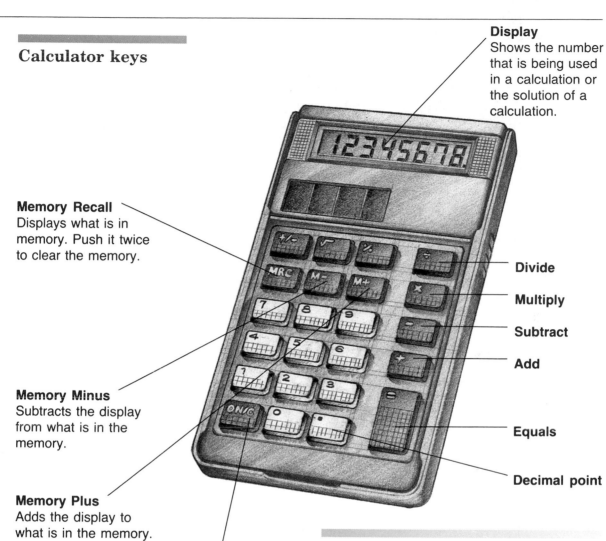

Calculator key sequences

▶ **Order of operations** Press 2 ⊞ 3 ⊠ 4 ⊟. If you get 20, your calculator does operations in the order they are pressed. If you get 14, your calculator does multiplication before addition.

▶ **Automatic constant** Press 2 ⊞ 3 ⊟ ⊟ ⊟ ⊟. Then press 2 ⊠ 3 ⊟ ⊟ ⊟ ⊟. If your calculator keeps adding 3 or multiplying by 2, your calculator has an automatic constant.

Problem-Solving Help File

Use these pages to help you solve problems more effectively.

Problem-Solving Guide

There is no recipe or magic formula for solving problems. But keeping a problem-solving guide in mind can help you become a better problem solver.

PROBLEM SOLVING
GUIDE

Understand
QUESTION
FACTS
KEY IDEA

Plan and Solve
STRATEGY
ANSWER

Look Back
SENSIBLE ANSWER
ALTERNATE APPROACH

Understand
QUESTION
► What are you asked to find?
► Try to state the question in your own words.
► Is an exact answer needed?

FACTS
► What facts are given?
► Is there too much or too little information?
► Is data needed from a picture, table, or graph?
► Do you need to collect some data?

KEY IDEA
► How are the facts and the question related?
► Are there groups that are part of a whole?
► Are two groups being compared?
► Are there groups that are joining or separating?
► Are there groups of the same size?

Plan and Solve
STRATEGY
► What can you do to solve the problem?
► Can the problem be solved by computing?
► Estimate the answer.
► Choose a strategy. Try another, if needed.

ANSWER
► Give the answer in a sentence.
► Do you need to interpret a remainder?
► Is rounding needed?

Look Back
SENSIBLE ANSWER
► Did you check your work?
► Did you use all the needed data?
► Does your answer have the correct labels?
► Is your answer close to the estimate?
► Is your answer reasonable for the situation?

ALTERNATE APPROACH
► Is there another way to get the same answer?
► Could you use the same strategy differently?
► Would another strategy be faster or simpler?

Problem-Solving Strategies

You might think of problem-solving strategies as problem-solving tools that you own and use when needed. One or more strategies might be used for a problem. And if one strategy doesn't work, try another one.

PROBLEM SOLVING STRATEGIES

Choose an Operation
Find a Pattern
Use Logical Reasoning
Make a Table
Draw a Picture
Try and Check
Write a Number Sentence
Work Backward
Make a Graph

Problem-Solving Behaviors and Attitudes

When you solve problems, do you give up quickly or lack confidence? Behaviors and attitudes can affect your work. So, remember these tips. They can help you become a better problem solver.

TIPS FOR PROBLEM SOLVERS

Don't give up. Some problems take longer than others.

Tips for Problem Solvers

▶ **Don't give up.** Some problems take longer than others.

▶ **Be flexible.** If you get stuck, try another idea.

▶ **Be confident** so you can do your best.

▶ **Take risks.** Try your hunches. They often work.

▶ **Brainstorm to get started**—one idea will lead to another.

▶ **Visualize the problem** in your mind to help you understand it better.

▶ **Compare problems** to help you relate new problems to ones you've solved before.

▶ **Think about your thinking.** Pause to ask, "How is this going to help me solve the problem?"

▶ **Share your thinking with others.** Explaining your ideas helps you think better.

▶ **Organize your work** to help you think clearly.

Mental Math Strategies

For simple calculations, mental math can be a more effective computation method than paper and pencil or a calculator. To sharpen your mental math skills, use the strategies shown on these pages.

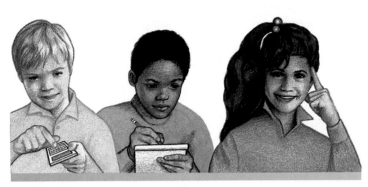

Breaking Apart Numbers

Break apart one or more numbers to get numbers that are easier to use.

54 + 23
54 + 20 + 3   Break apart 23.
  74 + 3
    77

68 − 45
68 − 40   Break apart 45.
28 − 5   First subtract 40.
  23   Then subtract 5.

87 × 2
(80 + 7) × 2   Break apart 87.
(80 × 2) + (7 × 2)   Use the distributive
  160 + 14   property.
     174

35 + 48
(30 + 5) + (40 + 8)   Break apart 35 and 48.
(30 + 40) + (5 + 8)   Regroup the numbers.
    70 + 13
       83

Compatible Numbers

Compatible numbers are pairs of numbers that are easy to use. Look for numbers like 1, 10, 100 or 3, 30, 300 that are easy to use.

40 + 30   **28 × 10**
   70   280

2 × 9 × 5
2 × 5 × 9
 10 × 9
  90

Look for factors of 10.

When there are 3 or more numbers, look for pairs of numbers that are compatible.

3 + 48 + 7
3 + 7 + 48
 10 + 48
   58

2 × 9 × 3
2 × 3 × 9
 6 × 9
  54

Multiply the lesser factors first.

Using Equivalent Forms

Divide to find "fraction of."

$$\tfrac{1}{3} \times 180$$

$$180 \div 3$$
$$60$$

Change decimals or percents to fractions to get a number that is easier to use.

25% of 32

$$\tfrac{1}{4} \text{ of } 32$$

$$32 \div 4$$
$$8$$

Compensation

Change one number to make it easy to use. Then change the answer to compensate.

57 + 29

57 + 30 = 87	Add 1 to 29 to get 30.
87 − 1 = 86	Subtract 1 from the answer.

165 − 97

165 − 100 = 65	Add 3 to 97 to get 100.
65 + 3 = 68	Add 3 to the answer.

Change one number to make it easy to use. Then change the other number to compensate.

66 + 19

65 + 20	Add 1 to 19 and subtract
85	1 from 66.

157 − 98 Add 2 to 98 and to 157.

159 − 100
59

Estimation Strategies

In everyday life, an exact answer is often unnecessary. For example, you can estimate while shopping to see if you have enough money.

When you do need an exact answer, estimation helps you find possible errors. Estimation is especially important for checking whether you pushed a wrong button on a calculator.

To help you make good estimates, use the estimation strategies shown on these pages.

Front-End Digits

Use just the first digit in each number to help you make an estimate.

$$
\begin{array}{rr}
173 & 100 \\
421 & 400 \\
+348 & +300 \\
\hline
 & 800 \\
\end{array}
$$

Since $73 + 21 + 48$ is about 100, you can also adjust the estimate by adding 100 to get 900.

Rounding

Round to the nearest 10 or 100.

$$
\begin{array}{rr}
37 & 40 \\
+22 & +20 \\
\hline
 & 60 \\
\end{array}
$$

$$
\begin{array}{rr}
88 & 90 \\
-42 & -40 \\
\hline
 & 50 \\
\end{array}
$$

$$
\begin{array}{rr}
425 & 400 \\
\times\ 4 & \times\ \ 4 \\
\hline
 & 1{,}600 \\
\end{array}
$$

Round both numbers up and both numbers down to get a range.

$136 + 243$

$$200 + 300 = 500$$
$$100 + 200 = 300$$

$136 + 243$ is between 300 and 500.

Substituting Compatible Numbers

Use numbers that are close to the original numbers.

6)$\overline{27}$
6)$\overline{24}$ or 6)$\overline{30}$
6)$\overline{27}$ is about 5.

4)$\overline{77}$
4)$\overline{80}$
4)$\overline{77}$ is about 20.

23)$\overline{476}$
24)$\overline{480}$ or 23)$\overline{460}$ or 25)$\overline{500}$
23)$\overline{476}$ is about 20.

24 × 78 × 4
25 × 78 × 4
100 × 78
24 × 78 × 4 is about 7,800.

Clustering

Look for groups of numbers that are close to the same number.

627
658
589
+613

Each number is about 600, so the sum is about 4 × 600 or 2,400.

Comparing to a Reference Point

Compare the numbers to numbers you can work with easily.

346
+438

Both numbers are less than 500, so the sum is less than 1,000.

Math Study Skills

Try these math study skills to help you do your best.

Before a Lesson

▶ **Preview the lesson.** Look over the lesson to see what it's about.

▶ **Set a purpose.** Are you about to learn a new topic or revisit a familiar one?

▶ **Recall what you know.** What have you learned about this topic previously?

Build Understanding

Reading the lesson

▶ **Read slowly.** Don't try to read a math book as fast as a story book.

▶ **Learn vocabulary and symbols.** Note new math terms and symbols. Use the glossary and index. Watch for words like "product" that have other meanings outside of math.

▶ **Read diagrams, tables, graphs.** Use a ruler to help you read rows and columns.

▶ **Do the examples.** Work the examples yourself as you go through them.

Doing Activities

▶ **Use materials.** Keep the materials organized. Use them to explore new ideas.

▶ **Work with others.** When you work with others, use the tips for working together given on page 560.

Check Understanding

Trying on your own

▸ **Note what you don't understand.** When you try some exercises, be aware of what you don't understand.

▸ **Reread the lesson.** When you don't understand, reread the "Build Understanding" section.

Preventing errors

▸ **Find another example.** When you need another example, turn to the "Reteaching" set at the back of the chapter.

▸ **Try again.** Keep trying until you feel you understand.

Practice and Problem Solving

Reading the exercises

▸ **Read directions.** Read carefully.

▸ **Read word problems.** Read slowly and reread, if needed.

Doing written work

▸ **Show your work.** Record what you did. Make your paper easy to follow and the answer easy to find.

▸ **Check your work.** Read what you write.

▸ **Find more practice.** Use the "More Practice" at the back of the chapter when needed.

After a Lesson

▸ **Look back.** Summarize the lesson. Can you explain what you learned to another student?

▸ **Connect to other lessons.** Think about how this lesson is related to other lessons.

559

Working in Groups

Working in groups during math class will help you learn and enjoy mathematics. You will also learn to work as a member of a team.

Roles for Group Members

When you work in a group, it can be helpful for each person to have a role. Some roles are:

- **Reporter**—This person summarizes the group's thinking.

- **Encourager**—This person encourages group members to take part and to work together well.

- **Recorder**—This person records the group's work.

- **Checker**—This person asks group members to explain their thinking or may ask others if they agree.

- **Materials Manager**—This person gets any materials that are needed and returns them at the end of class.

TIPS FOR WORKING TOGETHER

You can disagree without being disagreeable.

Tips for Working Together

Here are some tips for working well with others in a group.

- Involve your whole group. Help everyone to participate.

- Help keep your group on task.

- To make sure your group understands the task or solution, have each group member say it in his or her own words, summarize the steps, or give an example.

- Work as a group. If you understand, help another group member. Don't work ahead of the others.

- Be a good tutor. Make up similar problems or easier ones to help someone understand.

- When you are unsure, ask someone in your group for help or say you don't understand.

- Tell someone when he or she does or says something that helps you.

- Don't decide by voting. Try to understand which might be the best solution and why.

- Remember, you can disagree without being disagreeable.

Tables

Metric System

Length

10 millimeters (mm)	= 1 centimeter (cm)
10 centimeters } 100 millimeters }	= 1 decimeter (dm)
10 decimeters } 100 centimeters }	= 1 meter (m)
1,000 meters	= 1 kilometer (km)

Area

100 square millimeters (mm^2)	= 1 square centimeter (cm^2)
10,000 square centimeters	= 1 square meter (m^2)
100 square meters	= 1 are (a)
10,000 square meters	= 1 hectare (ha)

Volume

1,000 cubic millimeters (mm^3)	= 1 cubic centimeter (cm^3)
1,000 cubic centimeters	= 1 cubic decimeter (dm^3)
1,000,000 cubic centimeters	= 1 cubic meter (m^3)

Mass (weight)

1,000 milligrams (mg)	= 1 gram (g)
1,000 grams	= 1 kilogram (kg)
1,000 kilograms	= 1 metric ton (t)

Capacity

1,000 milliliters (mL)	= 1 liter (L)

Time

60 seconds	= 1 minute
60 minutes	= 1 hour
24 hours	= 1 day
7 days	= 1 week
365 days } 52 weeks } 12 months }	= 1 year
366 days	= 1 leap year

Addition-Subtraction Table

+	0	1	2	3	4	5	6	7	8	9
0	0	1	2	3	4	5	6	7	8	9
1	1	2	3	4	5	6	7	8	9	10
2	2	3	4	5	6	7	8	9	10	11
3	3	4	5	6	7	8	9	10	11	12
4	4	5	6	7	8	9	10	11	12	13
5	5	6	7	8	9	10	11	12	13	14
6	6	7	8	9	10	11	12	13	14	15
7	7	8	9	10	11	12	13	14	15	16
8	8	9	10	11	12	13	14	15	16	17
9	9	10	11	12	13	14	15	16	17	18

Multiplication-Division Table

×	1	2	3	4	5	6	7	8	9
1	1	2	3	4	5	6	7	8	9
2	2	4	6	8	10	12	14	16	18
3	3	6	9	12	15	18	21	24	27
4	4	8	12	16	20	24	28	32	36
5	5	10	15	20	25	30	35	40	45
6	6	12	18	24	30	36	42	48	54
7	7	14	21	28	35	42	49	56	63
8	8	16	24	32	40	48	56	64	72
9	9	18	27	36	45	54	63	72	81

Customary System

Length

12 inches (in.)	= 1 foot (ft)
3 feet } 36 inches }	= 1 yard (yd)
1,760 yards } 5,280 feet }	= 1 mile (mi)
6,076 feet	= 1 nautical mile

Area

144 square inches (sq in.)	= 1 square foot (sq ft)
9 square feet	= 1 square yard (sq yd)
4,840 square yards	= 1 acre (A)

Volume

1,728 cubic inches (cu in.)	= 1 cubic foot (cu ft)
27 cubic feet	= 1 cubic yard (cu yd)

Weight

16 ounces (oz)	= 1 pound (lb)
2,000 pounds	= 1 ton (T)

Capacity

8 fluid ounces (fl oz)	= 1 cup (c)
2 cups	= 1 pint (pt)
2 pints	= 1 quart (qt)
4 quarts	= 1 gallon (gal)

Glossary

Add To find the total when putting together two or more quantities.

Addend A number that is added. In $8 + 4 = 12$, the addends are 8 and 4.

Addition property of zero The sum of zero and a number is that number.

Angle ($\angle$) The figure formed by two rays with the same endpoint.

Area A number given in square units that indicates the size of the inside of a plane figure.

Array An arrangement of objects or numbers in rows and columns.

Associative property (Grouping property) The way in which addends (or factors) are grouped does not affect the sum (or product).
$(7 + 2) + 5 = 7 + (2 + 5)$
$(7 \times 2) \times 5 = 7 \times (2 \times 5)$

Average A number obtained by dividing the sum of two or more addends by the number of addends.

Basic Fact A number sentence that has at least two one-digit numbers. The sentences below are examples of basic facts.
$7 + 2 = 9 \qquad 16 - 7 = 9$
$5 \times 3 = 15 \qquad 8 \div 4 = 2$

Billion The word name for 1,000,000,000.

Centimeter A unit of length in the metric system. Your little finger is about 1 centimeter wide.

Circle A plane figure with all points the same distance from a given point called the *center*.

Circumference The distance around a circle.

Clockwise The direction in which the hands of a clock move. The hands pass the numbers in order.

Clustering An estimation method used when all the numbers are close to the same number.

Column A line of objects or numbers from top to bottom in an array.

Common denominator A common multiple of two or more denominators. A common denominator for $\frac{1}{6}$ and $\frac{3}{8}$ is 48.

Common factor A number that is a factor of two or more numbers. A common factor of 6 and 12 is 3.

Common multiple A number that is a multiple of two or more numbers.

Commutative property (Order property) The order in which numbers are added (or multiplied) does not affect the sum (or product). $4 + 6 = 6 + 4$; $4 \times 6 = 6 \times 4$

Compass An instrument used for drawing circles.

Compatible number A number close to the number in the problem being solved that is used for mental computation.

Composite number A whole number, greater than 0, that has more than two factors.

Cone A solid figure formed by connecting a circle to a point not in the plane of the circle.

Congruent figures Two figures with the same size and shape.

Coordinates Integers in an ordered pair giving the location of a point in a coordinate plane.

Corner (1) The point where the 2 sides of an angle meet. (2) The point where 2 sides of a polygon meet. (3) The point where edges of a polyhedron meet.

Cube A prism with all square faces.

Cup A unit for measuring capacity in the customary system. 2 cups equals 1 pint.

Curve A line that has no straight part.

Cylinder A space figure with two circular bases that are parallel and congruent.

Data A collection of gathered information that has not been organized.

Decimal A number used to name a whole quantity and/or a fractional part. It is written in standard form with a point to separate the whole number and fraction parts.

Decimeter A unit for measuring length in the metric system.
10 decimeters equal 1 meter.

Degree (of an angle) A unit for measuring angles.

Degree Celsius A unit for measuring temperature in the metric system.

Degree Fahrenheit A unit for measuring temperature in the customary system.

Denominator The number below the line in a fraction. It names the number of equal parts or objects. In $\frac{3}{4}$, the denominator is 4.

Diagonal In a polygon, a line segment that connects corners not next to each other.

Diameter In a circle, a segment that passes through the center and that has both endpoints on the circle.

Difference The number found by subtracting one number from another. In $95 - 68 = 27$, the difference is 27.

Digit One of the symbols used for writing numbers: 0, 1, 2, 3, 4, 5, 6, 7, 8, and 9.

Distributive property When a factor is a sum, multiplying each addend before adding does not change the product. $5(3 + 4) = (5 \times 3) + (5 \times 4)$

Divide To find how a total amount can be separated into an equal number of groups, or into groups of equal size.

Dividend A number that is divided by another number.

Divisible A number is divisible by another if the remainder is zero after dividing.

Divisor The number by which another number is divided.

Edge Segment where two faces of a polyhedron meet.

Endpoint The point at the end of a line segment or a ray.

Equal Things that are the same as each other in size or amount or value.

Equal fractions Fractions that name the same number. $\frac{2}{3}$ and $\frac{8}{12}$ are equal fractions.

Equally likely Outcomes that will happen about as often as each other.

Equation A mathematical sentence with the $=$ symbol.

Estimate A number that is close to another number. A term used for a calculation not requiring an exact answer.

Even number A whole number that has 0, 2, 4, 6, or 8 in the ones place.

Expanded form A way to write a number to show the value of each digit.

Face Flat surface that is part of a polyhedron.

Factor (1) A number to be multiplied. (2) A number that divides evenly into a given second number is a factor of that number.

Family of facts The related number sentences for addition and subtraction (or multiplication and division) that contain all the same numbers.
$5 + 3 = 8 \qquad 8 - 3 = 5$
$3 + 5 = 8 \qquad 8 - 5 = 3$

Flip A change in location of a figure by flipping it over a line, creating a mirror image (reflection) of the figure.

Foot A unit for measuring length in the customary system. 1 foot equals 12 inches.

Fraction A number that names a part of a whole or of a set. It is written in the form $\frac{a}{b}$.

Frequency The number of times a certain item occurs in a set of data.

Gallon A unit for measuring capacity in the customary system. 1 gallon equals 4 quarts.

Geometric figure A closed shape made with line segments or curves in a plane.

Gram A unit for measuring weight in the metric system. A raisin weighs about 1 gram.

Graph A drawing used to show information in an organized way.

Greater than ($>$) A relation between two numbers, with the greater number given first.
$8 > 5 \qquad 9 > 1.4$

Grouping Putting a known number of objects into each group and making as many groups as you can.

Hexagon A six-sided polygon.

Hour hand The short hand on a clock that names the number of hours.

Improper fraction A fraction whose numerator is greater than or equal to its denominator.

Inch A unit for measuring length in the customary system. A paper clip is about 1 inch long.

Integers The whole numbers and their opposites. Some integers are $+3$, -3, 0, $+16$, -16.

Intersecting lines Lines that meet at a point.

Kilogram A unit for measuring weight in the metric system. 1 kilogram equals 1,000 grams.

Kilometer A unit for measuring length in the metric system. 1 kilometer equals 1,000 meters.

Less than ($<$) A relation between two numbers, with the lesser number given first.
$5 < 8 \qquad 1.4 < 9$

Line A set of points continuing without end in both directions.

Line plot A graph that uses Xs to show information and compare quantities.

Line of symmetry A line on which a figure can be folded into two congruent parts.

Line segment Two points and the straight path between them.

Liter A unit for measuring capacity in the metric system. 1 liter equals 1,000 milliliters.

Lowest terms A fraction for which 1 is the greatest common factor of both the numerator and the denominator.

Meter A unit for measuring length in the metric system. 1 meter equals 100 centimeters.

Mile A unit for measuring length in the customary system. 1 mile equals 5,280 feet.

Milliliter A unit for measuring capacity in the metric system. An eyedropper holds about 1 milliliter.

Million The word name for 1,000,000.

Minuend A number from which another number is subtracted. In 95 − 68 = 27, the minuend is 95.

Minute hand The long hand on a clock that names the number of minutes.

Mixed number A number that has a whole number part and a fraction part.

More likely An outcome that will happen more often than another outcome.

Multiple A multiple of a number is the product of that number and a whole number.

Multiplicand A number that is multiplied by another number. In 27 × 3 = 81, the multiplicand is 27.

Multiplication property of one The product of one and a number is that number.

Multiplication property of zero The product of zero and a number is zero.

Multiplier A number that multiplies another number. In 27 × 3 = 81, the multiplier is 3.

Multiply To find the total when putting together groups of equal size, or to find the number that is "times as many" as another number.

Number pair *See* Ordered pair.

Number sentence A way to write a relationship between numbers.
18 + 27 = 45   9 > 6

Numerator The number above the line in a fraction. It names the number of parts or objects being thought about. In $\frac{3}{4}$, the numerator is 3.

Octagon An eight-sided polygon.

Odd number A whole number that has 1, 3, 5, 7, or 9 in the ones place.

Ordered pair A pair of numbers arranged so there is a first number and a second number, used to locate a point on a grid.

Ordinal number A number, such as *third*, used to tell order or position.

Organized list All the possibilities for a situation written in a certain order.

Ounce A unit for measuring weight in the customary system. A slice of bread weighs about 1 ounce.

Outcome A possible result of an action.

Parallel lines Lines in a plane that never meet.

Parallelogram A quadrilateral with opposite sides parallel and congruent.

Pentagon A five-sided polygon.

Percent (%) A word meaning "hundredths" or "out of 100." 45 percent (45%) equals 0.45 or $\frac{45}{100}$.

Perimeter The sum of the lengths of the sides of a polygon.

Perpendicular lines Lines that intersect to form right angles.

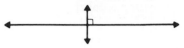

Pint A unit for measuring capacity in the customary system. 1 pint equals 2 cups.

Place value The number each digit represents is determined by the position the digit occupies.

Plane A flat surface that extends without end in all directions.

Point An exact location in space.

Polygon A plane figure made by line segments called *sides*, each side meeting two other sides, one at each of its endpoints.

Polyhedron A solid figure made up of flat surfaces called *faces*. Each face is a polygon.

Prime factor A factor that is a prime number. The prime factors of 10 are 2 and 5.

Prime number A whole number, greater than 1, that has exactly two factors: itself and 1.

Prism A polyhedron with two parallel, congruent faces, called *bases*. All other faces are parallelograms.

triangular prism
bases
rectangular prism

Probability A number from 0 to 1 that tells how likely it is that a given outcome will occur. The closer to 1, the *more likely* the outcome is to occur. The closer to 0, the *less likely* it is to occur.

Product The number found by multiplying numbers. In 27 × 3 = 81, the product is 81.

Protractor An instrument used to measure angles.

Pyramid A polyhedron formed by connecting points of a polygon to a point not in the plane of the polygon. The polygon and its interior is the *base*.

triangular pyramid   rectangular pyramid

uadrilateral A four-sided polygon.

Quart A unit for measuring capacity in the customary system. 2 pints equal 1 quart.

Quotient The answer after dividing one number by another.

Radius In a circle, a segment that connects the center of the circle with a point on the circle.

Range The difference between the greatest and the least numbers in a set of data.

Ratio A pair of numbers that names a rate or a comparison.

Ray A set of points that has one endpoint and that extends without end in one direction.

Rectangle A parallelogram with four right angles.

Regular polygon A polygon with all sides congruent and all angles congruent.

Remainder The number that is left over after dividing. When 20 is divided by 6, the remainder is 2.

Repeating decimal A decimal in which one or more digits

keep repeating, such as 0.518181818. . .

Right angle An angle with a measure of 90°.

Right triangle Triangle with one right angle.

Rotation A change in location of a figure by turning it about a point.

Rounded number A number expressed to the *nearest 10, 100, 1,000,* and so on. 368 rounded to the nearest 10 is 370; rounded to the nearest 100 is 400.

Row A line of objects or numbers from left to right in an array.

Sample Part of a group upon which an experiment or survey is conducted.

Sequence A set of numbers formed by a pattern.

Sharing Putting the same number of objects into each group when you know the number of groups.

Side *See* Polygon.

Similar figures Figures with the same shape but not necessarily the same size.

Slide A change in location of a figure by moving it without turning it.

Solid figure A figure that has three dimensions—length, width, and height.

Sphere A solid figure with all points the same distance from a given point called the *center*.

Square (in geometry) A rectangle with four congruent sides.

Square (in numeration) To multiply a number by itself.

Square products A sequence of numbers that can be shown by dots arranged in the shape of a square.

Standard form The notation

for writing numbers using the digits 0–9 and each place represents a power of ten.

Statistics Numerical facts that are collected, organized, and analyzed.

Subtract To find how many are left when some are taken away, or to compare two quantities.

Subtrahend A number to be subtracted from another number. In 95 − 68 = 27, the subtrahend is 68.

Sum The number found by adding numbers. In 8 + 4 = 12, the sum is 12.

Surface The outside of a solid figure.

Symmetric figure A plane figure that can be folded in half so the two halves match.

Tally chart A table to help with counting when collecting data.

Terminating decimal A decimal with an exact number of nonzero digits, such as 0.375.

Triangle A three-sided polygon.

Triangular numbers A sequence of numbers that can be shown by dots arranged in the shape of a triangle.

Turn A change in location of a figure by moving it around a given point.

Vertex *See* Corner.

Volume A number given in cubic units that indicates the size of the inside of a solid figure.

Whole number One of the numbers 0, 1, 2, 3, and so on.

Yard A unit for measuring length in the customary system. 1 yard equals 3 feet.

Index

INDEX

ACKNOWLEDGEMENTS

Design
Cover and Special Features:
SHELDON COTLER + ASSOCIATES

Art Direction and Production/
Core Lessons: Taurins Design
Associates, Inc./NYC

Rosa + Wesley Design Associates,
Jack Weiss Associates

Photographs
Cover: Richard Chesnut xi (tl):
Lawrence Migdale xi (bl):
Lawrence Migdale xi (c): Tony
Freeman, PhotoEdit xi (tr):
Lawrence Migdale xii (bc):
Lawrence Migdale xiii (t):
Stephen Frisch, Stock Boston
xiv–xv: Courtesy International
Business Machines Corporation
xvii (tl): David R. Frazier xviii (tr):
Jan Doyle, PhotoEdit xix (tr):
Scott, Berner, The Picture Cube
1 (tl): Alan Oddie, PhotoEdit 1
(br): Mary Kate Denny, PhotoEdit
ScottForesman photographs by:
Richard Chesnut 17, 34–35, 50,
104, 105, 130, 131, 163,
218–219, 248, 249, 252–253,
269, 311, 402, 403, 406–407,
418, 452, 453, 470–471, 485,
497, 517; Arie de Zanger 16,
72–73, 87, 228, 294–295, 310,
379, 485; Fred Schenk 2–3,
108–109, 148–149, 184–185,
311, 328–329, 340, 341,
358–359, 463; unless otherwise
acknowledged, all photographs
are the property of
ScottForesman. Clare Aich: 62,
74, 75, 76, 77, 110, 128, 156,
188, 189, 190, 202, 234, 258,
277, 302, 303, 314, 315, 342,
416, 417, 420, 421, 428, 440,
481, 509, 511, 512, 530 Alaska
Stock: Clark Mishler 459
American Museum of Natural
History: 458 Peter Arnold, Inc.:
Keith Scott Morton 148–149;

Erica Stone 218–219
Cameramann Int'l: Milt and Joan
Mann 309 Click/Tony Stone
Worldwide: Margaret Gowan 478
Woodfin Camp & Associates,
Inc.: Craig Aurness 438–439;
John Ficara 218–219 Comstock:
184–185 Beryl Goldberg 413
Judy Gurovitz: 118, 377 Richard
Hutchings: 18, 32, 37, 52, 53,
92, 112, 126, 127, 132, 133,
170, 192, 196, 202, 230, 238,
246, 272, 296, 300, 301, 330,
338, 349, 364, 366, 420, 426,
446, 521 The Image Bank:
Janeart LTD. 504–505 Image
Works: Bob Daemmrich 261
Brent Jones 412 L. A.
Lavenstein: 419 Library of
Congress: 136 Ron Morecraft: 8,
57, 94, 116, 158, 226, 254, 255,
256, 257, 263, 285, 299 New
York Public Library, Schomburg
Center for Research in Black
Culture, Astor, Lenox and Tilden
Foundations: 153 Photo
Researchers: Magendra 308
Stock Boston: John Coletti 165
The Stock Market 453; Thomas
Braise 438–439; Charles Krebs
149, 438–439; Eric Lawton
438–439; John Maher 438–439;
Roy Morsch 438–439

Illustrations
Elizabeth Allen, Jacque Auger,
Ron Becker, Dolores Bego, Ron
Berg, Eliot Bergman, Lloyd
Birmingham, Alex Bloch, Lee Lee
Brazeal, Dan Bridy, David Cain,
Susan Johnston Carlson, Jim
Deigan, Jim Delapine, Nancy
Didion, Kathleen Dunne, Mac
Evans, Mark Fisher, Robert
Frank, Janice Fried, Toni Goffe,
Franklin Hammond, Fred Harsh,
Steve Henry, Dave Joly, Mark
Kaplan, Robert Korta, Andy
Levine, Ron Lieberman, Peter
McMahon, Kimble Mead, Mike

Muir, James Needham, Eileen
Mueller Neill, Julie Pace, Charles
Peale, Bob Pepper, Brenda
Pepper, Nikolai Punin, Joe
Rogers, Claudia Sargent, Dan
Siculan, Susan Skoorka,
Suzanne Snider, Kirsten
Soderlind, Randy South, Barton
Stabler, Susan Swan, John
Trotta, Paul Vaccarello, Rhonda
Voo, John Walter Jr.

ScottForesman Staff
ScottForesman gratefully
acknowledges the contributions
of the following individuals.

Editorial
Karen Usiskin, Janice Ziebka,
Therese Smith, Clare Froemel,
Nancy Baty, Anna Belluomini,
Rosi Marshall, Lisa Kircher,
Colleen Mulvenna, Christine
Rakow, Iromie Fernando

Design
Barbara Schneider, Virginia
Pierce, George Roth, David
Dumo, Tom Gorman

Production
Mary Lou Beals, Joy Kelly,
Barbara Albright, Kathy
Oberfranc, Lois Nelson, Joan
Dixon, Sally Buehne

Marketing
Cathie Dillender, Nan Simpson,
Muffet Fox

Business
Elizabeth A. Dietz,
Elizabeth R. Semro

Picture Research/Photo Studio
Nina Page, Rosemary Hunter,
John Moore, Phoebe Novak

Photo Lab/Keyline
Marilyn Sullivan, Mark Spears,
Madeline Oton-Tarpey, Gwen
Plogman